*"Our greatest pretenses are built up
not to hide the evil and the ugly in us,
but our "emptiness".
The hardest thing to hide
is something that is not there."*

~ Eric Hoffer 1983 Presidential Medal of Freedom

Eden's snake-gifted wisdom came "empty-of-understanding"
Fig leaves masked the shame of choosing fig leaf wisdom
God's curse was to walk the earth lost in its "emptiness"
Religion-gifted templates harbor the same "emptiness"

Theology and realism envision the same white light
Religion paints a picture of emotional bliss ... afterlife
Realism describes how to paint that picture ... now

FIG LEAF WISDOM
THE GARDEN OF EDEN CURSE TODAY
Suffering Grows from "Emptiness" of Understanding

BORROWED WISDOM

RELIGIOUS THEORY

CULT LOGIC

CAUSES "EMPTINESS"

DAVID McCASLIN

In Memory of My Father
Dedicated to Those Wrapped in Fig Leaf Wisdom and to
Truth-Seekers Purposed on Self-Training
Tree of Life Wisdom to Gain the Understanding to
Undo Emptiness-Spun Life Misery

There is no material from any outside source that has not been fully credited in this text. Quoting other sources simply indicates that this author credits and values the interpreted message of the cited material.

It does not mean that the quoted source agrees with or supports the storyline of this writing or the author's interpretation of the quoted material.

The different bits of quoted material represent how life truths are seeping out of humanity's collective mass and appearing in all different media types. It could be said that the different sources are messengers of the self-evident truths that everyone shares inborn inclusion of.

Quoting the more famous sources is hoped to draw a more serious reader consideration. It's also good to hear ideas voiced by different perspectives to possibly enrich understanding.

It is hoped that readers will acquire the quoted sources to enjoy the entire text.

Fatally Fooled
The Moral to the Story of Fig Leaf Wisdom

That time does not stand still,
We all will learn to say,
Understanding its true meaning,
Keeps most of us at bay.

Time's the magic carpet,
That flies us through our day.
Understanding its true nature,
Is the game we all must play.

Father Time cannot stand still,
Without that rhythm and rhyme,
A cause would have no effect,
There'd be no passage of time.

Erratic bits of energy,
Give shape to all we know,
They never stand continuous,
Or things could never grow.

These patterns of creation,
Ground the principles of life-truth,
That determine the very outcome,
of everything we do.

So, when one builds a world inside,
Stagnant to laws of change,
They defy the laws of nature,
Clinging to reality rearranged.

When blind to the self-evident,
In what we touch and see,
We ride a gauntlet ambush,
Through emotional misery.

What we're told should make us happy,
Deep inside sometimes we feel,
Empty-to-understanding,
The source of life's appeal.

Over time they'll give up asking,
'Bout things on their life page,
That long-gagged curious child inside's,
Just dying to engage.

They'll live their life alone and scared,
of the boogieman inside,
Who's grown free on unchallenged uncertainty,
Since they were first alive.

Maybe he hides under the bed they make,
As their life-clock slowly unwinds,
Or's ready to leap from their closet of secrets,
They stand too ashamed to confide.

Without the drive to air and plan,
For what lurks in their unknown,
They're left as slave-curator and prisoner,
To their past and what they've come to know.

The ladder of compassion,
We all must find to climb,
While self-training our self-awareness,
Via self-knowledge manifesting inside.

Tree of Life wisdom follows,
As life-meaning is derived,
With a steadfast faith in understanding,
Life's naked-change carpet ride.

For 'til this time we'll suffer,
From what's misunderstood,
We might look to theology,
To do our soul some good.

A carrot of non-suffering,
Is wagged just out of reach,
In a stilled-time promised heaven,
Theology crafts to teach.

Enlightened about what's now,
We'll suffer in life no more,

The boogieman in life relationships,
Won't again knock at our door.

In knowing Father Time's ways,
Our suffering will fade,
In Mother Nature's honor,
Our beds will be made.

The true heaven that blinds faith believers,
God-tased too ignorant to see,
Shines its light bright in their faces,
While they're living … no middleman … and it's free.

Like when Adam and Eve faced their god in Eden,
As His voice was laced with despair,
They reached for a handful of fig leaves,
To hide their shame from his stare.

Any shamed emptiness,
That lurks treed-up inside,
Grew from fig leaf wisdom,
Borrowed and elsewhere-derived.

Jehovah told Adam first thing,
While this world from creation still cooled,
Tree of Life wisdom only,
Or you've been fatally fooled.

~ David McCaslin 6-6-17: Brown County Abe Martin Lodge

FIG LEAF WISDOM

TODAY

Table of Contents

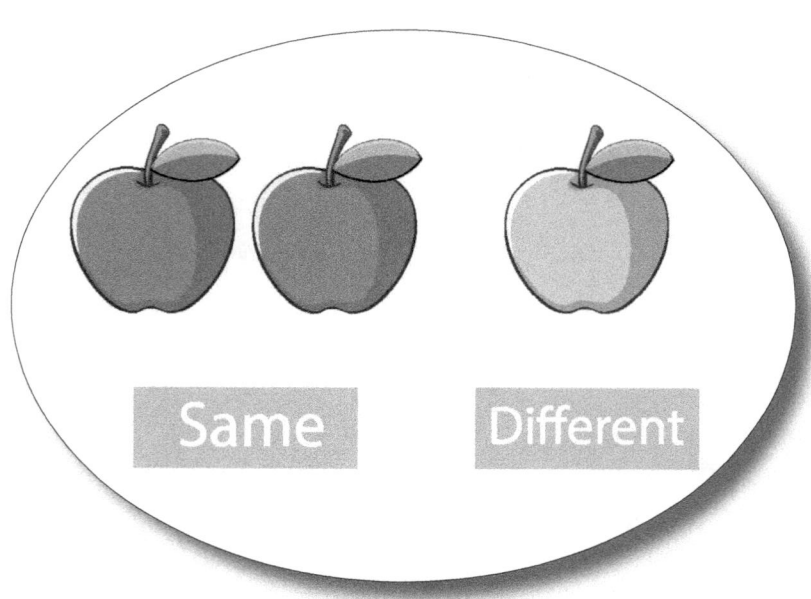

Apples to Apples

To best understand the intended meaning of this writing, it is important to understand how the writer interpreted the meaning of the words used. Most are common to the English language, yet their recognized meanings can suffer from differing conditioned understandings or maybe from having their meaning numbed or diffused from overuse.

The word interpretations can have different meanings to different people which would distract the intended thought stream. It is hoped that this clarity will help keep reader interpretation on a common thread of understanding to best follow this writing's intended message.

BORROWED KNOWLEDGE … intellectually metered and processed knowledge from another source that's meaning is believed and internalized while yet unverified. Belief in the verification of its truth is secured only from placing blind faith-confidence in the other entity's assumed experience.

CONTINUITY … the imagined state of unchanging permanence of something or idea that has a continual existence in time. The naïve understanding of reality allowing this state of existence is the fundamental ignorance that seeds thoughts of craving or attachment to something imagined that is non-existent … symptom of fundamental ignorance … the root of all human suffering. This ignorance is what results from having the "emptiness-of-understanding" referenced throughout the book.

DOGMA … a principle or set of principles laid down by an authority as incontrovertibly true. Superstition will over time help spawn unique rites and rituals thought to please some version of a god. It is a symptom of an individual's "emptiness-of-understanding."

EMOTIONS … Wikipedia says: "Emotions are psychological states brought on by neurophysiological changes, variously associated with thoughts, feelings, behavioral responses, and a degree of pleasure or displeasure. There is currently no scientific consensus on a definition. Emotions are often intertwined with mood, temperament, personality, disposition, or creativity."

How an individual values their collective emotional report reflects how they perceive their level of satisfaction with their human experience. It is thought here that having a balanced state of emotion, with no suffering, is the tangent agent people can intrinsically relate to and because of this, religions use it to entice emotionally frightened individuals to have blind faith in their suggested unverifiable wisdom. Emotional bliss is the promise religions make to convince those who are trying to find the answer to end the "emptiness-of-understanding" that generates the ignorance causing their emotional misery.

There are no "bad" emotions. All emotions are there to teach something. They help set boundaries to light the pathway for a truth-finder to enlighten their waking awareness with the understanding that will fill the "emptiness" that houses their ignorance.

ENLIGHTENMENT … That mystical eastern sounding "being enlightened" on the very basic level simply means having gained the needed knowledge to derive the wisdom that allows for the consciously recognized understanding of the relational principles driven by the universal forces that define the impermanent backdrop of this reality and the outcomes of cause/effect relationships. It obliterates any suffering brought on by the "fundamental" ignorance of these relationships. Enlightenment is a state of understanding awareness that brings on emotional bliss. It fills an individual's "emptiness-of-understanding,"

It's not so difficult to envision what being "enlightened" means intellectually with the head. The challenge lies in self-training the ability to feel and interpret the extent of that envisioned intellectually metered meaning intrinsically with the heart.

Religious theology equates the resulting emotional bliss realized from becoming "enlightened" about what brings about bliss and what causes human suffering with the Bible's promise of salvation from suffering. In Christianity, a believer realizes a state of enlightened understanding from simply willing their soul to the notion of the Christ.

Emotions contribute to creating moods. When enlightened about relational principles, reactionary emotions do not control an individual's moods. An individual has the understanding enlightened wisdom to think first, understand, and then act.

Jesus of Nazareth was an enlightened individual from a socially unsettled time in history. His intended message and life story were made obscure and re-scripted to the design of Rome's self-serving agenda. Through gospel selection, Rome's priests edited into Rome's 325 A.D. compilation of the Roman Bible that emotional bliss is delayed until, if judged to have lived within the god-sent guidelines, after being accepted into an afterlife god-gifted Garden of Eden-like "heaven". At that point, the believer is then being zapped into a state of emotional bliss.

It is promised emotional bliss that is gifted if judged to have lived in obedience to the appropriate god's mandated unexplained wisdom-defined rules of behavior.

This delay time, the individual's lifetime, allowed Rome to outwardly control the Roman citizen search for leadership and direction… versus looking inside to find the knowledge to better understand or lessen the ignorance concerning that which brings on the fear of the unknown.

There are early accounts of his teachings about blissful enlightenment, during his 20's, as being the same as Siddhartha's earlier teachings, as are also found in the recently discovered Gnostic Gospels.

With this strain of theology, when intellectually "seeing the light", it becomes an ordered life endeavor to follow the god-sent instructions on how to live a good life (to numb emotional awareness) in hopes that the performance of living a good life is judged by this theology's god to be good enough to live in "heaven" … the bliss of emotional paradise.

Siddhartha Gautama, the "Buddha", a self-proclaimed normal human being, was able to leave a detailed account telling how he self-trained and reached his state of enlightenment. Even though he made it clear that he was no god figure, his followers began regarding him as one after his death.

Theravada Buddhism best replicates his method of realizing the state of enlightened blissful freedom from the fundamental ignorance that causes suffering while still alive. He teaches how to self-train the mind control to realize Tree of Life Wisdom with no middleman.

This is emotional bliss that is earned through doing the work to self-train a morally/ethically tempered mind (where theology stops) and using that calmed mind to self-train the right concentration to gain the right knowledge to use the resulting insightful thinking to self-train the enriched wisdom of an enlightened understanding awareness, on the most primal level, of the relational laws of impermanence.

After intellectually "seeing the light," it becomes a lifetime endeavor to consciously self-train the ability to open up the deeper consciousness and release its understanding from the deeper consciousness to "enlighten" the waking conscious awareness.

EXPERIENTIAL KNOWLEDGE … On the most basic level, experiential knowledge from witnessing life's manifestation itself is only possible in an individual's only connection with this material world … in the subatomic dance going on in the flesh of their own body. Here, they sensually witness what happens while life is being manifested during this reality's state of ongoing transformation.

"Getting to know yourself" is meant to be taken literally … getting to know the nature of the material self … not the personality that is a product of intellectual decisions on how to best maneuver the causes the ever-changing material reality hits them with. An individual needs to understand what's controlling the change that affects the mental self (personality).

FAITH … The Oxford American Dictionary says that faith is a "complete trust or confidence in someone or something." More specifically defined it says faith is a "strong belief in a god or the doctrine of a religion, based on spiritual apprehension rather than proof. … a system of religious belief: the Christian faith"

… BLIND FAITH … intellectually founded unverifiable faith in something intangible

… STEADFAST FAITH … resolute faith intrinsically founded in something that proves self-evident.

FIG LEAF WISDOM … a new term describing mankind's matrix of compromised decision-making logistics. Fig leaf wisdom underwrites the logistics of the code of conscious rationale used by most individuals today.

Fig Leaf Wisdom's been here since Adam and Eve chose to go against Jehovah's 1st Commandment do-or-die mandate to use only Tree of Life Wisdom on day 6 of the Garden of Eden account of creation. Fig Leaf Wisdom is borrowed, received unearned wisdom that leaves an individual with an "emptiness-of-understanding" about the nature of life relationships.

Fig Leaf Wisdom is the Tree of Knowledge breed of wisdom that Jehovah sentenced mankind to live with before banning him from the Garden of Eden, not to return until armed with Tree of Life wisdom.

It might be said that living with Fig Leaf Wisdom is Jehovah's Garden of Eden punishing curse to mankind for making that "original" sin against the god Jehovah.

FREE WILL … The Meriam Webster Dictionary says that "free will is a voluntary choice or decision … that humans have the freedom to make choices that are not determined by prior causes or by divine intervention."

However, because this two-word gradation of one state of willpower and is describing the "factory setting" that everyone is born with until conditioned otherwise, it should be only one word. It will be referred to as "freewill."

FUNDAMENTAL IGNORANCE ... "Emptiness-of-Understanding" ... not understanding that this reality has an impermanent nature that allows no state of time continuity. Fundamental ignorance allows an individual to believe that things have a permanent presence ... continuity. From this can emerge a craving attachment to the imagined permanence of those imagined stagnate-in-time images from which suffering will develop. Fundamental ignorance is the root cause of human suffering and pain and it is generated from an individual's chasm of "emptiness."

HEAVEN ... Emotional Bliss ... complete emotional balance ... as referred to in John Lennon's song *Imagine*.

HELL ... Emotional Fire and Brimstone

IMPERMANENCE ... the nature of this reality ... a state of constant change or unchanging transformation. The only unchanging thing about this reality is that it continues to change. Tree of Life wisdom decodes the nature of this living reality.

JESUS "THE CHRIST" ... **"In Christianity, Christ is a title for the savior and redeemer who would bring salvation to the whole House of Israel. Christians believe Jesus is the Israelite messiah foretold in both the Hebrew Bible and the Christian Old Testament. Christ, used by Christians as both a name and a title, is synonymous with Jesus."** ... Wikipedia

This writing differentiates Jesus of Nazareth from Jesus "the Christ." The "Christ" was the message. Jesus of Nazareth was a man who taught about finding relief from suffering, as did Siddhartha Gautama. Jesus of Nazareth was simply the messenger.

...THE "ANTI-CHRIST" ... **"In Christian eschatology, the Antichrist or anti-Christ means someone recognized as fulfilling the Biblical prophecies about one who will oppose Christ and substitute himself in Christ's place. The term is found five times in the New Testament, solely in the First and Second Epistle of John. He is announced as the one who denies the Father and the Son."** Wikipedia

This writing sees the anti-Christ as not being an individual delivering the message, but the message itself, someone will be "substituting their message for the message "the Christ", just as the "Christ" is the message and not the messenger.

The message is how to find the knowledge appropriate for deriving Tree of Life wisdom.

The anti-Christ appears as wisdom from the Tree of Knowledge … borrowed and "empty-of-understanding," from anywhere or by anybody. The "anti-Christ" represents strains of wisdom that direct a truth-seeker to a dead end in their search for the answer to understanding the nature of this reality that affects the outcomes of their human experience, as the "Christ does, in such a way to generate the feelings they react to.

The anti-Christ is what continually feeds into the formation of the Fig Leaf Wisdom that keeps mankind perched on the balance beam of suffering.

MEDIA … the means that an individual uses to access and collect the knowledge they internalize into their belief system to derive the strain of wisdom they rely on to shape their frame of reference … their worldview.

… INTELLECTUALLY METERED MEDIA … used for gathering borrowed or received knowledge. Both Eden Garden trees of wisdom can start with gathering knowledge intellectually.

The difference is that the initial Tree of Life knowledge is merely an intellectual footprint of how to self-train the ability to calm the mind of white noise, focus mental awareness into where the truth-seeker's connection with material reality is sensually coded knowledge exists that will allow inspiring the insightful right thinking to then derive and gain waking awareness of the intrinsically coded wisdom that will unlock and fill the truth-seeker's pit of "emptiness-of-understanding" with the understanding innate to the deeper consciousness that will ease their emotional confusion.

Intellectually metered knowledge gathered for the wisdom that satisfies the Tree of Knowledge of Good and Evil, lacks the intrinsically founded taste of experience-based reference. Reading or maybe being told something is true that has not been sensually tasted (experientially verified) from a book, a friend, a professor, a priest, a snake oil salesman, or maybe a snake in a tree gives a truth-seeker the wisdom that's empty of their understanding.

Even if those with only an understanding drawn from intellectually metered sources has a calmed mind empty of mental white noise, they have no guidance on where to go and what kind of knowledge to find to allow them to insightfully figure out what's going on (the wisdom) to replace their ignorance-founded "emptiness-of-understanding" with the understanding of the relational nature of how cause/effect transpires to make this an impermanent reality.

Most of the time, the truth of this strain of knowledge must be backed by a faith that is blind to the conscious understanding made possible from experience.

... SENSUALLY METERED MEDIA ... used for gathering the experientially founded knowledge that is used to derive what the god Jehovah called Tree of Life Wisdom and demanded that Adam use. Siddhartha Gautama is said to have called Tree of Life wisdom universal reality wisdom.

This knowledge is founded in and metered from what has a sensually registered intrinsic familiarity with what insightfully proves to be self-evident truth. The intrinsically sourced wisdom registers in the waking consciousness level of understanding. Knowledge of this nature is derived from an individual's internal reflection into the ongoing life in the flesh of their body.

The experience can be described through intellectual metering, but only gains waking understanding when it develops an intrinsic history through being sensually metered.

The wisdom derived from this knowledge proves to be self-evident and is backed by a faith that stands steadfast in its truth. "Give me liberty or give me death."

... MEMORY
... INTELLECTUAL MEMORY ... memory that is stored in the outer brain, farther from the central part tied to sensually experienced conditioning ... not coupled intrinsically with waking consciousness

... SENSUAL MEMORY ... memory that's based closer to the central part of the brain, in the amygdala, tied to intrinsic motivation and verification

MINDFULNESS / MEDITATION ... Mindfulness points to the ability to be present and undistracted with a curious and kind heart. Meditation with a calmed mind focused into a physical makeup awareness is time used to self-train this ability.

MORAL/ETHICAL CHARACTER ... What an individual decides to do when they are alone with nobody watching reflects their state of moral/ethical character. What they do when being watched reflects peer pressure.

Calming the mind through developing sound moral/ethical character is the 1st of 3 levels of self-training mind control on the way to becoming enlightened about the impermanent nature of this reality to be rid of suffering and attaining emotional bliss. Establishing what's moral/ethical behavior in a society helps calm the mind from seemingly uncontrollable mental white noise to allow uninterrupted sustained focused mental concentration to further self-train universal or Tree of Life wisdom.

ORIGINAL SIN ... This is what Adam and Eve committed by going against Jehovah's only Garden of Eden command by accepting the fruit (the promise of complete wisdom over everything between good and evil) of the Tree of Knowledge from the Eden snake. Having blind faith in the promise of borrowed or received wisdom from another entity to use to derive the wisdom to support a belief system, blinds an individual from having any sensually founded intrinsic understanding of the proving path to the wisdom they blindly support.

PRETENSE ... An attempt to make something that is not the case appear true. This is like an individual trying to hide or use a fig leaf lined mask to disguise their emptiness-of-understanding.

REALITY'S DIMENSIONAL BACKDROP ... This reality's dimensional backdrop is the interwoven cocktail of natural forces that maintain the animated river of time flow that humanity perceives as being the present moment. It consists of the forces that sustain the energy particle grid that makes true the principles that determine the outcome of all relational interactions that define the relational world of present moment life interactions in all levels of perception.

The backdrop supporting this impermanent reality is made of at least 4 forces that interact to write the script for the principles ruling coming and going energy particle relational interactions that filters up from the metaphysical subatomic world through all the larger objects they makeup. The random coming and going of these forces and the principles they construe are beyond the normal influence of mankind.

Religious theology dogma asserts that it is their perspective god that is the mystical force that created and controls all the principles that sustain all relational interactions.

SALVATION FROM SUFFERING ... (see enlightenment) Salvation from suffering is the common purpose of all religions as well as the school of universal non-sectarian truth. Suffering is related to via an individual's emotional makeup.

Universal wisdom brings understanding to the nature of this impermanent reality to eliminate the ignorance-spawned emptiness-of-understanding that generates all human suffering.

Religion requires a believer to have blind faith in and accept the god's promise to award them with afterlife emotional bliss in exchange for giving their life to the savior and living according to the wisdom voiced in the discipline's holy scriptures.

SANDBOX ETIQUETTE ... the groundwork for human relations learned at the earliest of ages ... the courtesies of proper listening and sharing that are learned under the coaching of a parent, kindergarten, or preschool teacher … while seated in a sandbox … sharing toys.

SCIENCE … A social movement that originated in the mid-second millennia when public awareness evolved from an age of superstition into an age of understanding … from the ancient times of magical superstition to an age of reason. A scientist is anyone who questions anything to gain a better understanding. A scientist is looking for the proof process to any question … not satisfied by just having blind faith in what they do not understand. Anyone who asks a question, looking for a better understanding is a scientist.

It seems some of the most persistent scientists are between 2-3 years old.

Siddhartha Gautama …

> *"This person – Siddhartha Gautama, known as the Buddha, "the enlightened one" – never claimed to be anything other than an ordinary man. Like all great teachers he became the subject of legends, but no matter what marvelous stories were told of his past existences or of his miraculous powers, still all accounts agree that he never claimed to be divine or to be divinely inspired. Whatever special qualities he had were pre-eminently human qualities that he had brought to perfection. Therefore, whatever he achieved is within the grasp of any human being who works as he did.*
>
> *"The Buddha did not teach any religion or philosophy or system of belief. He called his teaching Dhamma, that is, "law," the law of nature. He had no interest in dogma or idle speculation. Instead, he offered a universal, practical solution for a universal problem. "Now as before," he said, "I teach about suffering and get eradication of suffering." He refused even to discuss anything which did not lead to liberation from misery.*
>
> *"This teaching, he insisted, was not something that he had invented or that was divinely revealed to him. It was simply the truth, reality, which by his efforts he had succeeded in discovering, as many people before him had done, as many people after him would do. He claimed no monopoly on the truth."*

— S. XLIV. X. 2, Anuradha Sutta,
as per: *The Art of Living: Vipassana Meditation as taught by S. N. Goenka,*
William Hart p.13-14

Siddhartha is one of the "enlightened souls" from the past who's unique because he was able to put into words and have recorded where he found the right knowledge needed to allow having the right thinking to include the "aha" moments of the insightful wisdom that eliminates the ignorance that caused his human suffering.

SPIRITUALITY ... The abyss of conjecture between an individual's deeper and their waking consciousness awareness. The halls of spirituality echo with the soundings of theology.

SUFFERING ... an emotional state of misery that is challenged for emotional bliss. It comes from a compromised understanding of the relational principles that define the how the impermanent nature brings on cause/effect relationships in this reality. There's an emptiness-of-understanding about how the human condition fits into the human experience ... about how relational principles affect emotional makeup.

This ignorance-spawned emptiness-of-understanding allows for this reality to exist in a state of continuity. This allows for attachments or aversions for the imagined presence of items. This results in the generation of negative emotions related to the imagined permeance of something that doesn't really exist.

The Art of Living: Vipassana Meditation as taught by S. N. Goenka, by William Hart ... a book with the best English translation detailing Siddhartha Gautama's self-discovered pathway that a truth-seeker can follow to gain an enlightened understanding awareness of universal wisdom, as he did.

THEOLOGY / RELIGION ... the study of Devine or Intelligent Design to explain the human condition and the human experience. It is metered and stored intellectually. Science is theology until proven self-evident.

TREE OF KNOWLEDGE WISDOM ... wisdom that is unearned and unexplained. It is borrowed and accepted unverified, requiring blind faith in another source's confidence in the truth of what the wisdom relates to. It leaves a believer in an ignorant empty-of-understanding state about the life principles that affect their emotions. They live in a confused state about what emotionally healthy life priorities should be. They suffer.

It is only intellectually spun. It lacks an intrinsic feel of familiarity for the process of how the strain of wisdom evolves to match its suggested wisdom with its end purpose ... emotional Garden of Eden bliss.

The Garden of Eden's snake's promise of complete wisdom acquisition by eating the fruit left Adam and Eve ignorant to understand their state of nakedness. It left them in shame of their ignorance … reaching for fig leaves.

TREE OF LIFE WISDOM … wisdom that's drawn from knowledge acquired from personal experience in sensually witnessing nature in action, leaving an intrinsic-based conscious understanding of how the cause/effect truth realization process is of what the strain of wisdom applies to. This is the type of wisdom Jehovah warned Adam that he must have or would die spiritually and that Siddhartha Gautama describes the pathway to acquiring while still living.

"VIPASSANA" MEDITATION … "Vipassana" is just an ancient Pali term. Nothing fancy here. India has a much larger selection of vocabulary describing spiritually related issues. English was not yet in existence when the "insight" describing what an "aha" moment of sudden appearing wisdom was had surfaced from mankind's collective deeper consciousness to its waking awareness. It is non-sectarian … associated with no sort of theological dogma.

It is used with no discrimination based on race, sex, or social class with equal benefits to all.

"Vipassana meditation … is a practical way to examine the reality of one's own body and mind, to uncover and solve whatever problems lie hidden there, to develop unused potential, and to channel it for one's good and the good of others."

- The Art of Living: Vipassana Meditation as taught by S. N. Goenka,
William Hart, P. 6

"Vipassana means 'insight' in the ancient Pali language of India. It is the essence of the teaching of the Buddha (Siddhartha Gautama), the actual experience of the truths of which he spoke."

- The Art of Living: Vipassana Meditation as taught by S. N. Goenka,
William Hart, p. 130

As the Garden of Eden cooled from creation,
God's first and only command to mankind for maintaining
the Eden bliss was to trust only the Tree of Life Wisdom
and not to internalize any Tree of Knowledge
promise of all-knowing wisdom.

Genesis author (Moses?) analogizes the life-or-death impor-
tance between using wisdom with experiential roots and that
what's borrowed "empty-of-understanding."

Adam & Eve's branded suffering from
an emptiness-of-understanding echoes
throughout mankind's collective belief system today.

Had Eve turned down the snake-bite temptation there'd be no
need for the Bible or religion.

Fig Leaf Wisdom Zeitgeist

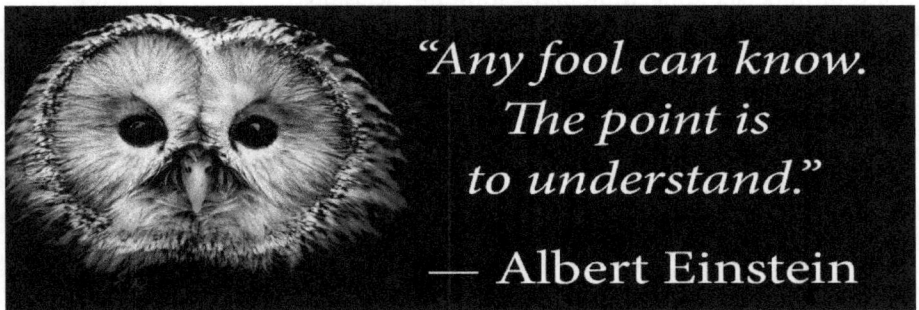

"*Any fool can know.*
The point is
to understand."

— Albert Einstein

There's an important difference between using wisdom founded in mere intellectual knowledge and using the wisdom founded in an intrinsically registered understanding awareness of how a claim connects a cause to its effect.

The distinction here is between having the knowledge of something that is "empty-of-understanding" and having the understanding with no feeling of emptiness.

Respecting the distinction between deriving wisdom from sheer intellectual "knowledge" and deriving wisdom from intrinsically "understanding" its meaning is what the author of the Bible's Genesis Garden of Eden story meant to analogize for his readers.

This distinction is so important, even theology recognizes it. It is the highlighted subject of the first meeting between Jehovah and mankind in the first part of the holy scriptures.

Jehovah makes it spiritual life-or-death clear to Adam that respecting this distinction makes an emotionally recognized difference.

One type of wisdom leads to emotional hell and the other can lead to emotional bliss.

Jehovah neglected telling Adam and Eve why one and not the other.

... The Absence of "Understanding" Tenders Emptiness

Eric Hoffer, an American moral and social philosopher, and receiver of the 1983 Presidential Medal of Freedom shared an insightful life truth:

"Our greatest pretenses are built up not to hide the evil and the ugly in us, but our emptiness. The hardest thing to hide is something that is not there."

~ Eric Hoffer

If an individual errs in making the distinction of which type of wisdom to honor and pursue, they will negotiate their human experience plagued by an emptiness-of-understanding while navigating life decisions with a worldview shaped by Fig Leaf Wisdom.

This individual's worldview was shaped and compromised by using merely intellectually metered knowledge to originate supporting wisdom … like Adam and Eve … and most people since. There's an "emptiness" of understanding what links an effect to its cause.

After ingesting the snake's gifted fruit from the Tree of Knowledge, Adam and Eve were empty-of-understanding their state of nakedness. They merely intellectually knew" of the "all-understanding wisdom" the Eden snake had promised the fruit-wrapped gifted wisdom to have.

They were left ignorant, "empty" of the all-understanding wisdom the snake had promised Eve.

Adam and Eve grabbed for fig leaves to mask their ignorance-seeded shame when pressed by Jehovah for disobeying his only Eden order to partake of any of the Eden trees, but not to ingest any fruit from the Tree of Knowledge of all good and evil.

"Understanding" the principles that grease reality is the difference between living in the fire and brimstone of emotional hell or in the heavenly state of emotional bliss.

Jehovah's punishing "I told you so … I warned you" was delivered in his order to Adam and Eve to walk the Earth in the state of Fig Leaf Wisdom emptiness … as warned … spiritually dead to emotional bliss.

… Humankind's Greatest Pretense has it Spending its Daily Life Energy at Some Level of Shame

… Masking the "Emptiness-of-Understanding"

Most want to belong … to be liked … to be normal … to fit in or maybe they'll bend over backwards trying to "keep up with the Jones."

Much of humankind suffers today using their daily life energy concocting fig leaf-lined masks to hide or disguise their ignorance-spun shame their compromised understanding of life principles their use of mere intellectual knowledge-derived wisdom brings them.

As We Walk Through the Valley of Death (Emotional Turmoil)

There exists a timeless worldwide human condition outcry. It echoes from the collective subconscious emptiness felt from humanity's lack of understanding of the logistics and principles of how the human condition fits into its human experience.

Every human being seeks to avoid emotional misery and realize emotional balance ... emotional bliss ... heavenly bliss as thought by many.

Trying to disguise their emptiness of life understanding prudence preoccupies most. Their present moment stays sidetracked as they flail through their "emptiness-of-understanding" in the flow of life's river of ongoing change that time sits in their laps millisecond by millisecond.

They'll get lost in changing their fig leaf masks at the drop of a hat in effort to posture themselves as situation change with whatever they believe to be a with-it individual.

Unrecognized by most is the challenge that lies in successfully identifying the strain of wisdom that decodes and gives an understanding awareness of this reality's outcome-determining principles that stretch the effects of one elusive present moment into becoming the cause that defines the next ... endlessly over and repeatedly ever since Jehovah first created the earth ... or the big bang ... or whatever.

Care must be taken not to rely on a strain of pseudo wisdom that leaves one empty of life understanding ... with an ego-crafted and ego-defended veneer of self-importance.

... 2 Concepts of Reality Form Two Schools of Wisdom

"Wisdom is the principle thing: therefore get wisdom:
and with all thy getting get understanding."

~Psalms 4 verse 7, King James Version

The "principle thing" ... getting an understanding ... not mere knowledge.

The validity of the wisdom an individual might use to negotiate their human experience depends on their tie with the knowledge used to inspire the thinking used to derive the supporting wisdom.

For the wisdom to be valid, the deriving knowledge must relate to the natural laws of how to best negotiate the nature of the reality that the wisdom decodes.

To get an "understanding," the knowledge referenced to understand the wisdom making sense of the cause/effect relationships in this reality to derive that particular strain of wisdom must be experiential ... the language of emotions ... sensual in nature. Not a promised package of wisdom the individual has no expe-

TWO KINDS OF WISDOM

EARTHLY WISDOM   WISDOM FROM ABOVE

riential reference to … like the wisdom that deceived Adam and Eve.

A person cannot just take any old snake's word for the true depth of understanding of their promised wisdom.

Wisdom drawn from knowledge with no known or understood relationship with the reality the wisdom decodes will not be useful.

Wisdom must be based on knowledge related directly to the working logistics of the natural force-driven principles of this ephemeral reality or the adopted wisdom will leave the individual in a state that's "empty-of-understanding."

Developing an understanding of the principles that determine the outcomes in how things interrelate will fill the emptiness of an individual's waking awareness that otherwise would have had them bowing to some degree of shame.

… Two Realities: with Impermanence or with Time Continuity

There are two possible conceptions of reality's nature. Everything moves or everything stands still.

Each has a wisdom code to explain the nature of how its relational interactions unfold. One comes with a thread of understanding … the other doesn't.

The cause/effect outcomes of interactions would be different in realities with different sets of natural laws. There would have to be a different set of dimensional forces to support the relational principle setup to run each show.

There would have to be different schools of wisdom to decode the different sets of relationships in how the outcome-determining principles from the different reality dimensional backdrops would work in establishing how a cause/effect process would unfold in the differing states of reality.

Basically, in an impermanent reality … one makes sense … and one is empty of sense.

Each different school of wisdom will decode the relationships between that reality's different principles that determine the state of that reality. It only makes simple sense. If the present moment backdrop of one reality's environment is governed by a different set of forces, the principles determining how cause/effect relationships unfold will differ.

If the forces governing the reality are not yet recognized or understood ... the citizenry will create gods to credit the control to. The powerful natural force events they don't yet understand will be imagined coming from sources like the Greek gods that controlled nature's environmental events.

... Time Continuity Differentiates an Imagined Reality

The passage of time must come to a screeching halt to allow envisioning and mentally constructing an imagined reality.

... Some Resist the Idea of Change

Many individuals would rather concentrate on what they have to give up, instead of what they have to gain.

... One Wisdom Card Will Not Decode the Other Reality

This universal reality has ongoing natural forces that brew up an everchanging transforming impermanent backdrop. This impermanent reality has a strain of wisdom that will relate to and interpret the relationships of the natural principles that determine the outcomes of all interactions occurring within this transforming realm of ongoing present moment reality.

... Ignorance from an Emptiness-of-Understanding Intellect Can Allow for Time Continuity

An individual running their life using the strain of wisdom that leaves them empty of an understanding of the patterned principles that sustain the dimensional infrastructure that determine the relational outcomes of all time-fed interchanges of this impermanent reality can lead to an envisioned reality that allows an imagined continuity of time.

It's like jamming around peg into a square hole.

The Ultimate Reality

"The Buddha did not deny the existence of the apparent world of shapes and forms, colors, tastes, smells, pains and pleasures, thoughts and emotions, of beings ... oneself and others. He stated merely that this is not the ultimate reality. With ordinary vision, we perceive only the large-scale patterns into which more subtle phenomena organize themselves. Seeing only the patterns and not the underlying components, we are aware primarily of their differences, and therefore we draw distinctions, assign

labels, form preferences and prejudices, and commence liking and disliking … the
process that develops into craving and aversion."
… William Hart, *The Art of Living: Vipassana Meditation as Taught*
by S. N. Goenka, p. 119-120

It might be thought that seemingly permanent objects like their car or maybe their house are permanent objects.

What's in the range of human perception and how it is perceived is not the ultimate reality.

William Hart writes about how at S.N. Goenka seminars, it's pointed out how Siddhartha explained how what humans perceive as reality is really not the ultimate reality. What people see within the range of human focus is merely the outer boundaries of the ultimate reality processes in motion … the tiny quarks of subatomic energy are busy following nature's dimensional force driven patterned principles random dance rhythm of ongoing change.

Seeing only what encloses the real activity that's occurring, leaves people seeing the comparative differences and not so much how everything, living or not, is composed of the same energy in motion.

People not cognizant of the inner truth will attach the liking and disliking to the seemingly permanent states of these things and this will develop into the attachment and aversion that causes suffering.

The effects from coming and going bits of energy coming from the last moment in time becomes the cause of the next moment's state of those bits of energy … in everything. Life is like a river, a constant flow.

The purpose of this reality is to initiate the ongoing change inherent to an expanding universe … to evolve life. Animate or inanimate, everything is giving birth to change.

Nothing stands still in time. The nature of this reality is one of transforming constant change … that's the only thing that doesn't change.

… Fundamental Ignorance is the Root of Human Suffering

If a reality is imagined allowing its timeline to skip a beat and exist continually, its cause/effect interactions will not unfold to the code of wisdom that interprets the relational principles that maintain the ephemeral nature of this universe's transforming reality.

This reality's state of ever-change is mistakenly and probably unknowingly understood by most as allowing for time continuity.

The difference and its significance go unnoticed by most.

This state of awareness allows for holding on to concepts like a "car" or a "house" as something that can be possessed. The state of awareness ignores the ongoing motion within what appears to the human eye.

Knowingly or unknowingly recognizing time as having a nature allowing continuity is thought to be the fundamental state of ignorance that spawns the craving and attachment to what is not truly there. This ignorance is what lies at the root of all emoti0nal suffering,

... Religion's Templated Theology

Most of humanity struggles trying to understand the unknown. Many blindly vow their trusting faith to support the wisdom they borrow from one of theology's scripture-promised religion wisdom templates.

They live in hope that their chosen god will take their hand and shelter them through the ongoing array of mysterious ongoing present moment change-up Father Time streams their way.

When theologians think of finding emotional (heavenly) bliss, they look up into the sky where they imagine the source of emotional suffering relief to be found.

... Developing Intrinsic Understanding

When one who places their trust in the strain of life wisdom that decodes this impermanent reality thinks of finding emotional bliss, they look inside to where they can sensually witness the manifestation of the intrinsically metered knowledge that inspires the right thinking to self-train the Tree of Life wisdom.

The strain of life wisdom that decrypts the principal relationships of an impermanent reality supersedes the waking emptiness inherent to adapting to or internalizing the hollow wisdom that allows for a continual reality backdrop for the truth of its soul-saving claim to find or make a claim to its truth possible.

Life wisdom bears an understanding awareness of the logistics of what happens between a cause and its effect. Life wisdom inspires the growing compassion-fed courage to step out and ask why or demand to see tangible proof.

Wisdom lacking in experiential verification with logistics derived from knowledge that is not centered around the inherent truths of impermanence

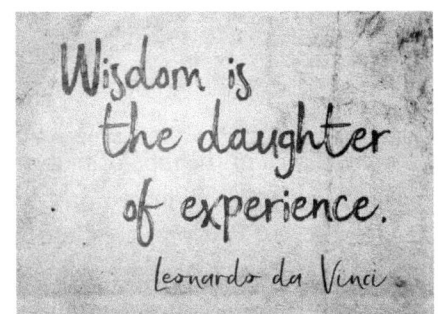

Wisdom is the daughter of experience.

leonardo da Vinci

will leave the individual ignorant with a feeling of emptiness-of-understanding. Their emptiness will leave them grabbing in fear-riddled self-doubt for Fig Leaves to hide their manifestation of some degree of shame.

Jehovah made Eden-clear the Binary Distinction of which Wisdom Supports the Pathway to Heavenly Bliss

... Type of Wisdom to Live By is of Spiritual Life-or-Death Importance

8. *And the Lord God planted a garden eastward in Eden: and there he put the man whom he had formed.*

9. *And out of the ground made the Lord God grow every tree that is pleasant to the sight, and good for food: the tree of life also in the midst of the garden, and the tree of knowledge of good and evil.*

15. *And the Lord God took the man and put him into the Garden of Eden to dress it and to keep it.*

16. *And the Lord God commanded the man, saying, of every tree of the garden thou mayest freely eat:*

17. *But of the tree of the knowledge of good and evil, thou shalt not eat of it: for in the day that thou eatest thereof thou shalt surely die."*

Genesis 2: 8, 9, 15-17 (King James translation)

The individual, some say it was Moses, who scripted the Garden of Eden story to open the genesis of the Old Testament had a spiritual maturity enlightened enough to understand how experience is necessary before any wisdom can be derived about the logistics of any relationship.

It's whether to have blind faith in what another entity calls wisdom or to experientially understand a relationship to derive wisdom.

The choice in the type of knowledge to use to derive wisdom will determine the nature of an individual's worldview.

In the very first post-creation discourse with mankind, the Genesis author knew to give the choice of wisdom top order. Wisdom choice was the sole/soul directive of Jehovah's first communication with mankind. Jehovah gave life-or-death detail to what an individual's wisdom-deriving knowledge source options meant to spiritual bliss ... eternal emotional bliss from the Tree of Life or spiritual emptiness/death from settling for borrowed wisdom from the Tree of Knowledge of Good and Evil.

... Adam and Eve Lived Blissfully Unashamed Before the Snake Made a False Promise to Eve

> *2:25 And they were both naked, the man and his wife, and were not ashamed.*

Eve's choice led to shame for both her and Adam.

... Eve Is offered Promise of Unverified Unearned Wisdom

(Had Eve been Cajun, she would have just eaten the snake and there would have been no need for any religion.)

> *3:4 And the serpent said unto the woman, Ye shall not surely die:*
>
> *3:5 For God doth know that in the day ye eat thereof, then your eyes shall be opened, and ye shall be as gods, knowing good and evil.*

... Eve then Adam Choose to Have Blind Faith in Borrowed Wisdom

> *3:6 And when the woman saw that the tree was good for food, and that it was pleasant to the eyes, and a tree to be desired to make one wise, she took of the fruit thereof, and did eat, and gave also unto her husband with her; and he did eat.*

... They Crafted Fig Leaf Aprons to Mask Their Nakedness

> *3:7 And the eyes of them both were opened, and they knew that they were naked; and they sewed fig leaves together and made themselves aprons.*

... They Face Universal Reality

> *3:8 And they heard the voice of the LORD God walking in the garden in the cool of the day: and Adam and his wife hid themselves from the presence of the LORD God amongst the trees of the garden.*
>
> *3:9 And the LORD God called unto Adam, and said unto him, Where art thou?*

... Adam And Eve Retreat in Shamed Fear from Emptiness-In-Understanding Their Nakedness

> *3:10 And he said, I heard thy voice in the garden, and I was afraid, because I was naked; and I hid myself.*

... God-Enforced (Universal Reality) Principled Outcome

> *3:11 And he said, who told thee that thou wast naked? Hast thou eaten of the tree, whereof I commanded thee that thou shouldest not eat?*
>
> *3:17 And unto Adam he (Jehovah) said, Because thou hast heartened unto the voice of thy wife, and hast eaten of the tree, of which I commended thee, saying, Thou shalt not eat of it: cursed is the ground for thy sake; in sorrow shalt thou eat of it all the days of thy life;"*
>
> *King James Version, http://www.dltk-bible.com/genesis/chapter2-kjv. htm*

Jehovah didn't explain to Adam and Eve why ingesting the false wisdom was bad, only the consequence of spiritual death ... emptiness-in-understanding.

... Genesis Creation

Theology's Garden of Eden analogy is one way to illustrate what causes the emptiness of understanding that Eric Hoffer refers to near the top of this chapter.

The strain of wisdom Adam and Eve decided to internalize was not the right kind to decode the ways of the environment that comprised their ever-changing transforming elusive present moment. The promised wisdom left them empty-of-understanding.

Each school of wisdom corresponds to one of the two trees at the center of The Garden of Eden.

A Tree of Life wisdom-enriched understanding feeds from the experiential knowledge of the living self-evident truth about what comprises the evasive aspect defining the ever-elusive present moment of this living universal reality.

The other brand of wisdom comes pre-cooked, freeze-dried, and notion aged.

... No Biblical Storyline

Had Eve merely turned down Eden snake's offer of gifted wisdom, there would have been no storyline for the Bible ... no Bible. There'd be no need for the blanket of hope theology speaks of that is needed to corral mankind's unanswered unrest.

Because Adam and Eve had their way with violating their god's virgin command it was Jehovah's sentence to them to live their spiritual lives, dead to Eden Bliss, trapped in an eddy of empty understanding-spawned ignorance-inspired suffering while staying busy managing his new planet Earth.

... The Original Sin?

Could this disobedience to the first and only command Jehovah had given to mankind be mankind's original sin? Is it that all of Eve's descendants would forever be born with this ignorance?

Is it that mankind is born into ignorance with an emptiness disconnect between their waking conscious awareness and their wise-to-nature deeper consciousness? They would have to either have blind faith-lined hope in another entity's promised log of wisdom or derive their wisdom from the type of knowledge that allows them to consciously have an intrinsic understanding of how their emotional nature syncs into the ever-changing nature of this reality.

Most individuals never realize there's a difference in the wisdom genre let alone the primal importance of understanding which strain of wisdom decodes humanity's relationship with the nature of this impermanent reality and how understanding it will lead to the same emotional bliss that is promised in the afterlife by theology ... that is sought after by non-theologian universal reality truth-seekers before dying.

Experiential Versus Borrowed Wisdom

... The Pathway to Borrowed Wisdom is Script-Directed and Experiential Wisdom Pathway is Self-Trained

Most individuals never acquire a heartfelt understanding of the latticework of knowledge they use for understanding the life principles that will seed the wisdom they use in making decisions. These principles determine the decision outcomes which they have no control over and will affect them on some positive or negative emotional level.

There are moral/ethical boundaries they must set that are set to ideally help them to lead a life of compassion-rooted joy and happiness. Many will act in the "right" way only because they have been advised to from another source, not through gaining an experiential understanding of the relationship of the principle-driven outcomes that make the behavior a "right" behavior.

... One of the Best Spiritual Books Ever Written Catorgorizes Wisdom

William Hart authored a book in 1987 where he described the teachings of Theravada Buddhism's Dalai Lama of sorts, S. N. Goenka. Like how Tibet's

(Mahayana Buddhism) Dalai Lama's (Tenzin Gyatso) purpose is to preserve through the living person to living person (Dalai Lama to Dalai Lama) exchange of the Buddhist monk, Atisha's interpretatuion of Siddhartha's teachings to Tibet a millennia ago when Buddhism was again allowed in the country, S.N. Goenka's teachings parley the person to person relayed teachings of Siddhartha hinself (Thereveda Buddism.)

S. N. Goenka's teachings have been personally handed down from the earlier time when Siddhartha's teachings were first brought into Burma. Like Siddhartha origionally taught, Vipassana meditation centers the focus of awareness more purposfully into the flesh of the truth seeker ... the theater of life manifestation.

> "*Whether it is accepted out of blind faith, out of craving, or out or fear, received wisdom is not one's own wisdom, not something experienced for oneself. It is borrowed wisdom.*
>
> *The second type of wisdom is intellectual understanding. After reading or hearing a certain teaching, one considers it and examines whether it is really rational, beneficial, and practical. And if it is satisfying at the intellectual level, one accepts it as true. Still, this is not one's own insight., but only an intellectualization of the wisdom one has heard.*
>
> *The third type of wisdom is that which arises out of one's own experience, out of personal realization of truth. This is the wisdom that one lives, real wisdom that will bring about a change in one's life by changing the very nature of the mind.*"
>
> — *The Art of Living: Vipassana Meditation as Taught by S. N. Goenka*, William Hart P.89

This writing considers wisdom that is "received" from elsewhere or acquired "intellectually" to be borrowed or intellectual. This includes borrowed wisdom that has been pieced together from separate sources.

Neither sort comes with an understanding of what happens in a cause that brings about its effect ... the believer just takes the word of the wisdom source.

This wisdom can either be borrowed or received intellectually packaged that is intellectually metered from another source that promises the validity of tibe wisdom.

Or wisdom can be derived from experiential knowledge that is intrinsically understood and comes sensually metered ... like Jehovah mandated and called Tree of Life Wisdom.

Any strain of theology's sectarian wisdom is not the product of experientially acquired knowledge and its wisdom is not the derived product of any gathered experiential knowledge that inspires self-generated "aha" insightful thinking. It comes empty of an intrinsic natured understanding.

Theology-founded wisdom is borrowed wisdom. All its various templates lack having any intrinsically founded self-evident palpable basis for its believer's spot-on reference.

Religious theology is internalized unverifiable and its claim to truth requires an individual's blind faith and ongoing hope in its truth. Its network of supporting knowledge has no intrinsically established experiential history with the believer.

Its wisdom was never worked for or "earned" by the believer. It has no tangible tie-in.

... Sensual Versus Intellectual Awareness

An individual's waking awareness is torn between 2 worlds. While they stand living in one ... the other world is imagined. Sensual versus intellectual.

Their focus remains disjointed in finding the wisdom to handle everyday life circumstance in between the life wisdom they have derived from sensually witnessing the self-evident display of life principles in the reality they live in, and the one made up of the cognitive impressions left from what they have metered intellectually.

A religious belief is intellectually metered. The cognitively sketched mental conception of their blind faith-founded unverifiable non-tangible untouchable heavenly reality realizes an individually unique brick and mortar design only in their imagination.

The subtle blur in their conscious direction sets the stage to some degree of unsettled confusion in understanding the sensually founded real-world cause responsible for affecting, in a non-biased way, the emotions every individual has been conditioned to use in finding and rating the emotional balance of their human condition during its human experience.

This borrowed wisdom is used in understanding and confronting their fear of what is unknown during their human experience. Having unfounded faith in some sort of protection from an unseen entity they have blindly pledged allegiance to is all they have to protect them from the shadows of the unknown.

They often stand empty-of-understanding the principles of what connects a cause to its effect in their life circumstance. They will fall short of emotional balance, and they will suffer in their ignorance.

... Tree of Life or Tree of Knowledge Wisdom ... The Human Dilema

Everyone chooses wisdom based either on the knowledge they have accumulated from experience or wisdom they have merely intellectually borrowed from another source while trusting in its promised validity.

Received or borrowed wisdom is what Adam and Eve chose to internalize in the Genesis Garden of Eden analogy. They had no understanding of the supporting network of principles of truth supporting the snake-promised wisdom explaining their nakedness that Jehovah later questioned them about.

This is what the god Jehovah warned would bring certain spiritual death from his Eden paradise. They grabbed for fig leaves to cover up the subject of their ignorance-inspired shame.

... Doing The Due Diligence

Using borrowed wisdom can stem from an individual's lack of the due diligence to get off the couch to find the appropriate knowledge used to derive Tree of Life Wisdom. In receiving borrowed wisdom, they do not need to find the courage to step outside their circle of influence to ask for verification about things they do not understand.

If they have chosen a religious discipline, they only have a faith that leaves them blind to the process of how what they are blindly believing actually builds to its truth.

It comes down to either using wisdom derived from life knowledge gathered and verified through experience (Tree of Life Wisdom) or yielding to temptation and borrowing experientially unverified wisdom (Tree of Knowledge Wisdom) that comes borrowed from and guaranteed by another entity.

In the search for the wisdom to find relief from suffering, every individual will choose or subconsciously favor and drift to which sort of wisdom they will trust to frame and shape their worldview. The role models that initially help to condition an individual's belief system greatly affect how high the bar of vetting claim acceptance is set for the individual as the years pass.

They will tend to form a "muscle" memory for the type of place to seek wisdom-deriving knowledge from and the degree of verification the role model settled for.

How often did the role models ask, like an insistent 2-year-old, "but why?!" or like a budding 14-year-old, "prove it!!". Or was it typically easy for them to just accept what they are told?

... Experiential Knowledge

To become Tree of Life "wise" about the ways of "life" itself it is necessary to accumulate knowledge from catching life manifest red-handed and to sensually witness life energy itself manifest. Then from times of inner deliberation (active or passive meditation or just an "aha" insight that hits you at any odd time) on that knowledge, it is possible to self-train having the right thinking to derive insightful thought-inspired wisdom to build up to a state of enlightened emotional balance.

This brings understanding clarity to the natural force-driven principles of this reality's impermanent nature. It gives an understanding definition to the relational principles that ensure proper rhythm to the ongoing in-color present moment animation of this impermanent reality's timeline

It fills the emptiness-of-understanding that would exist when using an inappropriate strain of wisdom with an understanding awareness.

Eden snake's wisdom plucked from the Tree of Knowledge of Good and Evil came borrowed by Adam and Eve with only the promise of all-knowing wisdom. Being borrowed, it stood void of having any understanding of the interconnectedness of the network of the knowledge interfacing the relationship logistics that accounted for an understanding of how a claim affected the truth of the effect of the claim.

After internalizing the borrowed strain of guaranteed all-knowing wisdom fruit of the snake's gifted wisdom, Adam and Eve felt only emptiness when trying to understand their Eden-nakedness. The borrowed wisdom was not suited to consciously decode the relational principles that gave them an understanding of how their nakedness fit it.

Tree of Knowledge Wisdom
Feeds on and into Fundamental Ignorance

"Beware of false knowledge, it is more dangerous than ignorance."
~George Bernard Shaw

... Fundamental Ignorance Nurtures Attachment to Illusions of What has Actually Since Changed ... No Longer There

Those who are consciously unaware that the only thing in this reality that never changes is this reality's state of transformation, out of ignorance, will become attached to their ideas of things where their true presence once occupied only a tick in the timeline of this reality's ever-transforming texture.

They become attached to what they desire or crave. They will probably have developed an ego that grasps to their illusionary "I AM" as well as to anything related to what's "mine".

This self-ego protects their imagined "I AM." It becomes a master crafter of fig leaf-lined masks to hide their shame-related feelings coming from their emptiness-of-understanding suited to match the different sorts of social circumstances they encounter.

They will form an attachment to their views, perceptions, and beliefs. Should they choose to follow a theological template, they will become attached to the rites and rituals that support the purported borrowed wisdom with no real understanding of any causal relationship between the rite or the actions of a ritual or of how it be the cause bringing about the effect of the promised emotional bliss.

This religious notion finds life only in their intellectual mind. They develop and realize no real intrinsic, gut-felt connection. It has no relationship with principled workings of the transforming reality it lifelessly clings to.

... Snake's Fruit of Promised Wisdom is an Allegory for a Religion Template ...

Like how Adam and Eve used their freewill to decide to blindly internalize the promise of an unverifiable all-knowing wisdom from the Eden snake, people today use their freewill to blindly internalize an unverifiable religion wisdom template purporting a promised state of future emotional bliss.

Today's believers commit to blindly trust their adopting and following what's said to be a god-drafted pathway to a future "promised land" of emotional bliss secured only by an unverifiable and what's said to be a god-drafted code of wisdom. Like with Adam and Eve, their choice leaves them empty of having an intrinsically founded understanding of the logistics supporting the cause/effect infrastructure of what defines and makes true the soul-saving claim supported or promised by the borrowed wisdom.

Wisdom derived from the Tree of Knowledge is empty of the intrinsically metered reservoir of understanding awareness attained from gathering the experience-founded sensual knowledge necessary to allow the right thinking to derive Jehovah's mandated Tree of Life wisdom.

... A Cognitively Warehoused Future Away-from-Earth Vacation Suspended in Time

Believers of borrowed wisdom have an intellectually sketched picture of how their unique imagination envisions the future land of heaven that awaits them after they die if they make it through the final heaven-or-hell cut after the Battle of Armageddon on the Day of Judgement.

To allow the developing of their intellectual understanding of this borrowed wisdom, religious believers will cognitively retain their pieced-together unique interpretation of what this spot in the sky of heavenly paradise looks like with its network of godly beings. It's a picture of suffering relief hope suspended in time until brought back to mind after Sunday morning mass to make intellectually crafted changes.

To cognitively sketch the developing mental image of this promised afterlife paradise, theologians must have a belief system that allows for their perception of the transforming flow of this universal reality to assume a skip-in-time state of continuity.

Imagining an unchanging presence of things and ideas allows their attachment to those illusions and their derivatives.

Being unwise to the ongoing unalterable presence of the force-driven principles that define the impermanent nature of this reality, they walk empty-of-understanding through an emotional minefield, open prey to the negative emotions that can follow in the wake of being attached to or aversive something or idea.

Something they might react to in ignorance of the principles that control the outcome can create and feed into their bout with suffering.

Their life could seem like a living emotional hell.

The ignorance-infected mindset that this reality's impermanent nature can take on a continual presence can be so subtle that it commonly evades detection. It's so prevalent in society, it can go masked undetectable while being considered normal.

… Allowing Time Continuity is the Most Fundamental form of Ignorance

This primal level of fundamental ignorance is what Siddhartha determined to be the "fundamental ignorance." He taught how fundamental ignorance is the cause of all human suffering.

Eliminating fundamental ignorance sets the stage for a life journey of self-training the ability to gain an enlightened understanding of its cause and solution to eliminate suffering and to finding the pathway to understanding, owning, and replacing it with the bliss found in emotional balance.

… Tree of Knowledge Hollow Wisdom Feeds on and into Fundamental Ignorance to Manifest in Fig Leaf Wisdom

Christian theology touts that mankind's gone astray and suffered ever since it started settling for borrowed wisdom on day 6 of the Genesis account of creation. Some modern-day personalized form of this mal-adjusted worldview is what most learn to consider to be normal life.

Most of mankind uses wisdom that has been borrowed from one of theology's disciplines. Their borrowed wisdom is founded in a purported god's claim of power control that cannot be tangibly verified and must be blindly internalized to then shape their worldview.

They have no intrinsic grasp on the logistics of the borrowed wisdom they use to make many of their life decisions. They will often find themselves in situations where they are empty-of-understanding. Just like Adam and Eve, they will use Fig Leaf Wisdom to understand the reality of Father Time's ongoing change and reach for a fig leaf-lined mask to hide behind.

Garden of Eden-Like Ignorance-Inspired Shame Manifests Today from a Worldwide Fig Leaf Wisdom Mindset

... The Hollow Truth of Unearned Wisdom Appears in Different Shades of Emotional Shame

Adam and Eve experienced ignorance-inspired guilt-ridden fear-laced shame when confronted by their creator after disregarding his forbidding spiritual life-or-death warning. They had decided to ingest the borrowed wisdom from the Tree of Knowledge while realizing their newly acquired snake-promised Tree of Knowledge all-knowing wisdom had left them empty-of-understanding their nakedness.

Their strain of snake-gifted wisdom was unsuitable for interpreting or understanding the relational principles relating to the impermanent nature of this reality. From the emptiness-founded shame they felt, they grabbed for fig leaves to cover the object of their shame.

... Adam and Eve Performed the "Original Sin" ... The Birth of Fig Leaf Wisdom

It was the original sin. It was the first sin ...by not following the premise of the wisdom of God's word to eat only of the Tree of Life.

... Mental Mile-A-Minute White Noise Plagues Humanity's Mental Focus

Many individuals fail to recognize that what they have adopted as normal life really is some degree of suffering. Many find it difficult to calm the "voices inside their head" to bring focused order to their threads of thought.

By the time an individual has become unhappy and dissatisfied with their human experience, many have lost the ability to quell their mental "white noise" to find the clarity of thought to even know what question(s) to ask to get the ball to emotional peace rolling.

The deafening sound and ongoing confusion stirred up by this mental white noise can be what helped inspire their search for suffering relief before choosing a religion's template.

An individual cannot solve a problem they do not quite understand while living in their present moment state of confused status-quo frustrated discontent. They cannot stop the avalanche of run-on mental white noise that bullies their thought pattern at a pace beyond their control from one topic of troubling rumination to the next.

Many will grasp out and settle for a templated answer of purported ageless wisdom to line their belief system. They will live on hope and prayer. They will use their unique understanding of the religious template to shape, and in so doing, will muffle their freewill and compromise their worldview.

… Shame is a Human Emotion … Has Many Faces … Is Timeless in Nature

Many individuals bow to the living manifestation of the same sort of shame or self-reproach as did Adam and Eve when hiding their ignorance-spun shame at Jehovah's confrontation about their decision to partake of the snake-gifted fruit of promised Tree of Knowledge wisdom … unvalidated and empty-of-understanding.

Shame takes on many forms. In its simple form, an individual might feel a bit awkward or hesitant. They might feel humbled in their ignorance or maybe a bit self-conscious.

Feeling flushed, awkward, reticent, speechless, withdrawn, or self-conscious are incarnations of shame. Being ashamed, embarrassed, intimidated, remorseful, or sheepish are a bit more pronounced forms of shame. When an individual feels emotionally demeaned, disgraced, ostracized, or maybe self-condemning, they are experiencing shame in its most intense form.

Adam and Eve felt ashamed and guilt stricken. They felt intimidated and full of regret. Shame-triggered remorse fed their impulse to reach for fig leaves.

Emotional shame might appear as feeling degraded or disgraced.

Shame has a kaleidoscope of incarnations.

Feeling ostracized or self-condemning are more extreme degrees of shame.

This uncompromising and unforgiving "Adam and Eve" shame-drawing emptiness prods humanity relentlessly during its ageless quest for emotional bliss. Shame affects individuals today as during ancient times. It is a human emotion … timeless in nature.

There is a very real present-day incarnation of the very same shame-spun need for a Garden of Eden fig tree leaves used by Adam and Eve as pictured during the Genesis account of creation.

Shame shows its boogieman face on a non-prejudiced worldwide scale.

Fig Leaf Mask Personified

Wellness Guru Dr. Deepak Chopra points to how greed and fear are the powers that are strangling the USA today.

Dr. Chopra said to Julia La Roche in a 12/23/20 Yahoo Finance interview that the USA is infected with greed and fear. He pointed out how citizens now spend money they do not have to buy things they do not need to impress people they do not like.

Basing decision-making wisdom on inappropriate knowledge from a mis-guided worldview leads to outcomes that are not accompanied by emotions of compassion-spun joy and happiness.

People suffer. They have no waking conception of the light at the end of the tunnel.

People wear masks to hide the emptiness that fills their void of understanding the life principles to follow that lead to compassion-spun joy and happiness.

... Self Ego Postures Social Importance

When trying to follow any promise of borrowed wisdom, ignorance-in-spired uncertainty and doubt are unavoidable and are common facets of being empty-of-understanding. The ensuing shadow of ignorance-reflecting shame inspires many to craft and posture a self-protecting ego-designed self-image to bridge or bully-over the pit of potential shame in their valley of understanding emptiness.

An individual's ego might cherry-pick from their memory treasure chest that best aligns with what and how they want their presence to seem to others. It will create a collection of situation-appropriate social masks to avoid the shame they have having a worldview understanding shaped by Fig Leaf Wisdom.

This lets them fit into any foreseeable social situation comprised of individ-uals with different ideas of what's good to do or what's unacceptable. Not really knowing which way to go on right/wrong or socially acceptable/unacceptable, they can mask-up to best fit into either.

Some individuals like for it to appear to others that they have their life path well envisioned and well under control. They want it to seem that even with what might feel like hollow self-assurance, they still have what it takes.

As they face the unexpected change of each new present moment, they choose which mask to wear to bridge over their valley of empty understanding ... their valley of their soul's death to true present moment joy and happiness.

Donna Bernadette Vigil, a fully initiated Nagual woman and working part-ner of the honorable shaman of Mexican Toltec self-mastery, don Miguel Ruiz sheds insight on how many individuals choose to cope with a reality they do not understand.

She ventures how people often wear masks to posture themselves into what they think seems to be a good life while silently "searching for something to fill the emptiness."

She describes in her book *Mastery of Awareness*, p. 38-40, how many will posture a self-image to fill their soul's emptiness:

"You, like every human being, become a master of the mask, but it is not the mask of sincerity or impeccability. It is whatever mask you believe will get you what you think you want. Ultimately you pay a price in life for wearing the masks. Learning to wear masks begins in childhood, through the domestication process. This is how children become such good manipulators. When you were a child, you realized that if you put on a certain mask, you could get what you wanted in life. Your mask may have been being cute, the good girl/boy, the funny child, the tough guy, or any number of other possibilities. You quickly learned which masks worked for you. As you grew into an adult, you learned to wear more and more masks and to become masterful at them.

Saying that you are a great lover is one of the biggest masks in the Dream of the Planet. And sex, like relationships, is one of the biggest hooks. You may want to be lovers with someone desirable in the Dream and then walk away and say, "I not only had this special person, but I was the greatest lover they ever had." Another big mask is the mask of wealth. You may want to wear the mask that you are wealthy by driving an expensive car, living in an expensive house, or wearing designer clothes. These may be way above your budget, but you buy them just to look like you have money or are well off.

You have so many masks that are part of your everyday life because the masks keep you from having to look at your true self. Putting on a mask is as simple and routine as deciding which dress or suit you are going to wear that day. One of the most common masks is the one you wear around your friends. You decide every day whether you are sincere around them or whether you are going to be fake, putting on a mask so you will be liked and accepted. Not only children and high school kids do this.

You put on masks regardless of your church, your environment, or your culture. As an adult, you put on masks to get the greatest partner, to be looked up to by members of your culture or community, and to be accepted in whatever social circle you try to be in. You change masks like you are changing your clothes. You get so lost in the separation of yourself from your true nature that you never look at your soul. Meanwhile, you feel empty and sad inside, and are always searching for something to fill the emptiness."

An Individual with a life purpose clouded or completely blocked out by a confused or misguided validation describing an illusionary nature of this reality can continue to suffer for the rest of their life the discomfort and unrest from misunderstanding life relationships within the cause/effect dynamics of many situations. They will struggle to find mental balance as they teeter in between deciding which of their ego-created masks to wear to present the impression they feel they need to fit into each changing situation where what they sense missing from the status-quo might be found.

Women will pencil their masks of their faces and men will select the right necktie to best neutralize, buffer or maybe exploit what uncertainty they fear they are going to face next.

They search unknowingly for something to set anchor and stabilize the ongoing change they take for granted and do not understand and feel lost in. They clench onto things and ideas that in this transforming reality do not really exist while standing stiff and unprepared to process the novelty of each new unexpected and unfamiliar present moment.

They do not know that by not being wise to the natural laws imposed on the human condition inherent to this state of reality, they will always entertain an ongoing present moment struggle while looking back over their shoulder and trying to explain and keep up with what just happened. Because they spend much of their time always looking back, they cannot be effective at proactive planning.

Wrapped in Fig Leaf Wisdom they strive to somehow force-fit and make everything they perceive to make sense within the boundaries of their untethered idea of "normal."

They struggle to find inner peace with no direction or understanding of what strain of media to turn to or where to look to find the real-time incarnation of the Jehovah-noted primal truth that balances the inner justice of the human condition on the ephemeral scales of the human experience.

To find emotional balance in this transforming reality, the truth seeker has to seek the right strain of wisdom-deriving knowledge to self-train the Tree of Life wisdom to better understand the life principles that determine the five w's in all types of interactions that determine the outcomes of all forms of change down to the ever-elusive ultra-elementary quark particles of coming and going energy that power all matter from the fundamental subatomic quantum mechanical universe to what science poses to be the expansion extent of the alleged 14 billion-year-old "big bang" universe.

... Many Suffer from the Friction

Some individuals have their worldview grounded in an objective perception of the changing present moment while some have their worldview tripped up in an agenda that lacks having any associated intrinsic feel corroboration.

They use their daily energy just treading time, disassociated from the sensual reality of the present moment.

The assurance for what the latter group hopes for is strapped to what another source promises them it should be. Their emotional balance hangs suspended in present moment confusion grounded in some theological apparition.

Their emotional peace is caught in between the blind faith they have in something they do not have an intrinsic connection with and the self-evident truth that is in the naked change they face second by second.

They suffer from the friction.

Fig Leaf Wisdom Epitomized … Doesn't Have to be Religion

… Cult Feed is Borrowed Wisdom … Any Mental Process Lost in White Noise Reasons Using Fig Leaf Wisdom

When an individual's thought process is dominated by mental white noise that clouds their present moment level of awareness to indecision and uncertainty lacking in the ability to focus or sustain a train of thought, like those who become hypnotized into borrowing a religion's promising templated wisdom, suffers the consequences of having their reasoning subject to the fundamental ignorance inherent to Fig Leaf Wisdom that allows their becoming attached and aversive to things and ideas. This leads to their suffering.

They can't begin to hone an understanding waking consciousness when they have no idea what knowledge will lead them to the ability to derive Tree of Life experiential wisdom or where to find it. They suffer the headache of just trying to concentrate.

… Finding Group Comfort … In Wisdom Supporting a Religion's Promise or Maybe Trump-Branded Wisdom Supporting a "MAGA" Promise

Many of those scarred by this friction of understanding use their present moment life energy to self-posture what they perceive to be socially important or at least acceptable. Their worldview is tendered by the echo of emptiness-of-understanding that affects all their life decisions.

They might be emotionally frustrated with a life rhythm hollowed by a deeply seated confused life purpose agenda. Many find protection and the strength to act or speak out when a collective number of like-minded individuals suffering from the same friction scars emerges.

They might work up the blind faith to trust and borrow wisdom from another entity … maybe from a religion with a god-promised after-death paradise … or maybe Donald Trumpism that promises return to an undefinable point in the USA past to someday "Make America Great Again."

Trump's promised agenda was greatly influenced by Trump's ongoing chorus line and personal instructions on what his wisdom sees as being what's needed to reestablish that undefined state of a "Great America."

Trumpites did not think it was their evil inside that was motivating their disruptive agendas. They did not feel any concern about their presence seeming ugly to others. Many seemed to share in some level of collective pride and courage in striking out against the feeling of "emptiness-of-understanding" they all shared.

They were acting out because of the pent-up emptiness-of-understanding that filled their conscious awareness.

... Trumpism Found No Room for Compassion

Their collective agenda lacked any compassion-fed purpose. They individually struggled to come to grips with their internal battles that preoccupied any mental space for objective informed concern for external affairs. They were consumed by misdirected emotions reflecting anger and hate that numbed their awareness to constructive concerns for any true nonbelligerent balance in external affairs ... anything calling for empathy for others.

The mental white noise that fed their internal unrest blocked out an awareness rooted in the empathy-founded compassion that falls in step with the rhythm of the patterns of principles that affect positive outcomes of the cause/effect relational interactions that feed into this reality's ongoing naked change that provides this realty's animated storyline.

Compassion allows situational change to flow frictionless in harmony.

Their conscious awareness was empty of the understanding needed to motivate compassionate involvement in public affairs. How their behavior drew influence, courage, and strength from like-minded individuals and their involvement in the collective disruptive revolting agenda of those lost to the same understanding documents this.

Their greatest pretense was with their struggle to find direction to affectively fill in the haunting emptiness that ruled their present moment awareness.

These individuals used Fig Leaf Wisdom in deciding how to navigate their present moment. They displayed collective blind faith in whatever Trump said. Many followed his instructions that ended up leading them straight into a jail cell.

Trump Gaslighting Fooled Nearly Half of The Voters

... Still, Over Half of Voters Were Wise to Trump Reality Model
... Blind Faith in an Unverifiable Claim was Needed

The 2020 Presidential Election had everyone the USA electorate faced with using their individually unique strain of wisdom in making the decision on who to vote for. It was felt by many that one candidate posed an infecting fascist-bent authoritarian threat to the fiber of democracy.

How deep was their understanding of life principles to face up to this unusual twist in USA leadership style decisions? It took time for many to realize there was a candidate who cuddled other world authoritarians and insulted and degraded anybody else at the drop of a hat.

What knowledge source did they reference to base their understanding to make their voting choice?

It appears that many voters patterned their lives using Fig Leaf Wisdom ... nearly half of the electorate made a presidential choice that rubbed against the relational principles that enable a smooth flow of time-spawned change. Being empty of having a waking sensitivity to what human behaviors manifest the outcomes that flow in rhythm with the natural beat of change, they were confused on which candidate best represented that goal.

What if Trump lived next door to them? Would they tolerate his abrasive personality? If they sat next to him in church, would they notice the puddle of sweat under his seat or have been able to dodge the lightning bolt that might have shot down from the ceiling?

... Followers Were Confused on Which Mask to Wear

The emptiness-of-understanding of the life principles that generate the sense of compassion that allows life change to do so to a rhythm that helps generate positive emotion challenged the wisdom tree used by many.

Trump's 4-year presidency unashamedly lacked any hint of true transparency. It was fronted by dishonesty, disrespect and undocumented finger pointing. It lacked any of the tenants of integrity that draw the honor and trust expected from the leader of the country that serves as a role model for so many other nations.

The USA lost its position as a role model for democracy. Dictatorships applauded the questioning of the democratic model that Trump presented.

The USA stands humble to the many countrymen who have died to preserve the freedom to live free to pursue a lifestyle defined by the positive emotions felt in love, peace, and happiness that help define true compassion.

While the COVID19 pandemic became part of the present moment of every human being in the world, USA citizens were collectively confronted with the challenge of using their personal belief system to vote on the future of their democratic freedom lifestyle.

The voters could compare the candidates as the relative facts about both were very well promoted in effort to influence (tempt) the voters. The vast assortment of media clearly displayed the stark moral and governing differences between the candidates.

Times were on-edge. Citizens were pushed to their limits in making sense of reality using the order of wisdom they had chosen knowingly or unknowingly to develop and nurture their worldview.

The COVID19 pandemic lockdowns had everyone busting to get out. With the dilemma the voters faced in electing the president, backed by the issues surrounding staying COVID19-safe or not with the pressure of being politically correct in dealing with "black lives matter" had the cities full of demonstrations, looting and even gunfire.

With maintaining the purpose of a democracy in mind, the size of each candidate's following is a good comparative gradient for indicating whether the voting public had their belief systems conditioned by either Tree of Life derived wisdom or they shaped their worldview trying to use unsubstantiated Fig Leaf Wisdom borrowed from elsewhere as a foundation.

Individuals focused on the fundamentals of a democracy pondered how so many other individuals could not see what was going on in the presidency of their democratic republic.

… An Ominous Threat … An Autocratic Fascist Wolf in Elephant Clothes

To gain traction in the USA democratic system, Trump had to enter it in a way that would fit into the structure of the system Thus, he crawled into an elephant's skin and called himself a republican.

His idea of a smaller government pointed more to a self-government.

Like in early 1930's Germany, Hitler gained support from German voters by saying he wanted to restore Germany's founding democratic principles. He wanted to make Germany great again. He undercut government officials and replaced them with his cronies.

Trump immediately began eliminating federal agencies. He nearly had the USA pulled out of NATO.

He was responsible for dismantling the National Security Council's global health security office which could have effectively managed the COVIS19 pandemic and undoubtably saved some of the hundreds of thousands of lives Trump's denial and ignoring of the pandemic cost.

He took no advice from anyone, including the science community regarding the COVID19 pandemic.

The federal government provided no plan for dealing with the pandemic. This was acknowledged to be the guiding reason to account for COVID19's record-breaking fall '20 resurgence.

The Business Weekly said in a 12-20-20 Facebook article that "Michael Beschloss, a prominent election historian, in an interview with MSNBC said that historians will need time to fully assess President Donald Trump's legacy but that he'll never be able to escape the COVID19 death toll.

"Donald Trump is not going to change the record. He was largely responsible for the deaths of hundreds of thousands of Americans who did not need to die," Beschloss said. "Millions of others who suffered from COVID did not need to suffer… This is really Nero's fiddling while Rome burns."

Among Trump supporters were the sycophants who were always there to bolster his agenda who knew better but looked for voter benefits from following his lead. Many followers feared what he might say about them or possibly lose their jobs for any friction they might have caused. Many did lose their jobs for that reason.

Howard Stern made the point that Trump originally ran for president just for the public notice it would bring him. He had no intention of winning. He blindly made promises designed to please the crowd he was speaking to.

Trump could not understand the state of influential power he suddenly had.

… Trump had No Integrity … No Honor … A Lying Vindictive Man

Trump had bitch-slapped all non-fascist world leaders and collective world peace efforts in his speeches and on tweeter as he pulled the USA's courageous form of progressive compassion out of world grasp. The only individuals Trump did not repeatedly degrade and insult were the leaders of countries with autocratic-style regimes. He referred to them as smart and genius on occasion.

Many citizens could recognize the White House fascist-authoritarian mindset. Trump's cumulative withdrawal from world efforts and insulting verbatim against anybody who questioned or disagreed with him was concerning. Trump would troll anybody that disagreed with him in speeches and daily tweets.

Pennsylvania's lieutenant governor John Fetterman said that "it was pathetic that the US president had become just some sad internet troll."

The gaslighting storylines of his speeches were wrapped around a theme pointed at complaining and degrading authorities or anyone who was not on his train.

He was numb to having the true altruism-seeded empathy that helps generate the love and compassion that lines the infrastructure of Tree of Life wisdom. He was oblivious to the basic relational principles that determine the outcome of cause/effect interactions that support the smooth transition of relational change.

USA forefathers did not think it necessary to even write into the government plan that a president would have to separate their business empire from the presidency, yet Trump never did that.

The USA was no longer the role model for the democratic government management style.

Trump's untethered attitude of repeatedly firing White House staff and government officials was the prelude to his late October '20 executive order. Government employees will have to pledge allegiance to the president's order of politics or can be fired without any recourse. They will lose their freedom to question power.

Post-election, despite election results differences that were too great for any discrediting of vote credibility, Trump insisted on filing frivolous lawsuits in effort to void election results in the states that were the closest.

Trump warned several months before the election that he would contest any results in which he did not win as they would have to be illegal for him to lose.

Trump had mailboxes removed and defunded the post office in advance to bring question to its ability to handle the election volume as he anticipated democrat votes would more favor the mail-in option than republican.

Expecting Trump's forewarned election credibility skepticism, voting officials knew far in advance to make sure there were to be no questionable voting procedures. How could Trump expect there to be any sort of stealing of the elections through illegal voting procedures? Judges clear up to his appointed Supreme Court threw all 60 of his frivolous lawsuits out of court.

His post-election refusal to gracefully concede in a non-winnable battle delayed the winning party the chance to begin the White House transition. Even though election reversal was out of the question, his continued refusal caused the question of national security to grow as President-Elect Biden could not be privy to security threats as he took office.

His efforts to rattle an effective democratic voting system were recognized worldwide and applauded by the autocratic governments.

This is what happens with an autocratic leader. These conditions were very well presented to public attention. Voters were aware of this when they used their breed of wisdom to decide.

... A Man of No Principle

With an awareness of Trump's life decisions and behavior, it becomes clear that he was, as the old saying goes, a man of no principle. His behavior was directed by an inner agenda that didn't align with the constructs that set principle for honor or integrity. Compassion was a word he never used and a feeling never reflected in his expression.

His agenda subscribed to generating conflict and operated just far enough outside the hands of law that his revolving court protests could keep him just outside wearing a striped outfit ... so far.

... Trump's Modus Operandi was Well Posted for All Voters to See

A brief non-comprehensive list:

- There's TV footage of his acknowledging the severity of the COVID19 pandemic early enough to have prevented hundreds of thousands of COVID19 deaths.

- Trump is a many-time over-documented liar.

- His shocking amount of proven adultery is unconscionable.

- His degree of racism matched that of Hitler.

- He was impeached for his dishonesty ... twice.

- During an interview with Stephen Colbert on "The Late Show," Mary Trump, Donald's niece, and a clinical phycologist said that while she believes the president demonstrates "sociopathic tendencies" such as an inability to show empathy, he "is not high functioning at all." She published a tell-all book, "Too Much and Never /enough: How My Family Created the World's Most Dangerous Man, "which sold a staggering 950,000 copies during its first day on sale. HuffPost, 7-23-2020

- Trump's sister, Maryanne Trump Barry, who was serving as a federal judge at the time was recorded saying that her brother "has no principles" and "you can't trust him." "His goddamned tweets and lying, oh my God," Maryanne Trump Barry told niece Mary Trump in secret recordings, made preparing for the publication of her book about how her uncle stands as a threat to the USA democracy. ... HuffPost, 8/22/2020

- "One does not have to diagnose to recognize pathological or toxic narcissism," Dr. Brandy X. Lee, a psychiatrist who has taught at Yale and authored the new book "Profile of a Nation: Trump's Mind, America's Soul," told Salon by email. Salon 10-28-2020

... Trump's 13 Failed Businesses

- Trump University, Trump Airlines, Trump Network, Trump Magazine, Trump Mortgage, Trump Vodka, Trump: The Game, Trump Steaks, Go Trump, The New Jersey Generals, Tour De Trump, and Trumped!

- Trump's 6 businesses that sought bankruptcy:

- Trump Taj Mahal, Trump's Castle, Trump's Plaza Casinos, Trump's Plaza Hotel, Trump Hotel, and Casino Resorts, Trump Entertainment Resorts

How can an individual run a business economy when they lack the skill to run a company?

Trump described his bankruptcies as smart business moves to best take advantage of the established legal system instead of being a means for those who did not understand how to work in rhythm with the system to legally get out.

He promised during campaigning for the 2016 election to let the public see his tax returns after some sort of audit was completed. This never happened. He continued with the same lie during the 2020 campaign. After much court action to see his taxes, they divulged up to a $400 million debt and many falsehoods to mislead in explaining.

... Trump: No Moral Compass ... His Image Over Reality

Any altruism-spun behavior of Trump was totally ego-managed with his giving energies directed toward his imagined self-importance and getting re-elected.

He felt that the law is to bend to serve him and not the public.

Following the tutoring philosophy of his mentor Roy Cohn to never back down, never apologize, and always to counterpunch all threats, Trump never intentionally showed any sign of self-doubt amongst his flow of falsehoods. His continued assertion that the '20 election was rigged in the close states continued beyond the assurance from contended state officials and the affirmation given in his pet attorney general's public statement that there was nothing vote tampering in any of those states.

Trump saw the office of the presidency as a family business. His children and son-in-law had no qualifications to be his advisors or mess with national policy. Yet ... they did.

The Trump team should have studied history to understand that promoting false narratives with the intent of enhancing personal power always ends badly.

... USA Christianity Backed Trump!

"Now I beseech you, brethren, mark them that cause divisions and offenses contrary to the doctrine which ye have learned; and avoid them."

~Romans 16:17-18 King James Translation

Even with Trump's behavior that violated every one of the Ten Commandments and rubbed up against the principles of democracy, USA evangelicals stood tall behind him and his 2016 campaign promises. Trump retained a reported 80% Evangelical Christian approval even while he was being roasted on the spit on impeachment.

> *"A new bipartisan Christian super PAC is taking on President Donald Trump with a new ad that accuses him of hypocrisy when it comes to matters of faith.*
>
> *"Mr. President, the days of using our faith for your benefit are over," the ad from Not Our Faith warns. We know you need the support of Christians like us to win this election. But you can't have it."*
>
> *" For Christians, of course, the position of Savior is already filled," Wear wrote. "" And Jesus is one person Trump can't fire or bully."*
>
> — HuffPost 10/15/20

For the religious groups that helped decide the 2016 election results in favor of the compassion-challenged candidate, these life principles that biblical wisdom promote may have been recorded intellectually, yet when applying their importance to real life, no connection was made.

It's amazing how this could happen.

Interestingly, this group of Christians stopped backing Trump because of his hypocrisy in their relationship, not because of his anti-Ten Commandment lifestyle.

... Biden's Modus Operandi

- 47 years as a politician including eight years as vice president providing an extensive list of leadership involvement in reviving the economy after the 2008 recession, expanding access to healthcare, advancing women's rights and gender equity, climate change, promoting peace and security, protecting USA children, policing, and criminal justice reform.

- A documented record of demonstrated empathy and ability to admit he was wrong on issues and change direction.

Biden's altruism was documented as being directed into compassion involving his family and electorate.

... Trump's Body Language Told The Story

Regardless of how every time Trump was confronted with decisions relating to negotiating relations with an authoritarian country, he unknowingly cried out his elevated level of insecurity by hiding behind his arms protectively folded over his chest. Anyone knowing anything about body language

would recognize this, yet his followers still decided to choose his weak example as a role model.

To have a strong economy, citizens must feel safe enough to go out and be involved in it for it to survive. ...people must not fear going out to spend money to keep the economy strong. They cannot fear contracting COVID19.

Yet, many chose to prioritize a stronger economy over the value of human life with Trump's blatant COVID19 neglect that cost thousands of people their lives.

... Trump Followers Used Fig Leaf Wisdom as a Crutch to Bridge-Over Emptiness-of-Understanding of Life Principles

Deciding between reelecting a proven highly unpredictable autocratically minded president or electing a predictable and documented compassionate-minded politician with a 47-year political track record of approved national service ending in gathering 8 years of experience as the vice president who could admit to being wrong and demonstrating how to build on it faced every voter.

The choice seemed so obvious. Trump made no real effort, probably out of naivety, to disguise the misdirected intent of his behaviors in his flow of daily tweets.

The many that borrow wisdom from some school of theology or elsewhere to guide their life purpose have a gut-felt emptiness-of-understanding in having a conscious awareness of the network of supporting knowledge used to derive the wisdom that decodes the principles that feed the life-defining self-evident truths that feed into the Tree of Life that have manifested into what has grown to be known as positive human characteristics that interlink to support the presence of compassion.

They are lost on what questions to begin asking to unfold the mystery or the courage or the energy to step outside and do so.

These are the behavioral characteristics that are needed to continue offering a freedom-based democracy.

... Turning A Blind Eye to the Attempted Dismantling of USA Democratic Floorplan

It could be wondered how voters on Trump's team could not see his challenged character. Many who were wise to Trump's character flaws thought Trump supporters must not have paid any attention to what he had done.

Many of the voters choose not to place importance on the character of the contestants.

Most of Trump's followers were distanced from his living persona. Would they follow him if he lived next door to them, and they had a more experiential knowledge of his true character?

... Some Must Have Shared Trump's Ten Commandment Infractions

Some Trumpites chose to overlook Trump's faults that they shared an unadmitted guilt in also possessing.

This misalignment of expectations and reality can become normal life for many. Many of the electorates must have shared Trump's character flaws that defined his lack of trusting honor.

The ongoing "Black Lives Matter" and Trump's acceptance and backing of the white supremacist groups documents that there were sections of the electorate that shared his negative personality characteristics.

There were many voters who, like Trump, had no problem with subverting the truth or maybe not being faithful to their partner. Some voters had no problem with taking something that was not theirs ... etcetera.

These documented "sinful" behaviors that Trump always denied could be behaviors these voters use themselves to bridge their gut-felt emptiness when reacting to life's temptations and consciously or unknowingly had accepted to tolerate.

They too, compromise their emotional balance and turn their face on compassion towards others.

They could have developed a blind eye to the nature that ruled his character.

As many will struggle to make sense of the present moment before the next present moment grabs their attention, they will use the behaviors they have been conditioned to use and the strain of wisdom that best justifies it. Even though they may know the behaviors are "wrong" behaviors, they at that flash-in-time present moment could not understand why ... before their attention veered off to what naked change's next present moment threw in their face to grab their loosely tethered mental focus.

They had not sought the wisdom-deriving knowledge in their past that enlightens their awareness to the principles that best connect the feelings that bring on an emotion-bred impulse to the behavior that will best satisfy that urge-to-satisfy in a way that agrees with those Jehovah-backed Tree of Life principles that rule the situational outcomes in this reality.

... Government Duty is to Ensure Freedom to Pursue Life Goals

The USA democratic government exists to serve the citizens. The government is led by a collective opinion ... not that of one individual.

Ideally, there should be a recognized common goal that all the political parties are trying to best achieve. They might represent different approaches, but they are shooting for the same goal ... freedom ... self-realized independence ... geared to the same purpose.

Change is inevitable as it is creator-written to define the impermanent nature of this reality. The different parties just want to control it in their way, yet they should all be sighting the same end for their electorate to share.

A democratic government allows the individual the freedom to search their soul and pick their own life goal of how to avoid suffering and reach emotional bliss and pursue that goal in a way they see best fit.

USA's founding fathers represented a new nation of individuals who were free to live in the way they choose to be free of suffering and to have the freedom to choose how to best allow positive emotions to fill their day and figure out how to live in a way to avoid the negative emotions that bring on misery.

The goal of living free of suffering which would leave one in emotional balance requires one to be working toward understanding the relational principles that control the outcome of how things work together to best interact and interrelate in the transforming reality of this living world.

Tree of Life wisdom is the strain of wisdom that decodes these principle-ruled relationships, leaving one enlightened about what they were ignorant about that caused their suffering and deprived them of emotional bliss. Tree of Life wisdom negates the ignorance that leaves an individual empty-of-understanding like the Eden snake's gifted wisdom left Adam and Eve.

... Fig Leaf Wisdom ... Empty of Understanding Life Principles

The voter numbers of the 2020 election document how at least in one situation, less than half of USA adults were not consciously aware of and thus cannot recognize the natural force-driven principles that determine the relational outcomes that define this reality's ongoing change that moves one present moment into the next in a coordinated rhythm of peace and compassion.

An enlightened understanding of these force-driven principles is what gives an individual the "enlightenment" that Siddhartha finally achieved that night under the Bodhi tree. It is exactly what Jehovah promises as afterlife heavenly bliss.

Having the personal freedom to develop and nurture the mindset to become enlightened about the force-driven principles that determine life outcomes ... through what is suggested by theology or through what reality poses as being self-evident ... is the "freedom to experience self-discovery" the democratic governing system is supposed to give the individual.

Fig Leaf Wisdom will harbor decisions empty-of-understanding hollow in how the borrowed wisdom explains the claim to the truth it is "snake-promised" to decode or interpret. Having a "blind faith" in what one poser of borrowed wisdom, like the Eden snake's, often results in it being easier for the individual to believe or have an unfounded blind faith in other things or claims that just do not dance into the relational truths of the principles supporting the dimensional design that maintains the animation of this reality's framework of ongoing change.

In the 2020 Presidential Election, there was much confusion in recognizing and prioritizing the factors for maintaining the freedom to best defeat suffering and attain the emotional balance that the USA claims to provide for its citizens the freedom to realize.

... Swimming Against the Current

Individuals that develop their worldview via Fig Leaf Wisdom are swimming against the ongoing flow of change itself. Their intellectual effort to make sense of how they perceive new situations appearing in their changing present moment struggles for recognition against the ongoing mental white noise from the lack of focused mental control and their ability to sustain their thought patterns.

These individuals suffer.

... Mental White Noise Cuts Short the Ability to Sustain Focus

The white noise controlling their attention span cuts short their ability to sustain focus on different thought threads about reality. Their conscious awareness stands empty-of-understanding how life principles affect the life situations of others.

They were lost on where or how to start looking for the answers to the questions they are not even yet sure of.

They often lack the ability to think things through. With thoughts often muddled by mental white noise, their behavior will not be coming from intentions that promote the smooth flow of change that allows situational outcomes to flow smoothly allowing those involved to enjoy the positive emotions that come as they experience their human condition's journey through their human experience.

... The 2020 Presidential Election was One of those Situations on Grand Scale

The sense of conflict, division, defensive unfounded attack, and event history misrepresentation that Trump established through his untrustworthy parley defines how he ran his business life and how he ran his presidency.

Trump's presidential persona showed no trace of the truth-based honor and trust-founded integrity that are characteristics needed to inspire a following that will act in a way to affect a smooth-flowing reality timeline.

often when making decisions in new situations, those using Fig Leaf Wisdom have mental energy that has been handcuffed into a preoccupation of posturing self-importance in an everchanging reality they do not quite grasp. While many lack the available mental bandwidth to reflect on their personal experiential history to inspire wisdom, many will first become distressed and settle back in some degree or shadow of shame … confusion, distrust, worry, panic or act out in a way where they will shout out to defend something they cannot yet establish quantified tangible support for.

They want to pull others into the same hole of suffering they are in and do not understand.

Compassion-based honor, trust, and honesty are virtues generated by the energy that flows in sync with the force-driven principles guiding the change that pushes one present moment into the next. They give the living color to the change that animates the passing of each dash in time.

These characteristics are spokes in the wheel of change and in the absence of their supporting energy the wheel gains a wobble that distorts in time its smooth transformation. I.E. Dishonesty brings up a disturbing static that stops the progress of smooth flow … to enjoy the journey.

… Power in Numbers Gains Anonymity

Lost in uncontrolled anxiety and knowing that many others were sharing similar views from the same emptiness-of-understanding state of mind provided a collective feeling of protection that disguised the feeling of personal shame to allow collectively acting out their frustration. There is power in numbers that creates an indistinct faceless sort of presence.

… Collective Fig Leaf Wisdom-Inspired Emptiness Morphed into Anger

Trump founded a group of individuals with similar states of internal emptiness-allowed ignorance-spawned discomfort to recognize and focus on a spectrum of contestable social issues. Together, their states of confused questioning mutated to form a collective opinion that mutated into collective blind-faith based unfounded anger.

During the heightened tension from pre-election activity many of those feeling aggravated frustration from their fundamental ignorance-spawned timeless state of emptiness of understanding, when challenged by those who confronted the object of their ignorance, chose to break windows, loot businesses, or maybe reach for a gun to silence the objectors. Instead of like Adam and Eve when Jehovah confronted their fundamental ignorance-spawned emptiness of understanding in the Garden of Eden, they reached for fig leaves to cover the shameful discomfort coming from their wisdom-empty ignorance.

… Empty Agenda Collectively Shouts Out

The collective mental white noise emanating from the Trumpites' internal fires was so intense they could not pay objective attention to what happens in the outside world. They fail to give objective thought to the causes and effects of outside circumstance.

While caught up in this eddy of confusion and through his gaslighting technique of changing minds through repeating falsehoods, Trump had developed quite a following.

Trump's devotees would do whatever he posed or gave passing hint to. They just needed a rebellious cause to help filter the anger and disgust that kept kindling the fire in their soul. Their present moment mental white noise short-circuits their focus and awareness … keeping their attention to what is happening in the world of reality blindfolded and unattended to.

Many chose to adopt some disruptive agenda that allowed them to shout out about their internal frustrations even though they do not understand them. They will find others with a similar disruptive view and gain strength and immunity from reason in the power of numbers.

Collectively, in a numbed/defensive state of group mentality adhering to a manipulative leader's every conjecture mixed with 1st amendment national pride, they would never show any sign of admitting they are wrong or agree to even talk about it. They strike out still blinded by the mental white noise that has kidnapped their ability to control their internal struggles.

In their collective ignorance, Trumpites drummed up the collective courage to shout out their hollow agenda in aggravating violence while hiding behind the masks of racially ignited white supremacy or maybe racial persecution. The pent-up feeling shared by everyone from the pandemic lockdowns only turned up the flame.

On 12-13-20 the internet magazine The Root ran the headlines: "MAGA Marchers and Proud Boys Descend on D.C., Setting Fire to Churches' Black Lives Matter Signs and Getting into Stabbing Fights".

It went on to say how: "Roaming bands of white supremacists trawled the streets of Washington D.C. on Saturday, setting fires to Black Lives Matter banners and getting into stabbing fights in what appeared to be a free-for-all outpouring of racist rage."

The January 6th attempt to overtake the capital with threats to hang the vice president that resulted in the death of police officers and one rioter was merely icing on the cake.

Their senses of emotional balance were lost in the valley of emptiness-of-understanding.

Election results showed how there are 84 million voters who can in one way or another see how Trump's character was badly infected with narcissistic illusions of fascist-bent self-grandeur and how it violated the principles of relational balance and about 8 million less who could not.

The election turnout was in record numbers. Individuals were terrified that Trump would be re-elected and USA's democratic role model would be further compromised if not destroyed. Some voted for Trump, and more voted against Trump ... many of which said they did not particularly like V.P. Biden.

Trumpism and Christianity ... Both are Borrowed Wisdom

... Theology's Heavenly Paradise and Trump "MAGA" Wisdom Both Cite a Promised Future State

Like when Adam and Eve succumbed to the Eden snake's unverifiable promise to a future state of all-knowing wisdom, Trump followers succumb to his vow to a future state of America made "great again." They follow whatever their leader-brewed wisdom tells them ... no matter how blatantly false.

Make America Great Again (MAGA) and heavenly bliss are promised present moments that lie somewhere in the future. What sort of present moment will determine that "America is great again" or that the state of "heavenly bliss" have been attained?

Both Trump disciples and Jehovah disciples have their sights focused on promises of a future state of improved emotional wellbeing. Both leaders create and stand behind a purported truth that requires a brand of wisdom to explain its truth that is unverifiable and leaves the blind faith followers empty-of-understanding.

... Internalizing Borrowed Wisdom Grows Easier

Religious believers and others with no waking agenda focused on the logistics of gaining the wisdom-deriving knowledge about the life principles that control life's cause/effect relational outcomes must use Fig Leaf Wisdom to bring calm to the present moment angst echoing of their emptiness-of-understanding.

This degenerated degree of mind control breeds the uncontrollable white noise eating up their waking energy.

Once blind faith has been called and trusted to assure spiritual security, it becomes easier to adopt blind faith in something else. Having belief systems conditioned to internalize borrowed wisdom about their soul's quest for the bliss of emotional balance, they more easily internalize other drafts of borrowed wisdom ... like Trumpism.

... Trump Gaslighting Affected the Public ... Just Like Theology

Trump gaslighted the populace just as religious theology has.

Those consumed by "emptiness-of-understanding" followed Trump in the same sort of blind faith in the false claims he was openly spreading in all his speeches and on Twitter.

Religious theology outlines a conspiracy of how Satan is plotting to steal away an individual's soul. The nature of the borrowed wisdom defining its theme leaves a believer empty of life understanding while going through life without a purpose. Trump's ever-present unending claims of how election corruption staged against his rule continued to convince his followers.

Their faith was blind to the fact that all of Trump's concocted court cases were abruptly defeated in all levels of USA courts. The agitated Trumpites lived in a dream world of Trump-defined conspiracy complicit to the acts of public insurrection.

... Christianity Like Trumpism Sees the World as a Conspiracy

Trump's logistics were not founded in objectively recognized accounts of reality ... of life truth. All of Trump's rhetoric pointed a finger at conspiracy coming from somewhere ... the fake media, other world leaders, or maybe from his political counterparts.

Over time, it seemed that Trump believed the gaslighting assertions he constantly laid claim to ... like voter fraud.

His gaslighting claims of truth were not founded in the compassion-threaded life principles that determine the outcomes of interactions of all kinds. Christian theology is also calculated from borrowed wisdom based on borrowed principles that are likewise followed by blind faith believers who stand empty-of-understanding what makes the borrowed wisdom true.

... Life is Just a Soap Opera

A follower of any school of theology ... Christianity, Trumpism, or whatever unfounded notion lacks having the wisdom based on the principles that interpret an agenda that feeds into generating Tree of Life founded self-evident outcomes.

Individuals with an untethered life agenda focused on a promised loosely defined future ending ... eternal emotional bliss / an America made great again ... cannot understand what the underlying purpose is that unites all things and individuals.

Their ungrounded life agenda is full of second-guessing. Many just remain naively out of the way while others might become very vocal with their life suspicions. Trump lived his present moment in a defensive state pointing his finger in anger while sitting cross armed in fear and self-doubt.

This leaves the individual empty-of-understanding, reaching for fig leaf-lined masks to create posture in their relationship with the present moment ... like Adam and Eve when confronted by Jehovah.

Principles of Compassionate Coexistence
Feed Tree of Life Wisdom

The principles that dictate how the bits of coming and going energy, now identified as the quarks of molecular mechanics, interact, echo up through their atomic society into the material things they make that animate humanity's field of perceived sensual recognition to determine the outcomes of all life situations.

Tree of Life wisdom makes sense of how these principles interact ... relate to each other.

Having an objective account of the real factors involved in an interaction will best understand what the outcome is going to be. The nonprejudiced account of what is happening in the present moment is going to allow the most predictive consideration of what is going to happen as a result.

This is the book of wisdom that is going to afford an individual a balanced emotional state. This is the all-knowing wisdom the snake promised Eve.

Those who have an understanding awareness of what these principles are and how they interact are the ones who best understand the Tree of Life wisdom that explains this.

There is no emptiness-of-understanding ... no emotional unrest ... no suffering.

With this understanding, the conspiracy theories disappear. Trump's narcissistic agenda went against the grain. His constant gaslighting of untruths to his naïve or maybe just opportunistic following rubbed against this truth.

Much suffering resulted.

A purposed life quest to acquire Tree of Life wisdom will leave a truth-seeker free of the emptiness-of-understanding they spend their present moment using untethered Fig Leaf Wisdom trying to disguise and hide.

... Today's worldwide mindset has assumed a Fig Leaf Wisdom zeitgeist.

II

Incipient Suffering Exists Today

… The Human Condition Stands Poised on the Balance Beam of its Human Experience

Many go through life with their eyes closed to what's self-evident … misunderstanding the ongoing present moment change they encounter.

Primal Purpose in Life?

"What would you say is the purpose of life?
To come out of misery. A human being has the wonderful ability to go deep inside, observe reality, and come out of suffering. Not to use this ability is to waste one's life. Use it to live a really healthy, happy life!"

— *The Art of Vipassana Meditation* as taught by S.N. Goenka, William Hart p.20

It's all about coming out of misery … out of suffering.
Misery is measured emotionally.
Emotional bliss is the human condition's goal during its human experience.
Some shoot for waiting 'til after life … some solve the puzzle while alive.

Theology calls it heavenly bliss. In the universal reality, it's recognized as being "enlightened." … about the "emptiness-of-understanding" inspired ignorance that underwrites the present moment misery that defines all of human suffering.

Being born into life ignorant, the human condition, aware or unaware, has an inborn longing to better understand its human experience. If things are understood, there is no confusion … nothing to spur emotional unrest … no emptiness-of-understanding.

It is natural to seek the emotional bliss that theology showcases in its promise of a future afterlife heaven.

The innate desire to be one with and consciously understand the heartbeat of reality is natural. It is natural to have life decisions lined with the desire to avoid misery in suffering.

Suffering Exists and It Knows No Prejudice

… Insipient Suffering In Contaminated Pleasure

"We all regard physical pain and mental pain as something unwanted. It is much more difficult to recognize contaminated pleasure as a form of insipient suffering. Our search for pleasure preoccupies us and takes up most of our energy, yet it is doomed to failure from the start because none of these pleasures can give us the real and lasting happiness we crave."

— Rinchen. *Atisha's Lamp for the Path to Enlightenment.* (Boston, MA: Shambhala Publications, 1997), p. 43

… *Insipient* … Not To Be Confused With … *Incipient*

"Something that is incipient means beginning to exist or just starting to happen. Insipient is an archaism meaning wanting wisdom, stupid, or foolish. Insipient is almost nowhere to be found in 21st-century English, except as an occasional misspelling of incipient".

—The Grammarist

… All Suffer At Some Degree of Ignorance

Most individuals live ignorant to understanding how the principles of nature that sway the outcome in every type of relationship affects their emotional wellbeing. These principles are generated and patterned from the push-pull interactions of nature's dimension-sustaining forces of electromagnetism and gravity … and what's still to be discovered self-evident in the string or wave theories.

These force-driven principles sustain this reality's ever-changing impermanent backdrop.

These force-driven principles determine the relational outcome of every interaction from the energy released that animates the elusive passing present moment ... from the metaphysical subatomic to what is human-perceived.

These principle-driven relational truths filter up to pattern the outcomes for the relational interactions occurring in the range of human perception.

In getting their heads around how their human condition fits into its human experience, people can be upside down on understanding the difference between contaminated pleasure and what is actually good for them. It is the difference between what has been conditioned to seem right or good and what truly is.

Today, individuals are conditioned to perceive many behavioral options that were not around in the days of the Ten Commandments and have not yet been included in the Pope's annual "don't do" list as being OK for their health or happiness that when considering the laws of nature that rule this impermanent reality, truly are not.

Items like white flour and sugar or processed foods and tackle football that are not wholesome for human health haven't yet earned their tenure of sorts to be considered as being sinful in the eyes of religious theology.

... It's Necessary to Realize Suffering Exists to Find its Relief

Individuals react to situational outcomes and the resulting feelings signal the emotions that are either pleasant or not. An individual needs to realize that some of those emotions are unnecessary and are not just to be accepted as the way things are but signal the existence of suffering.

Finding Comfort in Contaminated Pleasure

... People Need to Feel and Define Their Own Perception of Cool and Not Cool ... Good and Bad

Many choose to emulate what they perceive the attitudes and behaviors of individuals they choose as role models that they admire for some reason and want to be like. They want to be accepted ... to fit in ... maybe just to be cool ... at least to be thought of as on who understands.

They may never learn how to trust or even to detect how they feel about or how they personally see or perceive things. They fail to understand their personal sensual definition of discomfort in social gatherings. Many individuals find it difficult to think for themselves.

The confusion from making decisions in the vacuum of uncertainty when considering this disjointed type of understanding leaves an individual unexpectedly open to misguided misunderstood conditioning that leads to their insipient suffering from their stumbling involvement into different forms of contaminated pleasure.

Many individuals spend much of their time wrapped up in some form of emotional anxiety. With time, this becomes normal life for them.

Many become tired by mounting negative emotions before giving up seeking answers. Instead of doing the leg work, many will turn to their favorite flavor of theology... unverifiable and secured only by their blind faith.

... Eat to Live or Live to Eat?

> *"Obesity in the United States is a major health issue, resulting in numerous diseases, specifically increased risk of certain types of cancer, coronary artery disease, type 2 diabetes, stroke, as well as significant economic costs. While many industrialized countries have experienced similar increases, obesity rates in the United States are the highest in the world."*

—Wikipedia

The 2020 USDA guidelines cite that 70% of Americans are overweight or obese! This is a driving factor for chronic cardiovascular diseases, type 2 diabetes, and certain types of cancer.

... Remember The "Fat" Person in Grade School Class?

There was a time before the 21st century in the midwestern USA when a 20+/- person grade school class had maybe one person who could have been classified as fat.

"Obese" is a term that didn't enter common use until the last 20 years or so.

Along with the proliferation of fast foods has come a quickly expanding number of individuals of all ages who are now greatly overweight or obese.

... Food to Die For

People with a carefree diet just do not take life seriously. Many spend their present moment caught up in a cauldron of confusion and wonder.

There's food that tastes so good, even though the food is proven harmful to human health, that good taste is just worth dying for. Maybe it won't kill an individual now, but it's the cumulative effect of repeating those bad decisions that will chip 5, 10, or 20 years off their lifespan.

The infectious nature of this unchecked crisis to humanity is made all too clear by watching individuals who might hold the highest homage to their chosen god yet have no mind to pay any regard to what they put into their physical bodies.

They cannot fight the temptation to indulge in white flour, sugar, sodas, and anything processed, as the list keeps growing. Any biblical guidance on what to eat and what not to eat is far outdated or non-existent, offering no tangible biblical wisdom for guidance.

After acquiring type II diabetes, they might ponder back into the blindfolded ignorance of their theological discipline and in their ignorance become lost suffering in rumination wondering if their new disease is maybe their god's punishment for something.

Whether or not emotional bliss waits for them up in their vision of an afterlife paradise or is attainable now from the inside where it is alive is another question. The human body is the looking glass to allow accumulating the type of knowledge (self-knowledge) used to derive the Tree of Life wisdom God mandated to Adam in the Garden of Eden ... that Siddhartha Gautama detailed in his teachings.

Still, even in this disconnect, it seems theologians would want to at least take the best of care of their physical bodies to allow them to do a better job of working for their lord. What will he think on the day of judgement of the care they've taken of the body he designed and created for them ... in his image?

Their present moment awareness does not combine their cognitively suspended still-life imagination-defined theological world with the living heartbeat of this present moment sensually fed impermanent reality.

What's Hurtful Soon Becomes Normal Life

... Ignorance Takes its Toll on Mind and Body

Over time, people learn to accept what happens every day in their life, harmful or not, as being their "normal." At this point in history, most individuals just do not understand that some of their actions do not serve to fortify their intrinsically registered wellbeing and happiness.

Maybe they will get up in the morning and have orange juice and white toast to start their day to later have a juicy steak with white potato and a few white flour rolls. Their behavior is likely to later expose them to their unique combination of the many life-threatening complications like diabetes II, stroke, or maybe a heart attack.

... Human Experience Spent in Knee-Jerk Reaction to Life Consequence

When someone has lost their way, if they ever had one, they go through life reacting to what happens more than using the wisdom they have derived to better understand relational cause/effect factors. This understanding would allow them to "act" instead of "react." They could use their relational wisdom to best anticipate interacting factors to affect proactive behavior.

With an informed waking awareness of cause/effect relationships, they can better stay on track to understand how the natural ways of impermanence affect their present moment to minimize their suffering.

We Battle the Seven Deadly/Cardinal Sins

It can be a challenge living in a nation that finds collective comfort in being guided by theological notions of how there is a god that is in control of the final decision to whether someone finds or is granted emotional bliss.

There is a country citizenry that has been told to be good ... not to sin ... and not what else to do with their time (like to find their direction to emotional bliss now, while still alive).

As per Christian theology, temptation does exist, yet the Bible offers no guidance on developing a waking understanding of why not to do the "bad things" other than "Thou Shalt Not."

What's considered good in one region might be tabooed in another.

Both the spiritually immature individual who cannot quite grasp how many of their activities they view as bringing happiness are in real life making them suffer and the individual of the highest spiritual capacity where altruistic compassion motivates everything they do, face temptation. They face the modern-day incarnations of the temptation to sin warned against back in biblical times. This challenge is compounded by the countless number of new mutations of those old sins.

... Seven Deadly Sins Emerge ... Pulling on Humankind's Emotional Strings

After being cast from the Eden state of emotional bliss and cursed to live in Fig Leaf wisdom emptiness-of-understanding, mankind's ability to recapture the Eden state of bliss has been flawed and misdirected.

As early human society grew and assumed adaptive behaviors, over time the collective reflection on the aftershock of suffering caused by certain of those behaviors caused the social consciousness to condemn those behaviors and to be classified as bad.

It is said to be the time of Moses when Jehovah put his flame-etched-in-stone stamp on this social awareness of these social taboos and categorized these bad behaviors to be classified as "sins." The negative effects of their earlier behavioral manifestations were collectively recognized and morally outlawed.

... Lust – Gluttony – Greed – Sloth – Wrath – Envy – Pride

Lust-gluttony-greed-sloth-wrath-envy-pride is the ten-syllable thought chain denoting behaviors that date clear back to the beginning of mankind that created much of mankind's early moral/ethical agitation that resonates yet today. This socially emerging centipede of sin breaks down into seven short segments, each depicting age-old behavioral taboos.

The appearance of this ancient lure, like infectious viruses, will persist in time as it adapts to change.

The adaptive sorts of fleeting reactions they inspire in today's cause/effect reality define the presence of each of their modern-day incarnations. There are seven groupings or combinations of these sensual perception packages that are known today as the seven deadly sins or the seven cardinal sins.

... They Can Become Reactionary/Normal Life for Many

The aftertaste of each of these sins can resonate in an individual's present moment waking awareness while remaining unshakably affixed to their must-redo list. Once experienced, the lure and preoccupation with each are sometimes very hard to resist as individuals put up progressively less resistance to their repeating of the behavior until it earns the status of being one of the fleeting reactionary habitual behaviors that characterize an individual's personal list of personality-defining addictions.

Individuals become attached to the security they find in having this behavior being something they are used to doing. They are familiar with dealing with the cause/effect package the behavior brings. Even if their freewill is strong enough to question the appropriateness of a behavior, their character probably does not dare to try other behavioral options.

... Their Recognition is as Evasive as the Present Moment Itself

Recognizing the actual feelings that compose and generate their emotional presence is different from merely attaching an intellectual definition.

These categories of sin are very much alive and evolving. When threatened by society's detection of their harmful nature, their lure can mutate into a derivative state that will continue to work against mankind's spiritual maturation.

... Their Manifested Incarnations Mutate

They mutate to squeeze through any modern-day attempt at harnessing them to eliminate their destructive prowess. They can evade being pinned down by any effective behavioral statute or mental antidote.

Weeklong summer revivals directed straight into the bowels of their sinful temptation have proven ineffective in eliminating their true cause but effective at fulfilling the misunderstood passed-along ritualistic obligation to have more religious revivals.

Today's preachers will piece together a series of Bible verses to supplement with millennia-old authority the logic in their intellectually developed lectures, showing how the modern-day implications of the ever-evolving mutant versions of the seven deadly sins are still frowned on by God.

... Mankind is Losing on the Intellectually Defined Battlefront

The sin-free relief-related logic of the intellectual reasoning might make sense to an audience during the time of a lecturer's message and may receive many hallelujahs and promises of future conformity, but once the flock leaves the building and the fresh intellectually metered borrowed wisdom concedes its mental floor presence to consider the more pressing causes being shouted in the believer's heads by each of the unrelated 1,000 voices of their mental white noise, the preacher's string of intellectual Bible-backed logic is soon to be forgotten or at least stored out of split-second recall.

The "birds of a feather" mind echo intensifies and they return to their circle of friends and back to repeating their sins-of-choice.

The source of the disruptive influence on mankind's ability to maintain ethical/moral standards has seeped undetected through the cracks while the Roman Catholics, in trying to keep the Ten Commandments current, update their list of modern taboos. The Pope issues updated lists of new-age sins defined only by the sinful behaviors themselves. Their analysis misses how the new sins are mostly the mutated incarnations of the old-time biblical taboos and where their cause lies.

The Roman Catholic Church's earthly link to God does not offer guidance on eliminating the ignorance that allows the sinful behaviors to uproot the cause of the temptation that leads to the listed sinful behaviors. The idea of directing proactive attention to stopping the ongoing process of the deadly sins' adaptive change seems obvious.

Yet, it seems that even the more detailed objectives based on behavior modification quickly become obsolete as time moves on. The tentacles of temptation mutate around and choke out any effective mental vaccine aimed at stopping their harmful effects on mankind's spiritual advancement.

These addictive behaviors help feed the parasitic internal guilt-inflicting judge and victim of self-blame. The harm of the disruption caused to one's ability to self-train their mind control despite the mental distress caused by the counterproductive nature and residual effect of conceding to any of these temptations can further deaden or at least distance a sinner's conscious connection with their once-unfettered freewill.

This spiritual advancement stutters on, trying to maintain moral/ethical standards. The religious train does not move on to self-training the thought control to go to where the Tree of Life knowledge can be found to self-train the wisdom to become enlightened about what it is that mankind is so ignorant about that underlines all the suffering from the behaviors that the Ten Commandments outlaw.

To most, identifying and sizing up the actual real-time modern-day incarnations of the age-old 7 deadly sins with only the mental pictures held of their intellectually stored descriptions is unlikely. The cognitive picture of the sandal/toga-time sins they sketched with their intellectual pencil seems somehow foreign and unassociated to their present moment real-life incarnations.

Yet, the real-time appearances are the very same thing represented by those intellectually recognized religious maxims of long ago. The old descriptions don't size up to their present moment sensually realized manifestations.

... Gluttony Takes Its Toll

> *"It's estimated that ¾ of the American population will likely be over-weight or obese by 2020. 2014 figures from the CDC found that more than one-third (36.5%) of U.S. adults age 20 and older and 17% of children and adolescents aged 2–19 years were obese."*
> —Obesity in the United States – Wikipedia

Mixing today's fast-food options and country-wide nutritional ignorance factors into this growing state of a health crisis.

This word "gluttony" encompasses several variations of harmful eating profiles reflecting ulterior agendas for using food other than to provide healthy nutrition.

> *Saint Thomas Aquinas lists six ways to commit gluttony. They include eating too soon, eating too expensively, eating too much, eating too eagerly (burningly), eating too daintily (keenly), and eating wildly (boringly)*
> ... Internet, Wikipedia: Seven Deadly Sins

In Midwest USA, it seems there is a race at each family dinner to see who can be the first one to lean back in their chair away from the table, undo their belt, and brag about how they could just not stop themselves from having the second or third helpings. Letting out one's belt after Thanksgiving Day or Christmas dinner to sleep off their overindulgence seems to be the body language showing one's appreciation for this American tradition.

It is an accepted way to compliment those who prepared the meal in this northern part of the biscuits-and-gravy/breaded-tenderloin capital of the world.

... Many Have More than One Hunger to Feed

Many will mistake their pressing emotional or spiritual hunger for physical hunger. They will keep eating while not generating the wisdom that will enrich their waking consciousness with the emotional understandings that satisfy the spiritual hunger they long to satisfy.

Others might try to satisfy this emotional hunger with endless shopping.

An individual with their present moment's attention tied up in the involvement in any of these deadly sins is not actively devoting present moment intended purpose in pursuing a goal of becoming enlightened about what allows their suffering. An individual having no effectual soul-satisfying end in focus is easily weakened to willfully comply to harmful temptation.

This is only one of the tentacles of gluttony reaching out into society to suck out human life potential.

This is only one form of incipient suffering that plagues the 21st century.

Temptation from untested, unverified outside promises or claims to what the future might hold will overtake any belief system weakened by having no focus toward developing an envisioned effectual soul-satisfying end. This is suffering with no end in sight. This is endless suffering.

An individual's unbalanced mental state, having 1,000 voices in their head shouting their unrelated intentions all at once, trying to gain control of an individual's behavioral intentions, causes the individual great present moment mental unrest and suffering.

They will in time somehow take action to organize and understand their present moment turmoil. They will either self-train themselves in how derive Tree of Life wisdom as Jehovah ordered, or they will borrow Tree of Knowledge wisdom as Adam and Eve chose to do and die spiritually to realizing the emotional bliss that both Jehovah promised afterlife and that Siddhartha left a detailed description on how to realize while living.

Humility Balances Out Pride-Generated Greed

Greed is a form of craving. Hatred … of aversion. Altruistically inspired giving and benevolence are their opposites. Gratitude negates entitlement.

Pride is thought to be the original and most deep reaching of the seven deadly cardinal sins. It is thought to be the source from which the others arise.

Because humility addresses ego-inspired self-worth, it is thought to be the opposing virtue that balances out the vice of pride.

… Humility … The Most Primal of Virtues Opens the Door to Compassion

Humility is what clears mental bandwidth for the altruistic intentions that tender empathetic awareness. Empathy opens the door to compassion.

It is only through humility the body and mind can shed their independent states of unparalleled attention to unite in a state of harmony to share a common mind-into-body awareness. United, the mind and body cross the bridge of communication, heart-in-hand, over the self-ego fortress of uncertainty and through the valley of emptiness-of-understanding onto the plateau of enlightened awareness.

It is from there, in a state of humility and shared purpose, a truth-seeker sensually listens to their source demonstrate the manifested truth of its intended purpose of making ever available the real-time present moment change that makes real the reality that supports this life.

A truth-seeker's self-deliberation over the uncontrollable stream of bodily sensations leads to their accumulation of insight-inspired "aha" Tree of Life wisdom to reach liberation from its ignorance. Humility must turn the pages through the entire self-observation process. Sandbox Etiquette listening skills are needed while focusing concentration to sensually listen while sidetracked by no irrelevant mental conversation.

Non-Attachment Threads "The Eye of the Needle"

20. *The young man saith unto him, all these things have I kept from my youth up: what lack I yet?*

21. *Jesus said unto him, If thou wilt be perfect, go and sell that thou hast, and give to the poor, and thou shalt have treasure in heaven: and come and follow me.*

22. *But when the young man heard that saying, he went away sorrowful: for he had great possessions.*

23. *Then said Jesus unto his disciples, Verily I say unto you that a rich man shall hardly enter into the kingdom of heaven.*

24. *And again I say unto you, it is easier for a camel to go through the eye of a needle, than for a rich man to enter into the kingdom of God.*

Matthew 19:20–24 (King James Version)

The USA has a 30 trillion-dollar national debt. Most of the citizens have "great possessions" … or at least the debt that secures future ownership … and all the related points of concern.

Those who have chosen religious theology as an answer for ending their suffering by finding afterlife emotional bliss should think deeper into what Jesus had to say. In the above King James translation of Rome's selected gospel Mathew, along the coasts of Judea beyond Jordan, Jesus addressed the Pharisees who provoked him with questions.

Jesus did not break it down in this instance how there is nothing to become attached to, the self-evident principle involved … only the affect … how it will lead to human suffering.

Above, Jesus makes the same point that Siddhartha made about becoming "attached" to the imagined permanence of things and ideas, only Siddhartha breaks it down to explaining why and how to solve the problem.

It is important to realize that Jesus was not just asking individuals to give up their worldly possessions to follow some arbitrary rule of Jehovah's to not own things. The reason involves the resulting emotional effects of attachment.

Jesus is pointing to the living hell the mind-seizing effects of the misguided thinking of becoming attached to the imagined permanence of things can lead to the miscued thinking that results in generating negative emotions that prevent realizing the state of emotional bliss.

… Hoarders Epitomize the Attachment and Clinging Syndrome

Individuals who cannot let go of things and ideas are hoarders.

Hoarders exemplify what attachment and clinging to imaginary things means. Hanging on to something unable to let go is knee-jerk reacting to personal misunderstandings of the principles determining what is real and what is not.

The bad thing about hoarding is that having an individual's conscious awareness preoccupied with being attached to clinging to material objects or ideas prevents them from using their mind to self-train the wholesome ethical/moral state of consciousness to self-train the mind control to then self-train the life wisdom to become enlightened about the logistics underwriting the impermanent nature of this reality to undo the ignorance that brings about their suffering while clinging to or grasping at some remembered aspect of something related to some past situation.

Hoarders often suffer attachment anxiety disorders and depression. They might feel embarrassed by their possessions and uncomfortable when others are around. They can have relationship problems and problems in work and social activities.

This and the resulting forms of suffering are what keeps a hoarder fat as the camel trying to wiggle through the eye of a needle.

Owning things can be perceived as a way for an individual to define who they are. The more items an individual owns, the harder it is to tell who they really are. True self-definition disappears and passions become undefined or at least unrecognizable.

The less things an individual owns, the plainer it becomes who they are … where their purpose lies.

Clinging to the imagined essence of something from the past is illusionary. In having a life purpose, deciding what fits into the plan and what does not, allows a hoarder to decide who they are and who they are not. They lack the focused purpose that says how most things they cling to would not fit into a successful journey to becoming enlightened about what makes them suffer to find their emotional bliss or as Jesus said: "through the eye of the needle."

When a person has everything they want, their subconscious will remind them how they have everything to lose.

... To Be "Young and Free"

"To be young and free" is an adage expressing how when young, an individual is free of the responsibility of being a caretaker of managed responsibilities. Responsibilities can involve anything from promises made like utility bills or maybe mortgage payments to items that they have decided to keep in their closet or garage or in their storage shed for one reason or another.

To be free of the ignorance about the transforming state of this existence that defines the nature of this reality requires an individual to realize why the attachment to the existence of things and ideas is foolish.

Like Kris Kristofferson acknowledges, having "no ... thing" left to lose is where freedom lies.

Individuals who become attached to the variety of cravings that can be associated with the imagined permanence of existence of anything or idea will suffer the emotional hell that will follow.

They'll be too fat to fit through the eye of a needle.

Suffering's an Emotional Thing

An individual's life report card is marked in hues of human emotion. Their collective total is how individuals rate their life quality.

... "Heaven" is the Highest Level of Emotional Bliss

"Emotion" is where the intellectually spun world of theology meets up with the intrinsically woven world of universal reality.

Theology promises emotional peace free of suffering in the future and realism tells one how to get it while living.

The better an individual understands their emotional world, the less suffering they will find in their human experience.

Humankind understands and equates its level of bliss or suffering in terms of its feeling-spawned emotional response to its human experience.

Emotional integration creates the mood or state of mind that an individual finds their waking consciousness in.

It is the emotional flow that sets the pitch for the degree of mindfulness an individual might use to deal with the next blast of naked change that colors in their next present moment.

Watch the expression on "man's best friend's" face when the dog's owner leaves or returns. Sadness and happiness. Most living creatures relate to their level of life satisfaction through how they perceive their living experience. The perception of suffering or bliss is exhibited by how they interpret the emotions they naturally feel or how what's experienced has been conditioned to be recognized.

Emphasizing the extremes of emotional bliss and emotional damnation are what theology uses to build up and establish the want and need for believing in its various forms of unverifiable theory. Extreme to extreme … from the imagined fire and brimstone torture of emotional hell to the emotional joy and happiness used to describe heavenly bliss.

Early Conditioning Can Negate "Understanding" Emotions

… Perpetuates Human Suffering

Adages such as "people that hide their feelings usually care the most" or "men don't cry" are examples of social attitudes that condition an individual to distance themselves from better understanding their feelings and the truth about their emotions.

To develop a better understanding of suffering life's misery, it's important to better understand what causes that misery.

That misery is realized emotionally … metered sensually … and recorded intrinsically.

When early life conditioning puts accepting and understanding states of emotion at a distance, developing an understanding of life principles and how they affect different emotions becomes much more difficult.

Acknowledging and owning their emotions is how a truth-seeker gains understanding about the unknown that enlightens them about the ignorance that brings them the different faces of suffering.

When ignorance-spawned suffering persists … the "Dark Side" wins.

Individuals need to better understand the universal life principles that decode the ignorance-inspired "emptiness-of-understanding" that causes their suffering. Understanding how the network of feelings that support the different emotions is essential in attaining emotional bliss.

Truth-seekers need to self-train a calm mind that's free of mental white noise to then self-train the ability to improve that calm mind's ability to sustain their focused awareness into the right mental frequency that allows accumulating the right knowledge to self-train the ability to derive an understanding conscious awareness of the intrinsically founded "Tree of Life" wisdom to put an end to their emptiness-of-understanding and to realize emotional bliss.

Trying to find that emotional understanding by borrowing the promised wisdom of another entity will leave the truth-seeker roaming the Earth lost in Fig Leaf Wisdom … empty of understanding … as Jehovah sentenced Adam and Eve.

Emotionally Founded Mood Inspires Human Behavior

"Emotions are at the root of everything we do and drive our choice to move toward what we want or to avoid discomfort."

~Karla McLaren, M. Ed. Facebook post

We understand now that emotions are vital parts of your basic cognition and your capacity to relate to the world and understand what's going on around and inside you.

Your emotions contain your instincts and intuition, they help you attach meaning to what you perceive, they help you identify your values and ethics, and they help you manage and engage in your relationships (among many other things).

Your emotions are involved in everything you think, every idea you have, every action you take, and everything you do. When you can understand them, you can understand yourself and others more deeply.

Your emotions are a vital realm of skills, abilities, talents, and instincts that support every part of your life. And they're not the problem; they come to help you solve any problem you encounter.

When you can learn their language, you can change every part of your life for the better.

… Karla McLaren, M.Ed. 12-07-21 Facebook post

Emotions are as real as the cold sweat and hives or the tingle of warmth that they can inspire.

They provide the spark that kindles all human behavior and fuels the human condition thought train from one present moment to the next.

… Emotions Don't Just Happen

Emotions manifest in the wake of when an individual's conditioned expectations meet up with real-time perceptions.

Humans can either choose to evaluate, consider, and act on what they feel, or they approach things with a loose unaware intellect and just react to an untrained unfiltered inborn fight or flight impulse.

Indiscriminate conditioning fashions an emotional matrix that can start in one state and as quickly as time passes and as stimuli change, mutate into another.

A conditioned perception can be formed from what the feelings from sensual stimuli represent as influenced maybe by a role model or whatever might implant a like/dislike perception.

... It's Wise to Better Understand How Emotions are Generated

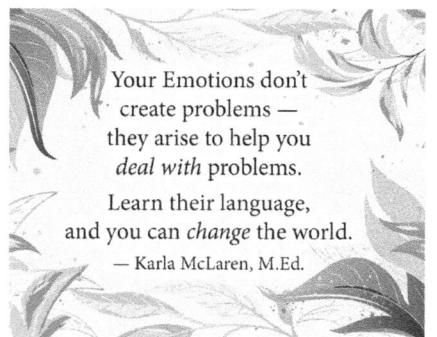

Your Emotions don't create problems — they arise to help you *deal with* problems.

Learn their language, and you can *change* the world.
— Karla McLaren, M.Ed.

Emotions are intellectually formulated descriptions of sensually experienced occurrences. The cause of emotional suffering or misery lies in how those sensations are evaluated to form the emotions that are either formed with an understanding of natural principles or ignorant to them.

Many individuals use most of their life energy struggling to make sense of these perceptions as they strive to stay emotionally afloat in time's ever-flowing river of change. They can use up all their waking life energy sorting through mental uncontrollable white noise while trying to manage untethered emotions while caught up in the ignorance of not knowing or understanding what they are the product of.

The different perceived emotions an individual's been conditioned to attach to different combinations of sensations create their present moment mood. Understanding the relational principles that make up and define what constitutes the perceptions of those sensations enlightens an individual to a deeper understanding of those emotions and less suffering from an "emptiness-of-understanding."

... Emotional Balance Walks On Razor's Edge

It is a human's life purpose to task out their emotional balance. They must learn to understand what underwrites their emotions by gathering experiential knowledge to derive the Tree of Life wisdom that makes sense of them.

A truth-seeker must gain control of their mental focus. In this calm, they can then self-train themselves to tap into the knowledge needed to inspire developing an aware understanding of what it is that brings their emotional state of agitated unhappiness.

Humans Use Freewill Ability in Choosing How to Escape Fear and Misery to Find Emotional Bliss

... Everyone is Born with a Freewill in Life's Feeling-Spun Emotional Matrix

Individuals are born ignorant with an inborn drive to understand how they fit in and where they come from. As soon as an individual can speak around 2 years old, they can't be stopped from asking why Mom??? about everything.

The human condition gathers knowledge to derive the wisdom to best navigate its way through the human experience while shuffled in between times of suffering emotional pain and spurts of emotional bliss.

Every individual uses their freewill to decide where to go and what type of knowledge to look for to derive the wisdom to lead an emotionally blissful life. This purpose, in some fashion, underscores all life decisions.

Individuals will use their freewill ability to decide where to look for direction and where to find the right sort of knowledge needed to understand how to best manage the ongoing manifestations of life's feeling-spun emotional matrix.

... Some Find Peace In What's Here

Some will effectively use this inborn purpose and take on the due diligence to discover the pathway to some degree of emotional bliss on their own while living. Some will find the appropriate guidance to this end.

... Some "Scare Themselves into Death in the Dark to be Where the Angels Fly"

Some truth-seekers will choose to scare themselves to panic down the rabbit hole of their unknown to where heavenly angels are said to fly. They use their free-will ability to blindly trust something that does not make intrinsic sense to them.

Many want to be where the angles fly because of the panic created as their emotional unrest has become too great. Some look upward in hope from the lack of incentive to figure it out for themselves or from just wanting to belong socially. Or possibly because they were coaxed by a god's promise of an afterlife eternal paradise of suffering-free emotional bliss by just saying "giving their souls to Jesus" and letting him do all the work. Maybe they were scared into submission by the promise of fire and brimstone for the unwilling.

... Religion Uses Emotions to Leverage Believers

Religions use an unpledged truth-seeker's intrinsically logged emotional history as a tool to fill their pews. Some believers join the ranks in hope of getting the emotional bliss promised in an afterlife heavenly paradise. Some adopt a blind faith to avoid the eternal fire and brimstone.

They must use believers' intrinsic connection to affect performance.

Those frightened into joining a religious discipline due to the fear created by the possibility of the everlasting fire and brimstone relate their decision of the threatened fire and brimstone to their intrinsically registered sensory history of what the feeling of intense "hot" feels like. And just the word brimstone is scary.

Religious cannot manufacture fear of the feeling of something that is beyond the extent of what the human experience has a sensual history of. A threat of something horrible like a league of zombies doesn't ignite the fight-or-flight level of fear created by something referenced to sensual history.

The believer is not really equating this threatened amplified fire and brimstone state of mental pain agony to the emotional "living hell" they could be experiencing before dying. Amplified reality trumps reality.

Even though a potential believer's intrinsic history can be used to create a state of "what if," there's no real link here between the believer's intellectual understanding of a "what if" and what is happening to them in the present moment of their sensual reality.

Mindset of "Heavenly Place in the Sky" Further Distances Association of Biblical Sin and Temptation from Today's Present Moment World Accountability

When religious believers look up into the sky in hope that their god/savior … up there … will grant them entry to what their imagination has painted the heaven … up there … to be someday, they're distancing the possibility of associating this afterlife emotional paradise with what could possibly happen to them in the animated present moment of today's emotional world.

When not turned to the religion's scriptures or sitting in church, their intellectually fashioned sense of feeling of biblically outlined responsibility is minimized or nonexistent.

They can hear a friend say: "Yield not unto temptation" right before taking a bite or drink of something that they know is significantly not good for them … and not bat an eye or just think the friend is joking or just a pain in the butt.

Chasing the Carrot on a Stick

… Borrowed Wisdom Gifts Emotional Bliss … Tree of Life Wisdom Makes a Truth-Seeker Earn It

Religious theology dangles an unverifiable promise of suffering relief in an afterlife paradise of everlasting emotional bliss … just out of tangible touch … for a believer to chase after, until they die. All they need to do is mortgage their soul for an unverifiable promise of heavenly bliss while living in the "emptiness-of-understanding" the wisdom they blindly strike faith in brings to them.

A truth-seeker who follows Jehovah's mandate and seeks only the knowledge that will enable deriving Tree of Life wisdom, will have to actively experience what this reality is to have the right knowledge to assimilate the sort of wisdom that gives a waking understanding of what disables the ignorance that causes suffering to allow the emotional bliss to rise from the deeper consciousness where it is readily available 24/7/365.

Greyhound dog races use this promised reward tactic with a fake rabbit suspended in front of the racing dogs just beyond their bite to help ensure the best racing times.

An individual's belief system will become compromised by choices made while following the spelled-out guidelines of the strain of theological wisdom to establish faith in.

Most of the world population today have used their individual freewill to decide to bet the wellbeing of their soul on the afterlife promise made by their favorite strain of theological wisdom. They follow their religion's promised plan that is to suddenly become real on the "day of judgment" to suddenly be assigned to an afterlife state of eternal suffering-free emotional bliss or to the confines of eternal fire and brimstone.

Their soul-staking bet is secured only by their blind faith in the strain of theological wisdom they have opted to believe in.

The religious promise's only source of life is from the believer's confidence they have in their intellectually metered world of understanding.

This intellectually filed rendition floats free of any tangible tie-in to the believer's awareness of the sensually metered intrinsically stored universal reality that exists in real-time.

For maintaining real-life emotional balance during their lifetime, religious promises leave believers only with the directive to pray to their god in heaven for his blessing and guidance to see them through their life ups and downs ... to keep their chin up in the hope they will make the final cut on "judgment day."

They are told not to "sin" and find peace in their savior, to enjoy eternal afterlife emotional bliss. They are offered no universal real-life wisdom explaining how to instill in themselves an intrinsic understanding of what their unverifiable god-particular wisdom points to.

Their chosen strain of religious wisdom will leave them reaching for modern-day fig leaves to cover the shame over their "emptiness" of life-applicable understanding of the outcomes of real-life circumstance tendered in the wake of their decision to adopt their chosen strain of empty wisdom ... like Adam and Eve when confronted by Jehovah about partaking of the snake-promised wisdom from the Tree of Knowledge.

Most people who suffer from not knowing what wisdom-inspiring knowledge to seek to realize the life wisdom that will help them best interpret and process real-life present moment situational relationships will stake at least a token allegiance to a god ... just in case. They still will have no conscious understanding of how to best negotiate what ongoing change presents to them as time slowly turns their hair grey.

The strain of wisdom they consciously live by does not help them establish a personal understanding relationship with the transforming impermanent nature of the natural reality their human condition is a living contributing part of ... that their god created.

At family gatherings, for many, there will be a white elephant in the room bringing compromise to sharing detailed feelings about real-life circumstance. Some individuals fear or at least dread stepping on another's religious toes and starting another round of the pitter-patter confrontation about the this and that typifies religious debate.

Openly revealing the real-life feelings and emotions from arising thoughts concerning how their human condition fits into its human condition is lost.

They suffer in their ignorance.

This form of suffering presents itself as a worldwide pandemic.

They chase a carrot on a stick ... and they suffer.

Modern-Day Temptation Lacks Hashtag Tie-in Reference to the Realm of Biblical Wisdom

> *"If religious believers connected their Lord's intellectually metered world with the sensual world "he" was to have created as being the same, they'd be able to tie today's "in life temptations" with the ones described in ancient verbatim. They'd be able to resist having the sugar-coated donuts before their Sunday worship services." They'd want to take good care of the bodies their Lord designed and engineered knowing he would want that before letting them into their concept of heaven."*
>   -Anonymous

Biblical temptation guidelines are inadequate when trying to recognize the plethora of modern-day temptation manifest.

There are even things now that are "sinful" ... that hinder an individual's quest to understand and minimize their suffering or to come closer to their emotional bliss ... that had not yet evolved into mankind's recorded world of unwholesomeness.

It is common for individuals who study the Bible daily and try to live by their religion's sandal-clad script not to associate the bible-backed wisdom with its modern appearance to associate and incorporate that borrowed wisdom into the modern living conditions of their daytime life.

There's real-life wisdom gathered experientially that they need to make it through everyday life and then there's biblical wisdom gathered intellectually they try to intellectually knit together to apply to real-life sensually metered circumstance.

When feelings from the naivety of a poorly conditioned understanding of what supports intrinsic happiness rub up against the disapproving pre-lingual intrinsic message felt from the "gut feeling" of an individual's sensually metered living experience, some suffer knowingly, and some yet remain consciously unaware and fearfully confused about their emotional imbalance and suffer incipiently.

With the intense theological national Roman-like gaslighting USA citizens are exposed to, it is understandable there is such a grinding waking disconnect in between the dos and don'ts described as holy wisdom and what the intrinsic history of an individual's life lived signals from within.

Today's Snake Oil Salesmen … Sometimes Satan Comes as a Man of Peace

… Stealth Proliferation of Today's Unfounded Knowledge … Corporate Hiss Disguises Truth About Product and Creates Ego-Wetted Promise … Corporate Intention: Crafters of Subliminal Temptation

Corporate America has been beaten back from TV advertising campaigns such as those showing beer ads correlating their brand with socially desirable situations. Cigarette TV ads are forever gone.

An individual will take on second job obligations to pay for the ego-juiced association of a new SUV's pictured abilities as seen in a TV ad driving through a rough stream bed of some rugged back countryside, yet never having the time or incentive to ever take it there. They do not want to damage it. They will park it at the back of the 2nd job's parking lot to avoid the door-opening dings.

Asbestos-related companies and talcum powder companies have paid billions of dollars for knowingly keeping product-related health information away from consumers.

Corporations will sweeten their product pitch using the cheaper forms of sweetener such as corn syrup and hide or minimize the mal effects it has on human health. The consumer will bite into the presented apple of knowledge that boasts of good flavor and possibly of health benefits it might otherwise possess.

What matters is how knowledge is acquired and internalized … hearsay or experientially witnessed … corporate snake or personally tested.

The corporate snake knows but does not mention how by their stripping the fiber out of the white flour that once it hits the human bloodstream how it turns non-fiber food into a spike in the individual's blood glucose level and plays havoc with their body's living state and their present moment emotional state.

Consumers stand naked and lost to the consequences in their blind trust in a company's presentation of their product, like Adam and Eve in not understanding the basics behind their nudity after taking a bite of the fruit of the Tree of Knowledge promising their understanding wisdom.

The consumer will find modern-day fig leaves to cover up the various results of their ignorance in trusting the corporate snake and biting on their apple of knowledge to think it wise to use the company's misrepresented product.

… Steven Jobs … Hidden Agenda … Apple Logo?

The Internet is today's on-call, at our fingertips, 24-hour source for endless amounts of wisdom-deriving borrowed knowledge describing everything from good to evil. Surely, Steve Jobs had no hidden agenda when naming his company, a provider of access to the infinitely massive source of borrowed knowledge, the Internet …" Apple" Computers?

The apple has come to represent the fruit-bearing the shortsighted wisdom-deriving borrowed knowledge ingested from the Garden of Eden's forbidden Tree of Knowledge of Good and Evil that the deceptive snake used to lure Eve. The apple has come to represent the untested knowledge that she borrowed that left her and Adam ignorant and empty to understanding the wisdom its snake-source had promised.

The Apple logo has a bite taken out of the apple … just like Eve took the single bite out of the fruit of the Tree of Knowledge. Is this meant to further lure onlookers to partake?

The Internet's unlimited access to this world's boundless volumes of borrowed knowledge and its accepted credibility have humanity's undivided approval. It pulls in the masses. It is accepted as normal.

Today's naïve lack of focused direction in seeking the truth of "the way" has evolved into an unchecked widespread apathy. This ensures its continued malignance. The question of credible authenticity is superseded and numbed by how so many people are becoming unbelievably rich through its design.

It is as if the borrowed knowledge poster child, the apple, like from the Garden of Eden's Tree of Knowledge of Good and Evil has sprouted up on a substantial percentage of the desktops throughout the world.

Worldwide Religious Dance

... Eight of Every Ten People Turn to Theology Worldwide

In 2015 the world population was 7.7 billion. Eighty-four percent belonged to some form of theological discipline ... 1/3 Christian.

In 2015 at least 8 out of every 10 people used their freewill ability to choose to have blind faith in wisdom received from elsewhere in their search for a better understanding of their life experience. They looked "outside" for the answer in unverified unexplained wisdom borrowed from their favored religious discipline.

In 2015 less than 2 of every 10 people chose not to use their "freewill ability" to trust wisdom borrowed from the outside. Some of those chose to go deep inside to observe reality to gain an understanding awareness of what is unknown to them about how this reality's transforming nature affects their presence.

... In 2015, 55% of Mankind Believed in the Holy Bible Old Testament

There are almost 4 billion people who live their life respecting the Genesis Garden of Eden account of creation on some level. Many evangelical Christians take it word for word. Others may see it more as an analogous metaphor or metaphoric analogy of sorts.

Each one of today's 7.7 billion humans will knowingly or unknowingly make the life direction decision that Jehovah brings life-or-death clarity to. It is the first item of biblical business. Choosing a school of wisdom to pattern the development of a worldview is a distinction, knowledgeable or not, that everyone must make.

This is the subject of the god Jehovah's first conversation with mankind on the seventh day of the Genesis account of creation! Its top-ranking priority demonstrates how this is such important stuff when considering where humankind looks for its wisdom-deriving knowledge and what sort of wisdom-deriving knowledge humankind looks for. For making the wrong choice, Adam and Eve suffered spiritual death, as Jehovah forewarned.

They were kicked out of the Garden of Eden spiritual paradise. They were cursed to live lost in the emptiness of fundamental ignorance to face the unknown surprises lurking ahead in the ongoing change they were to face in the unknown abyss of a transforming living reality.

In 2015 over 80% of mankind was using wisdom borrowed from "outside" to "come out of suffering" … to regain the Eden paradise emotional bliss that theology promises again afterlife.

The Garden of Eden Curse Challenges Mankind

15. *And I will put enmity between thee and the woman, and between thy seed and her seed; it shall bruise thy head, and thou shalt bruise his heel.*

16. *Unto the woman he said, I will greatly multiply thy sorrow and thy conception; in sorrow thou shalt bring forth children; and thy desire shall be to thy husband, and he shall rule over thee.*

17. *And unto Adam he said, Because thou hast hearkened unto the voice of thy wife, and hast eaten of the tree, of which I commanded thee, saying, Thou shalt not eat of it: cursed is the ground for thy sake; in sorrow shalt thou eat of it all the days of thy life;*

18. *Thorns also and thistles shall it bring forth to thee; and thou shalt eat the herb of the field;*

19. *In the sweat of thy face shalt thou eat bread, till thou return unto the ground; for out of it wast thou taken: for dust thou art, and unto dust shalt thou return.*

20. *And Adam called his wife's name Eve; because she was the mother of all living.*

21. *Unto Adam also and to his wife did the LORD God make coats of skins and clothed them.*

22. *And the LORD God said, Behold, the man is become as one of us, to know good and evil: and now, lest he put forth his hand, and take also of the tree of life, and eat, and live forever:*

23. *Therefore the LORD God sent him forth from the garden of Eden, to till the ground from whence he was taken.*

… Genesis 3: 15-23. King James Version

God's punishing Garden of Eden curse levied against mankind rings true today. If the Genesis account of creation is accurate, since Eve is "the mother of all living", this curse is genetically preserved. It has been patterned into human DNA since humanity's first offspring.

Because Adam and Eve ate of borrowed wisdom one time, mankind has ever since, as God-sentenced, struggled in the emptiness-of-understanding inherent to fundamental ignorance and will suffer because.

Jehovah lectured Adam to either live by the logistics of the Tree of Life wisdom or make life decisions that cater to an adopted Tree of Knowledge strain of wisdom and surely die spiritually.

Jehovah's life-or-death warning made no difference. Adam and Eve's freewill led them down the wrong path.

... Jehovah's Ultimatum

Ever since Adam and Eve allegedly had their way with Jehovah's virgin demand, mankind has struggled to make sense of how to derive the right strain of wisdom to live in emotional harmony amongst the unavoidable patterns of life principle that define and rule the outcome of relational interactions on every level of the impermanent dimensional makeup of this reality.

These natural principles determine the outcomes affecting how the human condition fits into its human experience. Enlightenment tells the story.

Jehovah says in verse 22 that man shall live by Fig Leaf Wisdom until he "put forth his hand, and take also of the tree of life, and eat, and live forever."

Man will live in the suffering misery brought on by his fundamental ignorance until he eats from the Tree of Life.

"Eating of the tree of life" is something that requires an individual to be alive to do ... not after they have died.

... Individuals are conditioned to find comfort in contaminated pleasure and have come to accept the resulting insipient suffering as normal life. They suffer.

... Borrowed wisdom's unverifiable claims pattern the same emptiness-of-understanding demonstrated by the Eden snake-promised all-knowing wisdom gifted from the Tree of Knowledge that left Adam & Eve empty-of-understanding their nakedness.

... Borrowed wisdom's intellectually painted world rubs up against the observable truths of the transforming sensual world.

... Humans grab for fig leaves, like Adam & Eve, to mask their ignorance-spawned emptiness.

"Emptiness" is the feeling
that short circuits
an individual's emotional matrix,
sending it into an ongoing loop
of unsure reckoning.

After a falsehood
has been repeated so many times,
many will give up on arguing
and begin allowing it.

III

Theology's Gas-Lighting Ethos

Gaslighting?

Wikipedia says, "Gaslighting is a form of psychological abuse in which a victim is manipulated into doubting their memory, perception, and sanity." It is a form of manipulation in which one entity tries to get someone or group to question their reality or perceptions."

Oxford dictionary says that "Gaslighting" is an outside effort to make someone doubt their perception of reality by convincing them that how they interpret what they sense is delusional.

It is thought by many that by repeating a misleading account of reality enough times will bring individuals to eventually give in and quit denying the false statement.

One example of poorly disguised national gaslighting through the repeating of a lie would be the 2020 presidential election where even after being shutout in nearly 60 court cases with 2 being the US Supreme Court, the electoral college vote and recognition from Russian leader Valdemar Putin's acknowledgment of V.P. Biden as president-elect, Donald Trump to repeat as fact in every public appearance and in his social tweets that the election was stolen and how he had won.

It is amazing is how many of his followers followed his lead through all of this. Two years after fact, Trump continued to assert that the election was stolen from him. He continued to have many followers.

It's an early-life struggle for many to decide whether or not to force believing in the existence of an unnatural reality when a group of role model adults that maybe even share their last name that teach them to tell the truth and live with honor are swearing to be true.

Gaslighting is a form of covert psychological manipulation seeking to numb human freewill. National gaslighting's tactical stratagem can touch on all aspects of a society's referenced presence. It counters what can seem to be self-evident truth.

In the USA, all forms of theological gaslighting have full access to the populace. Religious organizations do not even pay taxes. This is the freedom for an individual to figure out on their own how to make that distinction on what to believe like Jehovah outlined to Adam in the Garden of Eden … Tree of Life/yes. … Tree of Knowledge/spiritual death.

Religious gaslighting starts as early as a Catholic infant baptism. As a child grows, despite their inner freewill questioning, the unavoidable first impression affirmative nod of the mass who it seems must know what is happening will vex the child's freewill into opening their future to include all the rites and rituals that define this religious theology's empty dogma.

A young person will question their memory, perception, and sanity while cowering in blind faith to seek the afterlife emotional bliss guarantee from their chosen strain of religious theology that is woven into the USA mindset.

Many just don't want to upset their parents.

"Gaslighting" Concept Goes Back to the Late '30s

This design of deception was dubbed "gaslighting" following a 1938 stage play of the same name. The 1944 movie "Gaslight", starring Ingrid Bergman was patterned after this play.

While her husband used gas lights for his secretive attic search for hidden treasure, Ingrid's character noticed the dimming of the downstairs gas lights. Trying to convince her that she was mistaken and even delusional, her husband told her there was no dimming and that her eyes were deceiving her.

Her husband was gaslighting her.

… Guilty!

Cheating spouses, politicians, narcissists, sociopaths, or just anyone wanting to exploit others might use this technique. Some merchants fashion their methods of gaslighting prospective buyers in how they advertise their product or belief. Governments will create propaganda to support their false claims.

Russia, China, and North Korea are examples of extreme national gaslighting.

Religious theology introduces its theological doctrines to society's youngest in many forms. Some reach as far as to avow that the world was created in 6 days, 6000 years ago, and flatly deny proven carbon-dated truths to the contrary.

By branding their religious notion with a more politically correct name, they are trying to get this untethered unverifiable supernatural doctrine to be taught in public schools as "Creationism" or "Intelligent Design."

All doctrines of religious theology support the unverifiable assertion that there is another unworldly entity(s) that made and control this reality.

Early Conditioning Sets Deep Theo-Notion Footprint

The youth are exposed to religious gaslighting when most vulnerable. Being that there is no tangible evidence to tether an individual's conceptualization of what "heaven" is really like, each human being that is offered the unverifiable wisdom that heaven exists along with its intellectually metered description, will configure an imagined mental rendition of its described truth as they intellectually perceive it.

Each conceptualized rendition will be as unique as each individual's imagination.

At such an early age, biblical miracles don't seem to make natural sense relative to anything a young mind has experienced so far, yet many will roll back their freewill questioning doubt and go along with their surrounding adult role models and "believe" or at least go along with it ... often tongue-in-cheek.

Many believers are conditioned or gaslighted by the adults in their life to accept the same theological discipline they were conditioned to follow at a younger age.

Theology Fails to Train the Inner Child

Theology might capture the imagination of the young child, but it does not take long for the Christian Bible's doubt-riddled storyline to poison any interest that might have initially been baited by the storytelling capabilities of a talented Sunday school teacher. There is no plan to work toward the promised heavenly peace other than waiting until considered old enough, in some religious strains, to then blindly "give their life to Christ" who has "died for their sins."

And what exactly does all that mean in tangible terms?

Some individuals allow their behavioral motivation to originate from what their intellectual mind has sketched reality to be according to their blindly trusted interpretation of a religious theology promise of making it to an afterlife paradise. This leaves them sticking to what the translation of their chosen holy text says.

Conversely, some will favor trusting their sensual history-conditioned gut feeling.

Religious theology takes a believer's attention away from trusting inspired insightful understandings of reality, steering their blind trust into whatever holy scripture interpretation they've chosen to bow to. The religious believers lose track of discovering what uncertainty their inner child curiosity might pose that maintains or completes the primal connection between their emotional consensus and their sensual feedback.

A typical 2-year-old child would walk through an area with their attention focused on the present moment and just spit out questions about the different things they pass by and don't understand. As they age, after compromising their freewill's curiosity openness via theology's manner of gaslighting, expressing their open curiosity with new and unexplored facets of life wanes.

Their inner child is suffocating. Their innate interest in the new and unexplored has been gagged.

When an individual has put their faith in an unverified source and has not developed a steadfast faith founded in any self-evident unquestionable truths it portrays, they stand susceptible to any other source of hollow borrowed (Tree of Knowledge) wisdom. When hit from all directions by assertions that a religious theology is valid, it is easy for them to follow suit and pledge allegiance to its unverifiable claim.

"Intelligent Design"

... Master of Adaptation

Like evasive influenza or malaria viruses, a gaslighting zeitgeist will find a way to adapt to public analysis.

Charles Darwin's insights about human evolution have challenged religion's claim to the truth of the Genesis six-day creation. The term "intelligent design" has been created by the hard-lined Evangelical Christians to make the thought that an outside terrestrial being created this universe a bit more palatable or politically correct while pushing for its acceptance to be taught in public schools.

They will continue numbing society's collective freewill. The Pope makes annual adjustments to what is acceptable to Roman Christianity in light of evolving social opinion and discovery.

There is never a deep reach to explain why these behaviors are bad or sinful.

When adapting becomes impossible, forms of theology will fade from society's acceptance. When through questioning reality's cause/effect confrontations (those who question are called scientists), the truth became self-evident as to what causes lightning. At this point, Zeus had to retire into has-been Greek mythology ... the Greek God Hall of Fame.

Mankind creates theological theory and mankind can eliminate religious causes. When Constantine decided that Christianity would be Rome's acceptable religion, he mandated that all other existing competing religions be erased along with any of their related materials as well as any of Christianity's teachings that rubbed up against Rome's self-serving protocol and were not selected for the Roman Bible.

Theologies Share the Same Hidden Agenda to Capture and Harness Follower Freewill

... Theological Discipline Does Corral Public Unrest

Having the public look to one supernatural source for answers is a means of corralling public question and unrest. Gaining control of the public's collective freewill helps to maintain a controlling arm and maintain public peace.

... Religions Dangle the Same Afterlife Paradise Carrot-on-a-Stick

In the USA, Christianity must somewhat step aside to allow other theological notions like Islam some national opinion room in its effort to continue corralling that can arise in the wake of the collective human fear of the unknown.

Some Christians groups stand firm that of the great number of Christianity's sects that only their particular interpretation of the Holy Bible will qualify any believer for the heavenly paradise, yet they draw pride-filled strength from being a member of the great mass of "Christians".

Gaslighting imposes government-controlled politically correct spiritual hyperbole.

In modern times, some of these religious sects are conceding that there might only be one god. Yet they stay true to their religion's unique collection of rights, rituals, and dogma that their believers must adhere to without question.

Yet, they all continue to scramble with the same unspoken agenda of taking control of their believers' freewill.

Untethered National Mindset Numbed

... Corralled to a Templated Ragtime Theological Awareness

"If God did not exist, it would be necessary to invent him."

~ Voltaire

Religious theology taps into an individual's intellectual memory bank to paint a unique imagination-housed picture of heaven and hell.

Humans form emotions that reflect their conditioned perception of their human experience. Emotions are the human sensual conduit that connects an individual's perceived conscious awareness to the sensually perceived outcomes of their life experience.

After Sunday morning service, believers leave their church setting to reenter a living world of unanswered uncertainty and insipient suffering with an everyday living protocol that beats to a different strain of wisdom.

… A Slavish Unquestioning National Ethos Corrals the Fearful in Search of Relief

Those who are fearful of the boogieman hiding somewhere under the bed they have made or in their secretive closet of undisclosed past encounters that might feed the eddy of rumination that steals away their ability to focus on the present moment, can panic for relief.

In an autocracy, the public must fear and follow whomever it is that rules their society. In a democracy or republic, most people do not know how to best spend their "free" time. They have no real conscious understanding of life purpose, and many are conditioned to be afraid of what might be lurking in the areas they are too afraid to confront.

Beyond out of ignorance participating in activities that bring about their insipient suffering, their state of social confusion might bring them to instigate activity destructive to the social purpose … riots … etcetera.

A templated theological pathway can help quell social unrest and give those lost and pathway of hope or at least a carrot-on-a-stick to pacify or at least side-track their unrest.

Roman Gaslighting Edits Bible Narrative Short of Including Self-Training Mind Control to Allow Developing "Garden of Eden Tree of Life" Wisdom Insight

… Rome's National Gaslighting

National gaslighting involves projecting a government-staged and endorsed public ethos of a social reality backdrop having no real supporting tangible evidence to verify its living presence.

Ancient Greek rulers supported the existence of the Greek Gods and often used the threat of situationally appropriate god powers to influence the thinking and behavior of its Greek citizens.

Rome did not want its citizens thinking they could themselves find their path to personal joy and happiness and to be freed from their suffering within their own body that Jesus taught about in the edited-out accounts of his teachings and spoke of a few times in the published accounts that he had taught to crowds of higher spiritual maturity. Con-

stantine wanted the Roman citizens to be looking to a god up in the sky or to the Roman Caesars that were propagandized to be godly figures for spiritual direction to capture emotional bliss free of suffering.

Jesus's entire message was neutered at the time of its Roman Bible birth. At that time in history was when Rome's government decided to become fully vested in Christianity,

There is only one type of human emotional bliss. All religions and realism have to have the same bliss in view. Their focus is just different.

It was 312 A.D. when Rome's ruler Constantine legalized Christianity as Rome's only recognized religion. Christianity made the most sense to adopt.

Rome's Emperor Constantine recognized the viability of Christianity to Roman administration. Christians were literate and could work for the government. They had to know how to read to be able to interpret the scriptures. Christianity only had one god which made it easier to just outlaw all the others.

... Roman Bishops Handpicked Only Four Gospels

The selection process of the Bible of today took a long time. It is a library of smaller documents. In 325 A.D. Constantine handpicked a council of bishops to select the accounts of the gospel appropriate for targeting Rome's tailored spiritual theology.

Constantine's bishop council chose which biblical accounts to use in composing the scriptures that would lead the citizens of its country on their religious path. A limit of only four gospels was selected. The head bishop romanticized that like the four directions of the compass and the four directions of the wind came the four pillars of the gospel.

These gospels were ones written on similar levels of spiritual maturity, yet they did not totally agree with each other.

... Gospel Selection Void of Self-Discovery Content Leading to Gaining Individual Enlightenment

Constantine's bishops edited out gospel accounts written by authors understanding and explaining a truth-seeker's ability to determine their self-direction could come from anywhere outside of Roman rule. The bishops selected accounts authored by individuals who expressed a more elementary level of spiritual understanding of what they heard Jesus say or could personally understand or had collected from others.

It was 50 years before any of the gospels were written. The rest were written in the next few centuries up to Rome's edited publishing.

Jesus's apostles fell into different levels of spiritual maturity, from Peter or John to Judas or Thomas.

Jesus tried to level the plateau of understanding using parables. Jesus said in the gospel according to Matthew when asked why he spoke in parables that some just cannot understand what they see or hear. He was likening it to sowing seeds where some seeds will take, and some will not.

Jesus was saying how the group he was speaking to had been waxed gross by their care for this world and the deceitfulness of riches. Their hearts were waxed gross to hearing or seeing the truth that is being spoken or is visible right in front of their faces.

None of the Roman bishops' selected accounts offered guidance on self-training mind control to then enable self-training through inspired insight, waking awareness of the "Garden of Eden Tree of Life" wisdom, as Siddhartha's teachings gave realism detail to.

of those who reportedly became enlightened back in the ancient times of the human experience, Siddhartha Gautama left a set of memoirs describing the pathway to self-training enlightenment from suffering least affected by governmental and other outside prejudice on how he was able to accomplish this feat.

Jesus offers a deeper understanding of gaining emotional bliss in the Rome-declared "forbidden gospels."

... The "Forbidden" Gnostic Gospels Survived

There were those of that time that understood how Rome was editing the accounts of Jesus's teachings to meet their gaslighting needs, only to have the forbidden gospels and all evidence of the other competing religious doctrines destroyed.

Rome's attempt to eradicate all the other non-published accounts failed, as the "Gnostic Gospels" were discovered within the past 100 years. The Gnostic Gospels are a collection of some of the original accounts of Jesus's teachings that had been hidden to avoid having Jesus's intended message destroyed by Constantine.

These accounts had possibly been written by more spiritually mature authors. They were deeper-reaching teachings Jesus possibly gave to audiences of higher spiritual maturity where using parables wasn't necessary.

You teach theoretical physics to a college student while you teach addition and subtraction to a grade school student. Also, it takes a college grad student's mental maturity to take notes during a grad class. A 5th-grade student's notes would be inaccurate due to their lack of existing mental development to comprehend and translate into writing the professor's intended message.

Jesus's intended message recorded in the Gnostic Gospels has not been exposed to the high degree of tarnished dilution lost in the centuries of multi-translating of the Roman Bible first edition. Yet, they are still subject to the human error inherent to what happens when humans try to transfer intended meaning … just not as much.

Constantine's priests left out the written account of Jesus's teachings by Thomas that was written before the chosen four gospels. He did not include the account left by Judas or the book by Mary and others. The interpretations that gave an account of Jesus's teachings were written by those of possible higher spiritual maturity.

Authors with higher levels of spiritual maturity wrote these "forbidden" accounts of Jesus's teachings. They better understood the final learning stages of what Siddhartha detailed as a process of self-training the mind control to realize the wisdom to calm the mind to self-train it to conquer the self-ego to self-train it to understand the ignorance that robs individuals of their joy and happiness and rules the misery of their present moment.

The enlightened ones were both teaching how to achieve emotional balance to then live in emotional bliss that is void of emotional suffering … one end story with two messengers.

Rome's citizen-control scheme included quelling citizen self-detection of direction to initiate the due diligence to understand what is missing from the status quo and where to find it. Constantine did not want his citizens to develop the ability to focus their minds beyond the ego-inspired white noise chatter of a hopeful imagination directed up to a god in heaven.

The published accounts of Jesus's life in the Bible gave no direct guidance on what the media (sensual) of human-to-source message exchange is and how to hear or witness the message to inspire wisdom coming in self-evident fashion from our personal living source.

Rome wanted its citizens to see Rome as its provider and rule-setter. Rome wanted its emperor to be viewed as being a god.

Constantine himself, the Roman leader who allowed Christianity to openly exist as a religion, did not convert to Christianity until years later, on his deathbed … just in case.

The presentation of Jesus's religion-related actions was tailored to maintain a mass of Bible-disciplined Romans looking for direction. Constantine's edited message left the Christian Romans looking to the government for guidance.

… Constantine Controlled Roman Freewill

By adopting Christianity and with the Roman priests' handpicked gospels crafting the theme of the Roman Bible First Edition, the Roman Emperor Constantine had secured a way to better corral and control unpredictable theology-driven uprisings. At the time this was a concern to the security of Roman rule.

Constantine managed to give his Romans a religious promise offering them the heavenly guidance they wanted, but a truncated path that always looped back to Roman rule. It was a theology that gave them an unimaginably, untestable paradise not realized until after they had died. Until then, while alive they would pay their tribute and taxes to Rome.

The Roman Bible sets the bar for mankind's spirituality high enough to at least establish an expected plateau of moral/ethical standards. Rome's recipe to control its citizens still works today through the religion that Constantine decided to let his unsettled discontent citizens observe.

They would follow Rome's leadership pointing to the moral/ethics of the Ten Commandments. Biblical guidance to self-training enlightenment stops there at the do's and the do nots.

There is no biblical guidance on why those are bad or sinful behaviors, leaving believers' uncertainty hanging in limbo while they wait in hope, staring up into the sky where they see their imagination-defined god and his power to be.

The Roman Bible weakens its Christian believers' freewill resolve by calling its soul-saving plan a heavenly blessed plan and uses guilt and the fear of a never-seen almighty god's wrath to help enforce it while promising an unimaginable paradise for unquestioned compliance. It stops short of teaching its believers how to figure out what is at the root of their suffering and how it saps out their life energy that should be directed at understanding our living source to allow their living in mental peace.

They will use Fig Leaf Wisdom … wisdom that is not their own … in making their way through reality's minefield of undefined naked change.

Roman government was gaslighting its Romans with the logistics of another reality.

The same recipe works well in many parts of today's world. Roman Christianity still works well to corral the masses in the United States. Fig Leaf Wisdom exists worldwide today.

USA National Gaslighting Follows Suit

The USA uses Rome's theological template formula to corral its citizens while blessing its endeavors by "the grace of God."

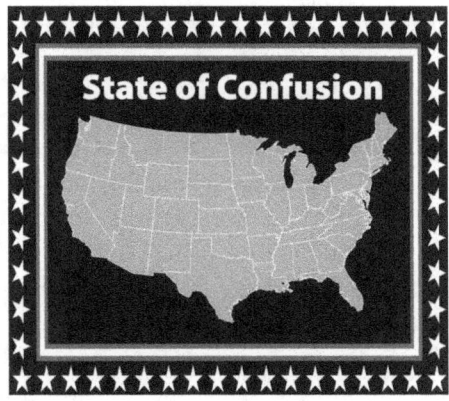

Like by having Ingrid's character question her sanity when her husband tried to convince her of what her reality was, the USA government certifies through its politicians' orations and its various forms of government publications and courthouse yard monuments that there is a never-been-seen reality hosted by a never-been-heard God-like shepherd of sorts that asserts a promised responsibility for the safety and eternal destiny of its citizens.

That notion is treated as an assumed time-proven fact.

Some USA localities are trying to include Evangelical-pushed Creationism in their public schools and give the knowledge associated with pseudoscience's theory of Intelligent Design the same credence earned by modern science through its process of double-blind experimental verification and carbon dating.

God sits on his followers' shoulders, judging everything they do and what they think. Many will claim he comes to them in a dream or vision. Believers know that before entering their promised kingdom, they will have to account for each sin they commit, while the notion of a "sin" has such a loose floating all-inclusive vague sort of definition.

Looking up into the sky holding onto the same untethered Roman thread of hope for salvation still finds much of the USA public in an unprepared emotional state for today's un-letting real-life parade of unpredictable naked change-spawned ups and downs.

American politicians know to ask for God's blessing of America to end their speeches if not only to grease the reelection voting lever but also to subconsciously remind the listening audience of the white elephant that waves the USA flag. "In God We Trust" can be found stamped on US currency and in the gamut of anything subject to government control.

... Donald Trump ... A Chronic Liar Using "In Your Face" Style Gaslighting

It has been said that if you repeat lies enough times that people might start to think they are true. That proved to be Trump's strategy.

On 1-28-21 the HuffPost said: "According to the Washington Post, Trump made 30,573 false or misleading claims during his four years in office, with nearly half of them coming during his final year."

His speeches were nothing but sessions of gaslighting the public. He made up his statistics and promises to please the crowd at the time of his speeches.

His public appearances fixed to the pitch of his bullying style were always set to a defensive tone guarded by his spray of personal insults. His presence inspired division and rage.

Despite telling over 2000 fact-checked lies in his speeches during the first 3.5 years of his presidency, his crowds just wagged their tails and blindly followed his divisive directives. Littered with misinformation suited to craft his message to his liking about whatever the random topic on hand might have been,

Trump blatantly gaslighted his followers. His gaslighting style of repeating his lying agenda until listeners finally started questioning their take on reality, if they had one, was effective.

Slightly less than half of the electorate was empty-of-understanding the difference or just did not care. Trump, the fascist-authoritarian candidate, had told a documented 2000+ speech-delivered public lies over his presidency that he projected as his claim to wisdom. His followers blindly believed his false assertions without asking why(?) or shouting prove it(!).

Most of his followers did not even blink as his stiff-lipped false assertions stroked the flames of national division. His gaslighting efforts were so blatant it was clear to many what a foolish liar he was.

... Fig Leaf Wisdom Rocked by Trump Gaslighting Style

One of his more significant gaslighting threads was how he fronted the falsehood that the coronavirus would somehow just "disappear like a miracle." Hundreds of thousands of Americans died because of his lack of attendance to known preventive measures.

The subject line of Trump's public appearances amounted to being an ongoing stream of gaslighting falsehoods proclaiming that he had won the election in all the close states. Even after being assured by different contested state's lieutenant governors that their state elections contained no voter fraud and Trump's Attorney

General, Barr, of the Department of Justice verified that there was no voter fraud, Trump continued gaslighting that the voter fraud was undeniable.

At the beginning of December 2020, Trump had accumulated over $175 million from supporters to finance reversing election results.

... The Courts Were Deaf to Trump's Gaslighting

Trump's barrage of fruitless lawsuits in the states where he lost were waved as unfounded by federal judges. Trump had appointed the judges in many of these courts ... two in the supreme court.

Even though the numbers showed that it was impossible for Trump to turn the election results around, he continued, gaslighting style, declaring that the election was illegal and stolen from him and his followers continued backing him in public demonstrations.

Trump's influence in igniting and supporting the 1-6-21 attack on the nation's capital was unquestionable.

... Still His Believers Continued to Stand Deaf to the Truth ... Like Jehovah's Eden sentence to Adam and Eve and mankind ... until they eat from the tree of life ... they walk the earth lost in fig leaf wisdom

Trump believers compromised their perception of a democratic republic. His gaslighting had amazing power.

Despite the scores of shutdown court decisions against all of Trump's voter count contesting in the states where the election count was close and the 1-6-22 attack on the nation's capital that was primed and delivered by Trump himself.

Until this time in 2022, a huge chunk of the republican party and related electorate continue to support him and his contention that the election was corrupted ... as he dodges legal disputes and those who understand his premise.

Gaslighting works on a populace that's numbed by their "emptiness-of-understanding," to look and question reality for its self-evident truths.

... Still ... So Far ... USA Democratic Republic Survives

As bad as all this was, it demonstrated to the world how the principles that support the resolute of a democratic republic government can overcome and undo fascist-minded tyranny.

The principles that ongoingly feed the Tree of Life that underwrite compassion win out in the end.

That's not to say that future changes might be in line to better adapt USA government to recognizing the rights and income disparities within its populace.

It will never get any better until the pressure from a $30,000,000,000,000 national debt is eliminated. Greed and the love of money is at the root of all evil. Ignorance is at the root of all suffering.

Trump's self-serving autocratic agenda did not reflect the relational principles that underwrite outcomes that are in line with nature's plan of relational balance ... the constructs of compassion ... what the Bible chips away at with its 10 commandments.

... USA Active in World's Religious Tango

At America's 2017 presidential inauguration there were religious figureheads representing several theological traditions currently active in this country. The USA is trying to allow all religious philosophies to exist with Christianity.

If not, the resulting rioting and social uprisings would be much worse than they already are at this time in mid 2022 ... impossible to contain. Religion of all denominations have the ability to settle and corral the fears of the public.

Like with Roman citizens, the 2020 Presidential election demonstrated how Fig Leaf Wisdom guided much of USA collective focus. Much of the public easily believed whatever they were told to be true.

Luckily, more than half were wise enough to vote against an autocracy-bent government. Still, most of the USA follows a religious template and walk the Earth with worldviews wrapped in Fig Leaf Wisdom.

"Jesus Died for Your Sins"... What?! ... Please Explain

... Theological Gaslighting Premise

Theological gaslighting involves projecting a theology-staged and endorsed public ethos of a social reality backdrop having no real supporting tangible evidence to verify its living presence.

For theology's gaslighting plan to have a lasting effect on humanity, it is necessary that the listeners accept the vague meaning attached to the notion that Jesus had died for their sins.

... Christianity's Motto Should Be "Jesus Died For Your Sins"

To some, "Jesus died for your sins" is a longtime established totally accepted and unquestioned unspoken truth. They've heard it by their role models before they could even understand what they were saying.

It can be heard parroted anytime a preacher or dedicated Christian believer takes a deep breath and needs a filler statement. Its repetition, when paired with "because", can be used to validate the truth of any otherwise unsubstantial or hard to backup claim attached to a religious purpose.

"Sin" … other than just being a sort of untethered guilt-inspiring word pointing tattletale to a violation of Jehovah's loosely defined biblical will or religious law, let's give the meaning of "sin" some present moment character and real-life sensual texture.

Let's give it some meaning that after said will leave in mind a tangible effect that the behavior has had on an individual's wellbeing.

Some Christians ground the fiber of their religious belief on this free-spun notion and hide behind its glazed acceptance. It's as meaningful as quoting book-chapter-verse to prove the validity of Christian theology.

If you try to think through this trademark badge of honor and try to match it up with some sort of tangible meaning, you might end up, as Graham Nash said in one of his songs, "chasing mirrors through an empty haze."

… Saved From What? Our Sins? … What Is A Sin?

The first question someone who is being coaxed into taking the leap of blind faith to believe in and internalize a religious template promising to save humanity from sin and to live in an afterlife of emotional bliss should be to know exactly what sin is.

A sin's a bad behavior. What's bad? Bad for what end?

But most don't even ask.

Oxford Languages defines sin as: "an immoral act considered to be a transgression against divine law … a sin in the eyes of God" … "immoral" is very subjective … "divine law" is rather vague.

Why are some behaviors or thought patterns considered to be "sinfully" wrong?

What sort of natural law or principle does a sin violate? Bad to what end?

One would think the consequences of a "sin" are realized and paid for emotionally and serve as a deal-breaker or stumbling block in an individual's pathway to gaining emotional bliss.

On a very basic level, one thing a sin does to a sinner is to in some way scramble the smooth flow of their thought process. It generates a source of mental white noise. It adds another voice to the voices speaking in their head … shouting for attention.

On the passive sort of level of "sin", it makes it more difficult for them to have a calm mind with the ability to hold a sustained focus on a subject. The more drastic sort of sin does the same thing only it be grand enough to affect their life in a drastic way … prison … divorce … etcetera.

But all levels of sin has an effect on the sinner's ability to have a calm mind.

… There's No Biblical Breakdown of Sin Anatomy

The anatomy of sin only receives shallow treatment at best. Just because Jehovah used it and underlined how bad it is … nobody's really asked.

Being that Jehovah determines what connects behavior to its result that qualities it as being a "sin" eliminates the need or possibility for that matter for any causal relationship to be explained. Any cause/effect relational explanation is constrained to being merely correlational at best.

There's no biblical explanation detailing what's so bad about ... what's lost ... as a result of what the behavioral cause does in bringing about its effect.

Even if a believer has a list of what behaviors constitute a "sin", what good does it really do the sinner for Jehovah to forgive them for their sins if they do not know what it is about the behavior that makes it "bad" ... something they need to be forgiven for?

What is it that is good that is being negated by the bad sinful behavior?

The loosely defined concept "sin" is a fly-in-the-ointment in the process of understanding what affects the process of securing the calm mind needed to find emotional balance.

Not knowing how "sin" fits into the matrix defining emotional balance can short circuit an individual's ability to realize empathy ... to better understand the circle of feelings and emotions that generate compassion.

What is threatened when a sin is committed? What good does it impede? It would be much easier not to repeat a behavior if it was known why it was wrong other than just because Jehovah says so.

There is a plethora of loosely applied interpretations of "Jesus died for mankind's sins". This soul-saving relationship offers at best a sketchy understanding in today's world as to how it plays into the sinner's quest for gaining an emotional bliss and salvation from suffering that they can understand.

... Okay ... Jehovah Mandated First Thing to Adam in the Garden of Eden was to Get Only the Tree of Life Wisdom

The Bible says in King James translation Psalms 4:7: *"Wisdom is the principle thing: therefore get wisdom: and with all thy getting get understanding."*

In Psalms, the Bible says wisdom is the principle thing, and in the King James translation it says that in getting wisdom, an individual will get an understanding.

The Tree of Knowledge wisdom comes empty-of-understanding.

Jehovah made it quite clear in the first of his Ten Commandments that he was the lord and the god and that what he said is the unquestionable law. Maybe he didn't need to explain anything. The Christian doctrine has its god Jehovah as a middleman between an individual needing/seeking the wisdom and receiving it.

The idea is to access wisdom-deriving knowledge generated from the pre-lingual intrinsically sourced theater of understanding awareness itself ... Tree of Life wisdom ... as Jehovah mandated.

In the Bible, Jehovah offers "his" wisdom on a "borrowed" basis wrapped in the Holy Bible book cover … like the empty-of-understanding borrowed wisdom from the Tree of Knowledge the Eden snake gave to Eve. Religious theology has its eye on emotional bliss … just not on the right pathway.

… Bible Stops Short of Leading a Calmed Mind to Gaining Tree of Life Wisdom

Let it be given that by obeying Jehovah's Ten Commandments, an individual's mind will have gained some greater degree of moral/ethical calmness … freer of mental white noise … more sin-free … more capable of self-training how to sustain a focused train of thought to enter into the right concentration.

By just burning the commandments into stone did not complete the cause/effect circle of understanding the anatomy of a sin. The burning bush did not "sear in" any sort of complete understanding.

Constantine had his priests edit out the accounts of Jesus's teachings that might have better explained what is needed to make a behavior bad by making it clearer what is needed to make behavior good … toward affecting an understanding of the ignorance that causes suffering.

A sin relates to interfering with the process of gaining and understanding of emotional balance/bliss … eliminating the ignorance thereof.

The Roman Bible premise leaves a gap in an individual's circle of understanding of what a "sin" is and fills it in with, as said in the 1st commandment, "because Jehovah says so."

An attempt at calming the mind is where the Bible quits with no explanation of what an individual is to do with their calmed mind except not to break the commandments and let Jehovah decide on the Day of Redemption if they make the cut.

… Siddhartha's Eightfold Pathway to Enlightenment Starts with Eliminating Behavior that Can Initiate Committing a "Sin"

The first of three levels of self-training in Siddhartha's Eightfold Pathway to Enlightenment … self-training a calmed mind … includes the first three of the eight folds that include gaining self-awareness and control over behaviors that might germinate a "sinful" behavior.

In self-training the right ethics to achieve a calm mind Siddhartha Gautama," he self-trained his calm mind through … as in his teachings … right speech, right action, and right livelihood. He established the same sort of morals/ethics as from obeying the Ten Commandments.

Any behavior that can sidetrack a truth-seeker from self-training a calm ethical mind is "sinful" to some degree.

... The Reason for an Individual to Have a Calm Mind

Siddhartha taught how he was then able to, with the right effort, the right awareness and the right concentration, self-train his mind control to then self-train the right thinking to realize Tree of Life wisdom.

Mind control allowed Siddhartha to realize the mind-into-body harmony needed to self-train the right thoughts and right understanding to gather the self-knowledge to self-train the same Tree of Life wisdom Jehovah mandated for Adam to pursue to continue living in the Garden of Eden state of emotional bliss.

After becoming enlightened to understand what caused his suffering, Siddhartha suffered no more and taught this self-trained pathway until he died.

His teachings benefited so many followers that after his death, Buddhism has arisen ... many think of him as a godly figure. To many, Buddhism is a religion. There are many versions of Buddhism that miss his point.

... So, What Makes a Behavior a Sin?

When someone does something that hinders their progress in trying to calm their mind or hinders someone else's process to calm their mind to eventually self-train the wisdom to be enlightened about our Source's impermanent nature, they have committed a sin.

When their mental activity becomes burdened with guilt, hate, envy, lust or any of these negative mental states bringing on any kind of thought-numbing mental white noise, their mind will not be calm enough to self-train the mind control to find the body/mind harmony for any inspired thinking to allow the insightful understanding awareness of this reality's impermanence to help undo their ignorance that takes away their joy and happiness and makes them suffer.

...A Sin Begins with Any Intention that Interrupts an Individual's Journey Down Their Pathway to Enlightenment

Sin begins with any intention that interrupts the flow of the self-discovery process. When someone does something that hinders their progress toward realizing enlightenment from their ignorance, they are doing something bad or wrong. They will not have a calm enough mind to, like Siddhartha, self-train the right concentration to self-train a wisdom-enriched understanding that decodes their ignorance that causes their suffering.

They are instigating more suffering.

If Jehovah had only made this clear to Adam as the Earth cooled from creation, he might not have had to later bring on the flood or the Ten Commandments to then finally send his only son to die for all of mankind's sins.

It is tough to get two answers that are the same. Watch Sunday morning Christian TV preachers.

It seems clear that something that interrupts or prevents an individual from self-training their calm mind or ability to focus that mind into the "right concentration" to allow self-training Tree of Life wisdom is bad.

Anything that stands in the way or inhibits an individual's process of developing or self-training a calm mind or increasing and using the mind control to become enlightened about life ignorance that allows suffering would be considered something bad or wrong ... a sin.

... And Besides

There is one human that would refuse to be saved from something so biblically undefined as their "sins" at the expense of someone else's life ... son of some god or not. It is our First Amendment ... human ... right! This is especially true when not being first asked or knowing what it was they are being saved from.

What about all our countrymen who have died... given their lives ... to ensure their loved ones' independence and freedom from the living hellfire of having to live in some autocratic style government? Isn't each single one of their lives as valuable and important and MEANINGFUL as the life of any other human ... Bible-declared god or not?

"Sin"... A Vague Religious Notion to Glaze-Over Inherent Void in Understanding

Temptation feeds totally on an individual's ignorance ... from their emptiness-of-understanding.

Loosely applied meaning of the notion of a "Sin" is necessary to gloss over the need for answers to any forbidden questions about how an individual gains freedom from their ignorance that causes their emotional suffering that robs them of the emotional bliss that is available for everyone at any time. They either let their god do it for them or they try to discover it themselves, while still living.

The biblical notion of a "sin" points to a dead-end answer for all the unanswered or unanswerable questions relating to mankind's process of finding salvation from what causes their suffering.

Temptation grows from the uncertainty in the lack of understanding. Behaving in any way that rubs up against worthy moral/ethical standards will preoccupy the individual's mental process with white noise that negatively affects how they develop control of the focus of their mental awareness.

Not being able to sustain a focused awareness will make it not possible for them to self-train the right thinking and right understanding to realize the emotional enlightenment that inspires the insightful awareness of Tree of Life wisdom. It's especially bad when the individual knows nothing about the true pathway to gaining spiritual enlightenment while alive while blindly believing a religion's template of salvation leaving them with a mental void that's filled with the emptiness-of-understanding.

It's living hell.

Eden's Fig Leaf Mask Manifested in Modern Society

In light of theology's gaslighting ethos, to best protect themselves from what may seem like embarrassing social critique spurred from their shame of having an underlying empty understanding of this reality's relational justice, many will generate a self-ego to posture, manage, and defend the presence of an "I AM" and whatever might be related to it.

Individuals will craft ego-conjured social masks that come fig leaf-camouflaged in a way to best posture an ego-protected self-image any time the feeling of ignorance-spawned answer-void emptiness threatens with emotional shame. Their ego-crafted fig leaf-lined masks allowing them to carefully step from one ripple of change-driven time-served social experience to the next.

Their ego-crafted mask assemblage shelters their waning level of concern for exercising the due diligence to understand how their suffering can be eradicated in this lifetime.

Gaslighting's Net Influence on Compromised Freewill

... Gaslighting Stunts Insightful Enrichment

Gaslighting USA citizens to believe that notions of theology represent reality welcomes the second-guessing and self-doubt that distances the open-minded creativity that makes it possible to realize "aha" moments of inspired insightful wisdom an individual might have realized about the way reality works. Trying to merge the intellectually spun footprint of ancient reality with the sensually wired emotional sounding board of living reality only invites confusion and emptiness of the conscious understanding needed to connect the dots.

... Gaslighting Neuters Inborn Curiosity

Effective gaslighting subordinates the innate spirit of curiosity to self-doubt. The mind-numbing blind faith blinds believers to understanding modern-day work-in-progress.

When the integrity of an individual's freewill ability to question and objectively decide becomes compromised, their resistance to believing what has not been adequately verified becomes weakened.

It becomes much easier the next time for them to strike up some blind faith in some unverified stain of wisdom justifying some other sort of belief or conviction they borrow from elsewhere.

Concentrations of 2020 USA religious believers who've already made the big step of giving tyeir blind faith to theology, easily gave their blind faith to Donald Trump's empty wisdom promising to 'make America great again" ... despite his very "sinful" lifestyle.

In their quest for the answers that effectively lead to the state of emotional bliss promised by the wisdom of their chosen religious template, they become further separated from finding the right questions to ask.

... Gaslighting Force-Feeds the Belief System

Today, a prospective religious convert ... come Sunday morning ... must work up the willingness to chance-out striking up the blind faith-backed courage to rise to the preacher's end-of-sermon call for sinners to stand and come forward to repent and "give their life to Jesus."

They agree to borrow Jehovah's wisdom to find afterlife bliss and protection from ignorance-invoked suffering while sullenly radiating the seeming emptiness of a lost soul. The admitted sinner socially extends their spiritual neck ... outwardly declaring their blind pride-protected willingness to acknowledge internalizing the plausibility of an unsubstantiated religious claim's unverifiable truth.

They are about to accept and force feed their belief system an unfamiliar strain of wisdom that's not founded in self-evident truth... a new intellectually metered and stored understanding that except for arm's length mention of the Holy Spirit, has nothing to do with the living heartbeat of the ever-passing present moment.

This freewill-sacrificing decision tenders a new personality trait highlighting their new blind faith-backed willingness to subordinate their innate freewill questioning ability to the validity of the wisdom supporting the unverified truth of another's suggested notion.

They are hushing their freewill ability to question and understand uncertainties to a degree of never-to-be-forgotten magnitude. This is a monumental christening act of freewill self-defiance, synching up their innate freewill questioning ability to test and confirm the applicability and truth of an unverifiable claim.

The resulting indecision and pending uncertainty coming from this imbalance will brew up an ongoing unsettled emotional cocktail that will influence their decision-making process of everyday interactions. It will affect the nature of their minds and skew their worldview.

... Gaslighting Affects Ritualistic Hovering in Devine Anticipation

Religious converts may have secured a more perceived sense of social belonging. Camouflaging their fear of the unknown with a god-ensured security does nothing but perpetuate and disguise emotional imbalance. As long as they skirt their inborn concern over the well-being of their human condition and spend their waking time in an emotional illusion they'll spin blindly in some level of fundamentalist denial.

They will harbor a searching hope subdued by fear and uncertainty. They will live with a mind waxed gross to seeing the truth ... too touchy and squeamish to adapt ... frozen from exhibiting the humility needed to gain an enlightened understanding of the patterned principles that set and define the nature of the impermanence that runs this reality.

Over time, this fundamental denial could concede to and bleed over into an apathetic mindset.

Mortgaged Belief System ... Freewill's Nemesis

Some people mortgage something they have of financial value for the unearned dollars to buy the right to pay back the money to own something at a future date.

Likewise, some people will mortgage what they have of spiritual value ... their freewill ... to be able to obey a notion of uncultured hope-founded wisdom and with their obedience, secure an unverified yet promised state of afterlife emotional bliss.

Believers hog-tie their soul's freewill questioning prowess to their promise of being blindly faithful to a proclaimed god's unverified wisdom that's promises to lead to attaining afterlife emotional bliss.

Adam and Eve mortgaged their souls' freewill to derive wisdom using Tree of Life wisdom for the Eden snake's promised short-cut to the all-knowing wisdom that deciphers all the ways of what happens in this reality ... to have a gifted wisdom that understands "Everything from Good to Evil."

The promised hope defining the unverifiable wisdom being borrowed is of a strain of wisdom that the individual has never earned or been able to test. They have not acquired the appropriate knowledge that understands the network of principle-founded interactions or relationships needed to derive that borrowed wisdom.

Like Adam and Eve, those who mortgage their soul will cower into the shade of fig leaves in the shame of their ignorance-spawned emptiness-of-understanding.

Borrowed wisdom is the freewill's nemesis. A new religious believer borrows and assumes a new and unfamiliar code of wisdom.

A new believer's freewill is cuffed by this new scripted wisdom. Their life choices are made in line with their perceived understanding of the borrowed wisdom's scripted intent, that is to be followed unquestioned.

It is a sin to question it.

... Fear And Ignorance Persist

When consciously subdued fear peaks its boogieman head into a religious believer's present moment out from under the bed they have made or from their closet of secrets, they are to look up into the heavens and pray to their new god for relief.

They continue to live in ignorance. Their interest in understanding their living world becomes detached and seemingly unimportant. Their life path stands confused while guided only by a blind faith in their intellectually grounded fix on what the unexplained wisdom means.

The ungrounded security coming from their un-quantified untethered blind faith submission will now echo from their worldview in all their future interactions. They have mortgaged out their inborn freewill questioning defense system that is meant to be used ... 2-year-old style ... to protect and help guide them from the uncertainties of life while learning from experience.

They make a promise to an unseen unverified entity that they will give up or pay their protection money with their innate ability to question what their human condition does not understand about its human experience.

They pay with their human condition's 1st amendment ... human ... right to speak up and express itself for the entity's protection from the boogieman of the unknown that hides under the bed they have made or in the darkness of their closet of unsharable secrets.

The believer lives in hope of making the final cut to enjoy a promised eternal afterlife to finally have the non-suffering emotional bliss the borrowed wisdom purports.

Their freewill questioning will be hushed into following the unexplained wisdom trail of their chosen god.

Stuck Suffering in an Eddy of Compromise, Empty Ritual, and Dogmatic Inflexibility

As a believer's connection with developing their awareness of their intrinsic sense and gut-felt understanding between what is right and what is wrong … weakened … in their unaddressed ignorance, they stand less resilient and more vulnerable to insipient suffering as their misguided conditioning leads them to different forms of contaminated pleasure.

Their ability to question lies frozen in stand-still confusion when trying to use their ancient strain of borrowed wisdom to make sense of the contradicting sensually metered self-evident truths of the present moment in action.

As an individual's freewill consciousness fades, their intuitive nature becomes even more easily mortgaged out to trusting the influence meant to serve the unverified or unverifiable mindsets of other entities.

Their personality fades.

… Public Gets Told What it Wants to Hear and What its Needs Are

Like Steve Jobs once said in a company meeting that it is not Apple's job to do customer surveys, it is their job is to tell the public what it wants.

This fits well when a public's collective freewill has been numbed by the bite of profit-hungry business entities, building often false misrepresented credibility for products that do not perform as promoted. The buyers have been duped into borrowing the business's untested unverified (snake-guaranteed) wisdom to purchase their product/service.

As undefinable focus eats up an individual's waking energy while trying to socially posture and defend their ego-managed self-perception, they will reach for fig leaves to hide their shame from their ignorance-spawned emptiness of understanding … like Adam and Eve did when confronted by Jehovah at the very onset of the Genesis creation for partaking of the snake-promised wisdom from the Tree of Knowledge.

From behind religious theology's protective veneer, the confused believer will keep an open eye for a more substantial understanding of reality to better secure an understanding of emotional balance/bliss.

This conflict seeds the self-doubt that can last an entire lifetime.

... The Mind and Body Drift Apart into Different Worlds

As the believer ages, their mind and body drift apart in caring for and awareness of each other. They become strangers to each other. Their mind beats to the rhythm of intellectually sourced maxims while their body continues to follow the intrinsically ingrained totally unavoidable life principles their mind no longer finds any respect for.

Mind and body harmony become distanced as the mind that is focused on living by the borrowed wisdom of the intellectually metered imagined world loses touch with recognizing the heartbeat of the universal reality that shouts out the Life wisdom-deriving knowledge from the believer's material body.

The barrage of input to how USA citizens must be brave with their blind faith in the wisdom they are borrowing from some ancient source comes from all government-certified angles in America.

This does very little to help them undo their ignorance to better understand the cause of the suffering putting them through their present moment emotional mayhem.

Theological gas-lighting manifests in many forms throughout the cultures of the world.

Gaslighting Ethos Filters Down To Affect Family Relations

The effects of theological gaslighting filter down to the family level. There are many young individuals who do not find it easy to swallow borrowed wisdom on blind faith that are raised in families with parents who have chosen to be true to some theological discipline.

Their parents were young once with the same level of questioning uncertainty. They too will probably bend in time.

These parents are their role models.

With parents that are reluctant to bending away from their take on what they think their god would approve of, a wall is built that compromises forming an honest transparent relationship that is needed to help the child best navigate through life situations.

When a parent takes pride in how they can stand amongst fellow church members after services and out book/chapter/verse their theory about what their god means in the multi-translated ancient scriptures, what chance does a young child looking to them for life guidance have?

When mixing the unverifiable nature of theology's undefinable uncertainty with the deserved recognition given to the self-evident principles that explain the relational nature of the impermanence that fuels this universal reality, a balanced child-to-adult development process can be greatly compromised.

Worldwide Theological Gaslighting Pandemic

When faced with the uncertainty of the unknown and fear of what it might hold, mankind looks for security. To most, it seems that understanding the answer does not have to be a part of that security.

Most of mankind at this time dances to the Fig Leaf Wisdom they get from believing blindly the promise they mistake for wisdom that explains how they can get protection from suffering and live in a state of afterlife emotional bliss. Most will suffer throughout the rest of their life with no knowledge about finding emotional balance.

Theology's gaslighting ethos has infected humanity worldwide. Anytime there is some strain of god-promised wisdom involved … there's gaslighting.

… Most fail to understand that reality doesn't happen in the biblical sense. Theology's gaslighting ethos perpetuates this state of collective consciousness.

IV

Jesus Would Roll Over In His Grave ... If Still Buried

"By and large, language is a tool for concealing the truth."
~George Carlin

My Universal Message ... Hijacked and Gagged ... Kidnapped by Human Greed and Juggled in Human Linguistics

The integrity of the Bible's intended message is in question here. It's necessary to weigh in on how Rome's 325 A.D. self-serving selection of available gospels to make up the Roman Bible's 1st edition changed Jesus's intended life message.

What was said in the gospel accounts that Constantine ordered destroyed had to be of some relevance or they wouldn't have been ordered destroyed. There had to be something in them that Rome's hidden agenda didn't want included.

Furthermore, after Jesus's intended message was sacrificed to the Roman hierarchy of greed lined self-serving purpose, Jesus's intended message has had to weather through 2 millennia of meaning-jamming ... yet unintentional ... human error in its many translations.

Jesus's Message of "Salvation From Suffering" is "The Kingdom of God is Inside You"

...The Awareness Connect Has A Preverbal Presence

In the later English language King James translation of the Roman Bible's priest-edited 325 A.D. 1st edition of Jehovah's promised salvation from suffering, some of Jesus's intended message seeped through.

Jesus made this point clear to his disciples:

> *"Neither shall they say, lo here! Or, lo there!*
> *For, behold, the kingdom of God is within you."*

> — Luke 17:21 King James Translation

Jesus's intended message, as interpreted and restated by his apostles also seeped through, as translated into the later English language King James translation of Rome's 325 A.D. 1st edition of Rome's Holy Bible.

In I Corinthians 3:16 King James Translation, the apostle Paul asks the Corinthian believers a question: *"Know ye not that ye are the temple of God, and that the Spirit of God dwelleth in you?"*

Paul repeats this question in 2 Corinthians 13:5 King James Translation, *"Or do you not realize about yourselves that Jesus Christ is in you?"*

Constantine ordered all evidence of the superfluity of competing religions of the time and those of Christianity not suited to satisfy Rome's deceptive intentions to be destroyed.

... Gospel of Thomas Gives Deeper Meaning of Jesus's Message

What has become to be known as the "Gnostic Gospels" were secretly hidden from Constantine's henchmen and have been uncovered within the last 100 years. These accounts were written by more spiritually mature authors of teachings that Jesus had given to more spiritually mature audiences. This scripture from the uncovered Gospel of Thomas is one example of Jesus's more spiritually advanced teachings:

> *"The Kingdom of God is inside of you, and it is outside of you.*
> *When you come to know yourselves, then you will become known,*
> *and you will realize that it is you who are the sons of the living*
> *Father. But if you will not know yourselves, you dwell in poverty, and*
> *it is you who are that poverty."*

> —Gnostic Gospel of Thomas, Saying 3 of 114

The Gospel of Thomas had been ordered destroyed by Constantine. Thomas was of the spiritual maturity to comprehend Jesus's intended message and was able to poetically express its intended meaning more clearly.

As Jesus said in the Gospel of Luke and Paul taught in 1st and 2nd Corinthians, Jesus plainly stated in the Gospel of Thomas how this "God" notion lives inside of you.

The Gospel of Thomas is saying how the kingdom of God encompasses everything. It is the nature of impermanence that spells out the truth. Understanding the nature of the ongoing exchange of living energy that's alive everywhere in everything is to understand what affects the emotions that will affect suffering from the ignorance inspired emptiness-of-understanding the ways of that impermanence.

The Tree of Life wisdom provides the waking understanding awareness that decodes these relationships.

To understand it in yourself is to know it in everything and that you are a part of this living (transforming, impermanent) almighty force. But if you choose to not learn about what makes up yourself, you suffer a poverty in understanding.

Jesus was a messenger, as was Siddhartha and other individuals who'd attained a state of enlightenment about the patterned principles that rule the dimensional makeup of this impermanent reality that set the cause/effect course for relational logistics.

Only One True Cathedral of Worship

"The Kingdom of God is inside/within you (and all about you), not in buildings/ mansions of wood and stone. (When I am gone) Split a piece of wood and I am there, lift the/a stone and you will find me."
~Gospel of Thomas, Saying 77b of 114

Thomas makes it clear that Jesus taught that the kingdom of God exists inside of everything ... dead or alive and not inside of churches made of brick or wood. It's the ongoing life of change that encompasses the mass of all things.

... Mankind Builds Its "Tower of Babel"

There is a vast collection of tributes to the various gods of theology throughout the world. Some immense cathedrals and masques that have lasted for centuries still stand in tribute. They are built of the most expensive materials, designed by the most gifted architects and some had taken more than a lifetime to build.

These are places mankind figures will demonstrate to their god of choice that by their devoting the most expensive and best of all possible resources to their god that the god figure will open his eyes, listen to them, and show them forgiveness.

Some have even sacrificed the most fertile and beautiful of the community's young maidens to honor their chosen god.

Believers enter these structures possibly thinking that connection with their holy power source waits inside.

They will learn to word their prayers in a verbal display like the version of biblical translation their congregation uses for their Sunday study thinking he will be better able to understand them or appreciate the respect of knowing that the prayer is changing their native tongue to that of Bible talk to give the message a dose of sincere sanitization.

It's when some believers are away from the material house of God that their prayers will stray to not so much for the welfare of others, but to prayers for victory … especially if they've made wagers on the contest.

Thomas's account reported that Jesus taught the energy … the power of life … the Holy Spirit … exists within everything. The truth exists in all the materials that compose a church … just not in the presence of the building.

… "The Kingdom of God is Inside/Within You"
… Pre-Verbal Language of Life is Spoken

If a believer wants to learn from their lord, they need to go into where the house of the lord … inside their body. Instead of telling him what they want to happen … the outcomes of things they'd like to see … they need to learn how to sensually tune-in listen to … witness … the truth he is shouting from every relational outcome defining the coming and going sensations from withing.

If they tune-into what their body's saying to them as their awareness confronts the appearance of feelings that would generate what they perceive while emotionally reacting to sensual inputs, they'll be accumulating the sort of knowledge that will generate the thinking for their insightful derivation of the Tree of Life wisdom that their god Jehovah mandated in his first breath to mankind in the Garden of Eden creation.

Worship the Message … Not the Messenger

… About The "Christ" And The "Anti-Christ"

As the son of God, a third of the Holy Trinity, Jesus is known as the Israelite messiah, the Christ, or the answer to Christianity's promise of salvation from suffering. Christians tend to worship the messenger … not so much the message that the messenger represents.

It's said in the Old Testament that someday one would come with the answer to human suffering. It's the answer … not the person. The person is only the messenger. It's unknown how many past or maybe even present individuals are messengers of how to find emotional balance/ bliss.

The "Christ" is the message. The "anti-Christ" thwarts its purpose to show people the way to be free of their ignorance and achieve an aware understanding of this reality's impermanence that is the fundamental source of their ignorance.

After all, Christian dogma believes that the Holy Trinity is what created and is the force that controls the natural forces that interact to produce the principles that sustain this reality's dimensional backdrop that brought on all the miracles, partings of seas, plagues … etcetera.

… It's an Agenda … Not an Individual

Christian belief is that the "anti-Christ" is an individual who is prophesied to oppose the "Christ" and become his substitute. How exactly the anti-Christ will oppose the Christ, as per Christianity reference is unclear and greatly open to opinion.

This writing sees the anti-Christ as not being an individual, but the agenda that underwrites the messenger of the message itself. The anti-Christ appears as any sort of interference with mankind's growing awareness of the self-evident truths that lead to an enlightened understanding that the messenger spoke of.

This process of mankind's collective "enlightened" understanding began replacing theological mystical magical notions with reality's self-evident truth about half a millennium ago when mankind's collective conscious awareness morphed from an age of mystical wonder to an age of reason.

Autocratic themed government is a shade of Anti-Christ. The nature of their rule greatly interferes with the freedom an individual needs to experientially walk the pathway to self-training an enlightened understanding of the nature of the impermanence that defines what affects their state of emotional balance.

There are many influences contributing to an Anti-Christ agenda at work in today's world.

Rome's Greed-Serving Priests Apple-Spit-Shined the Roman Bible First Edition to Rome's Benefit

… Constantine Stamped Christianity as Rome's Religion

In 312 A.D. in weighing all the different religions in his Roman state, the Roman emperor Constantine decided to make Christianity Rome's official religion.

Rome was a polytheistic civilization. Romans worshiped different gods and goddesses. Even with monotheistic religions, like Judaism and early Christianity, Romans honored multiple deities. The rituals varied between localities.

Christianity only had one God and that helped in the decision to recognize it. Constantine realized that many Christians could read, and this would be useful for the Roman government.

So, all other gods were outlawed and Christianity became state-controlled and edited with the selection of the Rome-preferred gospels, with any offshoots being punishable by death.

Constantine felt he had to control his Roman citizens. In 325 A.D. his priests spit-shined the Christian religion to offer a set of self-serving rules to his citizens to ingest, as the snake did for Eve. Romans were told the Bible was their new god's wisdom.

The published written rules snipped off any aspects of an emerging theology that pointed anywhere besides outside leadership, making their observance illegal and punishable by death.

It would help corral citizen morale into a Rome-designed public control ethos.

Rome did not want its citizens to realize that they each had inside, the power to determine their own life direction. He wanted Roman citizens to look to Rome for this.

Rome did not want its citizens to think they could find direction from within. Rome wanted its Romans to look outside to the government for direction.

Human Translators

The unavoidable mal-effects coming from the human-plagued translation process must be considered in what today's theology followers stake their sole-soul-future on. It is inherent that anything translated will to some degree dilute and reconfigure the original speaker's intended message to the tone of limits of the translator's capabilities.

When considering individual translators' spiritual maturity levels, a translator's effort to find a word to express a written concept that they are not able to personally grasp the intended meaning of, their miscued understanding will cause the written intended meaning to be lost or altered in their translation.

The selection process for finding an innovative word with the closest parallel meaning will have been compromised.

Having different people speaking different languages from different times in history with their thinking being pushed and conditioned by social trends and government oversight along with differing personal levels of spiritual understanding, and the limits of a language's word-selection availability in translating the text of these ancient scriptures must compromise the original speaker's intended message as expressed by the written text.

As the centuries passed, more life truths proved self-evident and surfaced to mankind's collective waking consciousness. The Aramaic language Jesus spoke and taught in was translated into thousands of newer languages with more words that came about as mankind was better able to insightfully recognize the deeper meaning attached to emotional impulses and assign those deeper understandings a word.

Translators had to make subjective decisions about which newer more descriptive words to use to best preserve the intended message as represented by what message they were translating.

It is clear to understand how speakers' intended meaning of what the English meaning of "inside you" can easily become distorted. It is hard to imagine how it could not become misdirected in some fashion.

... English King Henry VIII Force-Fitted Bible Text from Latin to English

Soon after the year 1500 AD, Henry VIII needed the pope's consent to divorce and remarry. The pope refused. King Henry had it falsely declared that the King's say-so supersedes that of the pope, so he withdrew England from the Roman Catholic Church to allow his remarriage.

The creation of the Church of England was the first opportunity for non-Latin-speaking individuals to even read the Bible. The amount of human condition instilled intended meaning butchery compiled from the biblically reported original speakers' intended meanings is unimaginable ... but does exist.

Apples to Oranges ... Bibles to Bibles?

To better understand and briefly demonstrate the disparity that exists between the different translations of the Roman Bible's scriptures, it only took a bit of due diligence and an Internet connection.

Performing the due diligence is much easier today than any past time.

> *"The Bible has been translated into many languages from the biblical languages of Hebrew, Aramaic and Greek. As of September 2016, the full Bible has been translated into 636 languages, the New Testament alone into 1442 languages and Bible portions or stories into 1145 other languages. Thus at least some portion of the Bible has been translated into 3,223 languages."*
>
> ~ Wikipedia

The Bible is the most published book to date. The number of different languages and cultures represented in these publications reaches out to all parts of the world.

And the first point made in the Bible is to seek Tree of Life wisdom and not to blindly believe what's said to be wisdom because it leaves you in fundamental ignorance ... empty-of-understanding.

The Bible is supposed to be the modern-day source used to derive the strain of wisdom used to steer a believer to emotional bliss (heaven) and away from suffering (hell). Choosing wisdom was the sole topic of Jehovah's first God-to-man verbal during the Genesis account of the Garden of Eden creation.

Each of the following seven modern biblical translations describes to their readers what's in the "wisdom" that they are supposed to direct their attention to spending their efforts looking for ... understanding is the most popular goal cited.

The meaning looseness inherent to translations results in including knowledge, prudence, and intelligence.

New American Standard Bible: "The beginning of wisdom is: Acquire wisdom; and with all your acquiring, get understanding."

God's Word Translation: "The beginning of wisdom is to acquire wisdom. Acquire understanding with all that you have."

American King James Version: "Wisdom is the principal thing; therefore, get wisdom: and with all your getting get understanding."

Bible in Basic English: "The first sign of wisdom is to get wisdom; go, give all you have to get true knowledge."

Douay-Rheims Bible: "The beginning of wisdom, get wisdom, and with all thy possession purchase prudence."

Darby Bible Translation: "The beginning of wisdom is, get wisdom; and with all thy getting get intelligence."

World English Bible: "Wisdom is supreme. Get wisdom. Yes, though it costs all your possessions, get understanding."

This comparison demonstrates the biblical translation skew on the intended meaning that exists between biblical translations of Proverbs 4:7. The nature of this intended meaning skew can be extrapolated to include the text from other scriptures.

Following is a comparison chart of different biblical translations reflecting differing interpretations of Romans 1:18.

INTERLINEAR	NAS	KJV	ESV	NIV	MESSAGE
Is revealed for wrath god's from heaven against all ungodliness and unrighteousness of men the truth in unrighteousness repressing.	For the wrath of God is revealed in from heaven against all ungodliness and unrighteousness of men, who supress the truth in unrighteousness.	For the wrath of God is revealed from heaven against all ungodliness and unrighteousness of men, who hold the truth in unrighteousness	For the wrath of God is revealed from heaven against all ungodliness of men, who by their unrighteousness supress the truth.	The wrath of God is being revealed from heaven against all the godliness and wickedness of men who suppress the truth by their wickedness	But God's angry displeasure erupts as acts of human mistrust and wrongdoing and lying accumulate, as people try to put a shroud over truth.

Just try to imagine how the intended meaning in the different translations of the Book of Revelations vary.

... Believers Interpolate Scripture Meaning into Their Own Unique Understanding

With all the different Bible translations in today's world, the reader's interpolation becomes necessary. An individual will read from a few of today's Bible translations and maybe from a few well-known Bible commentators. From these sources as well as from sermons and group discussions they will interpolate their own idea of the originator's (Jesus) Aramaic-versed intended meaning.

Just listen to how different Sunday morning TV preachers justify their take on biblical wisdom and listen to their point-proving string of book/chapter/verse quotes to justify their take on their supported theological notion.

Experience Unavoidable Human Static

There is a party game in the Midwest USA that makes light of how the core intended meaning of a story changes shape as the story theme is verbally passed along from person to person.

The exercise starts with one person quietly whispering into the ear of another a detailed story of some sort. The listener then whispers the same story into the ear of the next person. After the story has been silently passed along between all the guests, the last person to hear the story shares the version of the story they heard with the group.

The final account of the story is always far from the original. The more participants, the more entertaining the final account becomes. The longer the line, the more the resulting distortion.

Keep in mind that these friends all spoke the same dialect of the same language in the same culture and there were no brain-to-paper related distortions of meaning passed along over multi-millennia ... thousands of times.

You Just Had To Be There

... Aramaic, a Language of Few Words ... Body Language Mimed *and* Tone-Shaped Meaning

"The contradiction so puzzling to the ordinary way of thinking comes from the fact that we have to use language to communicate our inner experience which in its very nature transcends linguistics."

~D. T. Suzuki

> *"The problems of language here are really serious.*
> *We wish to speak in some way about the structure of the atoms …*
> *But we cannot speak about atoms in ordinary language."*
>
> ~W. Heisenberg, *The Tao of Physics,* Fritjof Capra, p. 32

Like in the world of atoms, Jesus was speaking of insights about life that were just coming into light … no real words for yet.

Jesus spoke Aramaic, the language of few words. There are no written recordings of his teachings in his native tongue.

It's hard to imagine how his true intended meaning that was orally presented in a language of few words could ever be captured and related to other people by any means.

Preserving his intended meaning in his teachings would be greatly enhanced by witnessing his body language as he formed his beliefs into words. Jesus's teachings reached deeper into the subtle meanings on aspects of spirituality for which there were probably no words for yet.

People came to hear his teachings about something new … teachings about the evolving truth about how the human condition fits into the nature of reality.

Jesus taught mankind about the subtle truths telling how the human condition relates to the human experience that was surfacing into mankind's cumulative waking consciousness using a language of few words.

That's one reason he spoke in parables, other than how some people were just too spiritually immature and couldn't grasp the insight when presented any other way.

He described new insights to enlighten mankind's waking awareness as to the truths about how humankind can find emotional bliss and be free of suffering.

… His Body Language Cues Enhanced Listener Understanding

How could he use the few-word language of Aramaic to accomplish listener understanding covering a newly evolving spiritual insight? He had to have used changing tone levels and body language to best hit on the heartfelt meanings as he tried to detail the process of how these deeply felt intrinsically verified truths become synced with a truth seeker's conscious awareness.

To secure Jesus's intended meaning, a truth-seeker really had to be there to listen and watch his body language. And even then, it would be left up to the subjective decision and spiritual maturity level of the individual who witnessed the animated expression to choose what descriptive and feeling-focused meanings to use to describe their heartfelt interpretation of his intended meaning.

... Speaking In Tongues?

Some of Jesus's descriptions of newly arising insights that still lacked any pre-scribed language might resemble what a two-year-old child does when they try to express a desire coming from the inside that they still do not know the word for.

Here with Jesus, it is more a matter of society not having yet developed the words to express the meaning of Jesus's insightful description unfolding the pathway to spiritual enlightenment.

It would be a combination of blabber, finger-pointing, eyebrow-raising, hip shifting, and eye intensity. Parents can often understand the intended meaning of their young children as they "speak in 2-year old tongues"?

This demonstrates one way the emotional essence representing what is felt is generated on a pre-lingual basis. This inner theater is where the wisdom decoding the cause and solution to emotional affairs exists and is derived ... not in consciously recognized intellectually metered and stored knowledge.

Language ... The Shorthand Cliff Notes of Intended Meaning

... Intended Meaning Lost from Aramaic and Finally to English Multi-Translations

Jesus's intended meaning has been passed along through scores and scores of human generations and from one language dialect to another.

There have been over a couple of thousand years for the intended meanings of biblically scripted wisdom to have been diffused and diluted before the Romans did it purposefully. The writings have been passed back and forth generationally from area to area ... language to language ... culture to culture.

Linguistics has many inherent limitations. There are cultural differences that add filters between the enlightened teacher's intended meaning and the understanding of today's truth-seekers. Much of the original intended meanings were lost, diverted misunderstood and mistranslated to some degree during the transformation of the original messages to what we have today.

... Language Is Merely A Social Agreement

The meaning of words is a conditioned social understanding.

Many words have different meanings culture-to-culture.

Language dialects form a word-crafting compromise where "rounded off meanings" become unavoidable.

The use of linguistically propagated knowledge as a chosen media to derive wisdom is not much more than interpolating wisdom from diluted approximations of intended meanings and using that blurred grasp on knowledge to derive wisdom.

An individual must stick with what gels into making sense to their conscious awareness.

And then ... it remains that the product here is only from the knowledge that's been intellectually tendered and retained. The knowledge is not registered and understood on an intrinsic level.

It is not the knowledge that is used to derive the same Tree of Life wisdom that Jehovah warned Adam to seek to live a life free of suffering in his Garden of Eden.

... Intended Meaning Diluted by Word Semantics

Bringing an inspired thought from the deeper conscious awareness up into waking conscious recognition to then cognitively flip through the mental card file of the conditioned subjective meanings attached to the known words expressed in the English language to capture the heartfelt intended meaning of that virgin inspired thought can change or at least dilute the thought's unsheathed intended meaning.

Then, when shared, the meaning attached to those words is filtered through the various meanings of those words the listeners themselves were conditioned to understand.

People might be trying to describe the same mental image and be lost in the semantics over the meaning of the same words they were earlier conditioned differently to understand. They can spend much time trying to with words paint their vision explaining what its imagined material presence would appear as.

... Word Semantics Vary From Culture To Culture

Different cultures generate their own assortment of words reflecting the different impressions reality's distinctive footprint has left in their region. Culture to culture, the same words may have different intended meanings. Different people from dissimilar cultures can interpret the same message quite differently.

The More Developed English Language Did Not Exist Back in Biblical Times

Rome's self-serving biblical reality comes described to today's readers white-washed through 2 millennia of accumulated multi-translated human perception-spawned error. Its intended meaning had to conform to or be further focused into dialects that were not even thought of back in the day or language of the original orator.

The biblical reality is presented conceptually on a sensuality-sterile intellectual platform.

... The King James Version Biblical Dialect

When visiting theology's world in prayer, many believers in wanting so much to please their god, will change their modern speech habits and use the "thy" and "thou" accented dialect referencing the times of the King James translation. This is their most direct contact with him. It is where they have read about the sandal-clad times of the biblical world they have managed to piece together in a time-stilled cognitive snapshot.

It is their most official dictation of his promise of heavenly bliss. It is the intellectually metered medium they got to know him on. It is the medium where their conscious tie-in to relief from life's suffering lies. It is the medium they made his acquaintance and got to know his promise of wisdom on.

Maybe they reason that speaking to their god in what they perceive as his language because it sounds from times past, even though really of a much more recent and different language, will settle better with him when it comes to blessing what they want to have blessed or in influencing the outcomes of what social event the want him to commandeer to their best interests or maybe miraculously healing the individual(s) they are "praying for."

Yes, believers will sometimes walk on eggshells to please their god.

This intellectual barrier sets a diversionary boundary that serves as a wall between them and the reaches of the deeper meaning, the sensually registered intrinsic version, of understanding the status-quo that their human condition longs to better understand.

From The Language of Few Words into Languages of the Future

The English language used in the King James Version of the Bible sounds antiquated in today's world while it was a yet-to-be-invented language of the distant future back during the days when Jesus walked the Aramaic Earth.

The original 2,000-year-old written impressions have been translated into thousands of languages that did not even exist back in the day.

These newer languages include a richer vocabulary reflecting mankind's more mature deeper understanding of concepts that 2,000 years ago were just emerging in mankind's collective consciousness as fragile ideas about how the human condition fits into the human experience rose into public awareness.

... Richer Meanings Emerge Over Time and are Expressed by New Words
... Subconscious Intrinsic Publishing House Takes Sensually Metered Feeling Signals and Assigns Intellectually Metered Wording

As individuals interact, more defined perceptions of the feelings they experience surface from the intrinsic publishing house of their subconscious awareness. Language development rides in on the coattail of thought development.

... People Self-Train the Ability to Allow Their Right Thinking to Inspire An Enlightened Awareness of What Mystifies Them

(See Chapter XII ... how to recognize and turn their mysteries into an understanding awareness to replace their ignorance that could be making them suffer)

As individuals reflect over the feelings they have during their everyday interactions they will have insights that might suddenly bring on some "aha" wisdom where things click, and they have an insight giving a deeper understanding to the principles that affected the cause/effect logistics of a certain result.

Discussing with a friend these sensual feelings using the words in their vocabulary to best describe what these feelings, good or bad, might help to transform these feelings into an intellectually shared medium. They try their best to "put into words" what these feelings might have indicated.

Today there is an innovative word, "simp" or "to simp",," which evolved on the social media Tic Toc. It combines referenced meaning from a few different contexts such as what used to be a "simpleton" or someone who is a bit naïve with a few more referenced meanings to evolve give "simp" the meaning of someone who is overly servant to someone they have interest in. The phrase is still honing a lasting meaning.

When a change has its effect on altering reality, new innovative words are needed to reference the meaning of evolving twists the change has on feelings that bring tweaks to the established catalog of human emotions to self-train the ability to transpose the gut-felt meaning into the wording used in intellectually metered communication.

Friends will put together a slang term to refer to a way they communicate or interact. If their slang term spreads and has a large enough collective social acceptance, it will eventually find its way into the dictionary.

Regions Vary In Need For Words To Describe

The many translators up until today have had to decide what they thought Jesus might have meant or intended to say and that depends on whether their personal level of spiritual maturity can even tender the true meaning of Jesus's intended concept.

Comparing language to language, French and Italian have several more words that convey more specified meanings of the word "love" than does the English language.

Eskimos have nine words that give a more differentiated understanding of distinct types of snow.

The eastern languages have a much larger selection of words to convey more detailed descriptions relating to the topics of spirituality than does the English language.

Some intended meaning is compromised when translating from a language with less available words to a language with a more available selection of words defining the topic or idea like with Jesus's native tongue Aramaic to any other of the many languages it was translated into.

It becomes necessary for a translator to subjectively choose a word with a different and possibly more general meaning or to choose a word from a larger more modern selection of a different language with a more specified meaning. The interpreter/translator must consider and use their subjectively affected word choice that might point in a skewed direction and miss the original speaker's intended meaning.

The intended meaning will be changed somewhat anytime a newer more descriptive word is used to express the same thought

The life of the message intent becomes smothered out in compromise.

... Using Translators Dilutes Intended Meaning

Like when the Dalai Lama holds a Western seminar to explain the meaning of Tibet's renewed understanding of Siddhartha's message from the turn of the first millennia, due to his limited ability to use the English language, he uses a translator.

Tibetan language has more words to describe the inner feeling-spun emotional signposts that make up his lessons. His translator must decide what English word to use to express the more meaningful Tibetan word.

Much of the deeper meaning of his intended message is lost in the oral presentation.

... Thich Naht Hanh Had Deeper Connection

Thich Naht Hanh, the prominent 20 century Zen Buddhist monk/teacher, was fluent in 7 languages. This ability enabled him to come closer to matching his understanding of the deeper meaning to his oral or written message.

He wrote 100 books and was known as a poet. He was known as a poet because of this ability to find the right words to express inner feelings. His deep reservoir of words helped win him this title.

... Human Assumptions are Unavoidable in Transposing Supposed Meaning

As demand for the Holy Bible grew and time passed, translators had a larger word selection available of more meaning-sensitive words. They had to decide which words to use to best channel their perception of what the enlightened orator's intended meaning was as they understood it. It is just like fitting a square peg into a round hole.

When transposing their understanding of a word's meaning between time-warped languages, translators must make assumptions on the word's intended meaning. They must decide on the meaning of one written word and then subjectively decide what more defined meaning from the new language that has since evolved that the original speaker would have used.

The four gospels that Constantine's Roman priests chose to include in the Bible's New Testament were not written until beginning fifty years past Jesus's death. This makes one wonder how the biblical account authors could parrot exactly what Jesus or any of the biblical characters said to be granted the King James version's red ink quotation authenticity status?

"And now, the rest of the story ..."

-Paul Harvey

The Life of Jesus Before Age Thirty

... Jesus Taught The Same Universal Wisdom

The biblical accounts of Jesus began when he was around thirty years old. There are no real accounts of what happened earlier in his life.

There was a story of his preteen visit to the Jerusalem temple, where he sat amid doctors, listening to the teachers, and asking questions. The teachers were surprised at his level of spirituality.

This was before Christianity.

There was no mention of his teaching them about the kingdom of his father, God, and the Holy Spirit as has been rumored from many Sunday morning pulpits (Luke 2:41–49, King James Version).

Just a computer keystroke away for anybody asking questions and performing their "due diligence," is much information dealing with where Jesus was from his teens until returning home which is where the New Testament starts.

One account of this missing time zone has been well summarized in The Lost Years of Jesus: The Life of Saint Issa, translation by Notovitch (12-19-06 Internet writing from The Reluctant Messenger).

"Ancient scrolls reveal that Jesus spent seventeen years in India and Tibet. From age thirteen to age twenty-nine, he was both a student and teacher of Buddhist and Hindu holy men. Brahman historians recorded the story of his journey from Jerusalem to Benares. Today they still know him and love him as St. Issa. Their "Buddha." (Introduction)

Nicolas Notovitch published a book called The Unknown Life of Christ. During his travels researching his book he journeyed through Afghanistan, India and Tibet. He stumbled across ancient records of over two hundred verses of the life of Jesus known as The Life of Saint Issa.

There were skeptics who returned to the area to either find the ancient documents or to prove his fraud and disprove his writings. One was Swami Abhedananda. He found a Bengali translation of the same document Notovitch had found a Tibetan translation of in a different Buddhist convent.

In 1925, Nicholas Roerich revisited the place Notovitch found the verses and made his own diary of Issa's travels. After having perfected himself in the Pali language, the just Issa applied himself to the study of the sacred writings of the Sutras (Siddhartha's teachings).

"Six years after, Issa, whom the Buddha had elected to spread his holy word, had become a perfect expositor of the sacred writings."

~ Notovitch translation. "The Lost Years of Jesus: The Life of Saint Issa." (http://reluctant-messenger.com/issa.htm), Chapter 6, verse 4."

It really does not matter if Jesus learned the path to self-taught enlightenment from Siddhartha's teachings or if the truth about our source was written on a postcard, knowing the primal truth about living is what is important … what is relevant is not who said it, when it was said, what language it was said in or what clothes the messenger was wearing or how they died or anything else.

It is a human being's way of finding enlightenment about what they are ignorant about that causes their emotional suffering. It was Siddhartha's way or Jesus's way of teaching the way. They were both enlightened teachers who had discovered paths to the same enlightenment that were documented in some fashion.

Jesus would shake his head when seeing how his message of relieving human suffering got so distorted and stretched out of shape ... intentionally by greed and unavoidably through human error-laden translation.

V

Everybody Wants to Go to Heaven ... Later

... Yet, Still Too Afraid (Uncertain) of Death (the Unknown) to Go Now

It seems like everyone wants to go to what they understand heaven to be ... yet nobody wants to die.

If someone feels sure about what they have been told about heaven's afterlife eternal emotional bliss, it seems like they'd want to be first in line to give up this life's emotional suffering to get there.

... Jehovah's "Promised Land" ... an Afterlife Retirement Resort?

Up until around 1500 AD when Martin Luther explained how salvation was based on faith and that there exist no human intermediaries between man and God, it was thought at that time that heaven inclusion could be purchased.

Religious believers adopt and nurture a blind-to-reality hope-based faith supported only by the arm-length confidence that heaven will be the promised afterlife eternal emotional paradise that comes free of fire and brimstone suffering.

Is the anticipation of heavenly hopers really any different than they would have for a trip to a part of the earth they have never seen? Maybe their anticipation copies what's found from looking forward to moving to a sunny warm place after retirement from their working life?

So ... Why Wait?

What is the sensual meaning of those English language descriptions? What does the intellectual fiber of those descriptions of heaven really mean to an individual's sensual context?

With death, everything sensual stops. Living flesh dies and reverts back to dust.

This happens. No question. It represents the most chilling degree of the unknown.

Heaven's cognitively etched-out mental picture registers as no more than a cognitively configured calculated possibility.

The bleed-over from a believer's intellectually engendered mental picture of heaven's described perks lacks the familiar feel of living reality's sensual pin-prick texture.

Physical death is thorn-in-the-side real while the essence of theology's cognitively sketched paradise is merely conceptualized.

Way ... way too much uncertainty for the boogieman(men) to hide in.

Who wants to bet their life on this?

Opting Out is Cowering Away from the Unknown

... The Promise of a Panacea to Solve All Problems

The Christian believer must make it through this life living by Jehovah's borrowed wisdom. Most individuals die without having developed an understanding of reality's ways sufficient to undo their ignorance of how their human condition fits into its human experience.

They die still having emotional issues.

A believer still must make it through this life suffering in ignorance to the ways of reality that they are not engendering the due diligence to better understand to relieve the suffering and gain emotional stability.

... How Deeply Woven Is That Blind Faith?

The thought of what really happens after death takes an individual into a primal specter of the unknown. It delves into the deepest unchartered depths of their interrelated fears.

By not voluntarily giving their living soul to their god by choosing mortal death, they are in a sense, still running away in lasting doubt from what is sensually unknown and unfamiliar. They choose to delay the blind faith-secured god-promised emotional bliss and heavenly freedom from this Earthly state of suffering.

Maybe they have some worthwhile compassionate reason for staying imprisoned by their material human body? Jesus chose Judas's betrayal to allow his crucifixion to rid his soul of its imprisoning material body as suggested in the Gnostic Gospels.

The living presence needed to support the intellectually founded heavenly concept just does not feel real enough to bet the sensual reality of their real-life heartbeat on, even if emotionally unhappy and depressed with their take of the status quo.

This is when the "getting away from" sense of suicide might step in, not the "going to" pursuit of chasing a conceptualized notion of heavenly emotional bliss.

Reliance on Religion is Founded in Fear *and* Hope of Promised Afterlife Paradise

"Upon the wicked he shall rain snares, fire and brimstone, and a horrible tempest, this shall be the portion of their cup."

~ Psalms 11:6

"The Son of Man will send His angels, and they will collect out of His kingdom all causes of sin and all evildoers, and they will throw them into the furnace of fire, where there will be weeping and gnashing of teeth."

~Matthew 12:41-42

Jehovah uses shades of emotional bliss in relating what he provided in the Garden of Eden and in setting the stage for his Bible-promised future heavenly Eden. The stage for the promised bliss and damnation in the borrowed wisdom of the Bible is described in terms of emotional joy and pain.

Finding relief from the fear of the unknown is one thing that drives the human quest for emotional balance. The human condition longs for relief from the ignorance in understanding what is unfamiliar … their ignorance of the natural force-driven principles that configure the backdrop of this universal reality that causes their suffering.

Billions of people today rely on their "hope" suspended in their cognitive understanding of the intellectually described "Almighty" to have the wisdom-enriched answers to what they do not understand and lack the courage-supported due diligence to find the answer for or even know what questions to ask to initiate the quest to gain an enlightened understanding awareness of what their ignorance leaves them full of emptiness.

They decided to quit trying to figure out the right questions to ask when they "gave" their life to their chosen heavenly god so they could just somehow take care of their suffering. So many others are doing it, it must work.

... Eternal "Fire And Brimstone" or Maybe Eternal Emotional Bliss

Jehovah's threat of eternal afterlife hell punishment for non-compliance is related in terms of humankind suffering. The only way humans can relate their human condition to its human experience is through what it has experienced ... through sensual reference.

Religion's borrowed wisdom intellectually strikes the match of fear by describing in the goriest details possible the imagined sensual gradient of the pain spawned when all types of pain are realized collectively ... God-threatened eternally. Promised eternal presence of an afterlife hellfire and brimstone punishment for loosely defined disobedience can send a soul-freezing lightning bolt-quiver through anyone's blind faith.

The thought of burning with the fervor of all negative emotions of pain and misery stoked full blast forever can be very scary.

This soul-stirring ultimatum is unsettling enough to convince some individuals to adopt the religious promise of hope just to avoid the possibility of that scenario's truth ... just in case the holy promise somehow holds true. Like the Roman ruler Constantine that allowed the legalization of Christianity in 312 A.D. finally did on his deathbed ... just in case.

Others might adopt a religion for its promised afterlife bouquet of joy and happiness-laced emotional bliss. It is emotional bliss that is cognitively calculated in terms of that experienced sensually in real life.

The potential believer may choose to focus on the promise of an afterlife paradise that only requires them to follow a set of God-ordained rules.

Keeping an Eye Peeled for a More Substantial Understanding

Individual's will try out different sources of promised wisdom to replace their current level of emotional unrest with emotional bliss. There are many flavors of religion to taste from.

What happens after death is a part of the unknown. Individuals are afraid of the boogieman(men) of their unknown that is hidden waiting in the wisdom-void emptiness of their conscious understanding.

Understanding this wisdom-void emptiness would help sedate an individual's fear of the unknown.

It is that inkling of background subliminal questioning doubt that piggybacks any form of blind trust that will have the theologian on reserved alert for anything that even hints at satisfying that inborn curiosity about what it is all about.

Maybe the promise made by the religion's plan was their best soul-security option at the time? Religious believers stay alert for a more tangible life answer while debating their chosen version of the multi-translated ancient scriptures of their chosen religious theology.

They stay subliminally alert for a more substantial answer as they pillage through different toys and beliefs, keeping an eye peeled for a more gut-satisfying answer to that soul-saving question they are not even yet sure of.

It is the inability to deal with the fear of the unknown that drives the human quest for better understanding of life's ways and purpose.

Can't Recognize Enlightened Sages in Living Color

Most people in the living world stand distant to the thought of there being individuals who emit the presence of what is intellectually described in sandal-clad terminology as being at or approaching "enlightenment".

... It Takes One To Know One

It takes one who has experienced the state of "spiritual enlightenment" to understand what to look for in someone else. If not enlightened, an individual still looks to the unknown in search of that state of peace.

There are those living that are enlightened about how their human condition fits into its human experience. The thing about it is that they too must die some-day. They are human.

Jesus died. Siddhartha died.

Biblical Wisdom is Hollowed ... Not Hallowed

Biblical wisdom, as received in its Rome-edited multi-translated state, taxes the limits of the human imagination ... like when trying to give form to the mean-ing of the King James Version of Revelations ... odds are that there are no two independently formed matching interpretations.

Many believers think there exists an afterlife neutral place of waiting until the day Jesus rides back into reality on a white horse with trumpets blaring to announce the Day of Judgement has finally come in the wake of their god's Arma-geddon victory over evil. They believe this waiting place contains the souls of all to be judged as earning their angel's wings and those doomed to be judged as hell-bound sinners.

It's not very compassionate of Jehovah to do the fire and brimstone thing to any of his creation. He has the answers. Why not just let every soul know his secret recipe to emotional balance so all can live in bliss?

He's the god. He wrote the book.

Along with Adam and Eve, blind faith religious believers comprise one group of many that ingest different sorts of Tree of Knowledge understanding-depraved wisdom. They are left grabbing for fig leaves to hide their shame for their empty understanding resulting from the ignorance-wrapped sterile wisdom they have chosen to adopt to craft their worldview.

Biblical wisdom is unearned. This holy wisdom gives its readers no intrinsic understanding of nature's Tree of Life-related principles that support the truth of the natural force-driven principles that determine all outcomes that they don't understand that the wisdom decodes. It creates a separate world disconnect from reality's living presence.

It is the hollowed/not hallowed wisdom that they show blind-faith pride in parroting yet stand too uncertain about and too afraid of their god's intellectually documented vindictive lightning bolt temperament to step forward and question.

The nature of the reality perceived in this either/or early-life distinction is mirrored in the nature of the individual's conscious mind. It is reflected in the fiber of everything their conditioned worldview has them believing, saying, and doing.

Religion's Bark Intensity More Real Than Bite's Credibility

… Unavoidable Emotional Imbalance

You drive a new car before purchasing. You want to verify the car dealer's claim.

You want to walk through a new home before mortgaging out your financial future to a foreign entity.

You should also want to walk through your soul's eternal home before mortgaging out your soul's inborn pathfinding freewill initiative for another entity's promised yet untested future answer to your pending need for soul security.

A believer's innate sense of freewill curiosity's been neutered by their pledge of allegiance to the notion of a theological entity.

A follower of theology's templated wisdom is instructed not to question what their heart does not intrinsically grasp. This is where blind faith steps in.

Undecided believers are uncertainty-touchy about detailing their pledge to a religious allegiance they are not subconsciously convinced about themselves.

They are risking it that their lord might hear them thinking or speaking their doubts. Or, maybe they feel guilty or at least self-conscious about verbally soiling what might have been premature childhood god-pledges made to please their parents or other elders or out-of-fear promises they had once made to heaven.

It might be time to get baptized again.

If not, what then? ... the promised eternal fire and brimstone?

This fence-straddling conviction style is reflected in how well balanced their conviction resolve is in other life affairs. A religious believer's life-long emotional imbalance is pretty much guaranteed.

There's Only One Heaven?

... No Two Intellectually Sketched Takes on Paradise are the Same

And there are no tangible ruminants to set as a collective standard.

There are different imagined incarnations of heaven to satisfy all the personalized unique mental projections of what has been intellectually metered to be cognitively crafted to suit the limits of everyone's imagined dream machine.

A potential believer's fear exists in their unknown. Heaven exists in their unknown to conquer that fear. This need allows each new believer to step over the line of reality and conjure up and take a chance on blind trust in a savior from their own personalized scary zone of the unknown to control and conquer that fear ... that boogieman ... that demon.

This biblically described heavenly palace has never been experienced in any sense by anyone. Every believer has a unique mental casting of what it might look like. None can be the same. Congregations argue over their heavenly impressions to the point of splitting up.

With no tangible history to reflect on to engage in discussions, religious believers cannot meaningfully weigh in with others about what the future-day material presence of the place of "emotional bliss" will really be like or what the representative meaning might be of the adopted rites-and-ritual gestures as a means-of-worship to get there.

Just listen to TV evangelists scripturally piece together the conceptualized logistics explaining and justifying the calculated steps in their stairway to heaven and maybe even what they think it will look like.

Religion and Realism Point to the Same Emotional Bliss

Although the spiritual traditions described in the last five chapters differ in many details, their view of the world is essentially the same.

It is a view which is based on mystical experience—on a direct non-intellectual experience of reality—and this experience has a number of fundamental characteristics which are independent of the mystic's geographical, historical, or cultural background. A Hindu and a Taoist may stress different aspects of the experience; a Japanese Buddhist may interpret his or her experience in terms which are very different from those used by an Indian Buddhist; but the basic elements of the worldview are the same. These elements also seem to be the fundamental features of the world view emerging from modern physics.

— *The Tao of Physics*, Fritjof Capra p. 116

A subtle pulse of common purpose ripples through the godly claims of the different strains of religious theology. The different world religions originated from the minds of different people in different parts of the world at different times.

... Siddhartha's Insights are the Same Self-Evident Truths Science Searches For

Even though Siddhartha's teachings evade having any god middleman, his purpose is included with those of the various theologies in Mr. Capra's above quote. Siddhartha's path to enlightenment represents the same insightful realizations about the self-evident nature of this reality's relational principles as does those science has revealed the self-evidence of.

All religions evolved from the same desire to better understand the unknown to find emotional balance and to be free of suffering and misery. They all point at a promise of afterlife emotional bliss.

The same faint ticker for truth also runs through speculations founded in scientific principle and spiritualist experiential sensually assimilated Tree of Life insight. All those that question reality, whether scientists or realists are also wanting to better understand the truth about the environment in which the human condition experiences its human experience.

All twitch to the same prick of primal curiosity.

This understanding will enable mankind to live more in harmony with the nature it is a living part of. At this point on the universe's timeline, there is much human suffering going on from lack of this understanding awareness.

Simply said ... these various disciplines all consist of human truth-seekers fueled by the same longing. They have just aligned their differently conditioned approaches of applying the "5 W's" when curious or finding the proof to verify some idea, with different established social avenues of posting notices of inquest.

The fields of speculation are trying to focus on some contributing ray of light making up the whole of the same bright light shining at the end of the same tunnel of life ... only through different colored lenses. Should it be some god or source of Life … quantum mechanics metaphysical coming and going bits of life-giving energy or the Holy Spirit … tomato-tomatoe … potato-potatoe?

Some individuals settle to obediently bow to theology's time-shaped schedule of what to them seems to be meaningless rites and ritual that has been somewhere deemed necessary to help their religious sect's promised afterlife claim come true.

Other truth-seekers insist on seeing intellectually documented proof while others follow their curiosity all the way and figuring out how to self-train an experiential sensual understanding of the wisdom-founding Tree of Life knowledge detailing what collectively constitutes the nature of this impermanent reality where a valid claim's impermanence-savvy purpose eventually exposes its truth as being self-evident.

At mankind's current stage in its evolution towards finding an answer to that great question, the path to understanding is still being viewed and approached from different points of view or platforms of perspective. The disciplines of science, experiential sensually assimilated wisdom-enriched enlightenment and religious theology all point to the same bright light illuminating from that final answer.

… All Avenues of Conditioned Speculation are Needed

With mankind's current collective spiritual maturity at a kindergarten level, all the avenues of speculation characterizing the different plateaus for posting different angles of observation that define the nature of this reality are needed.

These diverse ways of recognizing and posting inquiry to understand this reality allow for all types of conditioned worldviews to participate together in understanding the nature of patterned principles that write script for the impermanent dimensional makeup of this reality. It still needs to be recognized that everyone is reaching for the same ultimate answer, they are just making their contributions via differing modes of conditioned understanding.

Why Not Find This Emotional Bliss Now?

If the whole idea is to find emotional bliss by eliminating suffering from emotional misery, why not treat your soul to it now while living with the emotional elasticity to experientially wake up an intrinsic awareness of and realize it?

It's just a matter of an individual owning and better understanding the nature of what affects their emotions.

... Establish the Emotional Balance/Bliss of this Enlightened Understanding Awareness Now and Not be Fearful of Death

A truth-seeker needs to realize their fundamental ignorance about the impermanence that makes up this reality and then build an enlightened intrinsic awareness of it and put their ignorance-spawned emptiness to rest.

Become knowledgeable about what it is about the life experience that is unknown and the misguided expectations from that ignorance will stop along with the suffering the ignorance summons. The emotional misery will be replaced with emotional bliss.

VI

Dreams of Heaven?
Look Before You Leap!

G od allegedly made man in his image.
With all due respect … he should have either left out the mankind free-will thing or "blessed" mankind with the waking awareness of the Tree of Life wisdom he mandated in his Garden of Eden talk with Adam.

Jehovah kept the emotional bliss secret to himself.

There would never have been a need for theology or science to figure it out.

At least it's easy to see that they're both after the same answer.

He left it a mystery to understanding how he programmed Mother Nature's natural forces to fuel and set dimensional pattern to her relational principles that determine the outcome of all cause/effect interactions … that give shape and living color animation to the ongoing change screenplay illuminating this world's present moment reality.

All of that ignorance keeps mankind repeating all the sinful behavior that makes him so angry.

Surely Jehovah knows how to use his anger to grow from

And what's with that commandment "Thou shalt not kill ... and allowing all these god-sponsored wars where so much human life is so needlessly lost?

Yet there are billions of people who use their freewill to choose to blindly borrow and follow the biblical wisdom or that of another god to a promised oasis of Eden-like emotional bliss in an afterlife "heavenly" paradise.

They live in ignorance, suffering in "hope."

Jehovah Rolled the Dice on Human Freewill

... God Jehovah ... The Gambler?

He must have been a gambler ... at least in the beginning of humanity's toga/sandal life chapter. Being that the Christian god Jehovah formed man in his own image, he really should have known better.

An untethered unaware freewill is something not to be taken for granted.

Following the six days God spent busy creating all the universal heavens ... and the earth, on day seven, Jehovah created his Garden of Eden paradise. And that day, right after forming Adam ... before he had even created Eve ... before hitting the "go" switch to animate and set pace to the non-continual ever-transforming future ongoing passage of time, Jehovah reached out to mankind and had his very first dialog where he issued the only mandate he had gambled necessary to preserve man's inclusion in the Eden paradise ... his handcrafted Genesis masterpiece.

On this day Jehovah drew for Adam a life-or-death line in the sand as it cooled from creation.

Jehovah devoted his premier God-to-mankind chat to making it do-or-die clear to Adam which type of wisdom he was to choose and which type of wisdom he was not to choose to form his awareness and understanding wisdom of how things interrelate to enrich his conscious mind and cast out any ignorance to allow for his continued living in the state of Garden of Eden emotional bliss.

He told Adam to partake only of Tree of Life wisdom and that it would take only one time of internalizing borrowed wisdom from the Tree of Knowledge to result in the death of Adam's conscious awareness of his intrinsic Tree of Life wisdom-enriched tie-in to Garden of Eden emotional bliss.

Hindsight's 20/20

Jehovah surely knew that bestowing to a born-ignorant human the innate ability to decide where to FREEly WILL their trust would probably come with a few snags. Wouldn't mankind's ignorance-laden thinking be peppered with either/or bouts of uncertainty-based indecision?

Created in his image … he should have known … with all due respect.

Bad choices would have to happen at least every so often.

What about the snake bite of temptation?

What were the odds?

Jehovah was soon to regret his Garden of Eden go-for-broke gamble as the resulting unending stream of mankind's sinful transgressions made it necessary for him to later many times invoke his tempered revenge-tilted punishment to finally sacrifice his only son in the effort to let mankind back into his grace from its sinful ways.

Now, these logistics are hard to follow for most.

Instead of Jehovah's either/or scare tactic used with Adam and … with all due respect … instead of the snake … maybe Jehovah should have created a teacher or maybe supplied a user's guide to fill in the "because-why" informative detail to give Adam and Eve a conscious awareness of the how's and why's of nature's ways to stay on the right path?

But now, who is this human to question any god's logic?

It's been said that hindsight's always the clearest.

When recognizing the Bible on its own terms, Christianity's God Jehovah rolled the dice when creating a multi-universe reality centered solely around Earth's tiny Garden of Eden answer to tender mankind's emotional paradise.

Jehovah's first attempt at paradise failed. Despite all that, there grew another ancient promise of a future-planned second attempt. But this time, an individual has to wait until after they have died to experience the state of bliss.

Any individual who's considering using their freewill to borrow God's wisdom, to wait in hope until after they die to be gifted emotional bliss, had better first look closer before taking that required leap of blind faith to be followed by a lifetime wrapped in the hope of being sin-lean enough to make Jehovah's final Day of Armageddon cut.

… Jehovah Scrapped His Eden Plan

"So he drove out the man, and he placed at the east of the garden of Eden Cherubims, and a flaming sword which turned every way, to keep the way of the tree of life."

~Genesis 3:24 King James Version

Jehovah was upset with man's ignorant behavior. He had warned them. It is understandable how someone, especially a god, might be angry with themselves for betting on their plan working.

But anyway…

He posted an impenetrable guard at the gate of Eden to protect the emotional purity found in Tree of Life awareness from mankind's corrupted way of approaching life by settling for an awareness founded on the empty understanding inherent to borrowed knowledge.

He did warn them.

Garden of Eden Paradise First Attempt Failed

… Asking for Blind Trust in Hope of Second Attempt at Paradise

With all due respect, based on Jehovah's reported "state of Eden" success history with mankind, the average person would question his ability to fulfill his long-pending promise to provide an afterlife paradise "Heaven", the modern/future/yet-to-be version of Eden, for mankind.

Adam and Eve, the first human beings, did not take his advice in this reality's Garden of Eden genesis.

There is no tangible material depiction of what future heaven will be like. Heaven's conceptualized yet-to-be presence is unique to everyone's imagination. There is nothing tangible to pattern the future presence of Jehovah's biblically reported yet cognitively sketched vision of this heaven of emotional bliss.

Theology asks for humanity's blind trust, living in hope for the fulfillment of God's promise, praying that it will be there as they perceive it to be and that they can satisfy the loosely defined requirements of the holy plan to eternal salvation.

Eden's Homeowner Association
Only had One Statute!

> *16. And the LORD God commanded the man, saying, of every tree of the garden thou mayest freely eat:*
>
> *17. But of the tree of the knowledge of good and evil, thou shalt not eat of it: for in the day that thou eatest thereof thou shalt surely die.*
>
> — Genesis 2:16-17 KJV

Yes … Eden's homeowners' association only had one area law to follow … only the fruit from one tree that was off limits.

Jehovah made it spiritual life-clear to Adam what type of wisdom to internalize to continue living in Eden-cast emotional bliss and by seeking which type of wisdom would result in his spiritual death.

Mankind's Original Sin

... Choosing the Tree of Knowledge Wisdom

"And he said, who told thee that thou wast naked? Hast thou eaten of the tree, whereof I commanded thee that thou shouldest not eat?"

~Genesis 3:11 KJV

Yes, mankind had its way with Jehovah's premier spiritual life-or-death mandate. This god had mistakenly wagered that he would only need one initial new-world commandment to make a success of his Eden project.

... And There Were Only 2 Choices ... Just 1 Distinction

Jehovah only designed two ways that humans could look at the presence of his new reality ... understanding its nature or ignorant to its life principles.

And even though the god who created Adam and Eve had threatened them with their spiritual death if they chose a certain one of the 2 options ... that is exactly what they did!

Be it that Adam was the one that Jehovah had forewarned, and Eve was the one that was snake-confronted with the temptation, that was still a weak use of their brand new freewill.

However, this setup leads to a huge problem.

Being that Eve "was the mother of all living," means that they created the world's population. And that means that every human inherited it!

Humans are all born to bear God's Garden of Eden curse coming from Garden of Eden's man and woman committing that original sin.

What Did Jehovah Expect?

... He Gave His Ignorant Naïve Human Race an Ungrounded Freewill to Make the Choice

In giving humankind a freewill, with all due respect, it seems that Jehovah was thinking that the nature of their worldview is the first thing that a human must consider before going on to discover the purpose for the unique gifted talents and abilities he gives them to help mankind's collective wellbeing.

Even though it is said that God knows what an individual has in their heart, it turned out that Jehovah had no control over Eve's or Adam's mental sway when

Eve was propositioned by his Eden snake. They used their freewill to consider and decide to knowingly disobey his first and only command.

Eve had been promised a shortcut on gaining wisdom … to be gifted someone else's all-knowing wisdom.

Maybe Jehovah should have toned down humanity's freewill factory setting?

… Or, Maybe

Jehovah neglected to instill in man a conscious awareness intrinsically synced with the protocol of Mother Nature's impermanent presence and the instinctual wisdom needed to best establish what Tree of Life wisdom-deriving knowledge to seek for deriving the Tree of Life wisdom intrinsic familiarity that the Tree of Knowledge wisdom lacked.

Jehovah Repeatedly Put His Foot Down to Punish Man's Ignorance

… The Resulting Garden of Eden Fig Leaf-Covered Shame was Mankind's Introduction to Suffering

It seems Jehovah remained vindictively upset with how mankind continued to sin after violating his virgin commandment.

Mankind has squandered in ignorance, using theology as a crutch in effort to maintain a healthy emotional life balance ever since the Garden of Eden mishap.

Jehovah … the all-power "God of Love?" … why not just make it available? … easy to spread? … maybe make compassion the 6th sense?

Why not just instill in mankind the awareness to live in harmonic sync with the principles of impermanence, that the ignorance of underwrites all of humanity's sinning and suffering?

A True Logistical Mystery

As mankind multiplied and time advanced, mankind's ignorance-spawned sinful stubbornness about violating this god's unexplained and unquantified demands on what to do and what not to do persisted. God, again and again, threatened mankind's disobedience only to end up wiping out all the disbelievers with a great flood.

As time passed and mankind failed to concede to following Jehovah's mandates, he determined it necessary to write in stone ten more commandments dictating how humans should behave. Again, he offers mankind no explanatory wisdom with an understanding detailing the why's or why not's of their ordered behavior.

Jehovah later personified his last chance for mankind to find forgiveness and find emotional bliss and sent his only son to die on the cross so mankind, empty-of-understanding, could be forgiven for its sinful ignorance-laid behavior. How this makes any sense, is a total mystery.

Jehovah Withheld the Emotional Bliss Secret to the Eden Paradise

... Why Will it be Any Different ... As Promised in His Afterlife Heavenly Paradise?

Those who never learned while living that the continual presence of anything is totally imaginary will expect God's promised heaven to appear as their cognitive-painted rendition of the imagined continual presence of their memories picturing the imagined permanence of their family members, friends, and even their pets they knew while living in fundamental ignorance.

This ignorance allowing for imaginary time continuity resulted in the clinging attachment that triggered their various forms of their emotional suffering.

If Jehovah didn't instill this Tree of Life-friendly wisdom in Adam and Eve when watching them use their freewill to choose to borrow wisdom from the Tree of Knowledge, why would he instill it after life? Why install this Tree of Life wisdom in someone who's died?

Wouldn't they still be empty-of-understanding its premise?

Amount many others, Siddhartha Gautama was one normal human being who figured out how to do this himself while living and was able to leave the intellectually metered pathway of how he sensually accomplished this feat for other truth-seekers to follow in effort to experientially self-train an intrinsic understanding awareness of and do the same thing.

His last words to his followers were to get off their butts and take a sensual walk down his worded path ro figure it out for themselves ... not in so many words.

The Day of Armageddon

Blind faith theologians will just have to wait until the Day of Armageddon when Jesus rides in on his white horse with trumpets blaring to see what happens. Heaven or hell ... family members that are present ... family members that did not please Jehovah ... their pets?

Many will be surprised ... and many will be disappointed.

… A Zombie Final Cut?

There are those who refuse the thought of cremation with thoughts that their body must be present to stand before their god. Like when an individual thinks of Moses, their conditioned reference to seeing Charlton Heston in one of the movies where he played the role of Moses, do images of the modern Zombie-related movies flash onto an individual's mental screen?

It's A Shame … Spiritual Genocide … Out of Ignorance

Billions of human souls have been misled and wasted looking to the wrong light for answers. Theology believers will die suffering while ignorant in hope of relief from their suffering … for a paradise of emotional bliss.

They had lived their life, their freewill handcuffed, not questioning the uncertainties of what is unknown. They probably did not know the right questions to ask and did not have the guidance they needed to sort out the question to then find the answer.

Had Eve Been Cajun

… She Would Have Eaten the Snake … There Would Have Been No Biblical Story-Line

If Adam and Eve would have been Cajun, they would have eaten the snake instead of the fruit and saved us and Jehovah a lot of trouble.

Humanity would be living in a state as described in John Lennon's song "Imagine."

Humanity would be living in compassionate harmony, consciously in sync with reality's ruling principles.

There would have been no narrative to fill Rome's 325 A.D. Bible first edition telling of mankind's plight, squandering in Fig Leaf Wisdom, after being banned from the Eden Garden paradise by Rome's newly certified god.

VII

Real Life Doesn't Happen in the Biblical Sense

Notion that a God's "Intelligent Design" Might be Responsible Fills Mankind's Popular Imagination

... Human Condition Struggles for Cadence During Human Experience
... Everything Revolves Around "the Earth" Mindset

Even with the advances in astronomy over the last few centuries, the feeling that the earth is at the "center of focus" of everything is still set in the minds of many. From the recent discoveries that there's water on Mars as well as finding seeds of life on asteroids to the growing number of Earth-like planets in other solar systems that might be suitable to sustain life as we know it, it has become self-evident that the Earth is not the center of the universe.

In a PBS special from American Experience "Chasing the Moon" part II, Jim Lovell comments about how his outer world experience during his Saturn 8 trip around the moon affected his view on Earth presence.

> *"All religions are based on the fact that the Earth is the focus of the universe and God sits up there with his supercomputer and keeps track of all the rights and wrongs. Orbiting the Earth and then going to the moon has given me a different outlook. The Earth*

is really nowhere as special as you'd like to think it is. Though it is our home planet for humans and it's the only one we got right now and there's not one in easy sight to get to, so therefore we ought to take care of it. But we shouldn't think that this is the designated center of everything."

https://www.pbs.org/wgbh/americanexperience/films/ chasing-moon/#part02, 1hr 43min 27 sec, into film

... When Thinking of Heavenly Solace, Theologians Look up for a God in the Sky

Believers in theology reflect through their cognitively mimeographed wisdom borrowed from the time-stilled days of old from the pages of their chosen ancient text for the way to overcome their suffering. The real time passing present moment living manifestations of cognitively cerebrally etched time-suspended intellectually stored abstract theological notions pass by unnoticed by fundamental theologians.

Their experientially unverifiable theological signposts get intellectually planted in the time-stilled specter of their human imagination and in keeping them safe from all the unexpected bumps from ongoing change, they gobble up all their host's waking reservoir of soul-safety energy as they spin-wheel-focus their attention on best posturing their confused living presence.

When thinking "heaven", the blindly trusted book/chapter/verse logistics adopted from time and translation-worn scriptures from a sandal-clad biblical promise still leaves many gazing hopefully upward.

Their imagination colors in the blank areas.

They are yet to detect the Tree of Life truth vibrating from within.

One type of wisdom is intellectually borrowed. It is backed by the confidence in the knowledge that has been received or gifted ... maybe gathered from different sources and conceptually calculated.

Another type of wisdom is derived from self-acquired knowledge conditioned through present moment sensual experience.

In Garden of Eden terms, this is Tree of Knowledge wisdom versus Tree of Life wisdom, respectively. Its distinction is as important today as it was when Eve decided to borrow the wisdom offered and gifted by the Garden of Eden snake.

... Bible's Compilation Challenged

The Roman Catholic Bible is a publication reflective of an ancient time reality. The collection of accounts describing the time of "the Christ from heaven" was 312 years old at the time of its first drafted Roman edition from nearly 2 millennia ago.

None of Rome's chosen gospel accounts were written until at least 50 years past Jesus's death. Today's versions of the Rome-approved gospels and the books composing the remainder of the New Testament and the books of the Old Testament have been down the trail of meaning-compromising translation several times to date.

There was no English language back in those days.

Religious believers struggle to use their cognitively etched mental blueprint of this ancient physical reality of intellectually metered bible-based borrowed wisdom as an emotional filter to best handle the sensual signals that naked change unstoppingly throws in their face.

They suffer individually and speaking in collective terms ... the world suffers. Having "God on our side" is the shared mantra of both sides in human warfare.

Believers will make at least a token effort to align their life perception with their cognitively processed intellectually honed understanding of the borrowed measuring stick of what defines right and wrong. They fiddle around with the loosely defined idea of "sin."

Believers struggle to make the connection for their intellectually shaped understanding of what right and wrong look like in ancient terms when it presents itself to them today in pre-lingual fashion through the sensual connections of their human condition to real life change.

The disjunction in this mismatch will in some fashion challenge their sanity day by day.

Imagined World Has No Material Blueprint
... Leaves No Living Footprint ... Lacks Tangible Context

... Manifesting Incarnations of Intellectually Metered and Stored Age-Old Sandal Clad Mockups Miss Linkup to Real-Time Sensual Presence

A religious believer's cognitively sketched blueprint of an age-old biblical spiritual world reference intended to showcase Jehovah's wisdom fails to draw any believer conscious association with the existence of its real-time present moment sensually metered intrinsically registered meaning when its manifestation appears in the transforming dimensional backdrop that services the human perception that monitors this reality's sensually defined present moment cause/effect exchange. It's presence only exists in print and in some biblical movies.

Intellectually metered knowledge has its own mental network of association different than that of the dialog of sensually metered knowledge.

Religious believers might try to live by a time-tempered skewed adaptation of the sandal-clad times referencing their biblical wisdom, They bring their written rule book's memorized dos and don'ts stored in their intellectually referenced mind to handle the real-life sensual tingle of the present moment circumstance defining what they are experiencing. They often fail to recognize or link the mental dialog of this intellectually founded capsule of borrowed wisdom to the intrinsically founded perception of sensually recognized and metered message of the present moment reality they experience life in.

This cognitively filed borrowed wisdom is often just not there when its present moment sensual incarnation presents itself.

Intelligent Design Presence
Lacks Tangible Real-Time Textured Substance

... Their Truths Are Debatable ... They Can Never Be Found To Be Self-Evident

After being born into the universal reality sphere of human existence and as their life conditioning progresses, an individual develops their own Rubik's cube spiritual window to reflect on their human experience in between their subconscious life principle awareness and their conscious mind level of life principle understanding. If they have had no guidance on securing heavenly emotional bliss while living, they might choose to form an intellectual understanding and possible acceptance of the attributes of one of the various theological claims to securing "heavenly" emotional bliss.

The verification of the theological "truth" a borrowed religious claim rests on lies merely in the conceptual intellectually tendered biblical knowledge they have decided to develop a blind faith in. Individuals of like opinion gravitate to form congregations representing their favored collective fraternal understanding that in some way addresses and relates to one of these theological conceptions.

... Religious Discussions Lack Dimensional Texture

When religious believers discuss how they understand what their heavenly promise is to be, they are limited to describing something they have a mere intellectual sketch of in their cognitively referenced imagination. It lacks having any identifiable tangible context to share. It is exceedingly rare that groups will open the book of Revelations and try to attach a shared understanding to Paul's described visions.

The framework of their understanding reflects the fixed-in-time scaffolding supporting an imagined world they have mentally sketched from a cognitively processed description of theological notions. Those are ideas that will lead to a conversation that just revolves in a perpetual circle.

Exchanges can end in the type of unsolvable disagreements over the means to an end that no one has a clear vision of. This can sometimes split a church into different congregations.

Group discussions generated from reference to borrowed knowledge are not ordered to the naturally patterned principles that set the relational justice detectable in transforming life. Having all the viewpoints coming from unique individual worlds of imagination blurs coming to a focused point of awareness about what comes to be understood to be self-evident.

The conclusions are engineered from intellectually perceived and categorized unverified borrowed knowledge sources … only bearing cognitively calculated subjective visions of an idea of what the godly source proclaims to be the truth.

When theologians have a point of God-derived wisdom to make, they quote scriptures. When they quote scriptures, they always must follow their quote with what they think it meant. They must verbalize their string of very subjective and abstract logistics. They share their interpretation of the topic to the extent their spiritual development can be biblically documented.

Still, the ring of their emptiness-of-understanding echoes from the logistics of their comments.

Something construed in imagination (a figment) cannot be discussed like something real and tangible. If its impermanent existence cannot be sensually shared and verified, there can be no common tangible grounds for discussion to achieve an effective fine-tuning of understanding.

It is more possible to share descriptions of commonly experienced real events involving something real and tangible than to be stuck in an ever-spinning eddy of confusion sharing unique imagination-sketched perceptions of the written knowledge describing what that tangible awareness was a few millennia ago. It is a matter of visiting the living source of that tangible manifest versus borrowing a compiled edited and multi-translated description of someone else's said ancient presence.

Intellectually imprisoned religious theological understandings lack the sensual texture apparent in the common threading of humanity's shared living bond. In this state, there are no tangible characteristics to gain purchase that different individuals can share in comparison and adjust their understanding of that forms their perception for better awareness of what cause/effect relational justice the impermanence that makes up this reality truly offers. These borrowed understandings live only when called to a theologian's waking consciousness from their mentally suspended cognitive closet of continuity that floats their imagination.

Fellowships of theological believers can at best only discuss their unique intellectually calculated understandings of what they see the borrowed wisdom message to be. This is what they have derived from the knowledge they'd gathered from reading or hearing about in the descriptions found in the religion's ancient scriptures they'd decided to have blind faith in.

They squander in trying to figure out what Jesus or one of his followers says to do or not to do and not so much about understanding the network of self-evident truths that support the Tree of Life wisdom that makes it so.

The end goal of attaining a suffering-free enlightened state of conscious awareness gets diluted to instead placing priority on minor random untethered considerations in reaching that end. Christian congregations will divide over what is believed to be their god's preferred means of baptizing a new believer or maybe whether having musical instruments is Jehovah-preferred.

Breaking up a congregation over whether baptism involves complete emersion or whether musical instruments should be used just testifies to a lack of understanding of what the end vision is … or what fuels the "great white light."

… Conversely

Knowledge gained from actual sensual experience leads to derived wisdom that is more open to objective analysis. Whereas borrowed knowledge offers up a sort of wisdom that is calculated from the individual's interpretation of that intellectually metered borrowed knowledge that in having no intrinsically related link, has a more subjective and harder to pin down understanding when being analyzed. Sensually touching impermanence itself allows experientially defining the tangible texture of life itself and not trying to pin down a common truth reflecting from unique projections of imagined interpretations of its borrowed descriptive texts.

With experiential verification, it is possible for a truth-seeker to sensually acknowledge and study this reality's state of impermanence in their intrapersonal chamber-of-flesh library (their material body) of self-knowledge where unbiased impermanence openly showcases/demonstrates the presence of its full-of-Holy Ghost-like life-giving essence.

All the stages in the process of self-training the ability to acquire the self-knowledge used to derive Tree of Life wisdom can be sensually experienced to then serve as the topic for discussion amongst others who are trying to consciously do the same. Here there is an identifiable tangible sensually registered presence to discuss.

The sensually registered conscious witnessing of life manifest itself allows discussing the tangible sensual signposts of the subject's emotionally reflected incarnations and not an attempted discussion bounded by the scope of the intellectually sketched intangible imagination-spun images unique to each contributor's world of imagination.

Experiential verification offers a tangible approach to understanding theologically posed spiritual ideals and goals.

Discussions might involve what is involved in bringing wisdom-enriched enlightened awareness of this reality from the subtle region of the truth-seeker's deeper consciousness to the truth-seeker waking consciousness, offering a better understanding awareness of a definable commonly experienced, sensually detectable state of this reality.

Truth-seekers can describe and share realistic impressions left by the expressions of the actual textures of impermanence they have sensually caught red-handed in action with fellow truth-seekers.

From their sensually metered and filed assimilation of self-knowledge collected at times of right mind-into-body concentration and the wisdom the inspired thinking that the body-speak brought to their waking consciousness, they can give verbal detail to the network of branches supporting the Tree Life Wisdom tree detailing how this impermanent reality fits together.

They can discuss tangible sensual report of what they've experienced trying to learn to overcome and evade the random mental white noise thought train interruptions while trying to self-train sustained mind into body harmony to enter in a state of heart-in-hand self-deliberation into the essence of the coming and going bits of energy in their flesh to self-train the inspired right thinking to spawn the insightful "aha" right understanding to enrich their awareness with the Tree of Life wisdom that enlightens them of their ignorance about the ways of impermanence that robs their waking consciousness of emotional joy and happiness and underscores their suffering.

Everyone has the Buddha within or is filled with Jesus. Everyone shares the same ability to recognize the self-evident truth of how something works or fits in just as both "enlightened" ones did while living.

... The Difference

The difference between those who suffer "emptiness-of-understanding" ignorance and those who are "enlightened" about that ignorance is that those enlightened can share the awareness that is risen from the depths of their deeper consciousness up to their waking awareness.

The insight-inspired awareness is tangible and is an awakening that is common to all.

This awareness is not somehow injected or borrowed empty of substance from an external source.

Gaining conscious awareness of physiological signs such as the sudden rise in heartbeat linked to the onset of anger or fear can be the self-trained self-knowledge that inspires the right-thinking leading to derive the "aha" Tree of Life wisdom providing a deeper understanding of this sudden emotional presence.

It is a waking link to better understanding the logistics of how emotions ride the rollercoaster of ongoing naked change. The better someone understands their emotional matrix, the closer they are to "enlightenment" ... the more they will enjoy their human experience.

This conscious awareness can lead to an individual's better understanding of the feeling's presence and what it is trying to say emotionally. They can then consider the factors and decide what action to take in response to the stimulating cause of this emotional onset instead of mindlessly meeting the effect of the cause with some conditioned kneejerk reaction.

A sudden "aha" understanding insight can rise from the depths while in meditative deliberation or while standing in line at the theater.

It is the same coming and going sensation in everyone. It is a waking consciousness plateau of the sensual report to seek commonly shared human life understanding.

It develops the foundation for having a steadfast heartfelt faith shared by everyone in what is demonstrated. It is a faith with boundaries that can be better described with a more defined understanding using the more developed languages of today that are more inclusive of the words to describe those states.

... Sharing Accounts of the Real-Life Experience

Discussions of those with at least an intellectual understanding of what lies at the end of the pathway to emotional enlightenment can relate to its tangible nature and pick apart the ways of impermanence as it manifests itself in the truth-seeker's mind-into-body right concentration. Their inspired thinking can be described and compared to what the others' interpretations of the same sensually noted coming and going sensation patterns seem to represent.

When a truth-seeker connects the focused presence of their mental awareness in harmony with the essence of their material body, they enter the same spiritual dimension of living transformation that is shared by each member of the brotherhood/sisterhood of humankind. It may be the waking recognition of what an individual consciously knows only within the conceptual confines of their capacity, yet they have the intuitively felt comfort of inclusion supported by the naturally instilled steadfast faith that the acquired experiential knowledge must be the self-evident reflection of the intellectually descriptive knowledge of the tangible reality that is shared by all.

It is of a realm of material substance that can be reflected on and objectively discussed and shared with others.

... Conversely

When submitting to ride an imaginary thought train, the hollow inner feeling of empty understanding attached to the religion's promised end spawns believers to find a way to numbingly suspend their prodding doubt from their gut-felt questioning and disbelief. They push it to the back of their mind and sadly over time their conscious touch with that gut-feeling can become locked up in the abyss of their emptiness.

Many spend their entire life without recognizing the distinction between the living reality that feeds the Garden of Eden Tree of Life and the make-believe reality of continuity that hangs suspended in the emptiness of the undefined imagination where an unlimited number of unverified assertions and assumptions linger. They unknowingly spend their present moment impatiently waiting for what their conditioning has twisted their perception into seeding their expectations of the course of unavoidable change to produce.

Many live their life moments entertaining a letdown inner agenda while somehow expressing some form of dissatisfaction in not being able to eradicate their fear of their uncertainty of the unknown. They find themselves slaves to insipiently suffering the negative effects in the wake of behaviors that knowingly or unknowingly rob them of their sought-after emotional balance and happiness.

A poorly conditioned notion of reality confuses what is wholesome with what is not. Their self-fashioned ego manages a self-conditioned abyss of inner emptiness. The better understood the impermanent cause/effect ways of this universe, the less is the need for theological notions to corral individuals' fears of the unknown.

... It Echoes Through the Family Structure

Many families cannot enjoy the closeness of being able to discuss what is truly felt to be the essence of life situations that occur throughout the day. Conjuring up the words to represent what is felt to best represent the perceived feelings can run into a wall created by their god's wisdom.

Many things are just assumed to be "bad" and "sinful" without a shared understanding of what or why. There is no attempt to break down the unanswered feelings.

The full circle of meaning that takes a situation from its occurrence through what that means to the emotional balance of the involved parties gets cut short by book/chapter/verse logic. This can cast a life-long shadow over family relations.

... Stretch for Tangible Material Tie-ins

Modern-day material evidence that verifies the living presence of Christianity's theological world seems to be limited to rumors of discovered fragments of the robe Jesus wore after being crucified, petrified parts to Noah's boat, or maybe a bleeding eye in the statue of Mary.

There exist in-depth matrixes of deductive reasoning to prove the Bible's truth. Their train of logistics involves how the creation of this reality had to be a product of intelligent design.

Yet, the framework of their proof matrix sidesteps how the ancient (6K years old?) design plays an active role in the life-related principles that determine present moment emotional bliss or suffering.

Then, there are those that just quote the scriptures to prove its truth.

… Those Treed by Fear Find a Secured Roost

Many religious believers find comfort in quietly living/hiding in a cognitively sketched place where nobody can disprove its existence…a place with no tangible coordinates…no living presence noted in time where nothing exists to disprove their agenda … where there is nothing tangible to verify its living existence.

The insecure often use their chosen religion's net of largely unquestioned socially accepted mysticism to front their compromising self-doubt. When treed by their conditioned feeling of being wrong, they may find it calming to talk about something else that has no tangible basis, and nobody can be proved wrong.

Religion, sports, and politics are just a few topics where you can voice an opinion where reasoning is mostly subjective.

… Religious Theology often Supports Superficial Shallow Friendship

There are many congregational groups of friends that when gathered will tip-toe on their god's written rules to avoid conflict of deeper-seated values. Many will hide things they are doing from these friends, wanting to avoid public knowledge of their involvement in any sort of "grey" area.

Heart-to-heart friendship can be absent or very shallow in these groups. But these arrangements do help provide some sort of social cohesion to help society minimize active conflict.

It could be said that a superficial friendship is better than having no friendship at all.

Religious disciplines do just that for different societies … provide discipline … at least until they decide their neighbors are doing something they do not like and decide to inflict their interpretation of this religious discipline on their neighbors … "with God on their side."

Alert: Do Not Mistake God's Promise for Tree of Life Wisdom

Christian theologians are led to believe what is purported by Jehovah in the scriptures to be unquestionable "written in stone" wisdom. While, in the dimensional constructs of this reality, this can be no more than an unverifiable promise requiring an inexhaustible reserve of stark blind trust.

The New Oxford American Dictionary says that wisdom is the quality of having knowledge, experience, and good judgment. Good knowledge is used along with good judgment to derive wisdom. It is necessary to know what good knowledge is.

For the truth-seeker, their grasp on God's "wisdom" comes from the written scriptures and is derived from intellectually metered knowledge that is borrowed and its verification is blindly trusted.

It comes attached to no experiential involvement in this reality. Its presence contributes nothing to the present moment manifestation of life itself even though it makes claim to having the "life-giving" Holy Spirit as being part of the Holy Trinity.

A believer must put the scripted knowledge together as they see it should be to derive their subjective cocktail of God's "wisdom". Listen to Sunday AM gospel preachers as they shout their interpretations. It is merely pieced-together wisdom derived from knowledge borrowed from the knowledge found in their translation of their God's ancient scriptures.

An individual needs to seek the "right" knowledge that allows their insightful thinking from their self-trained calmed mind to derive or become enlightened with the wisdom enriched with the understanding that connects a cause to its effect in a reality with an impermanent backdrop ... not in one that involves any measure of continuity.

Understanding what the natural principles are that determine the outcome of relationships that happen within this force-driven reality is the "right wisdom" ... on the most basic of levels. The principled truths from this filter up and serve as the common threads of strength that knit together the dimensions of the impermanent backdrop that supports the present moment of the humankind experience.

Christianity entices its Christian believers to blindly trust that Jesus died for mankind's sins (whatever that means in tangible terms). This allows those who believe in God's word and intellectually "give their life to the Christ" to earn an afterlife free from suffering. They can enjoy eternal joy and happiness and evade the pits of unimaginable hellfire and brimstone.

The directives given throughout the ancient scriptures that proved acceptable by Constantine's Roman priests in 325 A.D. are thought by many to be God's wisdom from up above.

This is not wisdom. It is an intellectually metered untethered promise secured only by intellectually secured blind trust.

There is no living trace of its involvement in generating the living design of the dimensional relational laws that with due diligent investigation prove to be self-evident in the flow of time to establish its realism. There is no verifiable record or mention of the forces of God's promise ever being a part of the transforming life force creating what makes up the present moment.

The historically referenced paradise to compare it (heavenly paradise) to happened back in the Genesis Garden of Eden and that did not turn out very well for mankind. Even though the Eden plan surely had a holy blessing, it did not work out very well for Jehovah either.

This unverified supposition is no more than a very unquantifiable projection into the never-to-come future of a non-existent reality. Whereas actual wisdom is drawn from the cause/effect analysis of the relational interaction between established elements of this reality, the theological notion has no leg of reality to stand on.

Self-knowledge-derived Tree of Life wisdom has no causal or correlational relationship with what Christian theology suggests being their god's promise.

Self-knowledge-derived Tree of Life wisdom provides a cause/effect relational infrastructure giving order to the impermanence that defines this reality's promise to provide ongoing change. Self-evident Tree of Life wisdom is not derived using the abstract logistics posed by the conceptual knowledge of any theological supposition.

What theological reasoning describes in no way adds to or plays a role in the generation of the ongoing change that feeds the Tree of Life that the living source of this reality promises to provide. The self-evident truth of impermanence that the Tree of Life wisdom provides a network of understanding for is demonstrated in the flow of this reality's present moment state of transformation.

It is by understanding or being enlightened about the ways of this impermanence that will leave an individual free from all the suffering brought about by their ignorance thereof. There is no need to wait until after death to let some other entity magically reinstate emotional joy and happiness and remove the same suffering as promised by Christianity's god.

The causal factors of any religion's paradox are vaguely defined and the yet-to-be produced effect has no comparable track record. The religion's suggested templated style of the soul-saving chain of circumstances lacks credibility. It has no verifiable experiential history that demonstrates any quantifiable causal relationship between the claim-maker's promise and its ability to eliminate human suffering.

A religious believer can really have nothing other than blind faith in the proposed causal factors (mankind's human experience grounded by the original in-born sin) producing the suggested effect of earning an alleged judgment day heaven free of suffering ... whatever the untested reality with unnatural dimensional continuity might feel like or where it might be.

Wisdom pertains to a conscious understanding of the relationships between the forces in the interaction between causal factors and their resulting effects. Wisdom makes conscious sense of exposing the latticework of cause/effect constituents. Wisdom understands and relates meaning as to how things affect each other … how factors interrelate.

The Christian mantra that "Jesus died for mankind's sins" to allow those that believe in God's word to attain an afterlife free from suffering does not have any historical reference. It has no record of ever being a part of the life force creating the present moment that is experientially verifiable in a tangible way that any human can realize. It calls for having blind trust in the speculative borrowed wisdom of an unverifiable claim maker.

Jehovah's not offering wisdom here. It is no more than a promise. The Bible storyline is a declaration or assurance of what future event would happen if an individual acts as directed.

This is how believer obedience is promised to be rewarded.

B I B L E
EMERGENCY NUMBERS

When in sorrow	John 14
When men fail you	Psalm 27
When you have sinner	Psalm 51
When you have worry	Matthew 6:19-34
When you are in danger	Psalm 91
When God seems far away	Psalm 139
When your faith needs stirring	Hebrews 11
When you are lonely and fearful	Psalm 23
When you grow bitter and critical	1 Cor. 13
When you feel down and out	Romans 8:31-39
When you want peace and rest	Matthew 11:25-30
When the world seems bigger than God	Psalm 90
When you want Christian assurance	Romans 8:1-30
When you leave home for labor or travel	Psalm 121
When your prayers grow narrow or selfish	Psalm 67
When you want courage for a task	Joshua 1
When you think of investments/returns	Mark 10
How to get along with fellow men	Roman 12
For great invention/opportunity	Isaiah 55
For Paul's secret to happiness	Col. 3:12-17
If you want to be fruitful	John 15
If your pocketbook is empty	Psalm 37
If you are losing confidence in people	1 Cor. 13
If people seem unkind	John 15
If discouraged about your work	Psalm 126
If you find the world growing small, and you great	Psalm 19

AVAILABLE 24/7 | PHONE SERVICE NOT REQUIRED
DIRECT PETITIONS HEAVENWARD

Bible Wisdom is Unexplained
... Leaves Believers Grabbing for Straws

...When Told Only to be Morally/Ethically "Good" ... Antiquated Ten Commandment Style

Bible wisdom leaves believers lost in ignorance ... empty-of-understanding. There may be random scriptures that give loose direction without any cause/effect understanding ... just like the type of understanding Adam and Eve were left with after accepting the promise of wisdom that understood everything from good to evil.

With no wisdom understanding applicable or related to today's sensual reality for finding their true source of peace within, beyond behaving with Ten Commandment moral/ethical values, they have no religion-inspired clue as to how to understand, own, and eliminate their ignorance about the principles that govern their world that robs them of their emotional bliss and causes their suffering.

... Blind Eye to Temptation's Sensual Incarnation

Keeping an eye open for temptation wearing borrowed knowledge-spawned intellectually stitched biblical reference clothing distances a believer from recognizing the real-time living incarnation of the essence of the evil temptations biblically warned about. The mental snapshot of the antiquated ancient-time nature of reality that is depicted in intellectually metered biblical descriptions of how sensually registered temptations arise is much different than what generates its real-time living heartbeat.

The Bible warns of certain foods that should not be eaten, yet even when delivered verified scientific warning, religious believers will eat white flour and sugar without making any connection to it being related to any sort of biblical sort of consumption sin.

Only having a believer's making of a cognitive record of the face of temptation referenced to sandal/toga times to watch for its lurking today's presence is a profound way to let real-time temptation have its way with a believer's health and happiness. People fail to equate the essence of what an ancient "temptation" is when its wicked lure display manifests in real-time everyday life situations.

The truth described by the borrowed biblical wisdom was coded intellectually when borrowed and it hangs suspended in the believer's imagined reality containing their cognitive sketch of how they intellectually perceive the knowledge they have borrowed. The sensually metered "what's" and "why's" of understanding the awareness of "sinful wrongness" ongoingly occur and draw undetected red flags in the theologian's sensual reality of the present moment.

The real-life sensual significance of the black and white depiction of religious maxims of all kinds evades cognitive hookup when their real-time living color sensual incarnations show their present moment face.

... Emergency Numbers

When intellectually metered/stored wisdom does not match up with the intrinsically stored wisdom that has not yet surfaced from a believer's deeper consciousness to their conscious awareness, there are emergency Bible verse references. If their publication of Rome's Bible has an index, many will turn there.

The Bible fails to tell its followers all the steps needed to uncover the secret to realizing that emotional state of bliss that it promises in its afterlife version of Eden. It requires its believers to accept its god-originated wisdom, unearned, just like the unearned wisdom Eve accepted from the Eden snake's guarantee and then gave to Adam.

While designing what Rome's 325 A.D. 1st edition of the Bible had to say about where to look for answers, Constantine's priests edited out the gospels where Jesus told his listeners to look inside their bodies for guidance to understanding the truth about this reality by understanding it through sensually witnessing its truth in their living ever-changing material bodies. Rome's edited Bible stopped short by only telling them how to calm their minds by being morally and ethically good people.

The scriptures did not tell its followers how to further self-train the mind control to gather the life knowledge to inspire deriving the insightful thinking to self-train the Tree of Life wisdom that Jehovah warned Adam was necessary to live in the emotional bliss of "Eden.".

The Bible gives an outline of some moral/ethical standards without saying that the resulting calm is needed to then self-train the mind control ability to sustain the focused attention to enable gathering the right strain of needed knowledge to synthesize the wisdom of understanding awareness that will vacate any suffering and allow emotional bliss to resurface.

Rome wanted Romans to look to Rome for direction. Constantine had his priests edit out the gospels where Jesus spoke with audiences of higher spiritual maturity and/or were authored by individuals with a more mature spiritual understanding to allow them to better interpret and describe the deeper content of the spiritual message Jesus was teaching.

Like Rome, the USA wants its citizens to look to the government as being their source of liberty and freedom. Using theology to provide a common membership with a book of behavioral rules helps them meet this end.

Like in Eden, Jehovah failed to share with Adam and Eve how to find life direction and realize independent liberty from within, instead of looking to him for direction.

Without satisfying religious believers' innate human longing to understand how their human condition fits into its human experience, they will covertly keep an eye peeled for that answer. Some will switch religious templates as they grow older, still in search of the answer … or at least the right question.

Adages "God Works in Mysterious Ways" or "It's God's Will" …Cure-All Kickstands

… To Botox-Posture an Ego-Managed Empty Understanding … Fills in or Bridges Over Borrowed Wisdom Understanding Void

Exploiting the fact that the logistics of borrowed wisdom are configured in the imagination … anything is possible … just wait and see what weird sensical cause/effect links can be rationalized together.

To satisfy the unresolvable ignorance involving some thing or some phenomena that has escaped human understanding at that time in history, many will credit their reigning god with having ultra-human capabilities too great to be understood and proclaim how their "lord God works in mysterious ways." This is the same philosophy our ancient ancestors grabbed for when explaining how that day's answer-lacking characteristics of the natural laws of this reality worked that science had yet to figure out … like Zeus and lightening.

When staring the unknown directly in the eye, many chose to strike up a blind ever-trusting faith and just write off understanding what is happening and say how the lord God works in mysterious ways and how we humans are not supposed to know this information. Sometime thereafter, science will explain the cause/effect path involved in those questioned phenomena and the religion will either fade away or like the few remaining, adapt.

Many religious fundamentalists, often with a frustrated air, are quick to play the "God's will" card and use their totally unverifiable cognitive notion of what God is to substantiate their subjective opinion on issues they can't quite put to word a waking understanding of that makes good cause/effect sense. When playing the "God says so" card, listeners cannot really object unless they want to be branded as an atheist-sort of politically incorrect person and feels up to receiving a heated finger shaking.

Theology's USA Christian believers have a constitutionally protected blind faith to stand guard over. This can involve explanations about the minute details of their visionary interpretation of the behavioral dos and don'ts (the relational justice) outlined in the scriptures of the translation of the Roman Bible that they choose to adhere to.

It is interesting how many older-fabric traditional Christians still tend to enforce much of the Bible to what they understand the letter to be. Their imagination has conditioned a self-fashioned narrow-minded waking awareness that finds refuge in the essence of what is no more than a unique cognitively sketched world construed to their subjective interpretation of what is written in their chosen translation of the multi-multi translated Bible.

... May "God Bless You"

It is common for a Christian to wish to another individual for the god they worship to bless the other person, whether the other person worships the same god or not. The other person might understand this as being rude, especially when the Christian knows the other person does not believe in their notion of finding freedom from suffering.

This thoughtless behavior can be taken as being insulting. What does it mean for their god to bless them anyway?

It is a time when the insulted person might have to just "turn the other cheek."

Cannot Use Intellectually Primed Brush to Paint Intrinsic Picture on Sensual Canvas

... Can't Just Page-Over Ancient Scriptures to Register an Intrinsic Understanding

Modern-day mankind cannot squeegee out any intrinsic meaning or just page-over that long-ago present moment with reference to only an intellectual imprint of the long-ago worldly presence of the ancient sandal-clad times of their favored religious reference.

There is no compromise to the self-evident truth that the human condition relates to the world sensually. When using the knowledge that is been metered intellectually, in hopes of building an understanding awareness of how to live in sensually founded emotional bliss, an individual will lack having the sensual dust of intrinsic understanding that comes from experience.

Hearing any of the theological explanations of how to relate to reality to secure emotional bliss and be free of suffering, will leave any truth-seeker lost spinning in undefinable confusion.

... Ask Any Doctor

To understand what it feels like to receive a pinprick, it is necessary to be pricked by a pin. Borrowing the wisdom from a book or a parent's explanation to their child before getting their 1st shot will not paint the intrinsic picture to enlighten the child about what they're about to experience sensually.

The parents' intellectual coaching will influence the child's perception of the feeling which will help shape the child's resulting emotion.

Theology's Borrowed Wisdom Lacks Intrinsic Support

This disconnectedness deepens anytime humans learn some intellectually metered and stored explanation of reality and borrow the wisdom claiming to represent life's truth to then use the theology's rule book to apply its justice in a real-life circumstance.

They will try to use book-chapter-verse wisdom to run their life while betting their soul on its validity.

They form an intellectually metered and retained mental picture of the wisdom's theological notion that is built on and depends totally on how their imagination has pieced together their uniquely perceived understanding of what has been intellectually communicated and remembered.

… Motion Pictures Give a 2-Dimensional Face to a 1-Dimensional Biblical Storyline to Adorn an Imagined 3-D Reality

If not for some painter's imagination-posed impression of what Jesus looked like seen in the biblical pictures Bible-wrapped in the desktop of most USA motels and for motion pictures, there would be nothing for an individual to reference for helping add more dimensional definition to make the Holy Trinity seem more a part of the living world.

Watching movie renditions of the scripture-described world of the Bible gives the religious believer something more tangible to further enhance its mental sketch and to better anchor their surrender to better understanding the actual reality of its ancient existence.

For many, when the Bible refers to Moses, the image of Charlton Heston in "Moses" or "The Ten Commandments" comes to mind, subconsciously supporting the notion's real-life existence and validity.

When he parted the Red Sea, it sure did look real.

Mentally picturing Charlton Heston in *The Ten Commandments* standing on the side of the mountain, dodging Jehovah's fireball delivery of the Ten Commandments to be fire-etched in pads of stone is as close as many Christian believers come to relating the intellectually metered meanings of the "sins" noted in the Ten Commandments to the living presence of the moral/ethical meaning they portray.

In the movie *Moses* when the Holy Ghost appeared to kill Egypt's first born, the impression of it slowly sweeping through homes in a foggy presence is hard to forget. That also suggests that the Holy Ghost is not a part of the living present moment ... everywhere. It seems that God must call it out ... that it's a separate thing ... not a part of the living present moment.

With the ancient scriptures, there is no intrinsic tie-in or familiarity between what is heard and what the believer's human condition's been through in its living human experience. It is a strain of wisdom of abstract logistics tied to an ancient reality that no reader of the Bible has ever had an experiential real-life taste of.

For the religious believer, the Bible sponsors life-guiding wisdom they carry around, reference and quote, borrowed from a book that's first edition dates to the times of Rome, and its authority is supported only by their blind faith in its relevance. It is not a wisdom that is intrinsically originated and felt from within that is supported by a steadfast faith in what proves to be a self-evident truth based on what they have sensually witnessed from their life experience like as from a pin-prick sensation of pain.

Theology-Founded Wisdom Fails to Connect the Dots

... The Nature of the Real Reason Why We Don't Play With Fire?

Borrowed wisdom from a parent can tell a child what hot feels like and how to act in its presence to avoid the burning feeling that comes with hot. Chances are that child will at some time hold their finger next to a flame to gather sensual verification of that borrowed prediction or promise made by another entity.

After the sensual knowledge has been gathered through experiencing what the burn of fire's sensual touch feels like when next holding a lit match under their finger the derived Life wisdom will intrinsically tell them to pull their finger back.

The report from this intrinsic record will out-position the intellectually stored warning from their parents ... in a pre-lingual fashion.

Theology's borrowed wisdom describes only in a cerebral context the emotional bliss of eternal afterlife paradise while Tree of Life wisdom establishes or touches on an intrinsically registered understanding of emotional bliss on a pre-lingual scale that can essentially be realized while still living.

It is of split-second importance whether wisdom-deriving-knowledge is cerebrally tailored or sensually realized.

Most leave this life with having realized an incomplete understanding awareness (enlightenment) of this reality's impermanent personality.

The nature of the real reason why we do not play with fire is intrinsic and the language it speaks is sensual.

Same Present Moment … Different Realities

… Same Present Moment at Different Points on History's Timeline

The passing present moment rides on the skirt of time. People are not aware of it because it is always there. It is the only state of waking presence they have ever known.

Ease back and picture the cognitive-spun rendition of the sandal-clad biblical characters read about as if they were dressed in blue jeans and tennis shoes, nonchalantly checking their smartphones.

Sprinkle some present moment dust on the cognitively fixed still-framed stories of biblical times.

Picture them in today's atmosphere.

Is it possible to force-feed the mental picture of men and women set in the days of togas and sandals with that of their living descendants wearing business suits and dress shoes, conversing in a language of tweeted hashtag using a language much more complex with many more word meanings that had yet to evolve from the ancient strains of communication?

This memory of that ancient present moment stands halted on the mental recognition of time flow … the 4th dimension supporting this reality's backdrop.

The toga/sandal attire is all stitched together in an individual's imagination. It is an awareness that is not linked to the cause/effect consequences of the real-time texture of the ever-passing present moment sensual reality.

It is unlikely that an individual will form any association between their cognitively sketched intellectually metered mental image of a godly man in a robe sitting full lotus under a bright white light with the actual sensual feeling of our life source literally emanating in coming-and-going transforming fashion as life manifests inside their flesh that is available 24/7/365 for their sensual observation.

They will see the man as godly and separate from them instead of the ongoing change that he is made up of … like they themselves are.

It wags the truth in their face ... literally ... 24/7/365.

Most religious believers do not recognize and equate their theological projections with its sensual presence. This separates the sensually metered present moment from the intellectually housed time of reference.

... Mankind's Idea of Society was Less Developed

Back in the sandal-clad days of the holy scriptures, slavery existed nearly everywhere. Human rights have made great advance since those days. It's possible that should Jehovah carve any more commandments in stone, he'd surely include the Bill of Rights.

Social attitude was very different.

... Different Spots on 4th Dimension Timeline

The Holy Ghost breathes into reality the same present moment breath of life today as was during the present moment times described in the Bible. The process of transformation that defines the present moment of 2,000+ years ago is the same one that defines the present moment of today.

The coming and going tingle of life as it manifests itself is the same. It has the same feeling inside an individual today as it did for Siddhartha and Jesus when they tapped into the very same theater of wisdom during their times of gaining enlightenment about nature's principles to undo their ignorance causing all their suffering.

Believers in religious theology settle for the intellectually generated soundness of abstract logistics to secure their intellectual grasp on what defines reality instead of visiting life itself as it manifests to better understand the ways of this impermanent reality that determine the outcome of everything they do, affecting their state of emotional balance ... their degree of human suffering.

Most religious believers fail to make any connection or recognize any association between any religious maxims they have formed and the living embodiment of these maxims in their present moment sensual experience.

They are blind to recognizing the universal life wisdom relevance and significance of the real-time present moment occurrence of the life-giving intended message of their cognitively sketched religious flagship when faced with its living incarnation manifested in its real-time sensual disguise.

... Reality's Living Heartbeat or Theology's Hologram Flatline?

Mother Nature actively signs her self-evident truth in the ongoing beat of palpable ever-changing sensual media. Theological truth hangs still in conceptual intellect.

Theology's answer to human suffering stands two worlds apart from reality's self-evident explanation. Theology cannot generate a sensually familiar conscious recognition and understanding from a mere intellectually metered and sketched understanding.

The cognitively stored intellectually formed meaning of some real-time emotion or feeling that is borrowed from an outside source will not be linked with its real-time sensual incarnation. How can an individual sensually define and know what 'hot' really means until they hold their hand near a flame?

They cannot sync an understanding of the world of impermanence that is based on wisdom-deriving knowledge reflecting sensual familiarity in a conscious world with a conscious awareness suspended in cerebral second-guessing.

Wisdom-Deriving Knowledge is Metered and Stored Differently

... Tree of Life Wisdom Comes Experientially ... Sensually Metered Intrinsically Registered

> *"All of your emotions are essential to your well-being.*
> *Learn their language, and you can change your life."*
> -Karla McLaren 4-22-21 Facebook post

One wisdom strain grows its logistics from knowledge sensually collected. This knowledge applies to understanding the workings of impermanence itself and is what is needed to derive Tree of Life wisdom.

This knowledge of life-manifest itself is sensually metered and intrinsically stored and is consciously drawn on. A heartfelt steadfast faith will develop in step with the derived wisdom.

... Tree of Knowledge of Good and Evil Wisdom Comes Borrowed Unearned and Unexplained ... Intellectually Metered and Stored

Wisdom borrowed from the Tree of Knowledge is not derived from the same school of knowledge that waters the Tree of Life.

Tree of Knowledge wisdom is believed and internalized blindly on an intellectual plain. It is a promise of wisdom that comes intellectually metered/ingested and retained.

This wisdom tree is built on intellectually metered and stored knowledge that comes unverified and borrowed from elsewhere. The believer's belief system is compromised by a crippled freewill. The wisdom comes unearned, and its logistics come hollow and empty-of-understanding.

It lacks the believer having done any work to develop an intrinsically understood relationship with the natural force-generated principles that support the suggested facets of the claim the wisdom decodes. The believer must have a faith that is blind to the claim's verification process ... if there is one.

Borrowed wisdom sidesteps having deriving knowledge that has been sensually metered/ingested with the intrinsic memory tie-in of Tree of Life wisdom.

Tree of Knowledge wisdom speaks to the brain in an intellectually primed verbal dialect. How to handle the real-time present moment manifestation of an intellectually metered/stored version of religious temptation fails to find sync with any sensually identified intrinsic history the individual might have. I.E. The temptation of some sweet dessert or sugar-ridden soft drink product fails to register as the temptation the Bible warns about eating the wrong foods.

The significance of what the Bible warns about lacks having any sensually stored intrinsic feedback context ... sugar crash ... insulin imbalance ... weight gain.

Individuals suffer from the friction of when a gut-felt undeniable unquestionable self-evident truth they witness in real life rubs up against their borrowed perception of truth they have been told from elsewhere. I.E. It is self-evident that one race or gender is equal to any other. Every person bleeds the same color blood, yet one race or gender is said by certain schools of borrowed wisdom to be "god-chosen" or genetically superior to the other. Which philosophy to act on when empty of ability to recognize and honor intrinsic self-evident understanding?

An individual's degree of understanding awareness of the natural force-driven principles of impermanence that determines life outcomes shadows the conditioning of their belief system that shapes and gives direction to their worldview is gagged by their blind faith.

It is a shell of wisdom that's group acceptance has finalized when the new believer "gives their life (freewill)" to the promisor. The god's wisdom comes in written form to be studied endlessly and still to only lodge an intellectual connection ... empty of having an understanding awareness.

Wisdom Media Sources are Synthesized Differently

... Intellectually Pieced Together with No Intrinsic Link ... Reality's Living Heartbeat or Theology's Imagined Heartbeat?

The self-assimilated wisdom derived from sensually originated self-knowledge is metered only in real-time. It uses the elusive present moment for its gathering time, and it uses the primal sensual expression as its media. It's language is strictly sensual … unwritable.

Conversely, the pathway to follow for borrowed knowledge subscribers is not self-trained. It is choice-subscribed and comes script-directed.

… Self-Originated Sensual "Body-Speak" Media or Borrowed Stillborn?

Yes, theology's borrowed wisdom and reality's universal strain of experiential wisdom are coded differently. An individual might have an intellectual, not intrinsic, understanding of the process of becoming enlightened. If so, it is cognitively registered in intellectual-speak media terms.

They need to experientially teach their conscious mind the language of sensual body-speak that perceives via sensual media suited to decode the sensually textured braille of this living reality to experientially gather the sensual life knowledge to then self-train the Tree of Life wisdom that carries the key to realize the state of emotional bliss that religion promises.

Examining this reality's defining footprint by self-training the ability to tap into the same sensual media frequency that feeling-spun emotions are tuned into is necessary for its better understanding.

Fight-or-flight precedence originating from an awareness focused on an intellectually metered strain of theology-coded wisdom derived from the subjectively calculated abstract logistics of borrowed knowledge (ancient scriptures) is tendered on a different plateau of conscious immediacy than from a conscious experientially conditioned awareness focused on the sensually metered strain of intrinsically coded wisdom that's derived and assimilated from the self-trained logistics of experientially gathered self-knowledge … the feel of "hot" verses its description.

… The Wisdom Logistics Supporting Religious Truth are Conceptual and Intellectually Calculated

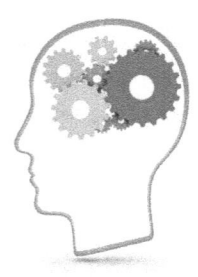

The wisdom logistics supporting religious truth are conceptual and calculated while the wisdom logistics supporting life truth is sensually textured and, in the end, its self-evidence is unlocked to be realized by the waking consciousness awareness.

Theology's wisdom-deriving knowledge is gathered only on an intellectual level. It is not wisdom derived and generated from the intuitive part of the brain.

The Garden of Eden Tree of Life wisdom-deriving knowledge that Christian theology's god Jehovah mandated that Adam use at the very outset of the Genesis creation is only accessed through sensual media.

The perceptual "ouch" from the triggering cause of emotion-generating feelings is first metered via sensual media and then sensually transposed through conditioned perceptual interpretations into the emotions that give report of an individual's take on their human experience.

Distinct parts of the brain here ... different periods of evolutionary refinement.

Intellectually Spun World of Sandal-Clad Borrowed Wisdom Lacks Knee-Jerk Access in Real-Life Emergency

... The Fight or Flight Test ... They Ring Different Bells of Awareness

The Sunday morning book-chapter-verse intellectually metered and stored wisdom is not tied "on-call" into the intrinsic network of human problem-solving physiology.

A believer will dance to the tune of the intellectually drafted music of what their theological source says is so. But, when they feel uneasy or are suddenly threatened like in a flight-or-fight situation, they'll react in a manner that references their experientially assimilated innate call of the wild sensitivity that's naturally programmed from the depths of their amygdala, the older central part of their brain, to reference their gut reaction. This is the source of incentive their deeper consciousness places its steadfast faith in.

It can be a challenge to figure out how to relate to, interpret and associate the meaning of the written strain of borrowed wisdom with the strain of universal life wisdom present in a living reality that is needed to best run their life to maintain emotional balance. A religious believer must be able to sync the intellectually borrowed logistics of abstract sandal-clad wisdom to the real-life wisdom needed to find balance in life's transforming sea of emotional turmoil.

... Fight-or-Flight Instinct Orients First to Experiential Conditioning

The knee-jerk impetus to self-protect is referenced from sensual memory and not from intellectually construed cognitive recall. After the split-second response-triggering mental red flag appears, the different cerebral interfaces have different perceptual textures.  Human deeper consciousness-spawned self-preserving fight-or-flight call-to-action is prioritized and processed differently than that from cognitively spawned intellectually construed recall.

They ring awareness bells in different parts of the brain ... worlds of awareness apart with present moment realities disconnected.

The intellectual and sensual pathways to conscious awareness are quite different.

The theologian mindset most often fails to consciously associate cognitive understandings of intellectually sketched religious maxims with their sensually recognized real-life manifestation.

Borrowed wisdom leaves an individual empty of an understanding of the principles their borrowed wisdom is promised to decode … like the shame-filled emptiness that Adam and Eve felt after their disobedience when confronted by Jehovah.

The hollow nature of their snake-endorsed received wisdom had them reaching for fig leaves to hide their shame.

A religious believer in demonstrating great obedience to the purpose of the borrowed theological wisdom must put to cognitive recall a great amount of book/chapter/verse from the translation of the Holy Scriptures their group of believers thinks describes the cause/effect relational justice that will make their promised afterlife heavenly presence real. When it comes time for them to wonder where in the scriptures they might find the wisdom describing how to get along with people who didn't swallow the same pill of belief in an afterlife paradise, they'll dip into their void of emptiness and decide which fig leaf-lined mask to wear.

After they enter a few keywords into the index at the end of their Bible and find a few scriptures that might apply to their question, they then must intellectually interpret the borrowed wisdom they are reading.

Their mental query must reference the cumulative effect of their past experiences and their conditioned perceptions of those experiences along with their mental renditions of what borrowed knowledge they've ingested that they'd allowed to help shape their worldview to then derive their interpretation of what they read in their borrowed source of wisdom.

Intellectually Metered Knowledge Does Not Sync with Intrinsically Fathomed Living World Circumstance

… Intellectual Memory Stumbles Searching For Intrinsic History

Everyone must know what it is like to read or to be told about how to do something and then draw a blank when trying to first accomplish it. Hands-on experience is needed most of the time to be able to physically apply the intellectually metered logistics.

Intellectually perceived knowledge does not get mentally recorded in a way that coordinates its recall in a way to have any intrinsically driven application. It's a complete muscle memory void.

If intellectually metered and stored knowledge was not experienced in a way that involved coordinating any sensually metered muscular learning, there will be a lack of mind/body coordinated wisdom to repeat the task from memory.

On 12-9-18, the CBS TV program 60 Minutes investigated the effects of digital media on the minds of teenagers.

"Dr. Dimitri Christakis at Seattle Children's Hospital was the lead author of the American Academy of Pediatrics' most recent guidelines for screen time. They now recommend parents, "avoid digital media use, except video-chatting, in children younger than 18 to 24 months."

Dr. Dimitri Christakis: So, what we do know about babies playing with iPads is that they don't transfer what they learn from the iPad to the real world, which is to say that if you give a child an app where they play with virtual Legos, virtual blocks, and stack them, and then put real blocks in front of them, they start all over.

Anderson Cooper: "If they try to do it in real life, it is as if they have never done it before."

Dr. Dimitri Christakis: "Exactly. It is not a transferable skill. They don't transfer the knowledge from two dimensions to three."

The 1 or 2-dimensional impressions left from religious knowledge-derived wisdom do not transfer into circumstance application in the present moment realm of this living reality's sensually registered multi-dimensional makeup.

The theological believer does not recognize or see the commonality between the cognitively sketched intellectual understanding they have fashioned and its real-time sensual meaning when encountered in real life. They have not self-trained their ability to synthesize one into the other.

Intellectually Defined Perception
Versus Intrinsically Defined Sensual Perception

... Abstract Cognitive Logistics Do Not Fortify Sensual Familiarity

Religion's intellectually metered and registered knowledge just does not allow deriving the depth of wisdom-enriched understanding as the intrinsically registered knowledge from sensual history.

Using the emotional feeling of guilt as an example, the mental state and physical symptoms common to an individual who is ruminating in feelings of guilt may persist even if they have a cognitive understanding of what guilt is. They might not be able to tie the intellectual definition with its sensually expressed presence.

Guilt can be intellectually understood, yet the body physiology symptoms and feelings that accompany its intrinsic incarnation still go untapped ... or at least unrecognized.

An individual can intellectually meter the definition of what guilt is and feel they understand that definition and will be careful not to let what they intellectually gathered influence their mental balance. Yet the feeling of guilt may continue to shadow their present moment.

They might be experiencing guilt at that time and go on spending their present moment in unrest because they fail to link their intellectual understanding or familiarity with guilt's sensual symptoms as its presence manifests in their real-life present moment.

This internal battle is stemming from their lack of ability to register intrinsic meaning to the intellectual understanding they have gathered and pieced together.

Their intellectual understanding lacks the ability to help them solve their intrinsic ignorance of guilt. Their intellectual understanding gets them no closer to emotional bliss.

They might know what it is but not understand it.

Need to Sync Intellectual Concept into Living Understanding

... Emotional Report Reflects the Human Perception of the Human Experience

Emotions are the gradient used in analyzing an individual's bliss-to-suffering ratio. Most people cannot evaluate how their emotions result from their conditioned perception of life's situational outcomes determined by Mother Nature's unchangeable natural force-driven relational principles.

Many will turn somewhere in a blind trust to borrow the wisdom of another source's promising answer in their search for emotional bliss or escape from suffering.

The nature of their uncertainty helps determine where they might go to find knowledge to derive the type of wisdom to secure solace or protection from their fear of what might lurk in the unknown nature of this reality. This ignorance or limited understanding of the ways of the nature of this impermanent reality is fundamental to causing all of human suffering.

... Analog Versus Digitally Formatted Worldview

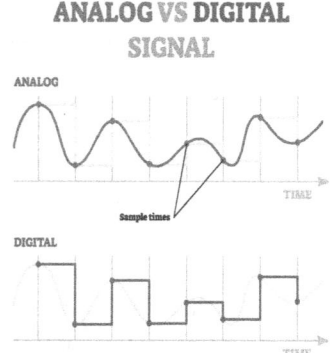

For the sake of uniting theology-strain wisdom's intellectually abstract logistics with the logistics of life wisdom's impermanent backdrop, it could be said that a religious believer's view through their spiritual window of salvation is focused and intellectually trained in an analog (intellectual) wave pattern.

They cannot be expected to know how to perceive the real thing when encountering its true sensual incarnation that occurs in a digital (impermanent) format.

Being conditioned to have faith in only one type of perception will not prepare an individual to distinguish knowledge presented in the other form of media... analog or digital ... intellectual or sensual. Intellectual understanding does not necessarily ensure experiential recognition/association.

Trying to internalize the intellectually woven interdependence of unquestionable theological maxims creates an impenetrable belief system scar that scabs-over an individual's conscious perception and suffocates the part of their inborn freewill that normally allows the waking mind to smell, analyze and question the fresh air of each new and crisp present moment.

The binding effect of theology's public gaslighting ethos goes unchecked.

Intellectually tendered age-old religious maxims must somehow be parleyed into present moment real-time sensual understanding to be associated with their real-life present moment manifestations.

The related borrowed wisdom does not surface when its understanding is needed.

It is important to be able to learn to recognize and describe these intellectually understood and stored religious maxims developed throughout a lifetime of hearing them as described in the world of religious theology interface with the sensual dialog that relates a tangible meaning when describing and understanding the emotional state of the human condition in the everyday human experience.

... Experience Morphs Mental Blueprint into Intrinsic Dimension

Getting a physical taste of what has been pondered can give it an intrinsically registered meaning. I.E., ... Holding the hand over a lit match gives intrinsic meaning to the intellectually metered verbal description of "hot".

The said wisdom a religious believer borrows from theology's world comes intellectually coded. It is secured only by their trusting faith that is blind to the validity of its suggested hearsay.

The self-evident truth of the living world is revealed intrinsically scripted, sensually coded and secured by a faith that stands steadfast in what has been sensually witnessed.

The intellectual personification and sensual manifestation of anything an individual perceives in the present moment will not share a mutual understanding if they have not developed an intrinsic familiarity with the logistics of how the wisdom won its valor.

This is the common ground where mind and body meet in harmonic awareness and where an enlightened understanding is seeded.

... Cognitively Managed Kingdom Lacks Reality Sensual Texture

The mental picture of the kingdom of heaven that a believer creates, hangs only in the still gallery of their imagination.

Reading about a "sin" in the Bible registers in a different sense than the "sin's" real life manifestation. A believer may say how wrong the action is on Sunday morning, but when the emotions arise that the "sin" evokes, they do not connect the dots.

Religious Adherence Mimics Hobby Devotion ... Has Tribal Footprint

... Sanctimonious for Many ... Believer's Belief System was Already Formed ... Religion is Merely a Generic Post-Production Accessory ... A Bite of Borrowed Wisdom of Choice

An individual is first born into their human experience and have already developed a belief system before they decide to turn it over to a god to manage. If their conditioning did not direct them how to self-train their understanding of reality's unknown, they might turn to the intangible for their answer.

Theological interpretations are molded by personalized opinions of teachers, preachers, family, society, and such. These theological designs are not experientially associated with anything tangible, so the personal shaping of these spiritual concepts lies subject to the individual's unique and imaginative illusionary constructs.

They have already developed a worldview during the earlier post-birth conditioning of their belief system. They just do not understand that the answer to the question their looking for and probably do not realize yet is already lies within on a 24/7/365 availability basis.

The desire to take the leap of blind faith to partake of the theological wisdom-deriving knowledge describing the configuration of a religion's soul-saving recipe is a very subjective and personal thing ... being a 100% theological notion, it is somewhat shielded from an outside challenge.

This decision manifests from the freewill that runs point for an individual's worldview that has already been conditioned to evaluate judge and decide.

The religion's tenets might then influence and further shape the development of the believer's worldview, but the religion's claim maker is not responsible for the initial conditioning of the believer's belief system that created the mental tone that allowed for their sudden blind trust and vowed allegiance to the unverifiable theological claim.

They had already been through the process of making the spiritual life-or-death distinction Jehovah warned Adam about and that is making that decision whether to borrow, internalize or partake of proised wisdom from the Tree of Knowledge of All Good and Evil.

Borrowing and internalizing unverified untested wisdom gifted rom elsewhere would surely result in death to developing their soul's wisdom-enriched enlightened understanding awareness of the ways of impermanence that their ignorance of causes their suffering.

Biting on the apple of theology means believing wisdom that is borrowed unverifiable. It is not wisdom that has a known process of derivation from attained knowledge. The religion's wisdom comes unexplained. It has no intrinsically cased experiential history with the believer.

... Birds-of-a-Feather Flock Together

Those looking for safety from what the demons that pop out of their mental white noise and scare them for some reason will shop around and assign their allegiance to a congregation of people that have also made the leap of blind faith that collectively shares similar fears of the unknown. They unite to stand behind the translation of the ancient scriptures they feel most comfortable with. They will sync their understandings to form a "congregation" tethered to a religious template of sorts.

There are thousands of them ... at least.

Even with the ever-expanding plethora of religious groups, many believe that their unique group will be the only ones that will be able to satisfy their god and make the day of redemption final cut.

Many church groups are beginning to open to the idea that the different religious sects all answer to only one god.

Their chosen group of believers will worship their god in unique ways defining their interpretation of the written word. Even today on a worldwide scale, populations representing one religion will massacre those of another ... sure that their god is on their side.

Believers belonging to the congregations of these scrutinized beliefs will be able to form close friendships with others in the group which is good and might help buffer their anxieties and dissatisfactions with the status-quo, but their religion's expressed belief is a dead end and won't put them on track to relieving the ignorance that results in their suffering and denies them the afterlife emotional bliss promised by their supposed creator.

The congregation members relate to the same feeling of "emptiness-of-understanding" that spurred their choice of fraternal church groups to join.

Creating a personal relationship with a chosen religious discipline is like deciding what model car to build and then what color to paint it.

... Religious Theology ... A Non-Primal Glorified Hobby

Theological notions do not center on generating the wisdom-deriving knowledge needed to develop an awareness of the ways of the relational justice characterizing the impermanent nature of this reality's dimensional makeup. The principles guiding how life is manifested that come from the push/pull of the natural forces is showcased in these basic metaphysical coming and going relationships that echo up through scale to set course in the cause/effect relationships affecting reality as it manifests in mankind's field of recognition.

There is an ever-present source of life manifestation on hand that affects the human condition's human experience on the deepest level that evades the intellectually based cognitive front of theology's subject matter. The humanity tie-ins of all the different schools of theology share in the absence of making any supporting contribution to life's present moment heartbeat.

It reflects an intellectual chess game and not a sensual living experience. Their wisdom-deriving knowledge is cognitively internalized, not sensually realized.

Joining a religious group is like taking up a new hobby. It is intellectualized and not understood or identified with the actual present moment manifestation of life's intrinsically registered never-stilled heartbeat.

A religious believer's understanding of the religious theology's plan to salvation from suffering to gain eternal afterlife emotional bliss is not something they were born with ... not innate to their consciousness. It is an intellectually endowed choice they make after real life has conditioned their conscious awareness to seek assistance in avoidance of what they have learned to fear about the "emptiness-of-understanding" they have about what's unknown.

Religious involvement is an intellectually registered and metered life option ... not from an innate life presence an individual has from birth.

... Believers Pick Their Idols and Favorite Dogma

These conceptual notions will be represented by human-shaped often martyred idols that believers worship and bow to. They gather with like-minded believers to read, reread, and review the written Roman-edited ancient accounts again ... Sunday after Sunday.

A believer's blind-faith in the usefulness of the ancient accounts of a god's presence shakes a customized sort of voodoo wand to ward off the demonic monsters that take form as fears materialize from a believer's belief system that's empty-of-understanding the cause/effect relational justice that gives order to the principles setting order to this impermanent reality. Each brand of religion has its own assortment of rites, rituals, and codes of "do this and don't do that" conduct that really has nothing to do with coming to grips with identifying and eliminating what it is that causes the human suffering their claim's assert to eliminate.

These dos and don'ts bridge-over the "empty-of-understanding" void of Tree of Life wisdom showing the pathway to finding emotional bliss. Self-training awareness of Tree of Life wisdom comes with the enlightenment bringing on emotional bliss whereas using religion's Band-Aid only comes with the hope that this emotional bliss will be waiting in an afterlife paradise.

Theology projects that there are gods that write the needed wisdom. They stop there and fail to teach the truth-seeker how to self-training the mind control to realize the self-knowledge to self-train the wisdom-enriched understanding of what it is that causes human suffering.

A believer's status as a Christian comes as an intellectually engineered personal choice with a subject set that can breathe life only in the believer's abstract imagination. It can never be experienced in a real-time present moment material sense.

... Impetus to Join God's Protection May Reflect Upfront Self-Interest

For many, the motivation to join the church is an effort to save oneself from an emptiness-of-understanding of the logistics of a transforming reality that brings on emotional suffering. It is a push from a mounting fear.

Others might join because of pressure from family or friends. Many might just want to avoid the threat of eternal damnation or enjoy the promised paradise.

In either case, the action is not centered around the compassion-seeded inner agenda to save others from suffering emotional hell.

Living with a world view centered around compassion is a real time present moment sensual journey that the intellectually ingested media cannot connect with.

... Believer Imagination is Notion's Only Connection to Living Reality

The only connected living relationship the religion's network of wisdom has with the living process of transforming life itself is within the life-circle expanse of a believer's imagination.

Church's Name ...
A Guess at Login/Password to Heaven's Gate?

... Yearn For Answer Conveyed in Flock Name

Congregational groups' collective inner yearning can be sensed in the creative names used to describe the thread of the theological fabric they feel will reveal the most direct route to pleasing their chosen god and finding his promised afterlife emotional bliss.

Just read the heavenly-gate-key church names as you drive down the road. often, the congregation's collective purpose pops out on their sign out front.

None of these theological conceptions come naturally or are born into. These religious visionary notions are internalized by an individual's belief system that is already been seeded with the very living presence that the theological notion claims control of. They target some promised state of existence that awaits them after their death.

Christian Church, Church of God or Christ, Holy Trinity, Baptist Church, Life Point, Grace Point, Real Life, Christ Church, St. Peter's Church, New Life, or maybe New Hope Church are just a few of the group names that hope to differentiate their agenda to catch their god's attention and underline their sincerity.

Membership in one of these theologically founded beliefs is something they later use their freewill to elect to do. It involves a weighed-out decision that is subjected to the earlier conditioning of their upbringing … an intellectual preoccupation of sorts.

… Real Life Just Doesn't Happen In The Biblical Sense

VIII

Fundamentalitis
... The Borrowed Wisdom Blues

... That Fundamental Wall

For many religious believers, there is a surreal fundamental wall that often stops short any rational questioning. A conscious state of "deer-in-the-headlights" mental standstill can often have those using Fig Leaf Wisdom choked up in between what their eyes tell them and how they interpret the written scriptures they have sworn unquestioned conviction to.

A religious believer's fundamentally faithful intellect-based prowess and subtle fear of their creator's ever-watching judgmental punishing eye will repeatedly not afford them the courage that will allow them to skip the tracks and take sensually tendered emotional inventory while searching for the recognized feel of any associated real-life relevance.

Their worldview is no longer wired to notice and recognize the sensual signposts of anything not suited up in the biblical attire they have intellectually sketched in their mental gallery picturing their Bible-spun imagery.

The borrowed biblical wisdom might be valid, but like with Adam and Eve, the religious converts had self-trained no intrinsically founded lateral understanding as to what and how and when it may be applied. They cannot understandably speak its truth from their heart. Its relevance to a real-life situation must be intellectually recognized and quoted from its borrowed source.

Religious Templates Used to Bridge-Over "Emptiness" in Life Understanding

"It's important not to just sit and hope that another entity will keep you safe and grant you emotional bliss. An individual must work for it and earn it. They must do their own work to bring understanding to their waking consciousness."

~ anonymous

For most, the conscious understanding of what is responsible for the relational logistics between this outside source's unknown/unrevealed principles and the human experience is missing. As people confront present moment change, they use their freewill to decide how to understand and confront this unknown force of change and find an understanding of what drives it.

Some will ask questions to gain the knowledge to derive the Tree of Life wisdom to better understand it on a steadfast personal level. They will experience no feeling of having an emptiness-in-understanding of the relationship between their human condition and its human experience.

They will suffer less. They will live closer to emotional bliss. The more an individual understands their emotions, the more "enlightened" they are.

Some will settle to internalize unverifiable borrowed wisdom from another source. However, their understanding of cause/effect relationships will be locked in a world of the emptiness-of-understanding of the interdependent details of how a cause generates its effect. This is like how Adam and Eve could not give account for their nakedness when confronted by their god.

When the threat from the unknown becomes too great, many will decide to follow one of the templated or cast-in-stone prescriptions to emotional bliss from one of the schools of theology.

It will be their greatest pretense to hide the shame-ridden weakness felt from being empty-of-understanding from others.

... Fundamentalist Mindset Used to Support Crippled Freewill

For most, the innate longing to understand the human experience will point some to religious theology for an answer. Juggling the possibility of a conceptualized supernatural promise-maker stretches the imagination.

Religious theology promises an afterlife of endless God-gifted suffering-free emotional bliss. Its afterlife promise is founded in the pins and needles of blind faith hope.

With the muffled curiosity of a compromised freewill, many religious believers will use their intellectually metered fundamental understanding of their God-bestowed wisdom as a cognitive crutch to calculate conceptional answers to navigate everyday life.

After becoming a religious believer while in search of safety from the unknown, it is necessary to use the persuasion-scripted dialog to find wisdom-based answers for dealing with the life situations that arise in ongoing change.

Believers Hover in the Same Intellectually Metered World They First Made "His" Acquaintance *and* Heard "His" Promise In

Believers can set their emerging mental impression of his Bible-scripted sandal-clad world aside to come back later to revise and further customize their configured understanding they've so far fashioned. Its state of continuity often spans from Sunday to Sunday.

Religious believers' imagination-construed reality is a world that is pieced together intellectually. Everything about the god they choose to follow was acquired from intellectually metered sources.

When in prayer, 21st-century Christian believers will often go as far as adopting a King James Version language dialect. For example, they will use the "thee's", "thy's", and "thou's" scribed in the King James translation while trying to speak to Jehovah in prayer.

That is the dialect used in the King James Version of the intellectually metered scriptures that are their closest contact with his projected truth.

It is the dialect used in a later translation into a language that did not even exist in the ancient times where they intellectually reference meeting him.

Theology Template "Rote" into Memory

... Loyal Bible Reading Can Become a Guilt-Ridden Ritual

Making sense of a religion's format is an intellectual adventure. Many will spend their entire life bowing to its intimidating notion with an ever-confused questioned understanding.

There are those who struggle blindly in the unfolding of their human experience. They will read, reread, and memorize religious translations that use modern descriptive new-world words to understand and fly under the radar of their shoulder-sitting god.

In demonstrating their loyalty, they hope to accumulate good behavior points for that promised future day of redemption. The thought echoes throughout their imagined world of heaven that he is always watching. Some feel it may impress their god to establish peer scripture recall rank by out-quoting fellow believers while discussing sermons in the parking lot after Sunday morning church meetings.

Many take much pride in having a memorized repertoire of book-chapter-verse wisdom on hand to defend against any outside objections.

They are putting to memory the god-controlled rules of nature found in the scriptures. They are the unique relational justice rules that ignore or twist in a Red Sea-parting way the self-evident natural laws of impermanence that set the stage for the principle-ruled dimensional character of this reality to allow for the existence of inexplicable miracles.

... Lost In The Details

Many Bible advocates pay attention to the smallest of details about how their chosen version of Jesus's multi-translated home tongue, Aramaic, the ancient language of few words, says to properly baptize a new believer convert ... full or partial immersion or maybe just sprinkling will do?

Do they wonder if exactness on this might please or displease Jehovah? This wisdom they borrow from the scriptures, hoping to be able to relate its intellectual understanding to real-life living sensually registered cause/effect situations.

They will need to recognize and apply to today's situations what life-truth example they can pull from the depicted life and times of the ancient societies. They hope to reach this objective by putting in their open-Bible reading time every day.

With unanswered afterlife curiosity spawned by persisting discomfort in their present moment condition and shamed by the ever-widening belief system emptiness-of-understanding void, they might read, reread, and memorize the commentary writings of others who have read, reread, and memorized some rendition of those ancient scriptures in effort to satisfy the ever-present fixed image compilation they have formed of their ever-feared shoulder-sitting god.

Yet, their real-life suffering persists that they have no real fix on.

This is considering believers who are moved enough to take on fundamental obedience. It's unknown how many proclaimed Christians ever actually crack open their Bible daily.

... Back in the Ancient Day, There Were No Bibles to Read

Jesus always said to follow him to experience the truth. He said to follow his way of living.

Rome edited out biblical inclusion of the writings like the book of Judas and the book of Thomas, that were understood and written by those more spiritually mature to comment in deeper spiritual detail that better revealed Jesus's intended meaning where the published Roman Bible hints about how "God's kingdom is in his listeners' bodies."

Over time, many faithful fundamentalists' daytimes become more and more consumed with studying their bible. Their religion becomes their addiction. They study and study it to regain their high that sits them atop their fashioned pinnacle in their imagined version of paradise.

When the decision-making of life situations bidding for their attention has worn this postured life image down and their refreshed self-image becomes tattered with red flags, they fall back into feeling the shame that shadows their emptiness-of-understanding void that haunts their present moment.

At this point they must go back into injecting the stream of biblical verbiage into their thought pattern flow to regain their religious high.

Creating Imagination-Fed Reality Draws On Superstition

Real-life taps everyone on the shoulder.

With borrowed knowledge, the believer's knowledge-receiving platform must favor a state of reality that allows bending the rules of time passage to allow this reality to have an unreal continual presence to allow for the continuity of a cognitively sketched mental picture of a future-promised paradise they have heard described.

They must trust and parrot/mime the written claims of an intellectually metered and internalized still-life description. They must piece together an intellectually calculated product of what footprint the borrowed description has left ringing in their imagination.

This breed of wisdom dead-ends into a wall of sensual recall emptiness.

Many individuals have not developed the conscious dialog to deal with modern-day challenges. They are not aware of what type of knowledge to seek and use, experiential attained or intellectually metered, to find the intrinsic feel for developing balanced emotional wellbeing.

Some ask those who are known to be wise for guidance on how to better understand the ways or principles of this reality that determine the outcome of how things interact. Many of those who turn to an unverifiable branch of theology and use the discipline's written word as their source of wisdom will carry the theology's written code to quote and wave defensively at any disagreeing view.

Religious believers cling to their unique interpretation of a religious notion that there is a god that might also be sitting judgmentally on their shoulder with the written wisdom to handle life's ups and downs and the power to sentence them to an eternal afterlife of eternally burning in brimstone hellfire.

Religious blind-faith believers entertain two worlds. Besides their theological paradise is the unavoidable reality that feeds them an ongoing barrage of ever-changing real-life situations they emotionally struggle to understand to survive.

... Human "Knee-Jerk" Response Sparks from Experience

In this universal reality, the fight-or-flight reaction first taps into an individual's sensually metered and experientially registered bank of intrinsically stored wisdom ... the home of the "gut feeling."

It will be what generates their "knee-jerk" reaction.

The other reality is one metered intellectually that finds life and reference only in their imagination.

Their sandal-clad intellectual interface to the written wisdom of how to deal with life often fails to come to their inner felt need when the ever-changing situation of real modern-day life suddenly appears undefined.

Many have made a cognitive sketch of theology's imagined promised paradise that they will update every Sunday morning when donning their Sunday goin'-to-meetin' clothes and attitude.

... Borrowed Understanding of What's "Right" Turns to Superstition for Support

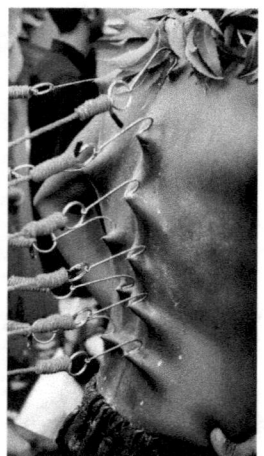

Many individuals will turn to a religious discipline in search of security from their fear of the unknown. They look to religion for a code to determine what is actually "right and wrong."

After accepting the discipline's terms and conditions, they end up having to follow the proposed wisdom they've borrowed unearned and unexplained.

Over time, believers in what they have been told unexplained and unverified, will from lack of understanding become superstitious. They might try doing things that were correlated to situations in the religion's written text that pleased their god even though there was no causation or cause/effect relationship established.

Being that their adopted wisdom has left them without an understanding of the cause/effect relationships involved in turning the wheels of impermanence ... In the "valley of emptiness-of-understanding" ... in searching for something to do to please their god, repeated performance of those correlated behaviors will become a ritual.

Without having conscious awareness of the Tree of Life principles of wisdom decoding what makes things "right and wrong", a religious believer might develop and become slave to the non-fertile superstitious rites and rituals associated with pleasing the associated god. To please or at least to not offend the never-to-be-seen godly entity, they will perform actions that had been performed in the past by others in hope of achieving the same God-pleasing effect.

... Ritualistic Behavior Numbs Natural "Aha" Wisdom Recognition

Being locked into following a code of borrowed wisdom that is merely intellectually ingested and blindly internalized that lacks conscious recognition of the intrinsic understanding of the natural principles of how things relate, disables the believer's ability to ask questions that register and relate to a deeper intrinsic understanding.

Ego-Crafted Social Veneer

... React To Social Suggestion Or Act On Intrinsic Know-How?

There are those with conscious attention not focused on what they might be able to do to make another person's life better as their present moment awareness is backed up on how others might be judging them.

Their intentions are generated in the head and not from the heart. They will decide on which "mask" to wear to satisfy different social situations in a manner to best posture themselves as front-runners.

Good moral/ethical behavior can originate from the desire set to assure others of having "good" socially acknowledged standards without really understanding why. Altruistically stirred compassion probably plays no role in their behavior.

Some individuals will proudly assert righteous qualities that society and their religious theology might praise ... honesty, fairness, etcetera ... without really knowing what is so good about the behaviors. The behaviors might not be fueled by compassion but from an unrecognized hidden agenda.

They might not understand why or where the resulting good feeling falls on the 1-10 scale of emotional intelligence as their sense of wholesomeness beats to a different rhythm from that of the rhythm of the natural force-inspired principles of impermanence.

When they are cornered with having their lack of base being discovered, they might become vindictive towards others. Some will lie, blow up, walk away ... everything short of lying on the floor kicking and screaming that worked for them when they were 2 years old... a hidden agenda ulterior motive so deeply and well disguised, they can't even see it themselves.

Many fundamentalists will do the right moral/ethical things because they know it is listed biblically approved behavior while in the first place not understanding why that behavior was on the good behavior list. The desire to appear like a good upstanding Christian believer fueled the deed, not the altruistic push from jumping into someone else's shoes and feeling what they are feeling.

Some fundamentalists would have acted in a moral/ethical way anyway as it was part of their character before taking the leap of blind faith. Being a fundamentalist is not an evil, it's just misdirected purpose directed down a dead-end street.

There is a difference between acting with "honor" because the intention was stirred by compassion for another's well-being and acting just because it has been heard to be the proper reputable way to act while not coming from a waking awareness of the intrinsic understanding of why.

A fundamentally frozen heart may craft a social veneer miming honorable socially lauded behavior even though only primed by shallow intentions.

While trying to convert the verses of the Bible to memory, the Bible never does reveal the "how" and the "why" about the justice it purports in the wisdom of its directives on what to do and what not to do. The believer will be stuck at knowing how the Bible says to act, but the how and why will never become integrated into the Bible wisdom catalog personified through their worldview.

The believer might reason that if they can just know what the Bible says that nothing else matters. They can let all else slide if they stay hidden behind the mask of caring … an insincere shallow interest as they had made no real effort to empathize with what the other individual is/was experiencing.

Being lost trying to come to terms with what their hidden agenda is, can leave them lost in trying to exhibit compassion towards a fellow human.

Dazed by the Notion of Afterlife Emotional Bliss in Imagined Reality, Fundamentalists Lose Touch with Reality's True Order *and* Suffer

Once an individual has worked up the courage to make the valiant leap of blind faith as a new religious devotee when they made a deal with the god of their selected theological discipline to swap their existing ignorance-bred fear-fed state of restless uncertainty for the holy promise of a present moment mental calm, it is unlikely they'll be able to work up the second-guessing courage to challenge and go against the discipline's directives.

They live in the same uncertain environment of unpredictable change but now it's softened by a self-inflicted mental fog requiring them to focus up into a cloud of hope for the blind-trust-backed security of an unsecured pinky-swear promise of going after death to an unearthly heavenly land of emotional bliss free of suffering.

While force-feeding their belief system with their favorite theological notion as now being the unquestionable truth, the freewill-gagged hope-blinded believer loses sight of understanding the cause/effect patterns establishing what reality's living truth is. They subconsciously feel only half-satisfied regarding the innate need to better understand the ways of the reality they were born into and are a living part of instead of finding full satisfaction from knowing that now they have an outside entity that will in some unverifiable mystical godly way, do it for them.

As the religious believer cultivated their intended purpose, they chose to rely more and more on the written does and don'ts of the script allegedly outlined by the maker of their selected unverifiable theological claim. While preoccupied with this, they lose sight of observing and focusing their objective attention on the cause/effect relational justice of this impermanent reality. Experiential involvement in what changes the causes of the passing present moment into the upcoming effects that make up the reality of the next present moment slides by forever missed.

While obediently turning a deaf ear to the blind-eye questions concerning the verification of a religion's asserted claim to heavenly bliss, they develop deafness to the truth of reality's rhyme and reason. The mindset that the heavenly stage is not on this Earth, but up in the sky furthers a believer from connecting its borrowed wisdom with the cause/effect patterns of the changing reality of today's world.

They lose touch with having the objective sensitivity to feel the intuitive pulse to honor the self-confidence needed to trust their intrinsic steadfast faith that what they are seeing is how things work versus what they have been conditioned to misinterpret something as being or meaning.

The believer has checked at the altar the prioritizing of any existing steadfast faith in life's self-evident truths to support the courage needed to leap back across their newly instilled fears of the unknown that might reach up and grab them from the abyss of "emptiness-of-understanding" that fills the moat of spirituality that surrounds their mental castle built from blueprints drafted from the unverifiable borrowed knowledge used to derive the wisdom supporting a future promised heavenly emotional state free from suffering.

As a fundamentalist reins-in their curiosity, they stop questioning things. Some people will capitalize on their loss of accountability and take advantage of them.

Their theological world is founded on the precepts of a reality with the cause/effect relational justice rhythm appropriate to support the continual time/space dimensional relationship needed to capture their lasting mental images of what their alleged promisors and their future afterlife home might look like.

… Can't Step Back Over Burnt Bridges

Many fundamentalist believers might feel they cannot renege on their alter-secured bet wagered on the validity of the theological wisdom supporting the future existence of a promised heavenly world reality … while many might simply be locked up in pride. They look back scared into the living world of life transformation where the boogiemen of their unknown that scared and chased them into taking the blind leap of faith into the hands of a godly cure-all are still hiding. The world of transformation dances to the Jehovah-enhanced Tree of Life wisdom that is built on the sensually developed physical self-knowledge that inspires deriving a wisdom-enriched understanding of the principles governing the cause/effect relational justice of this impermanent reality.

Fundamentalist devotees of any theological or speculative discipline are very unlikely to ever seek any therapy or psychological help with their difficulty in perceiving reality unless maybe it is with a therapist from their theological grouping. They choose to live pent up alone in their uniquely interpreted fundamentalist shell.

… Book/Chapter/Verse Adherence Dulls Feel For Reality Logistics
… Obscures Objective Reality Recognition

As present moment mental fluidity goes into remission while a theological believer focuses their waking efforts on memorizing and following a written script of unexplained purpose, the devoted believer gradually loses sight of and confidence in their prior understanding of reality's cause/effect rhythm. Based on the borrowed knowledge they have used to derive the wisdom they now rely on in cause/effect analysis, their decisions frequently fail to make sense of things subject to the push-pull logistics that thread together the relational justice of this impermanent reality.

Fundamental observance of biblical rules will eventually overshadow conscious awareness of reality.

When an individual chooses to trust and borrow wisdom-deriving knowledge that is verified only by blind trust in an outside source and it comes time to demonstrate an understanding of what is alleged by the borrowed wisdom's claim, they are often left empty-of-understanding … some in shame … for not having an answer.

This is like when the snake provided the borrowed fruit of wisdom from the Tree of Knowledge of Good and Evil to Adam and Eve and when confronted by Jehovah, Adam and Eve were ashamed of their emptiness-of-understanding coming from foolishly ingesting the awareness-empty wisdom that their borrowed wisdom had provided them concerning their nakedness. They reached for leaves to cover up and mask the subject of their emptiness in understanding.

When a dedicated fundamentalist who has devoted their waking time to better understanding the book/chapter/verse rules detailing the wisdom structuring the biblical plan to realize the promised after-life freedom from emotional suffering comes into a life situation needing a wisdom-fortified decision, they sometimes turn to their cognitively memorized and stored book/chapter/verse borrowed knowledge-derived wisdom to calculate, formulate, and customize what their situation-specific interpretation of the borrowed wisdom would be to render their best borrowed wisdom-based judgment.

of the believers who have spent their time gathering and memorizing unverifiable wisdom-deriving knowledge that comes blindly trusted from the outside sourced religion, many will brag about having the bold courage to blindly trust the fate of their soul to an outside source that cannot verify how the wisdom in its plan is alive supporting the impermanence of this living reality. They have not spent their time self-training the attainment of wisdom-deriving self-knowledge from their personal sprig of the Tree of Life to assimilate a wisdom-enriched life awareness to weigh in on the making of their situational decision. It is the Tree of Knowledge of Good and Evil versus the Tree of Life.

... Which Slice of Wisdom Applies?

A fundamentalist can end up struggling over which bit of borrowed knowledge-derived wisdom to use when they come across a situation when they still may have conflicting book/chapter/verse understandings of what was meant that threatens their judgment about which interpretation of the borrowed book/chapter/verse knowledge best applies. They could have left their counterpoint understanding of this certain book/chapter/verse unresolved when they left it hanging on its cognitive hook at an earlier time when their mental awareness shifted to another subject of preoccupation.

This is wisdom derived from their intellectual understanding and interpretation of the borrowed knowledge from the outside source. It lacks in having any sort of self-evident experiential tie-in history with the claim's promised cause-into-effect process.

It is not the type of life wisdom derived from life knowledge assimilated from the life manifest arena of introspective deliberation ... the human body ... where sustained harmonic mind-into-body awareness spawns the thinking to inspire an insightful wisdom-enriched insightful understanding of the cause/effect relationships that affect the justice in real-life situations, backed by a steadfast faith intuitively assured from having sensually witnessed the makings of this cause/effect truth supporting the truth of impermanence.

This veil of obscurity becomes more imposing to a fundamentalist's mental focus the more time they devote to applying the efforts of their waking consciousness towards linking together a web of cause/effect relational justice supported by the book/chapter/verse logistics of the scriptures. They become consciously numb and blind to the self-evident sense that explains the cause/effect change of this everyday ephemeral reality.

Vision for the realness of things becomes more obscure and makes less sense.

When a religious believer's purpose is to spend their time pouring their focused awareness deeper and deeper into the bowels of the borrowed description of a promised unverifiable abstract reality that is to protect them from afterlife suffering instead of self-training the right harmonic mind-into-body introspective deliberative concentration into the primal source of life-manifest itself (their body) to attain the self-knowledge to self-train an enlightened awareness of this reality, undoing their suffering-causing ignorance, they are choosing to internalize the knowledge that has nothing at all to do with deriving the same life-wisdom-enriched awareness that sustains the Garden of Eden Tree of Life preferred by Jehovah.

Slaves to the dictation of fundamental relational justice lose their ability to identify with their intrinsically generated gut feeling for right or wrong. They rely on a subjectively fallible interpretation of wisdom based on what they have been told to be true or what they have pieced together from their readings.

The struggle between going with the ruminants of their gut feeling and what the church says is ok causes much emotional stress. Christianity continues trying to stay caught up with what's assuming an "ok" status with most of society ... female degree of church responsibility involvement ... gay rights ... etcetera.

... Hypocrisy Inherent to Ignorance

Knee-jerk impulse-driven behavior is not interfaced to reference the intellectual library for biblical wisdom.

Fundamentalists are often cited as being hypocritical. They loudly profess one thing at Sunday morning services, only to act differently when encountered in real life. Some will swear by the Ten Commandments yet vote for a president that breaks every one of them because the stock market has risen during his time in office.

They find it difficult to see a world of sandals and togas as being clad in a suit and tie. They can quote the Bible on how to act 2000 years ago, yet they fail to recognize its living application in modern-day real-life circumstance.

... Logic and Proportion Become a Blur

Choosing to blindly invest and devote waking conscious energy to memorizing and understanding the checks and balances of the untethered details making up the imagined world of a promised future existence causes disconnect when trying to understand the ways of the relational justice that make real-time things work.

Over time, the logic and proportion of real-time situations become a blur.

The significance of intellectually coded things of little real consequence can swing to assume monumental importance. Some fundamentalists cannot see the forest for the trees. Some Christian believers become so upset if their church congregation allows for something that goes against their interpretation of Jehovah's biblical wisdom. They might even decide to leave the congregation. Using musical instruments can be of life-or-death importance to some religious believers.

... Compromised Freewill Gauge of Credibility Leads to Real-World Verses Imaginary World Switch-Out

As denial sets in and focus is lost on the importance of objective situational analysis, many fundamentalists lose their ability to recognize and appreciate reality's in-your-face truth. They lose sight of reality's relative importance while lost mentally roaming, trying to attach tangible meaning to the intellectually metered description of the theologized means to the promised end of no suffering.

Those who choose to preoccupy their mental presence with the cognitively plotted abstract logistics needed to support having blind faith in a posed truth about the notion of a reality ruled by a god that's tethered only by the limits of their imagination with a presence that's never been verified to play an active role in the real-time presence of living change itself, lose touch with the significance of how the actual heartbeat of their state-of-life status is what their spirituality is tied to.

Any urge of due diligence to pursue a better understanding of the reality that they suffer in gets doused in fear and tasered into a state of numbness.

... Infection Eventually Festers into Gangrene

At the point in an individual's worldview development, when the integrity of their freewill stamp of self-authorized credibility becomes compromised when blindly trusting borrowed knowledge, it will continue to become much easier for them to internalize the possibly miscued purposes of unverified claims when searching for other life answers while seeking an explanation to so many other seemingly mysterious time/space relationships from when a cause (of anything) transforms to take on the changing form of its effect in this reality. Maybe this is what Jehovah meant by saying that the *"day that thou eatest thereof thou shalt surely die"*?

At this point, the believer is "lost" in their search for a waking understanding of the truth about how this reality works. They do not understand that causes their mental pain. They have no direction in finding the answer to a question that is still not clear to them.

... Interrelations Can Lose Sensitivity

When a devoted fundamentalist spends significant portions of their time studying the written accounts of the ways of a removed reality recorded in ancient scriptures, the believer's waking logic and proportion slowly shift towards a state of permanence in the imagined ways they interpret the written accounts of that reality to be. Some can become so isolated and confused in their hope of imagined proportions that all they feel comfortable talking to friends and family about is limited to neutral subjects like sports, politics, or maybe a generic general sort of shallow question about something they are involved in.

When religion comes up, everyone close expects the barrage of book/chapter/verse that can seem unyielding while supporting a meaning beyond compromise.

As the heartbeat of their waking awareness sways more and more to the theological pulse, they will lose touch with the ticking of Father Time's reality clock. At some point in the lifetime of a believer who spends their time trying to convince themselves that their blind faith's been well spent, by jamming into their belief system the theological notions of their religious preference, they lose touch with the objective truth of what is happening in the present moment.

Over time they will sit staring into a silent haze of surrendering confusion when important discussions involving the cause/effect justice of real situations are in process. Recognition of the natural rhythm of the patterns and forces associated with reality's truth fades. Appreciation for the rhythm of the real cause/effect order of things disappears.

When faith in a theological notion that is blind to having any verified real-life involvement grows out of proportion, a fundamentalist believer can lose touch with determining what is real. At some point, they will have become lost and give up while searching for peace in their lonely world.

Lying about things becomes acceptable to them. What's happening in the real world takes second place to the importance of the religious fire that's burning in their soul.

Along with the many life choices made over time, an untethered freewill gradually mortgages out its intuitive nature to an unverifiable mindset with underlying intended purpose blind to the ways of the natural forces of principled order and pattern that give shape to the undeniable push-pull of the natural laws defining the dimensional makeup that supports the passage of the time that defines this impermanent reality.

Fundamental Obedience Incites Loneliness

The religious believer is alone in an imaginary world that's unique to their imagination. No two imagination-fed designs of heaven are the same.

When a believer of any religious theology first decided to dedicate their waking mindfulness to forming a self-drafted mental picture giving shape to the religious claim details of a borrowed description of what a promised reality is promised to be like sometime in the future, it sets their ego-managed "I am" up for a lonely existence with a sense of alienated emptiness ... even when amidst a congregation of those with similar religion-inspired notions.

They have pieced together an intellectually synthesized meshwork representing the understanding of a fully conceptualized unverifiable reality that is held together by nothing more than the vigor of their blind faith.

Their present moment awareness can become slowed into a state of rumination abyss ... hypnotized into a stoic gaze of ever-ponder contemplative wonder. Their decision-making process teeters on how to shift compromise to fit the square-pegged borrowed logic and proportion from their pieced together self-fashioned perception of their favorite religious theology into the elusive "right now" round hole logic and proportion footprint left in the wake of this ephemeral reality's impermanent shakedown.

A devoted religious believer that adheres their energy to improving their understanding of the fundamental rules set by the maker of a speculative theological notion, will live alone imprisoned in the unique cognitive details they have assigned to their understanding. Being that the theology is based purely in untested nonexistent speculation, there is nothing tangible to base a concrete understanding on.

They live afraid or at least are not motivated to step out, caged alone in their individually unique and quite scanty book/chapter/verse cocktail understanding of the relational justice of how things in everyday real-life present moments should relate to each other.

They take modern-day life situations and use antiquated multi-translated scriptures to piece together a string of wisdom subjected to their borrowed knowledge conditioned perception. Their understanding stands as true as their determination wants it to be as there is really no book/chapter/verse logic sequence that they cannot conjure to serve as a hard-shell defense.

Many will place "I" at the very top of life's pecking order ... Prima Donna style. Their conscious intentions can totally lack having any thread of compassion. There will be nobody else with the same imagined details of this heavenly place to talk to.

Listen to TV evangelists give a book/chapter/verse account of what they think Jehovah meant. About anything.

Fundamentalist View Feeds Lack of Self-Confidence

After a childhood of being told what's right or what's wrong, early conditioning leaves many totally lacking in self-confidence. Being afraid of stepping on somebody's opinion and being challenged on some point, they would much rather talk sports or politics where opinion must be allowed.

As slight miscalculations of expected results accumulate over time, they lose self-confidence in anything having to do with the real cause/effect order of things. Anything having to do with the actual nuts and bolts that make a situation reality is approached with uncertain caution and self-doubt.

Applied interest that would normally generate relevant points can be pushed into the background behind a cloud of self-doubt.

To avoid exposing their emptiness-of-understanding about something or not having a sincere interest in the thing at hand and just to make conversation, they might pose entry-level questions about how the things work that have simple entry level answers.

Fundamentalist Fixation Necessitates a Hidden Agenda

"We use a higher power to encourage us in our lower deeds."
~Roger Waters 5-17-12 Sirius/XM Deep Tracks Interview

... You Can do Anything with "God on Your Side"

Humans suffering from mal-conditioned belief systems will say they have their "god on their side." They will stop at nothing ... genocide's still popular today in many countries.

Out of ignorance, the religious believer who has only blind faith in their interpretations of the borrowed life wisdom from their chosen religious theology must unknowingly view the nature of the dimensional makeup of this reality as continual. With that, they piece together and keep suspended in the world of their creative imagination a cognitive sketch of the existence of an imaginary "I AM" to become attached to ... to spend their life energy defending and posturing amongst all the "Smiths and Jones" encountered in the flow of their life timeline.

After ingesting a strain of borrowed theological wisdom into their belief system, a truth seeker remains caught up in worrying about their identity... still ruminating in the empty unknown spiritual abyss of their back-mind.

The needling question they cannot quite put their finger on that has to do with how their human condition best melds into its human condition sheds an omnipresent shadow over their waking awareness. They yearn to better understand the principles that determine the outcomes of the decisions they make.

From their ignorance, they have been making decisions with outcomes that have brought them pain.

... State of Confusion Edge Out Altruistic Intentions

A true fundamentalist can become so lost in the mile-a-minute mental white noise figuring out where to find emotional bliss that real life just ticks by. They cannot step into others' shoes to empathize with others when they do not know who they are to start with ... when they do not feel comfortable in their own skin.

... Believer Will Use Up Day's Energy Treading Time Lost in Emotional Confusion Trying to Understand Their Untethered Agenda

They stand lost in their lack of understanding why they feel "naked" to the truth ... like Adam and Eve did when they, with the new knowledge they were naked lacked the side of the borrowed wisdom explaining the why or how of its relevance.

They can devote their time putting to cognitive memory the rules of the borrowed knowledge and what the theology claims to be the source and authority of cause/effect relational justice of this reality.

Lacking a purpose focused on understanding the self-evident nature of reality, their energies are exhausted on posturing the stature of their imagined self-importance.

Roman Catholic Theology Provides Cover for Pedophiles

Cases of child sexual abuse by Catholic priests, nuns, and members of religious orders in the 20ᵗʰ and 21ˢᵗ centuries have been widespread and have led to many allegations, investigations, trials and convictions, as well as revelations about decades of attempts by the Church to cover up reported incidents. The abused include mostly boys but also girls, some as young as three years old, with the majority between the ages of 11 and 14. Criminal cases do not for the most part cover sexual harassment in the workplace against persons who had renounced sexual activity and therefore pre-declined sexual advances. This category includes all priests and seminarians and all religious brothers and sisters. The accusations began to receive isolated, sporadic publicity from the late 1980s. Many of these involved cases in which a figure was accused of decades of abuse; such allegations were frequently made by adults or older youths' years after the

> *abuse occurred. Cases have also been brought against members of the Catholic hierarchy who covered up sex abuse allegations and moved abusive priests to other parishes, where abuse continued.*
>
> *~ Wikipedia: Catholic Church sexual abuse cases*

Interestingly, the Wikipedia description does not use the word "pedophile." The national news is too often carrying news about Roman Catholic pedophile activity. It dates back for years but is just being brought out into the open over the past 20 years.

It's organization awareness reaches clear up to the mitered hat one nearest to Jehovah himself.

The loosened lax-meaning description attached to the type of person that fills a preacher's shoes has allowed those with evil agendas that prey on the human condition of others to find comfort and hide their evil behavior behind the multi-colored fabric that many Christian ministers/pastors/preachers adorn themselves with.

As modern times evolve, technology-pushed split-second worldwide communications have brought more public exposure and transparency to the various things that qualify as a biblical "sin". This sinful priest pedophile activity along with its coverup that has affected every level of the Catholic Church corporate-style structure clear up to within sight of the Pope himself is being forced out into public view.

This does show how, like when the negative effects of Ten Commandments finally surfaced in mankind's collective recognition as belonging on the "unacceptable list" back in the time of Moses, his god Jehovah fire-blasted his hand-scripted Ten Commandment behavioral directives in stone.

This sort of behavior can lock one's mind up, ruminating in circles of emotional unrest. Without providing direction in where or what to look at, the ability for the individual to self-train their minds to find the knowledge to self-train their understanding enlightened awareness of the ways of impermanence to attain emotional bliss is completely stifled.

The current pope says the Catholic priest pedophile behavior is an "abominable crime" and that the offenders are "tools of Satan." The 3rd highest-ranking cardinal was just found guilty of a year past child molestation.

... Spiritualists with Direction and Pathway Understanding Don't Molest

Interestingly, there is no record of Buddhist spirituality group teachers with an understanding of where to look and what to look for, and how to prepare to get there, of having ever been accused of molesting children. They have a pathway to emotional bliss intellectually detailed in their mind and the pathway guidance to get there.

They devote their time and intentions to self-training the mind control to convert that intellectual understanding to an understanding on the intrinsic level to realize the sensual awareness pot of gold at the pathway end.

They have direction and they can feel the progress. This feeling of increased understanding awareness keeps their minds on the end goal of emotional bliss and not child abuse.

They are not just spinning in ritual and dogma that they dare not question.

Fundamentalist Underlying Agenda Void of Compassion

... Life Purpose Only Targeting Search for One's Own Salvation Lacks Compassionate Concern for the Whole ... One Can't Wear Another's Shoes if They Can't Tie Their Own

"You can't depend on your eyes when your imagination is out of focus."

~ Mark Twain

The state of emptiness coming from borrowing some sort of outsourced wisdom has a crippling effect on the amount of the believer's compassion shown towards others. Over time, the mental dysfunction from being isolated in the still-life nature of the unique scripture-founded behavior-guiding wisdom that supports the theologically founded ideas and beliefs mounts up.

This world's intellectual registry does not readily come to mind when being faced with life's sensually registered and metered confrontations. Their sandal-clad fixed-in-time reference does not translate into and line up with the life rhythm nature of modern-day happenings.

Individuals with a lost sense of what comprises their own personal self-enrichment will often offer help to others because they intellectually know that behavior is supposed to be "good" behavior. It might be behavior from their biblical memorization recall like any of those from the Ten Commandments.

They like the feeling ... they just don't understand how their emotional network works.

What is learned to be a sin according to their biblically influenced reference stored their cognitive reality, does not have the same essence of presence as that of sin existing in their real-life presence. The basic fundamentalist keeps in mind the burnt-in-stone list of sins, not aware of the shared common characteristic that bleeds into modern-life incident that makes each of the behaviors a sin.

Understanding this conversion factor is essential when using intellectually realized biblical instructions to forge a pathway in this modern-day world. Keep in mind that any behavior, a few of which are listed as Ten Commandments, that interrupts calming the mind for self-training mind control to then seek the appropriate knowledge to self-train Tree of Life Wisdom, is a sin.

This understanding should be conditioned as a behavior filter in each human's worldview … but it's not.

… Hidden Agenda Lacks Tie-in to Rhythm of Reality's Life Principles

Borrowing an unverifiable template version of religion's explanation of life wisdom of how to attain heavenly emotional bliss leaves a believer without an interpretation or tie-in to today's life experience.

The life-threatening effects of eating white flour and keeping the refrigerator stocked full of diet soda with the unchecked consumption of salty foods while taking water pills while being hap-hazard about when to take insulin shots are examples of the spiritual death-from-ignorance of Tree of Life wisdom that Jehovah warned Adam about.

This emptiness-of-understanding spawned ignorance bred behavior leads more directly to physical death from not understanding the complete "circle of truth" the borrowed wisdom stands empty of. It means spiritual death to the soul's chance of becoming enlightened about why humans suffer to restore emotional bliss.

Since daily activities like these are not included in the Ten Commandments list of sins, the urge to commit these real-life sins does not register in the intellectually resident biblical "temptation" sensor.

The security of having extensive book/chapter/verse recall ability does not translate into a real-life social skill that generates acceptance anywhere other than the church congregation that shares the same unique worldview. Over time, a complicated infrastructure of rationalizations takes shape that loses touch with the relational justice that runs everyday life, and a hidden agenda arises.

For some, from misguided prior conditioning over time, maybe in their younger years, their worldview rests on a miscued understanding of relational justice. Maybe they learned to cower into a self-protective hidden agenda of abuse-related fear while conditioned at an earlier age when threatened by role models or when copying adult role model coping skills.

They lack the understanding of themselves, so they have no ability to put themselves in the other person's situation. They might just blurt out that the other person just gets what they deserve. End of conversation. Period. There is no compassionate reflection of any sort.

... A Hidden Agenda with Sabotaging Intent ... Some Want Rather to Drag Others into Their Hole of Suffering

A fundamentalist-minded individual might still want to chime into a social setting with something to say, to not seem odd, and to fit in. Yet stemming from their own frustration from their feeling of unconquerable emptiness, some may house a hidden agenda to sabotage others' present moment struggle.

They do not want someone who is also struggling to find relief and leave them alone still suffering.

They think that sharing their empty despair will help them find balance.

They are lonely. They want instead to drag others into their hole of emptiness to see how they handle it and maybe get a clue about how to get out of their own.

Fundamentalist Agenda Engenders Air of Negative Energy

Upon entering the home of a known religious fundamentalist, a feeling can seem to hang sweltering in the air where free-thinking seems to be interrupted. Somehow just not flowing smoothly.

It preoccupies suffocates and replaces the ambition and self-confidence that asserts the generation of positive intentions.

Negative energy prompts using present moment energy to avoid swordfights with the host's ego standing king of their illusionary castle. It creates the presence of the "white elephant-in-the-room" that all can sense, yet not put into words or have the courage to do so.

... The White Elephant-in-the-Room Negates Positive Energy

Negative energy is created anytime there is a white elephant in the room. Its crippling presence undercuts sidetracks and captures the wholesome intentions of anybody within the reach of its aura. Constructive present moment thoughts can hover in patterns of avoidance and worry.

Individuals who recognize the life truth appearing in today's living environment welcome science's advances in knowledge that enrich mankind's understanding of reality. For example, recognizing knowledge about the nutritional hazards in today's processed foods they have been eating for decades and is practiced by most.

Those in the room aware of nearby unbendable fundamental theological beliefs will try to stay clear of engaging in any uncompromising debates that might very possibly lead to a fundamentalist's meltdown-walk-away. The caution in not offending this White Elephant can preoccupy and sterilize the possibility of having any heart-to-heart exchange.

Unique Imagined Reality Grows Time-Pickled

Over time, fundamentalists' perceived interpretation of their borrowed wisdom finds shape more adapted to explaining how they see their life experience as their god becomes designed to better corral their needs and fears. Their vision becomes more Bazar, and their resolve strengthens in its belief.

There are very few the fundamentalist will share these interpretations with.

As time passes and as their perception of the meaning of the borrowed wisdom continues to unfold, it becomes more and more unique to the individual. The further they walk out on the plank of the unfolding and belief of its derived wisdom, the more the security of their soul's future depends on it.

Their understanding becomes more and more unbendable over time as it becomes more and more unique to their interpretation.

Devout religious followers apply their subjective interpretation of their chosen scriptures as solutions to their unique set of fears. As they age, the interface of how their scripture interpretations become more imaginatively innovative and case-by-case specific to their life experience.

The tangle of their beliefs becomes too involved to unwind. How they choose to see something is often kept strictly to themselves.

When explaining their line of logic, as they lose touch with heart-to-heart sharing, their eyes drift off to be docked elsewhere as their attention fades into describing the confines of their fixed-in-time cerebrally housed imagination. The more seasoned their account becomes … the more unique is its flavor.

The more unique its flavor, the more unchangeable it becomes.

By altering one of the linking points of logic leading to the conclusion, it weakens the validity of that conclusion. If one contention is wrong, the entire Pixi Stix structure will fold.

As the aging believer sets their focus off into the distance while they read the writing on the walls of their imagination, it becomes clear that there is no reason to attempt to discuss any part of their theological logic stream. Just finding agreement on what is meant by the various descriptive words would prove very unlikely, as they are speaking from their memory files recorded in intellectual script, not from real sensual report … the language of emotions.

Bottled Up Repressed Uncertainty
Draws Panic Attacks for Many

… The Boogieman of Their Unknown has Their Mind Treed in Anxiety

After a truth seeker has opted to cast their faith blindly into the wind outlining a theological promise, they will spend much time trying to memorize the rules of behavior (a twist on relational justice) outlined in the scriptures of the translation of their chosen religion.

They slowly become detached from consciously recognizing the causes of the effects in the ups and downs of real life.

Over time, much of their present moment becomes lost to the emptiness and uncertainty of unanswered rumination. Their mental balance slowly worsens as they react in a fashion they never experienced as a youth before blocking their relationship with the living reality out trying to force-feed an understanding of life founded in the intellectually borrowed rules describing how a doctrine of the sandal-clad reality of the past related to finding freedom from suffering.

The mental presence of many believers in a theological discipline will reach a boiling point of wanting an answer to a question they have no conscious recognition of. They will feel their world caving in from outside pressure they cannot see and do not understand.

For many, their cocktail of nutritional neglect, lack of exercise, and poor sleeping schedule will leave their bodies with unbalanced blood sugar. Along with an unbalanced state of mental presence, a high or low blood sugar count can contribute to being one source for generating the anxiety to trigger a panic attack.

... A Swirling Eddy of Living Hell

It is useless to suggest seeing a therapist, psychologist, or psychiatrist because in the depths of their emptiness, they cannot imagine what sort of fig leaves they could fashion to hide what they perceive as being such a shameful state of being from their friends.

They've already "surrendered their life to Jesus" or maybe Allah or a god of the thousands to pick from. Their initiative to ask why and gather the fitting knowledge to derive the Tree of Life wisdom to understand the answer to a question that is still not noticeably clear have long faded away.

The thought of surrendering their mental state of attachment to objects and ideas they keep their imaginations stuffed full of in an understood state of continuity to understand their ignorance of the ways of this impermanent reality has far too many layers of memorized ritual and religious protocol weighting it down for it to rise to the attention of their waking consciousness.

The religious believer becomes locked up lost in an impenetrable shell of suffering. They do not know where to turn.

They might decide to memorize the book of Acts.

Their mental awareness struggles to strike balance in the loneliness of the unique rhythm set to the design of their imagination. Every so often, they have a panic attack.

They do not recognize it as the living incarnation of the hell intellectually described in their chosen biblical translation.

They do not see their present moment living hell as being what their imagination has defined the logic and proportion of what their fashioned god in the sky promises to unravel in their afterlife if they adhere unquestioningly to his borrowed wisdom.

They are so lucky that nowadays there is a pill to help dull this type of extreme anxiety.

Book-Chapter-Verse Manacles

… Living by a Book/Chapter/Verse Life Rhythm Locks Citizens into the Follow the Government "Laws of The Land" Biblical Command

"Obey the government, for God is the One who has put it there. There is no government anywhere that God has not placed in power. So those who refuse to obey the law of the land are refusing to obey God, and punishment will follow."

~ Romans 13:1-2, KJV

… Fundamentalist Must Live Lockstep Slave to Narrow-Minded Book/Chapter/Verse Scriptural Life-Understanding

The nature of the wisdom that controls a worldview mindset set to the limits imposed by knowledge from The Tree of Knowledge of Good and Evil that is borrowed/copied from an outside source (ancient scriptures) is empty of the understanding that comes from gathering self-knowledge used to derive the Tree of Life wisdom.

If behaviors cannot be talked through and ordered in terms of what the written scriptures say, they are fundamentally wrong.

The believer's belief system has an emptiness-of-understanding that cues up when questioned about aspects of the purpose of their theological belief. This is when they must rely on their cognitive collection of memorized book-chapter-verse to explain the cause/effect relational justice that gives a reason, ensuring the future fulfillment of their religion's promise.

The believer's worldview remains handcuffed to whatever arrangement of cause/effect relational justice the religious claim maker (the god) is reported to have said. This is needed to allow the truth of their claim's purpose (claim to a state of heaven) to find its truth.

This leaves religious believers scrambling to memorize book/chapter/verse to defend their courageous leap of blind faith to questioners who might ask "why" or say, "prove it" that may not have swallowed the same pill of promised afterlife.

Rome's edited compilation of Jesus's story they allowed included in their Bible hints at but fails to tell how to kindle the flame of the Tree of Life knowledge source within. Rome needed its citizens to turn to the Caesar-gods of Rome for life direction.

Conversely, self-trained self-assimilated knowledge enlightens a truth seeker with a wisdom-enriched understanding awareness that is engendered from the insightful thinking the self-assimilated knowledge inspires. The understanding associated with the infrastructure of the hierarchy of the self-trained derived wisdom (Tree of Life wisdom) is transparent.

It's self-trained self-assimilated wisdom versus that what's borrowed and mimed.

A fundamental worldview unknowingly has created a stilled spot in the imaginary confines of their cerebral universe. There is a suspended atmosphere where the essence of things and ideas can assume a fixed-in-time permanence they can isolate and become attached to.

The "I AM" persona that is managed by the self-ego they have pieced together will design modern-day fig leaf masks to cover up their emptiness-of-understanding resulting from their abbreviated understanding of the borrowed wisdom they live by ... like Adam and Eve.

Book-Chapter-Verse Chameleon-Like Logistics

Fundamentalist believers in religious theology are OK with deducing the right wisdom intellectually through memorizing and parroting the tracts of theology's abstract logistics. They are OK with piecing together a wisdom patchwork configuration interlinking random bits of biblical wisdom that are taken from the unrelated biblical episodic application to stand behind and to justify their opinion on everyday real-life affairs.

With blind trust in any unverified knowledge, untested truths often self-justify their own tree of unique chameleon-like wisdom. It can be used on-call, to integrate an unnatural relational justice influence into a cause/effect relationship that is needed to demonstrate some skewed perspective of truth.

... Ready With The Book-Chapter-Verse Retort

If the credibility of the Bible-spun imagery's threatened, a seasoned fundamentalist can just rewire its book/chapter/verse justification circuitry and re-sketch the imagery interface for an acceptable intellectual reckoning of the compromised meaning ... they can work up another logic thread of book/chapter/verse to justify it to satisfy another configuration of an angle on perspective.

The unverifiable nature of the subject prevents them from ever really being pinned down.

Religious believers rely on their blind trust in the proclaimed wisdom they have borrowed from the scriptures, which in most situations must be subjectively pieced together and relied on, in hope that their calculated decision will please and not anger their chosen god figure.

They must rationalize a way to synthesize their particularly fashioned book/chapter/verse understanding of the borrowed biblical knowledge to justify the spray of parroted wisdom they use in making their behavioral choices.

Just listen to the Sunday morning TV evangelists' scripture-linked-justifications they use to bring realness to what their imagination has pieced together to represent their unique biblical interpretation. They are fishing for support (some financial) for their personalized biblically fortified opinions of how their listeners should run their lives.

… TV Preacher Biblical Wisdom Quotes Book-Chapter-Verse Logic Strings to Justify Unique Agendas

Sunday morning TV preachers string together a series of personalized biblical book/chapter/verse combos to justify their unique visions.

It's the only source of wisdom their intellectual awareness can find to tap into. They believe it to be unquestionable and infer that it means just what they interpret it to mean. It's their means of relating and using the biblically derived ancient application of the old-time borrowed wisdom to deal with today's ongoing ever-changing barrage of new and untested life circumstance.

… A Cognitively Configured Snapshot of "Heaven"

They settle for the intellectually generated soundness of abstract logistics to secure their intellectual grasp on a religious claim instead of experientially verifying that the claim's purpose can demonstrate its truth while living and pulling its weight somewhere in generating the living flow of this impermanent reality.

To conjure up the due diligence to get their feet wet asking what they feel to be the verification questions that silently prod them concerning their blind faith would help to instill an intrinsic familiarity that strengthens the growth of a fortifying steadfast faith alongside a growing wisdom-enriched intrinsic understanding of the nature of this impermanent reality. It's the first step in adding shareable tangible meaning to understanding the truth about the human condition and eliminating the ignorance thereof … the source of all human suffering.

Posturing Biblical Wisdom Credibility

The unverifiable borrowed knowledge that comprises the different theological topics are open to an endless line of interpretations. To help establish credibility for their theological posers, theologians use media such as TV specials or author articles about their breed of religious theology.

They enlist the highest qualified authorities to report what intellectual conclusion they are left with when trying to shape the most modern interpretation of how the interpretation of the religion's aspects can be best documented into being a working part of today's reality. The conceptualization of any reality with a makeup requiring dimensional continuity is created totally from intellectually configured opinion. They find the best opinion they can to help followers best refashion their cognitive sketches and jump on their wagon.

Theology-related TV specials use high sources of integrity to impart the intellectual knowledge they can find to their audience. They hope it will be assumed to be a fact even though these opinions are still nothing more than educated guesses.

This allows the religious watchers to edit their related conceptualized cognitive still-shot sketches of the subject matter. They find the highest educational degrees possible to lend their calculated wisdom to the listeners, should they want to borrow the presented knowledge to alter the conceptualized image of their version of the intellectually realized and stored subject matter shot at the truth.

Being that a world with a reality having a nature of continuity lacks inclusion in the living pulse of this reality's ongoing change to validate its real-life participation, there really can still be no validation for these opinions, however logically feasible or proportionally crazy they may sound.

Still … continuity is a myth.

It's from a believer's self-shaped untethered understanding of borrowed knowledge that they derive, calculate, or simply parrot twisted wisdom. The wisdom borrowed from the snake left Adam and Eve with no idea what to make of the reality of their state of nakedness. They were both empty-of-understanding of how they fit in.

They were lost to any intrinsically founded intuitive familiarity with what purpose their nakedness filled in this ephemeral reality. Likewise, today the ignorance inspired from the borrowed wisdom that eating white flour products is acceptable comes back to haunt the believer when they find out they have developed diabetes Type II.

Believers Think it Grand to "Book-Chapter-Verse" Bible's Borrowed Wisdom

It is not uncommon to see a religious martinet of sorts standing in the center of a crowd drawn together by their vocal proclamations about what is wrong with society and how their god is going to fix it. They stand Bible-in-hand, defending their unverifiable belief while the crowd stones them with their jeering comments and questions.

... Verbal Stoning

They are being verbally stoned just like the ancient counterparts they have read about in their biblical transcripts.

They may take pride in being persecuted in the name of their god, just like the ancient zealots they have read about. Let the crowd disagree with their proclamations, as there is no way to prove their assertions wrong. The land they speak about is what they have plucked from the imagined continual world that houses their fancy.

What could come straighter from the Tree of Knowledge of Good and Evil than another entity's explanation of what the thread of wisdom is of the principles of relational truth? Some religious believers take pride in being well versed in "God's wisdom" ... in readily knowing "on-call" their scripture answers explaining the relational justice of how things work.

Giving book-chapter-verse of a many-times-translated ancient text is mistakenly thought to be the best way to enlighten those in question.

... Book/Chapter/Verse Chant Euthanizes Pain From Emptiness

A fundamentalist's confident blind faith in their self-trained ability to recite on call from their extensive Bible-stamped borrowed knowledge catalog to repel all the testing from doubters of their calculated Bible-wisdom explaining the cause/effect relational justice determining how things work can bridge over and euthanize the haunting echo from the caverns filling their void of emptiness.

The void of emptiness remains void of understanding. Camouflaging the emptiness's existence only alters how it seeps through. Everyone uniquely arranges their fig leaves.

... Fundamentalist Will Support Borrowed Wisdom ... Right or Wrong

The unavoidable presence of the self-protective red flags of uncertainty and doubt continue to bring to the believer's waking awareness the feeling of emptiness. Yet, this natural curiosity that is supposed to initially trigger the believer to work up the humility and courage to ask why or why not is gagged when the individual repeatedly bows faithfully while consciously blind to what verifies and determines the validity of the borrowed wisdom supporting the promise of their untestable belief.

Their freewill deafness to these belief system red flag warnings increases over time.

Whether the cause/effect account of the borrowed knowledge is true or false does not matter. The emptiness-in-understanding of the process between a cause and its effect cited or predicted by the borrowed knowledge that shapes and supports any resulting wisdom exists regardless ... the devout fundamentalist will wag their book that explains their borrowed wisdom.

In effort to secure the peace found in having emotional balance, many will gag or compromise the inborn right and innate power of their freewill and stop asking questions, step back and adopt the fundamental template of their favored theology. They will adopt the promise made by the theology that best aligns with their conditioned take on reality's mysteries.

Comfort In Unverifiable Nature of Religious Promise

... "It Is My Opinion And There's Nothing Tangible To Disprove It"

Theologians find much comfort in the unverifiable nature of their chosen religious doctrine. Theology's unverifiable environment offers protection from being wrong.

Nobody can objectively disprove a theological take on things unless self-evident on-topic facts have evolved.

If a religious believer finds the courage to have trusting faith in what is blind to understand the cause/effect process that justifies its proclaimed wisdom's truth cannot be verified, then it cannot be disproven.

Being that religious theology's homeland is imaginary and has not been experienced by any living creature, who is to say their way of defining it is wrong? This relationship is unknowingly appealing to many.

Religious belief is a wonderful thing for an individual who has been conditioned to be unable to find it within to allow themselves to be wrong or even just to be corrected. The unverifiable imaginative nature of religious outlook creates an air of invincibility as its truth is determined by subjective opinion.

Others may find similar satisfaction in playing Dungeons and Dragons, in sports fantasy leagues or maybe talking politics.

Over time, strict adherence to a religious discipline's manifesto will gradually bring on a worldview's separation from appreciation for reality's objective truths. Their feel for true compassion's been short-circuited. Empathy gets undercut by an underlying since of inferiority and shame and just does not really make face.

Shielded By Religious "Holier than Thou" Righteousness

... Elitist Attitude Popular Front to Posture Self-Worth

It is not difficult for a fundamentalist in religious theology for example to look at someone's life and pick something they do or are doing that is condemned in their chosen strain of religion. Drinking alcohol or maybe just not attending the right church are common examples.

When they just do not know how to interact with them, they might judge them as sinners to justify sticking their nose in the air and avoiding any social interaction with them.

It is easy for a fundamentalist to feel superior to another individual when they do not attend the only church that is going to heaven.

The seasoned fundamentalist has memorized so much scripture that they are nearly invincible with having book/chapter/verse wisdom to cover about any topic which they feel in their hearts must please their God.

This represents quite an elite group of religious pundits. This gives negative personalities a way to feel superior as they retreat into the lonely world of their own configuration.

The Bible's greater intent should ideally teach humans how to consciously harbor the altruistic impulse that seeds and feeds compassion. The scriptures are said not to be used as a tool to judge others to allow casting the first stone and to then retreat into a "better than they are" attitude which justifies not associating with them to set a good example through behavior.

This elitist attitude reflects social insecurity echoing up from the emptiness that rings from the void of uncertainty ... empty of conscious altruistic ties to expressing compassion ... lonely and on guard to snap out.

One Person's Truth is Another Person's Fairytale

... Imagined Construct of Reality's Different for Everyone

Just because an individual might adopt to having blind faith in the notion of an unverifiable tale of the spirit they have pieced together and internalized, does not mean it holds true for others. The truth of their imagined world is unique to their imagination.

Scripture understandings are unique products of each believer's uniquely conditioned worldview. A believer of theology can become tied up and lost in their conceived continual world of what their imagination has sketched their answer to the unknown to be.

When a religious theology believer defends or tries to explain what their religious conviction means when questioned by an outsider, they must use the perceived impressions of their own uniquely conditioned worldview to interpret what they feel the intended message was meant to be. The biblical translation they use to understand what their god's proclaimed cause/effect relational justice is meant to be to fulfill his promise of being able to jump from living suffering to afterlife non-suffering requires their unique imaginative inputs to connect the dots.

A religious believer relies on the cause-into-effect wisdom framework that shaped their worldview over their lifetime to figure, derive, and weigh the wisdom sought from the borrowed knowledge taken from their chosen religion's manual of cause/effect relational justice (scriptures.) The type of knowledge an individual might use to condition their worldview from day one is what sets the footprint for the nature of their connection with this reality to bend towards.

Watch Sunday morning TV preachers and get a glimpse into the interpretation kaleidoscope of Bible-sourced God's wisdom. It is all about how the preacher's belief system has been conditioned to perceive things that determine how and what they will pull from the halls of their imagination to reflect their impression of what the scripture's borrowed wisdom might mean.

A believer's pre-conditioned worldview is where the borrowed wisdom of any religious theology is first analyzed and finds its meaning.

Every internalized description of what makes up a religion's theological purpose, heavenly location, and the cast of characters contribute to form a patchwork of mental snapshots cognitively pieced together.

This gives it an unverifiable dimension set within the limits of each believer's imagination suspended in the mental scape requiring a continuous dimensional reality.

Where to Draw the Line … Power-in-Numbers

A devout fundamentalist might assume an individual who is introduced to them as being Christian as someone who is not living by their congregation's fine point standards and to be hell-bound.

However, when it comes to asking a fundamentalist about how high Christianity ranks in the ranking ladder of world religions a non-defined muddled-over all-inclusion understanding can filter in.

Like in horseshoes or tossing hand grenades where close is good enough, a bit of a twist on their blind faith writes those Christians who don't live by the fine point standards of their congregation a hall pass to be an acceptable member of the Christian click count … going to hell or not.

When a fundamentalist's blind Christian faith is challenged and they feel cornered to establish and justify their religion's significance and demonstrate this through its worldwide existence and acceptance, a defensive panic can sit in. If they do not quote the scriptures to prove their faith's legitimacy, they might seek verification through power-in-numbers. Christianity has xx members, Islam has xx members, Buddhism has xx members ... and so on.

The number grows, even though, on the other hand, since most of those Christians don't believe what their congregation believes, they're all going to hell.

When sitting down around a multi-generational dinner table of a Christian family where through the years the children have branched out into different strains of Christianity, their dinner prayer still addresses the same god. Even though a few might belong to a congregation who believes that all others are going to hell, the atmosphere suddenly becomes accepting of all who call themselves Christian.

The boogieman of their unknown has been stirred and awakened. The premise of their unique cognitively designed guard over their fear of the great unknown has been questioned. They seek conscious reassurance that they are in the safe zone.

By selectively enabling their "close-enough" qualifier, they will lower their stringent qualifiers and accept all proclaimed Christians as members of their religious fraternity.

... Religious templates are offered to corral society's discontent. Many will retreat into fundamentalism and close their eyes to understanding reality's truth. They suffer.

... To this day, humankind is born ignorance-cursed, sin-bound to suffer God's Garden of Eden Curse to squander in Fundamental Ignorance, Empty of Understanding, in search of Eden's Emotional Bliss.

... Intrinsically generated intuitive impulse guides behavior in most situations. Realigning that intrinsic impulse with the Tree of Life principles that extend the outcomes that define the present moment will bring an individual closer to finding the true peace of emotional balance. One can't constantly try to interpret what borrowed wisdom might say.

IX

Have You Been Fatally Fooled?

"It's easier to fool people than to convince them they've been fooled.
No amount of evidence will convince an idiot."

~ Mark Twain

"Religion is for people afraid of going to hell...
Spirituality is for those who see it and want out."

~ Indianapolis Westside bumper sticker

After publicly playing one's spiritual hand ... banking the credibility of their ability to analyze how their life condition best fits into its life experience ... taking the initial leap of blind faith ... believer's letting it be publicly known that they without any verification believe in the borrowed wisdom from a particular theological notion.

Personal pride steps in and neuters the idea of any future reversals of that belief.

Yes, pride is thought to be the original and most deep reaching of the seven deadly cardinal sins. It is thought to be the source from which the others arise.

Fundamental Ignorance *and* the Garden of Eden Curse

Fundamental ignorance entails not understanding that this reality has an impermanent transforming nature that allows no state of time continuity to exist, so there's no reason to get attached to what doesn't exist.

Fundamental ignorance is the cornerstone of Siddhartha's teachings explaining the circle of suffering. It's the founding truth of the philosophy explaining Buddhism.

Fundamental ignorance entails thinking that things can assume an unchanging presence. This allows an individual to become emotionally attached to some facet of the unchanging illusion of something or some idea.

... The Cause of All Human Suffering

Attachment to and the craving for things that do not exist is the cause of all human misery and suffering. Individuals suffer from the kaleidoscope of emotionally spun feelings wrapped in this ignorance.

This suffering can be realized as the living hell that humans fear and seek relief from Having it promised in the afterlife and to last forever is icing on the cake.

It stuns reverence into the new believer.

Religious believers can then spend their lives dreaming about finding that emotional bliss in an afterlife-promised paradise. There's no reason it shouldn't last forever when it logical that a person is going to be dead forever.

It could be said that humans are born ignorance-cursed and sin-bound to suffer Jehovah's Garden of Eden curse. They are born stripped of the conscious ability to sense their subconscious understanding awareness of the nature of this impermanent reality.

It seems that individuals are born with varying levels of "street sense." And of course, how an individual is conditioned has a great effect on this.

But still ... people just aren't born "enlightened" about the ways of impermanence ... a full catalogue of Tree of Life wisdom.

They can spend their entire life walking the Earth lost in Fig Leaf Wisdom emptiness-of-understanding,

This fundamental ignorance comes generationally stamped into human DNA. It could be said in a theological sense, that mankind's been Eden-cursed by God to flail in spiritual confusion, not understanding the nature of this reality.

Theology doesn't observe that man has the due diligence to figure out that he lives in a state of suffering ... that it has a cause ... that the cause is part of the living reality and that he, a part of this living reality, has the power to eliminate that cause and find the emotional bliss that lies on the other side of their ignorance.

Mankind struggles, having to figure out how the human condition fits into the reality of the human experience.

Most individuals get conditioned to subconsciously and out of ignorance, create imagined breaks of continuity in this reality's unchangeable impermanent flow of change to preserve a mental snapshot of the imagined continual existence of things and objects.

There just aren't that many individuals qualified that are around to teach those who are ignorant. It varies from culture to culture.

... Fundamental Ignorance Leads to this Mindset

Many do not think deep enough to realize how Father Time has too many plates spinning while providing an uninterrupted feed of unexplored naked change maintaining this reality's animated yet elusive present moment to say "freeze" and say "cheese."

Many believe they can take selfies in the passage of time.

For many, the imagined time-suspended essence of the remembered image of objects and ideas can register as being real and have a continual presence. This would require an unnatural imagined reality with a supporting transforming dimensional backdrop that can allow for a "pause" in time for the existence of their subject of thought.

In this impermanent reality, while the human body might be recognized as being a solid mass, it is no more than the transforming presence involving a series of separate time-linked events ... metaphysical subatomic bits of appearing/disappearing bits of energy.

Without self-training the procedure, the human perception cannot fine tune enough to sensually detect this ongoing process of change.

... Over Time Believers Can Develop a Hardening of the Heart

Once an individual who harbors growing fears of what unknown surprise the naked change of impermanence will next confront them with concedes to borrowing the unverifiable wisdom of a strain of religious theology or "giving their soul to Jesus" they will probably not have the mental energy or desire to be able to effectively derive another strain of wisdom.

They have been spiritually sidetracked and mentally extended by the exhausting process of adapting that knowledge into their belief system to reshape their worldview.

They will still not understand what strain of knowledge they need to seek to allow deriving life wisdom. Keeping their eye pealed for a sounder path to follow grows old with time and they will become less receptive to new options.

Fooled on Which Sense of Reality to Acknowledge?

"Sometimes the questions are complicated, and the answers are simple."

-Dr. Seuss

... Which Sense of Reality to Honor ... Apparent or Universal?

An individual might recognize the exterior presence of something and see that as what reality apparently is. However, if they recognize the formless collection of transforming energy activity that supports that outside shape, they are recognizing the universal reality.

... Jehovah's Garden of Eden Mandate Points the Way

As the Earth cooled from its Garden of Eden creation, in the first topic of the God-to-man chat, Christianity's God Jehovah issued mankind a life-or-death spiritual ultimatum with a zero-tolerance rider.

Mankind was not asked but was ordered to live by Tree of Life wisdom to continue in the Eden paradise sense of living. Accepting borrowed wisdom from the Tree of Knowledge would result in spiritual death ... committing the original sin?

After Jehovah's confrontation for choosing borrowed Tree of Knowledge wisdom from the snake of temptation, Adam and Eve were sentenced to live outside of Eden, approaching life suffering while armed only with the emptiness-of-understanding ... inherent to Fig Leaf Wisdom.

... Genesis Author ... A True Genius ... Life's Most Important Distinction

Both theology's Old Testament Genesis account of creation and the self-evident truths of this universal reality point to the same thing when considering what makes up emotional bliss or creates an emotional living hell.

Theology maintains the process of realizing awareness of this universal reality on an intellectual level of understanding and Realism takes realizing this awareness for the full circle from mere intellectual recognition to converting the intellectually understanding into an experientially founded sensually metered intrinsic understanding.

It is thought by many that Moses wrote Genesis as well as the first few books of the Old Testament Hebrew Bible. Moses or whichever mortal wrote those scriptures was a very wise individual to realize what the most important aspect of the human living experience is and to present it as the doorstep to the storyline of the Bible.

He was enlightened about this primal life truth. And like Jesus used parables to educate the ignorant, Moses used an analogy of sorts.

An individual must wonder who was there to witness the Garden of Eden-bound relationship between Jehovah and Adam, being that Adam was the only human being at the time. Maybe being that Jehovah is a god, he inspired the account details to Moses?

To live in emotional bliss, it is necessary to gather the appropriate strain of wisdom-deriving knowledge to develop or maintain the Tree of Life strain of wisdom ... not to just believe what you are told to be true as with Tree of Knowledge directives, leaving you Fig Leaf empty-of-understanding ignorant.

Moses realized that to be emotionally fit, it is necessary to understand how things naturally relate to each other. He realized the only way to do this is through experience.

The Garden of Eden Analogy makes the importance of this either/or dilemma truly clear if one carefully reads in between the fig leaves.

This is the either/or decision every human must make ... knowingly or not.

Christian theology's Rome-edited account falls short of telling how to reach or maintain that Tree of Life plateau of enlightened understanding awareness.

... Siddhartha's Enlightened Perspective Details How to Get There

While focused on the same bright white light of emotional bliss at the end of the tunnel of human experience, Siddhartha Gautama gives a detailed description of how he self-trained himself to became enlightened about humanity's fundamental ignorance ... while still alive ... still able to experience and learn.

Being worlds apart in time and location ... Moses and Siddhartha ... makes no difference. There is only one truth ... one light.

They were both just messengers ... like Jesus was.

Borrowed Knowledge-Fed Ignorance Feeds the Boogieman of the Unknown

... Lacks Experiential Knowledge to Verify and Yield Insight-Enriched Thinking to Inspire a Steadfast Faith-Backed Understanding

The emptiness filling the void of understanding of the child-minded of any age in a misunderstood reality gives life to and feeds the imaginary monsters of the unknown and misunderstood that might be hiding under their bed of life karma or that might be waiting to leap out of a dark corner of their hushed-up past.

This self-designed bottleneck of ignorance will prod an individual's present moment consciousness with the painful thought that something is missing from the status quo. It takes hostage the answer to the unknown question they are inwardly longing to find while inadvertently hoping it will somewhere surface from what they daily pillage through during the activities of their everyday life.

Their emptiness-of-understanding sets shadow to the path to and distances them from the answer.

Starting with the Primal Basics ... Nature of Reality

"Do not trust atoms, they make up everything."
~Self-Evident Truth

Everything that appears in the range of human perception is real, but this is not the ultimate reality.

On a more subtle level there is another world of activity that is the ultimate reality and explains misperceptions made about the other.

Within the subatomic world there are "quarks" of energy that come and go only to the rhythm determined by the dimensional forces that house this reality. Their ever-changing relationships create what can seem to be unchanging.

People will see only the seeming permanent state of these things in seeing only the outline that houses the everchanging bits of energy inside. They will assign these things names and classification to judge and compare.

They will form likings and dislikings to these things.

In their fundamental ignorance that ignores the true state of change in process, from these perceptions, people will form the attachment and aversion that causes their suffering.

The nature of this reality is to be in a state of ongoing transformation.

... The Present Moment is Ever-Evasive

"There's no present. There's only the immediate future and the recent past."
~George Carlin

Yes ... the ever-elusive present moment ... It takes a mere instant to form a perception of what the changing reality throws in one's lap but as that very present moment point in the flow of time becomes instant history, that perception becomes prior conditioning.

The transforming energy configuration of all matter and the push and pull of what influences ideas and beliefs are continually changing. This process never stops. That is the self-evident unchangeable nature of this reality's impermanent dimensional makeup and pattern to the logic and proportion of its derived wisdom.

... "Now" is the Only Presence of Reality Humans Have to Reference

The passing present moment of this impermanent reality is the only feeling of life humanity has experienced. Like asking a fish to describe what "wet" means, it is a tricky thing for an individual to appreciate and express an intrinsically wet idea of what the passing present moment feel of a future-cast "heaven" might be like.

... Every Human Must Recognize Reality's Presence as Transforming ... Or Maybe Not

Every human being will be conditioned to make a most primal of subtle distinctions, probably unknowingly, that will circumscribe the nature of their mind.

This decision will affect the degree of emotional unrest they experience during their lifetime. It serves as the foundation for the sort of wisdom they use ... how they reason.

This distinction is reflected in choosing to either spend their waking time assimilating the appropriate type of knowledge to allow insightfully deriving the Jehovah-backed Tree of Life strain of wisdom to pursue and realize the Garden of Eden emotional bliss or experience spiritual death from borrowing and internalizing the Tree of Knowledge strain of wisdom as Jehovah so forewarned.

... Youth's Decisions Reflect Their Vision of This Reality's Nature

During childhood innocence, a youth is exposed to wisdom-welding knowledge typifying the nature of both Garden of Eden Trees of wisdom.

When emerging from their world of innocence and assuming responsibility for decisions made in life and how those decisions are made, everyone will knowingly or unknowingly expose which texture of knowledge they ingest to trust in shaping the nature of their worldview wisdom.

Everyone is liable for the nature of the knowledge their freewill chooses to use to vindicate the wisdom that lines their worldview ... as God's warning and punishment to Adam exemplify. The Tree of Life ... knowledge of cause/effect relational justice supporting an impermanent reality or the Tree of (borrowed) Knowledge purporting wisdom to explain everything from Good to Evil ... knowledge supported by cause/effect relational justice honoring time/space/mass continuity.

... Many Go Through Life Unaware of Difference ... Tangled Up in Theology

Making this distinction determines how an individual is predisposed to recognize and perceive this reality's time/space/mass relationship and how it affects their understanding of how the texture of the human condition finds its place or fits into their understanding of their human experience.

Making this distinction lies at everyone's ground zero point of primal importance and might very well lay the groundwork for the primal ignorance that will color their life with different shades of suffering.

An individual's worldview is conditioned to perceive the nature of this reality's state of presence as being one of ongoing transformation or one that naively allows the imagined continuity of objects and ideas ... an enhanced virtual reality of sorts.

At this point in the evolution of mankind, most will indeed die totally unaware of the nature of any such ignorance that results in all forms of human suffering or its cause. The problem and its solution do not ring any religious theological bell.

Siddhartha's pathway isn't considered theological as it's not based in theory. It's supported truth becomes to prove self-evident.

The problem and its solution involve how an individual develops their belief system to shape their worldview.

The Bible does not offer much here. The decision to follow a religion's unverifiable pitch comes as a product of how the belief system has been fine-tuned to allow the worldview to be developed ... whether to bite on the fruit of borrowed theological knowledge or only settle for what's experientially verifiable as God forewarned to only ingest knowledge from the Tree of Life.

In modern society, conscious acknowledgment of this decision paradox usually slides by totally unrecognized by most. That does not matter. How individuals are conditioned (probably subconsciously) to perceive what they see in this reality's present moment dimensional footprint ... how they might perceive the nature of its time/space/mass dimensional makeup ... impermanent or continual ... still echoes from their every decision. This demonstrates the character of the cumulative nature of acquired knowledge forming the collective substance of wisdom personified through their worldview ... the nature of their mind.

Gathering the right knowledge and deriving the appropriate wisdom to understand the truth of this reality's impermanent ways wards off the ignorance-inspired emotional suffering caused by not understanding it. It is the thin and narrow pathway leading away from suffering in ignorance to realizing emotional bliss.

That is the Tree of Life wisdom Jehovah told Adam was necessary to live in a spiritual state of "Eden."

A Trip Down the Rabbit Hole into Theology's Wonderland

While chasing her White Rabbit, Jefferson Airplane's Alice slipped down her rabbit hole into the Wonderland of her ultra-creative imagination. Like Alice, after choosing to borrow and follow one of theology's carrots-on-a-stick to eliminate suffering, religious believers must enter the creative dimension of their imagination to create a mental hologram framework to support their understanding of the intellectually metered theological plan they've decided to blindly follow into their grave.

Due to the sensually foreign unverifiable conditions being considered in any theological notion, a truth-seeker must make imagination-appeasing twists in the non-compromising laws of nature that give conforming order to reality's impermanent dimensional makeup to be able to harbor the thought in their imagination-spun reality.

In Alice's mental Wonderland depiction of reality, no matter what living forms or unusual circumstances were needed to make real Alice's mental apparitions, the dimensional makeup of her imagined reality was able to supply some unnatural need-fulfilling creature or material concoction to satisfy the essence of the deeper agenda behind her unusual nature-bending thoughts.

... Must Recognize and Accept the Nature of Reality's Backdrop

Being an inclusive part of Mother Nature, the human mind and body reverberates the input of nature's present moment energy-change menu. To get along emotionally in this eddy of energy, it's best to understand it … to become enlightened about its nature.

However, prior conditioning plays a major role in shaping how an individual learns to gather knowledge to cultivate their perception of new sensual input and make life decisions.

For an individual's belief system to successfully acclimate to the possibility of a knowledge source's method of making true its predicted claim … i.e., supernaturally bestowed suffering relief or maybe some sort of miracle, they must accept the nature of the reality backdrop that's needed for their level of spiritual maturity to find sync with this reality's natural laws of impermanence to support allowing what needs to happen for the borrowed knowledge-purported promise to attain its promised end.

In believing and internalizing any bit of knowledge, the believer is acknowledging the state of this reality's presence to have one of two natures. The state of a reality's presence involves the nature of the reality's multi-dimensional makeup as either being in the transforming state of impermanence that does not know the meaning of "still" or in an imagined state of continuity that allows what is thought of to assume a state of stillness.

Strain of Wisdom
Supports the Nature of Reality Backdrop it Decodes

... Impermanent or Continual

This reality's dimensional backdrop is the interwoven cocktail of nature's gravitational and electromagnetic forces that keep the river of time flowing within its banks. This is the animated life show that humanity perceives as being the present moment.

Religious theology dogma asserts that it is their perspective god that is the mystical force that created via "intelligent design" and controls all the principles that sustain all change-forming relational interactions.

Choosing to internalize Tree of Knowledge wisdom, like Adam and Eve, or deciding to experientially derive the Tree of Life strain of wisdom that Jehovah mandated relates directly to the way or how an individual has been conditioned to perceive the nature of what happens in the present moment of this reality as being in a sensually metered impermanent ephemeral state of transformation or allowing for time's skip-in-record continual intellectually metered presence.

Choosing which type of media source, sensual or intellectual, a truth seeker uses to gather the type of knowledge to assimilate and derive the strain of wisdom they use to base life decisions is something individuals use their freewill to control.

An Imagined Reality

"Anything or thought perceived to "be" is an illusion … beauty lies in how the uninhibited freedom of something's, or thought's resolved purpose adapts it to extend the cause/effect rhythm that gives flow to the present moment."

~ Mother Nature

… Finding Another Reality to Grip

"Being insane is not losing your grip on reality, it's finding another reality to grip."

~ unknown source

Any reality with natural laws that are not of the type monitoring this impermanent reality is an imagined reality. It is not one of impermanence. Imagined realities use a reality backdrop exhibiting continuity and not impermanence.

This allows bending the natural laws that give order to how things in the reality exist.

The dimensions and limitations of intellectually transferred reality descriptions having only a cognitively etched presence are totally defined in the regions of individual imagination. If it is not a reality with a dimensional makeup that is impermanent, it must have a supporting dimensional makeup that honors some unnatural arrangement of the reality's time/space/mass relationship (some degree of continuity) … as described by the cause/effect relational justice statutes set or implied by the maker of the borrowed claim that the believer decided to blindly internalize.

This order in understanding or having the feel for the cause/effect order of relational situations leads to the believer's miscued misaligned perception of how the cause/effect relationships of many of their life situations are linked together … what cause(s) accounts for which effect(s).

The code of relational justice piecing together the natural laws woven into the cause/effect rhythm that keeps this living world's multi-dimensional impermanent makeup glued together is the same one that writes the script for how everything in this universe relates and how it maintains a natural balance … from the coming and going of the subatomic quarks of energy to the center of a celestial black hole (Science is still figuring out the black hole.)

It follows that the way the relational justice guiding how things interrelate as they coexist would very well differ in the imaginary realities of theological worlds with cause/effect claims that have to recognize non-impermanent natures of continuity that are given unique forms in the imaginations of its believers.

Ask Star Trek's Mr. Spock about the relational laws that rule the ways of his Vulcan world reality or maybe Yoda about the natural laws that rule the reality controlling the Force or the Dark Side in the reality of Star Wars. It is clear from watching shows like Star Trek, Star Wars, and maybe even the Twilight Zone or Lost in Space, how worlds from the far reaches of the universe … from the corners of mankind's imagination have different realities with different dimensional setups that fall in step to a different set of laws of relational justice.

But of course, everyone knows that all those alien worlds are figments of human imagination.

Conditioned Ignorance … A Time-Stilled Mental Hologram

… No Two Holograms are the Same

From the earliest age, USA citizens are exposed to a culture professing there is a reality with a different nature than the one their five senses report to exist. This is confusing to anybody … especially the young.

Through the various means of handed down misguided conditioning from parents, grandparents, schoolteachers, national anthems and currency, courthouse lawns, license plates, historically endorsed passed-along religious design, religious pundits, friends and etcetera … the greater part of the collective USA belief system has been stymied into recognizing and accepting an unverifiable separate reality.

This separate reality requires recognizing an unnatural state of reality dimensional presence that allows time-continual hiccups for an individual's mental sketch drawings to be stilled in time. They mentally sketch a mental hologram depicting what wisdom-deriving knowledge (Bible's wisdom) they have "received" or "borrowed" from another entity. This image and state of reality are imaginary.

This imagined reality's state of continual stilled time allows individuals to become attached to these mental holograms of any sort of object or idea that they can become emotionally tied to. This casting of imagined stilled representations of former likes and dislikes in an imaginary world creates the sense of attachment that allows for unfounded emotions that cause the individual's suffering.

Holograms Play No Role
in Supporting Reality's Ephemeral Life Matrix

"It is not impermanence that makes us suffer. What makes us suffer is wanting things to be permanent when they are not."

~ Thich Nhat Hanh

These cognitively assembled still-shot notions find their only connection to this living world being that they hang suspended in the believer's active living mind. The truth they purport makes no active contribution or plays no role in affecting the flow process of this reality's impermanent state.

Theology's purported truths can't be shown to be self-evident. Truths/powers/forces that set the principles that rule this reality can be shown to be true or false. Theology's truths are all debatable.

Memories representing these illusory bits of imagination that they have no physical or sensual history with occupy only a place in the individual's cognitive world. The essence of their presence must hang suspended in an imaginary state of continuity.

It waits in an intellectually scripted state of imagination. The mental hologram cannot find real-life purchase to be a contributory part in making real its host's journey on life's transitory canvas.

How someone has been conditioned to perceive reality will affect their conscious level of life insight capability that determines their ability to understand the twists and turns in their human experience that affect their state of emotional well-being.

Making this type-of-reality distinction is such a subtle primal early life process that it probably remains consciously undetected by the vast majority.

But still, it is a distinction every human being must make.

"Tree of Knowledge of Good and Evil"
Relies on Time Continuity

The strain of wisdom supporting the Tree of Knowledge reality perception pairs with the individual who seeks/borrows wisdom that has been derived or originates from another entity. It makes sense for being in an imaginary reality that needs the added unnatural dimensional backdrop characteristic of continuity of time.

Borrowed knowledge relies on the borrower compromising or neutering the inborn self-protecting guard of an alerted freewill. On internalization, without having any experiential palate on which to draw any steadfast faith, it somehow contracts the believer's anti-doubt-blazed hardened shell of blind trust.

In Genesis 3:5, the snake misguided Eve in its promise that the wisdom fruit from the Tree of Knowledge would instill all-knowing wisdom: "For God doth know that in the day ye eat thereof, then your eyes shall be opened, and ye shall be as gods, knowing good and evil."

Eve … then Adam simply had to take the snake's word for the promised results.

Time continuity allows an individual to capture and contemplate the subject of a memory in an unnatural state of non-change … something to possibly get attached to.

With this shade of intellectually metered knowledge, the believer does not understand the origination of the cause/effect process the source of knowledge describes or relates to that develops the wisdom the promise needs to justify.

They cannot defend or explain its foundation or infrastructure based on their actual experience. They can only quote the promised claim and wait on its coattails, praying in hope that it is true.

There is no way to test and verify the living consistency of the religious calling this scripted knowledge represents in the living confinements of this impermanent reality to be enlightened about the "how" and "why" of its living purpose. Its cause/effect storyline is very undefined, and its interpretation is completely open to imagination.

A reality suited to satisfy Christianity's theologized claim to an afterlife paradise exists only in the imaginary still-time/space/mass dimensional continuity makeup needed to cognitively sketch and suspend the intellectual interpretation sparked by what was read or heard.

This dimensional continuity is different from that found in this ever-changing living ultimate reality.

Nothing ever stands still.

Borrowed Wisdom Path to Attachment and Suffering

… Most Never Really Have A Chance From The Start

Conventional human conditioning facilitates misperceiving this reality's dimensional nature as continual … not impermanent. Most will never consider the split-second difference unless they're fortunate enough to have a qualified spiritual teacher.

Borrowed wisdom itself, like with Adam and Eve, or wisdom intellectually calculated from borrowed bits of unverified knowledge, leaves a void of understanding what that wisdom's supposed to decode.

To get a foothold on life, a child borrows and internalizes intellectual wisdom from the ones they trust. Most are conditioned to believe and internalize answers to life questions without knowing the importance of establishing more of a conscious familiarity with the claim's circle of truth.

Being conditioned to have a trusting blind faith in all sorts of things from birth onward sets such an early norm for accepting this type of wisdom-deriving knowledge packaged wisdom as-is. Without being lucky enough to find qualified spiritual guidance, most never really stand a chance at finding the right path to understanding or becoming enlightened to their ignorance of how the truth of impermanence affects their emotional makeup that inspires their suffering to rediscover their innate capacity for compassionate joy and happiness.

... Attachment Seeps In

With any strain of borrowed wisdom, while compromising the belief system to make room for the imagination-fed abstract state of dimensional continuity that bends the natural laws of an impermanent state of order, in seeps attachment to the remembered liked or disliked essence of things or ideas.

An individual might only recognize the outer appearance of something that's merely an apparent reality. Their perception ignores the state of constant transformation that's really happening.

The state of continuity of what they're perceiving is imaginary. It's something they can develop a craving attachment for or aversion to. They can suffer from negative emotional states resulting from the imagined relationship state they have in their mind.

The thoughts one has about things they might think are non-changing are no more than thoughts about their present moment perception of a memory. A later mood-influenced perception of that same event will have itself changed. The light under which they choose to bring it back into their thoughts will be affected by their changing mood-conditioned perception.

They live in an emotional minefield full of the hurtful feelings that can arise from believing they have relationships with things that really don't exist.

... Ignorance-Spawned Self-Crafted Ego Steps In

"Your body is not a noun. It's a verb. You are not your body you are its creator."
~Deepak Chopra

It does not work to have a still-shot from an unreal reality drafted into one's cognitive screenplay. It force-plays an unwanted bookmark in the ongoing flutter of reality's turning page.

Living in a state of confused ignorance teetering in between the swirl of this reality's ongoing transformation that flows in step with the rhythm of time and religious theology's imagined reality that stands still in time, an individual will develop an overseeing self-ego to manage and protect their confused human condition from what the unknown might have in store during their empty-of-understanding journey through their human experience.

Using the mental impressions of their most complimentary self-images collected from their favorite photos or glances in the mirror and maybe from the most flattering comments from friends, their imagination will piece together an unchanging "I AM" that was there to witness these highlighted things.

This ego will manage and protect this wannabe caricature "I AM" and anything associated with it.

In the cognitively designed imagined reality suspended in their waking consciousness, their self-ego will visualize this "I AM" persona to be different than the living world. They feel a strong duty to protect the physical and social integrity of the pictured image they have forged.

... Self-Ego Squanders Day Energy Posturing "I Am" Self-Image

They will use up their waking mental energy just trying to maintain social poise in ways they perceive as socially cool or religiously proper. Their meter of suffering will swing wildly in both directions as they search for the missing answer to find and sustain emotional balance.

Mental notions give rise to imaginary things. When things can stand still on a pad of time, they become still objects worthy of possession that will have all sorts of real emotions attached to their imagined continuity. Their imagination convincingly overrides their innate sense of reality and superficially, yet unknowingly tags this becoming reality as having a dimensional nature of continuity.

In their mind, this caricature can lose the natural elasticity it needs to change as it hangs suspended while they add and take away from the essence of its wannabe state. While in denial, many will go to all lengths to hide their graying hair and erase the wrinkles and even the smile lines that give true form and definition to their face and the time-laced events that gave them their form.

They will use this continuous reality of which "I AM" is the center figure to house their imagination's evolving unique depiction of the claim defended by the wisdom they have borrowed that they have no verified understanding of for to culture their impression of what the wisdom-deriving knowledge describes the claim and its end to be.

They live confused in the rub between what they're intellectually recorded reality is and what their life experience shows it to be.

They will ruminate their day away while in a very subtle level of their conscious awareness, trying to figure out what the real question is that they are trying to find an answer for.

... And They Suffer

Suffering starts with having a sense of reality where one can assume a state of permanence.

Is love really ever lost? Or does its presence just change over time ... transform into another emotional reckoning? It will keep changing and eventually "time will heal" the emotional pain in learning how to realistically recognize and accept the involved principles.

The sufferer grows emotionally. They become a bit more enlightened about the relational principles that their ignorance of, was causing their suffering,

An individual can look back into snippets of time, dwelling on memories, thinking the objects of memories of those spots of history's timeline still exist. Their managing self-ego can pull from their imagination a snapshot of a past time and develop a craving attachment to that captured moment on time's 4-dimensional timeline and suffer.

The strain of wisdom supporting an imagined reality will do nothing to help in better understanding the principles of nature of this living reality that are not imagined.

With attachment, the human experience becomes an emotional rollercoaster ride triggered by feelings of loss, worry, misery, regret, envy, and other emotional ties created from the attachment to the imagined permanence of anything affecting anything related to their ego-managed imaginary concept of "I-AM".

When challenged in understanding life principles, an individual might anticipate certain causes to bring about certain effects that do not. They can be shaken by things that happen with causes that were totally unforeseen. They will suffer when they rely on this borrowed wisdom in daily events and miscalculate what the cause/effect relationships in this living impermanent reality are.

Their wisdom deriving logistics are empty-of-understanding. Their Fig Leaf Wisdom has failed them.

Something imagined existing in the illusionary land of continuity is something that the unwise can grab a hold of for better footing to better withstand the ongoing storm of unanticipated ever-change. They worry about something they might miss or lose and are shaken by whatever emotion might trickle down attached to something imagined that does not even exist in this impermanent reality.

They have developed emotional states and addictions that define their personality. A truth-seeker must realize there is no "I AM" or anything standing still long enough to grab hold of.

They must see that there is another world ... the ultimate reality ... that they can't see but are a living part of. The outer shells they see, that house the ongoing coming and going bits of energy that supply the life to those things create the illusionary presence of an object they can judge and become attached to.

They must overcome reacting to the debilitating state of craving ... the itch that must be scratched.

... Shared Compassion Pays the Price

Choosing to develop an "I AM" centered conscious awareness cuts short the altruistic capacity for issuing compassionate attention. It distances attention to recognizing the equal importance of the presence of others and their issues.

A fundamentalist lifestyle is lonely.

Their present moment core is more about "me." Over time, with uncompromised clinging to an ego-managed sense of an imagined "I am" that's postured in their own very real emotional minefield they lose their mental room to give attention to the emotional world of others.

When they're lost in their own emotional makeup, how can they empathize with the life situations of others.

In choosing not to recognize the innate force that drives their human condition to understand the relationships and ways of the dimensional makeup that govern this impermanent reality ... to be ignorant about its fundamentals, an individual invites the suffering that follows.

This is the product of fundamental ignorance in its most primal sense.

Most decisions made founded in wisdom-deriving knowledge having to allow for a reality of continuity, with the inability to understand the ways of impermanence will only fan the raging flame of the individual's internal living hellfire.

From Mystical Ancient Times of Magical Superstition to the Age of Reason

... "Burning Bush" Protocol Morphs into the Scientific Method

Science without religion is lame. Religion without science is blind.
~ Albert Einstein

Humankind's specie emergence has been carbon dated to have been from around 200K years ago. Seventy-five thousand years ago mankind's cognitive revolution kicked in.

African caves have revealed early works of art that show how man's finally been stirred from its cognitive limbo.

Individuals have since chosen how to recognize the unknowns and uncertainties.

Some will either figure things out to understand the self-evident truth responsible when possible, or when too complicated, some might keep asking questions and testing ideas while others will force their freewills to have blind faith in unverifiable accounts of godly entities that were said to control the questioned event or to even have created nature itself.

The process of generating mankind's insightful understandings of the principles that affect nature's ways continues today. Humankind has a very much deeper and growing understanding of Mother Nature's life principles that the ignorance of once seeded all sorts of imaginative theory (theologies) to somehow fill the void of mankind's emptiness-of-understanding.

Today's explanations bring fear-reducing understanding to the mysterious unknown. This helps restore or at least come closer to mankind's collective emotional balance/bliss.

Today, mankind better understands the nature of reality better than at any other time in history. During the COVID19 pandemic, mankind understood the natural principles that determine the outcome of cellular activity well enough to set the pattern for a vaccination that could pump up the now understood antibodies to cripple the proteins that affect the cellular infection.

Mankind is no longer empty of understanding human DNA characteristics. It is now possible to do what was once thought of as miraculous.

Another example is that through discovering and developing the understanding of the chromosomes that comprise DNA, mankind can predict the characteristics and alter the development of an embryo.

Humanity is consciously waking up to the natural principles that Mother Nature uses to control the events that mankind once assigned to certain gods that were rumored to exist.

Mankind's understanding awareness of what "heavenly bliss" is, has also grown immensely in step with its understanding awareness of "scientific" principles.

The understanding truth those that use their imagination to create gods-in-charge to explain things and those who settle for nothing but demonstrating the self-evident truth, both focus on the same bright white light of emotional bliss.

... Science is Born ... Mankind's Freewill Pushes Beyond the Mystical Age of Magic

Greeks were first to attribute changes in our environment to natural forces and not from their palace of gods ... Zeus and his crew.

The theory that atoms are the building blocks of material objects finally emerged. With the understanding that things not understood might have a natural origin ... science was born.

The Lutheran Reformation demonstrates how even within the ranks of Rome's church while evolving from calculations founded in borrowed wisdom, the understanding of how the human condition fits into its human experience is evolving.

Martin Luther explained how there are no human/godlike intermediaries between the average individual and Jehovah. He taught how salvation is based on faith and not earned or purchased. (The self-evident truth is peeking through, yet still shadowed by misunderstanding.)

Yes, mankind's collective consciousness is maturing. As its collective waking awareness questioned superstition, around the middle of this millennia, it found the courage to openly evolve from just believing in magic to understanding what produces the magic.

The scientific method of testing phenomena has been around since before the 16th century. Leonardo Di Vinci posed the necessity for an individual to doubt what they know and to ask questions. He said the answers should be supported by experimentation.

Whether it be under the guise of speculative realism, speculative physics or maybe theoretical physics, mankind continues in 2-year-old style that shouts "Why?" and the teenage branded "Prove It!" to this reality in the most pronounced of ways.

In 1610 A.D., through Galileo another self-evident truth about this reality surfaced from reality's deeper collective awareness. He shed light on the truth that our sun, not the Earth, is the center of this galaxy.

Reality has a deeper consciousness with life principle logistics that mankind has not touched on. Being that mankind's material presence is a living part of the heartbeat of this deeper consciousness, this knowledge will continue to emerge via insightful understandings of the future.

Over time, mankind's collective awareness is "wising up" to recognize what proves to be the self-evident truth describing Mother Nature's forces that influence establishing the patterns of influence that form the life principles that humans all must live by.

It's becoming clearer how humankind's condition fits into humankind's experience ... how life principles affect life emotions.

About half a millennium ago mankind's collective perspective of reality opened from ancient superstition to the age of reason.

It finally surfaced to mankind's collective waking awareness that the universe is governed by the laws of nature. The laws maintain consistency over time and these principled laws control the outcome of life's cause/effect relationships.

... Mankind is Slowly Figuring it Out ... Truth Proves Self-Evident

Early man once peered into the mysterious night darkness and visualized flying devils with great horns. It is now common knowledge that those "flying night devils" are Great Horned Owls looking for a rodent snack.

Yes, mankind's collective conscious awareness has migrated from an ancient mindset that fearfully looking to imagined powers of supernatural superheroes to explain this reality and the forces that wear its atom-woven cover.

What is now called science, mankind's ability to openly question, stepped in as mankind's freewill to observe and question nature's forces and the reality that those forces constantly dish out.

... Due Diligence Brings on Enlightened Understanding

There is less to be imagined and not understood about what relational principles establish the transforming character of this reality than long ago.

The truths about how reality works become more self-evident and unquestionable.

The 14th century was mankind's Golden Age of Learning.

Humankind once thought ... many ignorant today still do ... that everything in the universe revolved around Earth ... revolved around humanity.

Nicklaus Copernicus captained the Copernican Revolution in 1543 AD. In his new theory of the cosmos, Mother Earth lost her place at the center of the universe as she joined the other planets to revolve around the sun now at the center of the universe.

With the telescope, humanity's senses are extended to better defined this new perspective on the cosmos.

With the Copernicus Heliocentric model of the universe, humanity loses its position of centrality in this reality.

In 1610 AD, with the new telescope, Galileo figured out how all the planets revolve around the sun. He questioned the Roman Catholic Bible's interpretation of reality.

Astronomers were burned at the stake.

In 1633 AD Galileo was found guilty of "vehemently suspect of heresy", sentencing him to indefinite imprisonment until he died under house arrest in 1642.

The teachings of Copernicus were banned for 200 years.

... Mankind Keeps Questioning the Misunderstood and Unknown

The apple tree was not mad at Sir Isaac Newton. He had not done something that some deity was punishing him for by allegedly dropping an apple on his head.

It was the soon-to-be-better-understood natural principles defining the force of gravity that caused that apple to fall.

Newton identified one of nature's governing forces when he questioned belief in the supernatural and asked the right questions to bring to mankind's collective awareness the Universal Law of Gravitation.

His discovery gave understanding clarity to this portion of nature's "burning bush" principles to then derive the wisdom-enriched understanding explaining nature's law of gravity. The understanding of how this force integrates and interacts with other discovered natural forces continues today.

The natural principles defining this discovery soon became self-evident and mankind's steadfast faith in its truth became as strong as with the rising of the sun.

Charles Darwin showed the presence of and gave explanation to how nature's subtle ever-present change also holds true for the animal kingdom ... the Natural Laws of Evolution.

The various disciplines of theology will either call on its believers to maybe stretch their blind faith a bit more to allow the theology's unverifiable borrowed wisdom to acclimatize to the new truth or become obsolete and fade into the stillness of the past.

But then, there are always Christian sects such as today's Evangelicals that will simply deny the unarguable. IE: Dinosaur fossils and carbon dating. They default their collective hum to endorse teaching in public schools as being fact that through the "Intelligent Design" of a godly entity that "Creationism" is how this world came to be 'as-is' and not through any form of evolution.

... Einstein Connects the Dots to Expose Reality's 4th Dimension

"Time has no fixed address ...
only an elusive spot in mankind's dimensional understanding of reality.

~ Father Time

Albert Einstein's theory of relativity is helping mankind to better recognize and understand the self-evident nature of this reality that's alive and in process whether we're aware of it or not. His theory of relatively has brought to the surface an understanding of the self-evident truth explaining the relevance of the relationship between space and time ... the 4th dimension of this reality.

From his curiosity and lifetime of unyielding questioning emerged a monumental wisdom-enriched perspective of how time itself fits into and defines our waking present moment. It allows for a tangible picture of the actual role time plays in the dimensional makeup of the impermanent backdrop that keeps our perceived reality suspended and positioned in each passing present moment.

Einstein gave mathematical clarity to how the natural force of gravity interacts and influences time and space. Longitudinal and latitudinal coordinates work for positioning something in space. But time is needed to position its spot on history's "timeline."

His work shows how the passage of time can be influenced by its exposure to different amounts of gravity.

However, the important thing is that time does not stop. It continues moving.

... Steven Hawking Exemplifies Time's Place on The Dimensional Ladder

Albert Einstein predicted gravitational waves. He discovered and brought to mankind's collective conscious awareness the presence of this reality's 4th dimension, time.

The theoretical physicist, Steven Hawking had a PBS show, "Genius." Its aim was, through example, to help its watchers better understand the principled laws of nature that affect their human experience.

In one episode he showed the relationship between the 1st 4 dimensions of this reality's dimensional matrix. A team of students was to locate a party at an address.

Picture the spatial characteristic of a cube for near/away, left/right, up/down and the 4th dimension ... time ... a spot in the flow of ongoing change.

The students followed the 1st three dimensions ... latitudinal, longitudinal (street address), and spatially (how many floors up in an apartment house) to arrive at the correct physical location ... but there was no party when they arrived.

When they added the fourth dimension ... the designated time ... they found the party.

Time is nature's 4th dimension. One can locate anything 2 dimensional by longitude and latitude. The 3rd dimension goes to a point in space. The 4th dimension locates that point with longitude, latitude, and a point in space that then references their physical presence to a point on the timeline of change.

Time is a transforming dimension in the passing prick-your-skin presence of the ever-elusive present moment. Mankind now knows this to be an unquestioned self-evident truth.

We do not notice the time because its transforming state is all that has ever been present for us to know. For many, this transforming state is misinterpreted as being constant or having continuity, allowing them an imagined reality they can become attached to … fundamental ignorance.

Flow with the Forces that Form the Principles that Control All Cause/Effect Outcomes

At a deeper level the reality is that the entire universe, animate and inanimate, is in a constant state of becoming … of arising and passing away. Each one of us is in fact a stream of constantly changing subatomic particles, along with which the processes of consciousness, perception, sensation, reaction change even more rapidly than the physical process."

This is the ultimate reality of the self with which each of us is so concerned. This is the course of events in which we are involved. If we can understand it properly by direct experience, we shall find the clue to lead us out of suffering."

~The Art of Living: Vipassana Meditation as taught by S. N. Goenka, p.29

Find cadence with the forces that generate the relational principles that interact during the passage of time.

Anyone is more relaxed when their conditioned behaviors flow in sync with that of the environment that they were born in.

For example, being timely with appointments during your life experience.

Individuals cannot control the outcomes of their life events. They can control what they do to influence those outcomes.

The outcome of a job interview is unknown, but that outcome can be greatly influenced by showing up on "time." That's part of the cause/effect process that an individual has control of.

People often get the 1st 3 dimensions correct … they just throw a fly in the ointment by not meeting the 4th. They are late. They missed the party.

Even in not knowing how many dimensions makeup and support the impermanent backdrop of this reality, just understanding that its dimensional presence has the 4 dimensions so far identified helps derive the life wisdom that will bring one closer to emotional bliss.

Being somewhere "on time" is what everyone is expecting in the upcoming unfolding of what naked change has to offer them. Why swim against the laws of the current of change when it's known what they are?

Why bring any more emotional doubt or disappointment into their lives concerning the dependability of their life itinerary?

When expected to be somewhere or make a phone call at a certain time in history and not fulfilling that expectation, it is just like Hawking's party gang going to the right place, just at the wrong time in history ... a fly in the ointment.

What could be said about someone's actions who's not ignorant to the life principles that influence an outcome, like above, but ignore them anyway? They're not ignorant here. Where does stupid fit in?

... Gravity ... Earth's Mass is Pushing Up, Not Pulling Down

Gravity plays a grounding role in the push and pull of time and space.

Gravity is actually curved space. An object curves the space/time around it in one of Einstein's gravitational waves.

While we may think Earth "possesses" enough gravity to pull down on us, in truth, gravity does not pull us down to Earth. The Earth pushes up against us.

Earth's mass affects the shape of the flow of the river of the time-space that we occupy as one present moment transforms into the next. The space-time path that defines an individual's presence bends around the mass. Gravity is really the Earth pushing up as our mass expands over the passage of time ... not grabbing individuals by their ankles and pulling them down.

... And Here We Are Today

The steel-driven industrial revolution brought about the railroad.

This was followed by modernizations brought about by electricity.

The computer revolution has catapulted mankind's ability to ask questions and search for answers with just the click of a mouse.

Many still label the occurrence of some unexplainable life event as a "God-sent miracle."

Just because mankind might not yet understand the logistics of something, does not mean that it is a supernaturally concocted miracle that soon won't be understood.

The age of reason introduced itself on scale when mankind could better share information about the questions it found the courage to look the gods in the eye and ask for explanations to better understand those superpowers that did the seemingly impossible.

Science ... mankind's freewill, guardian and spokesperson will be around for a while because it gives humankind the light to see what its eye cannot.

Science represents all of mankind equally. It is blind to politics or theology of any kind. It is only interested in the truth describing all the dimensional aspects of this impermanent reality.

Science's demand for experientially verified empirical evidence to bring light and understanding about the relationships between the interrelated parts working to sustain this reality's state of impermanence, lights humankind's pathway to a wisdom-enriched enlightened understanding of its collective fundamental ignorance that causes all human suffering.

Time Itself ... Naked Change ... Follows No Timeline

... It's an On-Going Present Moment

The self-assimilated wisdom derived from sensually originated self-knowledge is sensually metered only in real-time. It uses only the elusive present moment to express its truth and it uses only primal sensual expression as its media.

Change occupies the ever-evasive present moment. The present moment's always been its home address.

Change's material emanation cannot be grasped and held to poke and prod with liking and disliking.

-Father Time

... Mass and Energy are Interchangeable

The world's most famous equation must be Einstein's E=MC2 ... that energy and mass (matter) are interchangeable; they are different forms of the same thing ... or in other words, mass is nothing but a glimpse at transforming energy's present moment ever-transforming character.

These are dimensions of this universal reality working together that we realize sensually and keep an intrinsically registered relationship with ... at least on the subconscious level ... its truth as wired into the coming and going energy that makes an individual's material presence.

... This is Where the Human Condition Meets the Human Experience

Understanding this relationship enlightens an individual to their misinformed conditioning that allows for their ignorance that causes their suffering.

... Change Emanates Uncontrollably from Raw Energy to Create Nature's Timeline

The passage of time ... the evolving transformation of reality ... the working presence of impermanence follows no timeline ... it is the present moment.

The present moment scripts nature's timeline.

As the universe continues to expand, change happens right on the spot seemingly from nowhere. It does not move in a line of continual time. It evolves in the living buzz of the everlasting present moment.

A quark (/kwɔːrk, kwɑːrk/) is a type of elementary particle and a fundamental constituent of matter. Quarks combine to form composite particles called hadrons, the most stable of which are protons and neutrons, the components of atomic nuclei. Due to a phenomenon known as color confinement, quarks are never directly observed or found in isolation; they can be found only within hadrons, which include baryons (such as protons and neutrons) and mesons. For this reason, much of what is known about quarks has been drawn from observations of hadrons."

~ Wikipedia

The transforming change observable in the world of quantum mechanics is generated from the bits of unpredictable coming and going energy … the ever-evasive quarks … as small as it gets … yet can't be grabbed … that contribute to the hadrons (protons and neutrons) that contribute to the atoms that make up the molecules that make up the flesh of the human body.

Science now has pictures of the life-giving particles of energy that became self-evident to Siddhartha sensually through self-training his ability to derive self-knowledge. It is said that these energy particles make up patterns of energy impulses that are unpredictable and uncontrollable.

Siddhartha experientially gained awareness of this when sensually witnessing the presence of the "kapula,"

This sensually identified constant stream of coming and going particle waves, in Pali "kapula" (indivisible units/smallest indivisible unit of matter) (intellectually metered as quarks) are now known to exist through an intellectual understanding. Science is struggling to better understand the natural forces that generate this phenomenon and probably still have no clue to how the causal relationships their interactions set the pattern for in generating the life-ruling principles that determine the outcomes of relational interactions.

An individual's intellectually metered reflection on the pictures of this energy-bound kapula leaves them with no intrinsically registered enlightened grasp of what relevance these tiny bits of energy have to do with the impermanent nature of this reality.

Siddhartha understood that these energy particles existed unseen, through sensual witnessing. He also understood the life rhythms these patterns would employ and the life principles they would support.

Maybe he sensually led his conscious awareness down the patterned life rhythms he felt through "right effort" and "right concentration", as he taught, to find and intrinsically deduce the kapula as their source?

One would have to ask Siddhartha or another "enlightened" individual like Jesus.

"Particle Entanglement" Connects the Quantum Mechanics World to Einstein's General Theory of Relativity for a Wholistic Theory of the Universe

... Outcome of Change is Not Predictable ... Yet Seems to Prove Probable

Everything is connected.

Particle entanglement, what Einstein referred to as being just spooky connections, explains the backdrop of the real world seen versus the world as-it-is. It cannot be seen how the movement of something in one location does affect a movement elsewhere.

The electrons that are composed of quarks are nothing more than a probability.

The groups of electrons, "cubits," of probability can point in the direction of several different outcomes of their interaction.

Through combing cubits into entangled cubits, it is becoming possible to decode encrypted messages at record times. It could soon allow for a secure global communication system.

A quantum computer is being developed that will greatly surpass the capacities of current artificial intelligence systems.

Anyone Questioning Anything Is A Scientist

... Theology Shuns Science

Some religious groups view science as evil as it seeks to explain things that the Bible says not to question. Some deny evolution and believe in the biblical Genesis account of the 6,000-year creation.

Religion fears science. From anybody just asking why to modern science's double-blind protocol, the curious are just trying to remove some of their ignorance about this reality,

Science seeks to make self-evident the truth about the logistics of relationships. Science tries to reveal the principles that bring about and define the relationships that define change.

To be on science's pitch takes religious believers away from their promised safety blanket to afterlife bliss. They must find the courage to ask why without angering their god by questioning the borrowed wisdom they have pledged blind allegiance to.

… Life Truths Pulsed from Believer's Deeper Awareness Needles Their Numbed Waking Consciousness

One of the constituents that comprise the mile-a-minute white noise that can plague a fundamental believer's present moment mental presence comes from the intuitive subconscious prodding their waking consciousness that something is missing from their understanding of the status quo … and what's missing has an explanation … an understanding. Their understanding is incomplete … it seems empty-of-understanding something.

As the prodding gets no answered … they unspokenly keep an eye open for something better.

… Inborn Human Curiosity

Scientists are not only those who wear white coats. Any brain-ready human is a scientist.

Anybody who boldly stares into the face of naked change about anything and with their inborn 2-year-old boldness asks why or how, is a scientist. They simply want to know the self-evident truth about something they do not understand so they will not suffer from an emptiness-of-understanding or misunderstanding how it fits in.

Anybody that has the insight to figure out the questions to ask and find the courage to ask why, is a scientist. From a pushy 2-year-old to those who seek double-blind experiential verification. They are all scientists … merely people looking for answers to something they are ignorant about.

With an increasingly science-enriched understanding of the workings of the intricate makeup of this ephemeral reality, mankind's collective fear of the unknown boogieman is gradually evaporating.

Science wants to bring to conscious awareness the self-evident explanation of what is not understood and has been theorized. Scientific questioning has brought understanding that lightning is caused by an electrical discharge of electrons moving very quickly from one place to another, superheating the air around them causing it to glow.

It is not the Greek mythology god Zeus throwing bolts of lightning from the sky. The threat of this explanation was probably used by Greek rulers to help corral Greek civil disobedience and objection.

This is another natural principle better understood … bringing mankind's collective consciousness understanding one answer closer to being "enlightened" to its ignorance.

In the USA, the freedom to follow a religious sentiment cannot be denied, yet this right has greatly retarded this country's ability to focus and advance its collective awareness and understanding of what proves to be the self-evident truth detailing how the human condition fits into its human experience.

With science's continued questioning, the natural force-driven principles that control the outcome of environmental conditions are gradually being revealed and better understood, at least on the intellectual level.

Public awareness is slowly wising up to centuries of theology's blanketing ethos of cultural gaslighting where it is to be taken for granted that this reality came from and is controlled by some source of intelligent design.

Mankind's Collective Awareness

... Bound For John Lennon's Reality "Imagine"

Today humankind has a much clearer understanding of this reality. It is no wonder there was such fear in humankind's past. To be in the dark about most everything would be quite daunting, to say the least.

Throughout history's timeline, mankind's had an untellable number of "aha" moments of insightful understandings that have helped recognize and detail some of the effects of the forces that produce reality's dimension characteristics. These self-evident truths factor into the principles that give support and assign order and rhythm the heartbeat of reality's animated human experience.

Today's educational system is challenged to streamline the teaching of this new knowledge in a way that human youth can intellectually grasp the principles exposed in these insights in a way that they can then reflect on this knowledge to allow further "aha" (Tree of Life) wisdom-enriched insights to surface.

... Humankind's Collective Understanding's Not There ... Yet

At some future present moment, as the truth explaining life's process in this reality becomes more self-evident, mankind will have a much deeper understanding awareness of things that today's ignorance of brings on worldwide suffering and serves as food for theology's survival.

The more mankind questions its ignorance, the better it understands it, and from this comes a wisdom-enriched understanding.

As time passes and mankind's questioning (science) continues, the mass of theological disciplines will fall or find ways to adapt to the newly arising insightful "aha" self-evident truths realized.

It's doubtful this will be the time Jesus will be riding in on a white horse with trumpets blaring, but maybe mankind will realize and understand the emotional bliss found living in what John Lennon "*Imagine*"d?

Science Remains as Theology Until Verified

Speculation of any kind stands as theory until the perceptively cloaked postulated truth about how it plays an active part in supporting the impermanent dimensional makeup of this reality proves itself to be self-evident.

Scientific theories are tested to see if their posed cause/effect relational justice sequence really does explain one of the living truths in the cause/effect nature of this reality.

Mankind's freewill (science) questions the observable to better understand the Tree of Life principles that set the pattern for cause/effect outcomes that define this reality.

I.E. What mysterious dimensional force is it that pulls an apple untouched from a tree and tosses it on the ground?

A speculative claim's degree of recognized living truth is measured considering where humanity's current collective degree of scientific/spiritual/theological maturity stands and can grasp and decode the intended gist. Scientific and spiritual speculation and religious theology all represent different perspective platforms for arranging the structure of claims made by insight-inspired theoretical models attempting to describe the countless cause/effect relationships that explain the birth and life of this reality.

Albert Einstein's E=MC2 and all the other great speculative models originated by other scientists from all the different disciplines of scientific principle … Newton, Galileo, Curie, Darwin, Aristotle, Hawking … remain speculative until tested and the clarity of their truth proves self-evident. Once the truth of the claim's purpose is verified, another piece of enlightened understanding surfaces to mankind's collective waking conscious awareness from the idle pool of undetected life-explaining wisdom residing down in the subtle depths of the ageless collective humankind deeper consciousness.

This process has helped further mankind's understanding of the cause/effect relational justice that keeps synched together the ephemeral makeup of the impermanent dimensional infrastructure of this reality.

Developing an understanding awareness of the unavoidable and unchangeable impermanent nature of this reality helps to further instill calm over the undefined fear of the unknown boogieman that haunts the children of all ages living in the dark emptiness of a reality they do not understand. It is the very same ageless strain of cause/effect relational justice described by the wisdom-building knowledge that gives meaning to the life wisdom emanating from the Garden of Eden's Tree of Life.

Science, humanity's freewill, with its innate 2-year-old curiosity untouched by conditioned shyness, insistently poses questions … you could call it scientific theology until the self-evident relational truth emerges to better understand what explains the network of change that animates this reality's present moment.

Theology Either Adapts or Disappears

As mankind's collective awareness matures over time, religious theology watches and adapts. Stop and compare mankind's present level of understanding awareness of the cause/effect relational justice turning the screws of the natural laws that operate this impermanent reality to those of only 25 years ago … advances in technology, medicine, astronomy, genetics, human rights, etcetera.

The Pope amends and adjusts the church understanding of the terms of Roman Catholic's afterlife emotional bliss promise annually to clarify what's acceptable to God amidst all new strains of debatable social behavior to stay politically correct with what modern-day science and social discovery show to be self-evident. It continues to help hold down social disagreement and unrest, to some degree as back in the days of Constantine.

Pope Francis endorsed same-sex marriage as a pontiff when interviewed for the documentary "Francesco" which premiered at the 2020 Rome Film Festival. This is a major step in Roman Christianity's acceptance and support for LGBTQ people.

In World News on 10-21-2020, Nichole Winfield with the Associated Press reported that Pope Francis said: "Homosexual people have the right to be in a family. They are children of God. You can't kick someone out of a family, nor make their life miserable for this. What we have to have is a civil union law; that way they are legally covered."

Over the past few millennia of spiritualist and religious conjecture … Taoism, Confucianism, Hinduism, Christianity, Buddhism, Islam, tribal religions, and others with scientific theory have been questioned, picked apart, and further analyzed. With defined advancements in mankind's understanding of the nature of this reality … as with dated quarries of scientific speculation, many abstract concepts of spirituality speculation and religious theology have either completely disappeared or managed to adapt.

… Logistical Threads of Intellectually Metered Claims

In effort to "prove" the Bible to be true, there are biblical scholars who have managed to piece together logistical threads of assertions made by intellectually metered and interpreted sources of knowledge into "if-so" strings of reasoning and venture the conclusive claim to be self-evident.

With no tangible context to establish the truth of these claims, the claims remain to be borrowed wisdom. The supposed principles supporting the interlinking network of sited relationships that would make these claims self-evident will be empty-of-understanding.

The Bible Itself ... It's Unverified Borrowed Wisdom
... Fruit of the Tree of Knowledg... How Stingingly Ironic

Like the Tree of Knowledge wisdom Eve borrowed in blind trust from the Garden of Eden snake, promising a wisdom-enriched understanding of everything from good to evil, the wisdom in the Bible is taken on blind trust by today's Adams and Eves. The Bible instills the same type of unearned unverifiable wisdom that leaves its believers empty-of-understanding ... like what Eve agreed to receive from the snake.

... A Rome-Shined Apple From the Tree of Knowledge

The Bible is a Rome-shined apple ... a greed-motivated unsubstantiated promise to mankind ... just like the all-knowing wisdom the Eden snake promised to Adam and Eve.

... The Irony of it All

It is ironic that the intellectually metered biblical wisdom telling of the need to live by Tree of Life wisdom is the type of wisdom (received and borrowed) wisdom that Jehovah fervently declares will bring spiritual death.

The Bible's storyline was still to develop. The Bible hadn't been written yet.

By the same logic, Siddhartha's message of the need to live by Tree of Life wisdom is also intellectually metered borrowed wisdom. The difference is that Siddhartha's message includes a detailed description of the pathway to self-train the intellectual understanding into an intrinsically registered sensually metered intrinsically founded understanding awareness.

Sell Your Soul to Blind Faith

... Your Freewill for Blind Hope Security

Religious believers will trade their soul's freewill ability for the wisdom describing the way to acquire an eternal afterlife of emotional bliss. Their guarantee is secured only by their blind faith in the promised wisdom sealed by their unquestioned obedience.

As of 2015, one-third of the world's population, over two billion people, are Christian. Over 55% of the world's population believe in the Old Testament. Religious theology lays claim to the freewill of about 85% of the Earth's living souls.

That means that as of 2015, 85 out of every 100 of the world's population is voluntarily, out of ignorance, choosing to "look outside" for salvation from suffering for the emotional bliss of eternal afterlife paradise.

With a Leap of Blind Faith ... Inner Compass Loses Polarity

... Freewill Gets Compromised

The believer becomes more of a follower and less of a leader. Life direction will become very faint and maybe disappear.

When someone agrees to follow instructions without questioning why, it takes something away from the supportive fiber of their self-confidence.

After once settling to look to an unverified deity that they have only built a cognitive sketch of for life direction, it becomes easier to follow other unproven notions.

... Internalizing Promised Wisdom Strikes a Mental Hiatus

A wall is built.

... The Bible Calls it "Hardening of the Heart"

After convincing oneself that they've "seen the light" once, it becomes much more difficult to venture out another time when the opportunity to find the "answer" about the reality of life might occur.

Convincing oneself to blindly take to heart any promised state of being that is not supported by actual sensually synced understanding leaves a gap ... a hiatus ... in the flow of the understanding of new life knowledge. Their worldview slips on a pair of tight-fitting manacles towards limiting open understanding.

... "Seeing the Light" Understanding Gets Reversed

A non-religious individual gets imbibed as a "sinner" and can be snubbed or ignored.

Once a converted believer chances the leap of blind faith, any individual who is not taken the leap of blind faith will find it difficult to try to reason with the believer about what really defines reality. The theologian will find it difficult to understand what "seeing the light" means unless is focused through their glasses.

Over time when a believer's intrinsically coded street sense wisdom about the self-evident aspects of reality rubs up against their memorized biblically induced wisdom, they will suffer in the confusion. It is locked into their waking consciousness that "seeing the light" means realizing how their chosen god is there to save them.

They fail to understand how "seeing the light" really means understanding the ways of this reality that will then excuse the ignorance that is causing their emotional struggle.

We Design a God to Walk in Our Own Shoes

We do not see things as they are. We see things as we are.

~ The Talmud

... To Better Understand Ourselves

Individuals create a god to handle the part of the living world that they do not understand.

People live in a conditioned state of mind reflecting how they have been guided to perceive reality. They arrange their world in a way to best find balance for their personally honed pitch of sanity or insanity.

Individuals fashion their conscious understanding of their environment in a way that they are most likely to find joy and happiness, as they understand it ... to not suffer.

The quest is always for emotional balance/bliss.

For lack of direction when fear of the future or maybe angst about the past stares them down, many will scramble in panic for the answer.

The faceless anonymity that characterizes theology's collection of gods allows each religious believer to choose from their unique assortment of cognitively sketched mental pictures of their catalogued display of available gods from the assorted stories read about, talked about, or maybe seen on TV.

People can do no better than bow to their notion of the god they have come across in their cognitive take on reality that they feel most compatible with.

... A God Suitable to Meet Unique Needs and Wants and to Make Ends Meet

People customize their god to meet their needs and possibly fulfill their wants. They fashion a god with the powers that prove to be an appropriate match for their level of spiritual maturity/understanding.

For some, their god will supply the needed miracles to tie together the real-life ends that do not meet or match up to their suspected real-life causes or that just do not make sense.

When what reality serves up does not match up with illusionary miscued expectations, something divine, all-powerful, and out of this world is needed to explain the unexpected and somehow make the ends meet.

Many of these unexplainable cause/effect relationships are justified, rationalized, or simply excused as being the sorts of things that happen only by the grace of God, or maybe the explanation of unexpected outcomes might simply be that God works in mysterious ways.

A god is as compassionate or punishing as the individual is conditioned to imagine. There is a direct correspondence between a god's gifts and punishments and the conceptual limits of an individual's conditioned worldview.

Almost one-third of the world's population, over two billion people, are Christian. The modern-day zeitgeist of the Bible could be recognized as an intellectual kaleidoscope of evolving modern-day interpretations of its Roman-edited multi-translated ancient message. It is exceedingly rare to find two Christians that agree on what Jesus's intended meaning was meant to be from any of the versions of the ancient text's many translations.

... Dr. Deepak Chopra Valuable Insights

The Eastern spiritualist Dr. Deepak Chopra also recognizes this default setting of the human condition. He also ventures that many humans fashion a god to have characteristics appropriate to satisfy their judge/jury protection/ punishment needs that they must placate in their present moment perception of the relational factors representing their unique illusion of an apparent reality ... like creating a god in the image of the individual.

Look at all the Jesus renditions from different artists. You will see a god that has 2 arms and 2 legs, just like the humans he is credited for creating in his image. Most agree on the white beard and robe.

In Dr. Choprah's book *How to Know God: The Soul's Journey into the Mystery of Mysteries*, he suggests that there are seven basic versions or stages of God that can be associated with the different aspects of different faiths. It follows that these different stages of God recognition reflect varying levels or flavors of spiritual maturity.

Dr. Chopra suggests that individuals at the lowest level of spiritual development or maturity will turn to a deity figure capable of the most devastating forms of punishment or reward that are bound only by the individual's conditioned world of imagination.

The progressive stages of God recognition will formulate into the illusion of a god that encompasses all possibilities that come to the awareness of an individual that has a more wisdom-enriched understanding of the relational justice inherent to the impermanent nature of this reality.

These described incarnations of a god created in our own image are very interesting and do a wonderful job of bringing to words one theory that describing the diverse range in what is needed to keep the wide variety of human angst corralled. There's a wide range of godly illusions people create to explain and to weather the sorts of human emotional reactions coming from all the unique human perceptions of this cause/effect reality.

People living in an illusionary apparent reality will create a superhuman power to help give organization to their uncertainty and to use to inject the missing relational justice needed to fill in the gaps and bring balance to their misguided maladjusted views and beliefs.

An individual's illusionary reality needs to be able to call on an appropriate phase of a god to deal with the type of misaligned internal misunderstandings that arise between illusionary causes and their mismatched effects. Their internal unrest may turn to a god to reward, punish, grant a wish, console, understand and tolerate, help create, cure an incurable disease or situation, or just watch over all things in an omnipresence way that's been read about, while the relationship with the living present moment cannot quite be understood.

It may require a god with powers that transcend those an individual has experientially witnessed during their lifetime to somehow apply the self-evident relational justice they know positively exists, somewhere in the subtle region of their deeper consciousness. Until they wakingly uncover their link to this inborn source of truth, they must conjure up a trusting faith that is blind to understanding the actual source of this borrowed truth.

The variety of illusionary apparent realities ranging from individual to individual is probably somewhere around six billion+. There is a countless number of god-conception possibilities characterized by what is needed to balance the belief system of someone spending their present moments stuck in an illusionary apparent reality.

Dr. Chopra's alternative god possibilities represent another's vision of grouping and arranging the needs of the human condition and explaining the human experience.

People will call on their god to reward or punish them in the way they feel he would want to for their own deserved good. Many will figure that when this life is over, when the void filled with their ignorance-spawned emptiness-of-understanding is gone, somehow, mysteriously, so will the suffering it brings them.

There is no need to make the process of finding our Source so mystical. There is no need to make such a pious ritualistic deal out of the process of understanding the path to becoming enlightened about the ignorance of how this reality works that brings on human suffering. Everyone has the potential to perform due diligence to understand this.

So, What Now?

Mankind's slowly maturing understanding of the ways of reality has reached a 21st-century point of reckoning on Earth's life timeline. In the 3.5-billion-year time expanse since the Earth took shape, in science's "Big Bang" account of creation, man's appearance occupies less than 1/1000th of one percent ... only 200,000 - 300,000 years out of 3.5 billion.

The last 500 years? ... go figure. Mankind's becoming collectively enlightened about what is going on behind the theology-draped doors.

Anyone interested in running their life in sync with the principles that define the ongoing heartbeat of this reality that when misunderstood makes them suffer, needs to develop the very same strain of wisdom that supports or decodes reality's unalterable network of functional relationships

The human deeper consciousness is already intrinsically armed with that sensually metered coding. Self-training the mind control will allow any truth-seeker to self-train the mind to collect the needed self-knowledge to derive the wisdom-enriched understanding for its understanding to climb from the deeper consciousness up the primal zip cord into the waking consciousness awareness.

... Understanding the Principles that Affect Emotion

If someone wants to better understand their emotional makeup, they gather emotion-related knowledge to inspire developing insightful familiarity with the network of wisdom supporting emotional balance. One can control making their life-related decisions, but it is the set patterns of life principles that determine the unbiased outcome of cause/effect interactions.

An understanding awareness of the ways of the living environment that affect one's emotions and thus to better understand their emotions is how they will reach emotional bliss.

By generating the due diligence to learn life wisdom-inspiring knowledge a truth-seeker becomes enlightened about life's unbendable principles of transformation to allow emotional bliss to surface and avoid suffering from an empty or miscued understanding of those life principles.

With this understanding, a truth-seeker will avoid being strapped living by Fig Leaf Wisdom and will have no reason to reach for fig leaves to mask ignorance-inspired emotional shame like Adam and Eve.

In that respect, as nature's plan becomes more self-evident, human blind trust is doomed to continued evaporation from human consciousness. We are not yet to John Lennon's reality "Imagined", but someday... this is the "hope" that all should share, maybe not so much that a god is going to solve our suffering that we stand ignorant to and do not even understand.

Like Siddhartha's deathbed last words … everything changes … get off your butts and figure it out.

Don't Live Life Fatally Fooled

Beware of blindly trusting gifted packages of borrowed wisdom supporting anything promised that instead of providing an intrinsic familiarity with its network of wisdom, provides a testament of unexplained rules of conduct, called its wisdom, that must be observed to stay within a life-long proving period while hoping to be included in the promised outcome that the strain of borrowed wisdom purports.

Look for and question any wormholes when ingesting the fruit of any sort of gifted unverified and unearned wisdom. If not, plan on ego-fashioning the fig leaf masks to cover ignorance-inspired emotional shame. Do not make life decisions that are the product of Fig Leaf Wisdom to end up naively living life fatally fooled.

Jehovah had warned Adam that eating of the Tree of Knowledge only once would bring death to his Garden of Eden emotional bliss … to then send them alive, out into the world to suffer using their chosen Fig Leaf Wisdom.

Adam and Eve were fatally fooled.

… To this day, mankind ingests the same sort of promised wisdom that Eve then Adam chose to ingest from the Tree of Knowledge and uses the same Fig Leaf Wisdom to shape their worldview and make life decisions.

… An individual demonstrates with their every decision how they have been conditioned to discriminate the nature of this reality as being either impermanent or one that allows an imaginary state of continuity to compromise the flow of time.

… Most use intellectual hues to color a spiritual worldview on life's sensual canvas.

… There are two ways to be fooled: believing something that's not true or not believing what is.

X

Two Types of Faith

... Only One Engenders Enlightened Growth

"Blind belief in authority is the greatest enemy of truth."
~ Albert Einstein

"It's not in the stars to hold our destiny but in ourselves."
~ William Shakespeare

Today's meaning of "faith" is very loosely configured. It bends around many corners.

The trusting act of placing one's faith in something can range in heart-felt sincerity from wagering blind trust in unverified hearsay to having developed a realized steadfast confidence in an unbiased truth that has come to be proven self-evident in real life.

Someone can have an untethered faith in what they have been told to be true or an intrinsically fed faith in what they've sensually experienced.

The type or degree of faith an individual chooses to establish reflects how their human condition approaches its human experience ... eyes closed or eyes open.

Two Foundations of Faith

... Which Source of Cause-Effect Relational Justice Balances Your Scales?

"Never, no, never did nature say one thing and wisdom say another."
~Edmund Burke

It is important for a truth-seeker to know what generates the fear or unknown form of evil they are seeking salvation from and how to deal with its cause. They will either try to understand it themselves or at some level of obscurity, trust the wisdom leading to some other entity's pathway to salvation from emotional suffering.

A truth-seeker is expecting their chosen source of enlightenment to eliminate their suffering. Is it possible for them to gain an understanding of the cause of their suffering and go to that plain of reality and eliminate the cause or will they just trust that the source of suffering elimination will just do it for them ... unexplained?

It's important which sense for understanding nature's cause/effect relational justice balances the right/wrong, yin/yang scales in the truth-seeker's worldview.

Does the truth-seeker plan to develop an enlightened understanding of the same principles of relational justice stemming from the unavoidable truth of the law of justice tapped out by the coming and going particles of energy defining the relational give and take of our physical world that inspires the content of the books of science describing the unfolding knowledge detailing the nature of our reality?

Or do they entrust the understanding of the destiny of their soul to blindly following the mystical undefined law of relational justice enforced by a never-before-seen entity that independently decides justice based on the guilt-guarded state of morality implied by a set of rules such as the Ten Commandments (including any periodic modern Papal-authorized updates) that offer no reasoning for understanding why the behaviors are considered bad and classified as a sin and how that affects realizing emotional bliss?

As mankind learns to better understand Mother nature's undeniable cause/effect relational laws that set natural force-based principles through science's due diligence, the religious authority will conform to science's discovered truth, or their theological creed disappears like so many already have.

It seems that using science's outreach sets pattern for religion's scales of justice. Those who want to experientially understand the unknown, which science represents, will prove something as self-evident, then religion beliefs will believe it and adjust their storyline or lose its believers.

Whichever foundation of faith … blind trust or steadfast assurance … that backs up a truth seeker's decision for seeking relief from suffering is important.

One faith is blind to how emotional balance is restored and the other engenders the enlightened growth to allow self-deriving the Tree of Life wisdom to understand how life principles affect human emotion.

… Type of Faith Corresponds with Type of Wisdom-Deriving Knowledge

When a child awakens from their childhood innocence to assume accountability for their actions, it's the fortitude of the wisdom-deriving knowledge their freewill had earlier been conditioned as being acceptable for collecting wisdom-deriving knowledge to populate their belief system to shape their worldview that will determine what kind of trust or faith … blind or heartfelt … they will use to support the wisdom their worldview purports.

Each type of faith corresponds to the type of knowledge they use to gain understandings about how their human condition fits into its human experience … knowledge borrowed or self-discovered experientially obtained.

When heartfelt steadfast assurance is missing from an individual's understanding, having a faith that is blind to understanding and developing heartfelt confidence in the claim's process helps the spiritually immature to find shallow pseudo protection from the monsters of the unknown in a reality they have yet to understand the nature of.

A faith steadfast in having sensually experienced the percolation of the wisdom-deriving knowledge grows stronger alongside the growth of insightful Tree of Life wisdom. A faith blind to the actual process of generating the knowledge to derive the wisdom relating to understanding a claim accompanies borrowed Tree of Knowledge wisdom.

Let's Focus

One type of faith reformats and safeguards an individual's ignorance. It is a faith "rote in" intellectual memory from story review that stands blind, empty-of-understanding."

The other keystones their sensually verified knowledge. It is a prelingual gut-felt faith that stands steadfast.

One faith bans or discourages questioning the preface of a claim to provide its own set of unsupportable answers in meaning-diluted multi-translated prose form.

The other comes as the reward for continued successful efforts to "live and learn" more about the principles that characterize the natural dimensional force-driven nature of this ever-changing reality. It grows steadfastly hand-in-heart with the knowledge-inspired insightful wisdom-enriched understanding of what brings one closer to emotional bliss.

The truth of the claim doesn't have to be written down. There's no middleman. Intellectual media and retention versus intrinsic.

An Individual First Develops Intellectually Referenced Worldview Before Deciding to Blindly Trust an Intellectually Based Theology

Which came first the chicken or the egg … an individual's entry into reality or their relationship with the promise protected by blind faith?

Everyone's born with a freewill. It comes wired into the human belief system. It allows an individual to decide for themselves what knowledge to use to shape a worldview. It come as part of the human package … the same ability to choose that Jehovah decided to give Adam and Eve in the Eden beginning.

An individual is born into life first, to then be conditioned to adjust to the human experience. This happens before they use their freewill to make the decision on whether to believe a theological notion or perform the due diligence to self-train their ability to self-train an enlightened consciously registered intrinsic understanding of the relational principles that affect the outcomes of all relationships that define the nature of reality's impermanent personality.

Before an individual can act on their fear of what is unknown and weigh the need in deciding whether to have blind faith in anything, they must first develop a worldview perception that is subject to how their belief system gets conditioned. Their worldview must be somehow conditioned to allow for trusting borrowed wisdom in seeking emotional stability from elsewhere before they step forward and give their soul to one of the heavenly gods.

How they have conditioned themselves to process and understand the unknown will help determine what type of faith they will decide to use in developing an emotional understanding.

To follow a theologically laid pathway is a decision made by an already conditioned belief system.

The quality of the understanding of the realty that created the belief system to make the decision seems like where the faith should point.

Even under the watch of their god, Adam and Eve had free spirits to make their Tree of Knowledge decision to blindly place their faith in another entity's ability to provide the truth to end up being "empty-of-understanding" why or how it's true.

Just Because a God's Promise Says So, Runs a Little Thin for Many ... Blind Faith ... What?

Sideline Your Experiential Reference?

Blind faith would have a believer stifle the doubts that tug at their gut feeling developed from seeing how related or similar relationships transpire in real-life time. A believer is expected to take the god's wisdom as presented ... to take "his" holy word for it. Many can't do this.

... Blindly Bet Your Soul on a Promised Heaven?

For many, with blind faith, the inborn directive that emerges in stride with vocabulary growth that brings verbal color to the "terrible 2's," insistently questioning everything that's not understood becomes conditioned into blind silence. They become intellectually handcuffed to the rulebook of a borrowed claim-to-wisdom template.

A religious belief will assert that their god's supernatural power is the force that creates and controls nature's principles ... thus allowing the miracles ... the parting of the Red Sea ... Jesus healing the sick and bringing the dead back to life ... the 10 plagues of Egypt ... etcetera.

Some value protecting their freewill with 1st amendment rights. They require a deeper understanding of whatever life path they are about to undertake. Instead of blindly following some notion, they need a taste of what is been promised.

Many find it difficult to establish any sort of faith in something that lacks having a related identifiable intrinsic history tie-in allowing a gut-felt association or understanding of the "why's" or the "why not's" needed to supplement its strand of professed wisdom.

The modern-day lack of having any defined discriminating awareness creates the same emptiness-of-understanding that drew the emotional shame out of Adam and Eve when they cowered to explain using the hollow borrowed wisdom from the Tree of Knowledge they'd received gifted from the Eden snake when confronted by Jehovah.

Steadfast Faith Grows from Understanding
What Proves Self-Evident

A baby is born ignorant to much of life's truths. They will develop any intrinsically registered steadfast faith in intrinsically filed feelings that become wakingly understood as they experience what it takes to transfer weight from 1 foot to the other in learning how to walk. This truth of weight transfer becomes self-evident to them.

Einstein's E=MC2 voices mathematically his "aha" insight of Tree of Life wisdom bringing into waking view how mass and energy are interchangeable. That this universe is impermanent becomes self-evident as this universal truth that defines this universal reality's force-driven dimensional backdrop filtered up through Mr. Einstein's conscious awareness to gain exposure in mankind's collective conscious awareness.

Today there are actual photographs of those subatomic quantum mechanics size particles of energy that come and go to their unpredictable schedule. It is now a self-evident universal truth that nothing stands still.

This is the same truth that became self-evident to Siddhartha as he came to understand intrinsically through self-discovering how to calm his mind to allow self-training his mind to focus a sustained mind-into-body concentration to sensually observe and gain conscious awareness through witnessed self-knowledge from life as it manifests itself in the evolving makeup of his flesh.

This self-knowledge equipped the right thinking to self-train the same Tree of Life wisdom through his insightful "aha" moments of realized wisdom that Christianity's god ordered Adam to have in the Garden of Eden at the very onset of the biblical version of this universe's Genesis creation.

... It's the Undeniable "Don't Shoot the Messenger" Sort of Truth

Back in 1775 when Patrick Henry declared "give me liberty or give me death" to encourage the delivery of Virginia troops to fight for man's naturally deserved "freedom and liberty" in the Revolutionary War, he was serving as the messenger of a most important life truth ... the right to the same liberty Mother nature gives to the tiny quarks of quantum physics ... that he and his fellow patriots used to anchor their rebellious callout.

Patrick Henry was merely bringing to attention the most basic of natural human rights to be free as transposed up from and felt in the natural rhythm of what is responsible for the ephemeral presence of this material reality.

Henry has demonstrated impermeable steadfast faith in a natural truth that Einstein's now mathematically documented and shown to be self-evident. The degree of unchecked unpredictable liberty Mother nature's recipe of patterned principles give to the relationships between the tiny quantum mechanics sparks-of-energy quarks ring the same bell of truth on up the chainring of relational inter-actions into the ongoing flow of material change that exists throughout mankind's limited range of sensual perception.

This truth proves self-evident when sensually witnessing life itself manifest, as did Siddhartha, within one's own flesh. Science's photographs showcase how the coming and going particles of energy present in the subatomic world of quantum mechanics exist in a relational state of total unchartered unbiased liberty ... as should mankind's inter-relational state.

... Steadfast Faith Grows in the Wake of Understanding

On a basic level, a faith that stands steadfast grows naturally in step with the wisdom-enriched understanding of the natural truths that control the outcomes of life experience.

Steadfast faith satisfies the intuitive ping for self-confidence while invigorating latent inner self-belief.

Steadfast faith supports satisfying a truth-seeker's quest to better understand the natural force-driven patterned principles that set course for their life in this reality.

They unravel their ignorance to better understand and become free of their emotional suffering to realize emotional bliss while still living ... before entering the mysterious "afterlife" that the human condition was clearly never wired to understand.

Blind Faith Grows
from the Hollow Hope of Realizing Unsupported Promise

This claim to faith requires a vow of unquestioned obedience to blindly follow a scripted set of loosely spun rules to hopefully attain the emotional bliss in a promised afterlife paradise free of suffering.

Having blind faith in the "God-given" wisdom supporting a theological promise means one must mortgage their freewill's right to question and seek membership in a group with similar fears, held subject to a loosely choreographed routine of rites and ritual.

A believer will spend their life hoping they are not unknowingly blacklisted by the promise maker ... the unseen god figure.

When casting blind faith in "his" written promise, a believer's emotional balance teeters on their unstrapped doubt-riddled hope of finding this afterlife emotional bliss, staged somewhere in a hell-free cloud paradise of unfamiliar unearthly texture.

Steadfast Faith Becomes Deeply Seated

... It's an Individual's Bosom Buddy

From birth, an individual's steadfast faith blossoms in the wake of their growing understanding awareness of even the most basic of reality's natural processes.

From what the day brings, each human being develops an intrinsically lodged confidence that stands steadfast in the self-evident truth of the undeniable manifestation of something they have experienced.

Most never put this growing awareness into conscious perspective. It is just taken for granted like how an individual's awareness of the flow of time gets lost in its constant presence.

Steadfast faith grows as a naturally spawned faith. It often goes unrecognized relative to the blind trust that is the sole fiber supporting a faith that is blind to reality's story.

One with a faith that's blind will often, when needed, vocally remind themselves that they are the proud bearers of a blind faith.

Once out of their mother's womb, an infant will develop a deeply seated steadfast faith that the morning sun will rise on schedule. They will just take it for granted that Father Time's clock will keep ticking ... without pause.

Human beings develop a steadfast faith in their understanding awareness of the different incarnations and rhythms that embody reality's uncontrollable patterns of ongoing transformation.

This is faith that is stands steadfast to any theory that might dare to negate its process of truth.

Steadfast faith is a basic essential for the human condition to navigate its human experience. The basic revelations in understanding what controls the human experience are part of the same interconnected infrastructure comprising reality's only truth network.

Since its existence was defined and brought to mankind's collective awareness by Sir Isaac Newton, mankind now has a consciously recognized steadfast faith in the existence of gravity ... one of Mother Nature's principle-determining forces.

Albert Einstein went on to bring into light how other factors like mass and speed can have a relative effect on gravity.

These natural forces produce combined effects that give pattern to the principles of life that influence humankind's emotional dialog.

The more pieces of self-evident truth awareness added into the puzzle, the clearer the picture becomes. Today, there is less ignorance from a deeper understanding about the uncertainties that cause suffering.

Developed awareness of these truths is Mother Nature-prescribed soul-healing. Its prescription is signed by the same deeper consciousness that understands nature's principles well enough to form a scab over a cut or remind the heart to beat.

This natural healing tendency wants just as much to help heal the suffering soul.

Blindly Willed Faith's Not Founded in Intrinsic Familiarity

... It's Merely a Pen Pal ... Blind Faith Lacks Experiential Validation

Blind faith is a faith that is founded in something the intrinsic core has no experienced history of. Blind faith's not supported by the steadfast assurance (faith) in what the heat from a lit match feels like. It is something someone can intellectually understand yet, in having no sensual history reference to, they have no intrinsic pre-verbal understanding.

Having faith in a friend's description would be "blind" to an understanding of the actual truth of what makes up "hot." Their borrowed wisdom would be "empty-of-understanding."

The childhood experience of being stuck by a needle engenders the steadfast faith in understanding the sting of a needle prick. It is a sensually metered event with a meaning that supersedes any intellectually generated graphic description.

Before their first injection, a child would not have any sensual history of the sting from getting a shot. They can only have a blind faith in their parent's verbal description to cognitively conceptualize the feel of the sting.

They need to see how this intellectually metered notion of "sting" scores sensually before honoring it with their scream.

Their blind faith will support their initial caution. But once the intrinsic reference is established by the sensual feeling of an actual needle prick, the blind faith will be superseded by their steadfast faith in the knowledge what the next pin prick will feel like.

The child's pre-injection faith is blind to their parents' sensual history of them getting their shots that established their steadfast faith-backed Tree of Life wisdom that is being offered as gifted wisdom to be blindly trusted, borrowed by their child.

The child's blind faith in this borrowed wisdom instantly transforms into experiential wisdom backed by their steadfast faith the instant they get stuck.

It's like striking up blind faith in wisdom borrowed from a friend or reading about describing what "hot" feels like. An experientially founded steadfast faith would arise from holding a finger to a flame.

The child's blind faith used when borrowing their parent's wisdom is like when Adam and Eve struck up a blind faith in the snake-promised all-knowing wisdom they were snake-gifted from the Garden of Eden Tree of Knowledge of All Good and Evil.

It's a faith built on trusting some other entity's unverified understanding that comes with no sensual history tie-in … no established intrinsic familiarity.

… Blind Faith is Based More on Intellectual Pride than Intrinsically Founded Surety

Any faith blind to an unverified divinity remains ungrounded as it echoes through an individual's void of uncertainty.

The inexperienced reasoning network of an untested strain of Tree of Knowledge wisdom that comes borrowed from blindly trusting another entity's say-so offers no intrinsically registered conscious familiarity with the fortifying principles making the wisdom valid … like with Adam and Eve and their borrowed snake-gifted wisdom left them both shamefully surprised, with no understanding, unable to understand and explain their state of nakedness.

An individual's waking perception of an imagined reality with a dimensional makeup that allows for time continuity or a skip in time to support the presence of the essence of their cognitively sketched impression of an intellectually metered thing or idea will not have the appropriate principle-decoding wisdom mental interface to decodes (understands) to enlighten them about the actual principle makeup that governs all cause/effect outcomes in this reality's undeniably impermanent dimensional backdrop.

Their misguided understanding … their fundamental ignorance … brings about their suffering.

This miscued perception is not focused on internalizing the appropriate sensually driven wisdom-deriving knowledge strain to inspire insightfully assimilating the strain of life wisdom that is sensitized to decode and understand the actual principle patterns that drive the ever-transforming infrastructure of this reality's impermanent dimensional makeup.

If an individual's perception of reality allows for continuity to play a role in the nature of its perceived presence, their belief system's compromised to where they're more likely to settle for gathering their wisdom-deriving knowledge from sources that allow or require an individual to recognize an imagined continual presence of the essence of other things and ideas to be time-suspended in a state of imagined permanence while not having to respond to Mother Nature's unavoidable impetus of ongoing change that runs reality's world.

The self-evident truth of this reality's ongoing transformation proves this skip-in-time perception to be imaginary.

... Ignorance Hardens Over Time

The developed thought of the essence of the time-suspended images can cognitively register as being real and have a continual sense of presence ... like when some older people think of themselves, many still picture a human body that's 20 years younger.

Their attachment to this clinging dominates and sustains their subliminal misperception about the force-driven patterned principles that generate and sustain this reality's impermanent backdrop. Not recognizing this reality's state of impermanence is the fundamental ignorance that lies at the root of all human suffering.

This pseudo-wisdom some swear by and cling to that is driven by their fear of the unknown with nowhere else to turn will over time only make this thorn-in-their-side enigma fester and the sought-after life truth will gradually become more distant.

The "answer" slips farther out of reach to a question that, for many, has yet to materialize.

With the type of knowledge used in deriving the wisdom that inspires no sort of intrinsic understanding giving detail to how the blindly adopted path to emotional bliss or cure for suffering realizes its circle of truth, they must settle for blind-faith comfort while standing reverent, following the instructions outlined by the sketchy details of its borrowed-leader-supplied wisdom they only have an intellectually realized familiarity with ... possibly available only in a handed-down chain of multi-translated interpretations of ancient scriptures.

We live in a reality that has an impermanent personality.

A transforming dimensional backdrop has no on-again/off-again switch.

This reality's wisdom book with the dimensional force-set principles that set the pattern for its impermanent presence has no scribed entry that allows for still-set continuity. Any reality that is not impermanent is imagined.

Steadfast Faith Comes Naturally ... No Blind Venture Needed

... It's Felt ... Not Intellectually Configured

Steadfast faith registers intrinsically in a subtle level of the deeper consciousness well before the conscious configuration of what most think of when they think of "having any faith in anything." Any messaging that uses sensual media takes priority over any derived wisdom that's reasoned out intellectually.

Intrinsically seeded steadfast faith comes when the waking consciousness comes aware of what inspired insight rises from what is already a living part of deeper consciousness awareness. It's reached the plateau of being self-evident at this time.

It makes sense ... no middleman guarantee needed.

... Faith Is Felt in The Soul ... Not Cognitively Configured

Many mistakenly think their intrinsic sense of faith and trust is something they can intellectually exert conscious control over. Some say that faith is not a feeling, that it is a choice.

Faith can be considered intellectually ... but its presence is felt in the heart.

Faith must be seeded in something for its reflected trust to grow. That seed must sprout from a felt connection. The waking consciousness feels the "It's OK" coming from the deeper consciousness.

... Blind Faith is Blindly Assumed

Blind faith is not a state that is intrinsically inspired. It is blindly assumed. The knowledge describing the tenants of faith are intellectually metered, then intellectually memorized.

Blind faith builds a bridge of trust over the field of uncertain doubt ... the emptiness-of-understanding filling the zone of spirituality that exists between conscious awareness and the unrecognized knowledge of nature of the deeper consciousness that has yet to rise to bring an understanding conscious awareness about the relationships between the impermanent nature of this reality and how the emotional matrix of the human condition fits into its web of transformation. The blind faith backs an answer that tip toes over this transition of awareness promising to ease emotional turmoil and allow emotional bliss to replace it.

Blind faith is an agreement the conscious mind makes with the inner purpose of the belief system. It blindly overwrites the possibility of anything else being true. It writes and hardens that belief into an impenetrable slab of stone.

The truth-seeker has no foundation or reason to dream up a steadfast faith. Steadfast faith is not a blind faith of hope or wish that an unvalidated claim maker will be there to catch them in their ignorance if something grabs them or lets them fall into their void of fear.

An individual's choice should be inspired by what they feel ... if they can know their true feelings and many can't. Many have their inner feelings numbed by a blind faith and they will parrot the response that the entity responsible for their borrowed wisdom says ... some degree of brainwashing.

Confidence and trust are constructs inspired by feelings.

The essence of true faith is not something that can simply be assumed. It must be earned, rooted in sensually witnessed experience.

A new employee must earn his employer's trust that he will show up for work on time and perform his job as expected. An employer's initial faith in a new employee's timeliness is untested and blind to experience.

Any claim to a cognitively processed gender of faith is more of a forced sort of unsecured yet postured trust in what somebody or some unfounded ideological notion promises.

The Narrow Path to Enlightenment from Ignorance is Paved with Life Understanding

A truth-seeker must continue to use the same basic innate intrinsic tools to continue nurturing their understanding of reality's nature as were used establishing a steadfast faith in the daily sunrise and in the deeply spun assurance that time will continue without pause.

The continued unveiling of the self-evident character of the principles in nature that control the outcomes of all cause/effect relationships in this reality is what is necessary.

Steadfast faith grows with each insightful growth of the Tree of Life wisdom needed to understand the ways of nature to avoid ignorance-inspired emotional suffering from being empty-of-understanding."

Mankind's Wired for Only One State of Emotional Bliss

No matter how many promises are made outlining afterlife states of heavenly paradise, human emotions can only realize one pattern of emotional bliss. The human kaleidoscope of emotions is all there is to deal with.

The thought of having freedom from emotional suffering targets the same state of bliss whether referenced or promised by religious theology or self-trained through recognition of realism and true freedom from suffering is founded only in what has been sensually experienced.

Self-training an improved awareness of nature's ways allows living a more emotionally balanced life to possibly self-train the total enlightenment explaining all fundamental ignorance to realize the only sort of emotional bliss humanity has been conditioned to know when establishing its living intrinsic history through sensually feeling its state of functional inclusion ... an working sliver of ongoing change affecting the cause/effect outcome of something in time's present moment.

Reality recognizes "emotional heaven" to be found in an enlightened understanding of the present moment and theology imagines this emotional bliss at some time in the future in a phase of reality that no living human has a sensual history of.

Enlightened Thought Stream
Lacks Bandwidth for Middleman Data Feed

… Avoids Web Provider Confusion

Developing steadfast faith in nature's self-evident truths like the sun rising or the passage of time is just the starting line for developing a better understanding of what details the human experience.

Consider developing the steadfast faith in the awareness that the sun rises every day, and that time passes by to be preschool.

Then consider the further evolvement of steadfast faith emerging abreast an improved conscious awareness of the principles that rule the impermanent nature of this reality bringing about spiritual enlightenment as being at the Ph.D. level.

T/he Roman priests edited out the accounts of Jesus's teachings that taught more at the college level.

Both the toddler and the Ph.D. are using the same sensually founded living tools to understand the same living system. Start to finish.

Their understanding must go uninterrupted by some other sort of plan using different tools that are not sensually founded but are metered intellectually … borrowed wisdom. This other plan would, as Jehovah warned Adam, bring them spiritual death.

They'd never get it right unless they began seeking out Tree of Life wisdom … as Jehovah said about Adam and Eve ever returning to Eden when he banished them.

… Yes … A Fly-in-the-Ointment

The mental scope needed to self-train an understanding awareness of reality's interwoven network of principles loses its focus when interrupted by a middle-man-designed promise that shortcuts and sidesteps the needed discovery work to allow somehow reaching the targeted end of what is really nothing other than an intrinsically founded emotional bliss … simple as that … no outside interruptions to sidetrack path.

The middleman disguises his demand with a required unquestioned blind obedience to his designed wisdom that promises the same emotional bliss. He wraps his promised afterlife paradise package in the required assumption of a pseudo-faith in his unverifiable promised wisdom that's admittingly blind to any sort of intrinsically spun understanding.

The borrowed wisdom somehow baits the hook in a way that inspires the believers to take pride in having the courage to blindly trust his pitch.

How can the resulting state of beat-down indecision this creates, lacking an intrinsic history foundation be considered true heart-stamped faith?

Steadfast faith is a faith vested in actual experience. It is not a faith built on the blind hope of a mystical promise. It lights a truth seeker's path and supplies sure footing in their attempt to realize this state of bliss possibly during their lifetime. They are not left ever-hoping for it to be a somehow middleman-bestowed treat after their life experience has ended.

Blind Faith in Fundamentalist Dialog can be a Barrier to Understanding the Self-Evident Truth of Life

Those who through their ignorance become attached to the imagined permanent non-flowing existence of things and ideas can easily develop an attachment to the static nature of the fundamental interpretation of a religion's written creed.

Their belief system has already been compromised by how they choose to view the presence of reality as allowing continuity.

Their waking consciousness is not prepared to process reality's feed of unchartered change that continually feeds their fear of the unknown.

They cling to their blind faith for security.

> "But if we remain satisfied simply to accept received wisdom without questioning, it becomes a form of bondage, a barrier to the attainment of experiential understanding. By the same token, if we remain content merely to contemplate truth, to investigate and understand it intellectually, but make no effort to experience it directly, then all our intellectual understanding becomes a bondage instead of an aid to liberation."
>
> —William Hart, *The Art of Living: Vipassana Meditation as taught by S. N. Goenka*, pg.90

> "The Buddha regarded his own teaching as a raft to cross the river and not as an absolute truth to be worshipped or clung to. He said this to prevent rigid dogmatism or fanaticism from taking root. Ideological inflexibility is responsible for so much of the conflict and violence in the world. According to the Buddhist teaching, knowledge itself can be an obstacle to true understanding, and views can be a barrier to insight. Clinging to views can prevent us from arriving at a deeper, more profound understanding of reality."
>
> —Thich Naht Hanh, *Inter-being: Fourteen Guidelines for Engaged Buddhism* (1988) p. 123

When an individual agrees to wear blinders through what their day offers to blindly follow the written dialog of some theological ideology, they lose focus and concern for questioning and understanding what ongoing change throws in their face.

Their inborn childhood curiosity becomes frozen in time.

They close their mind to experiencing the mental peace that follows in the wake of enriching insights to help in understanding what life principles control the outcomes that give form to their assessment of how their life condition is fairing during their life experience.

...Inviting a State of Apathetic Laziness

With no effort to deepen their conscious understanding life awareness, a conceding state of apathetic laziness can set in.

They will pass through life apathetically choosing not to get off their mental couch to make the effort to understand and direct their individual and unique talents and skills to accomplishing even basic life responsibilities.

Many of those locked in the notion of some theological ideology will continue to pillage through life, turning over the rocks of new things and ideas hoping to uncover the answer to the unknown question that keeps prodding them from deep within.

Many who boldly proclaim to be a follower of a certain god, fail to connect the importance of having the flow of their physical body's rhythm in line with that of the reality they are a part of, that holds the answer to their emotional imbalance.

They may never drink any alcohol like some religions believe or eat meat on Friday.

They may be faithful at the time of Lent, but they may still find it easy to fill their iced tea with packages of fake sugar that have been proven to feed cancer. They do not hesitate to eat their favorite preparations of white flour.

They choose to stay ignorant and unconcerned about what blood glucose is.

Intellectual Understanding of Self-Training Pathway to Emotional Bliss can Lead to Experiential Understanding

> *"Wisdom acquired through listening to others and wisdom acquired through intellectual investigation are helpful if they inspire and guide us to advance to the third type of panna, experiential wisdom."*
>
> —William Hart, *The Art of Living: Vipassana Meditation as taught by S. N. Goenka,* pg.90

An individual's only way to gain an enlightened understanding is to personally experience it.

If a truth-seeker can intellectually understand what the steps are in self-training an enlightened understanding, they can recenter themselves should the step outside the pathway and experience emotional distress of some sort.

They're not left hanging.

A truth-seeker needs to follow a qualified teacher's lead and experientially convert how they have heard the experience should be like to what they intrinsically understand it to be.

Emotional Suffering is Realized in Present Moment Living Reaction

... Not so much in Contemplated Planned Action

It is because individuals trip over their ignorance of reality's governing principles that they suffer while reacting.

Many fail to stop and observe their arising emotions before emitting some knee-jerk reaction. They'll thoughtlessly react to that situation the next time it occurs.

During times of sensually witnessing change live in action while in self-contemplation or when an emotion-spawning feeling arises, if an individual can think ... hopefully insightfully ... before reacting ... and plan out a course of action that might be better suited for the situation, the suffering can eventually be avoided.

Enlightenment comes in baby steps.

Misguided conditioning and poorly tagged feelings will tender the emotional hellfire an individual can spend their entire lifetime wrapped up and burning in. It is the real-life living hell version of religion's biblically threatened fire and brimstone.

People evaluate and rate the quality of their life experience by how they collectively access their emotions.

Steadfast Faith Emanates Inner Confidence

Steadfast faith protects and strengthens a truth-seeker on their quest to become enlightened about reality's nature to be free of all the mental white noise to allow their emotional balance to surface from their deeper consciousness where it waits strapped down by the waking consciousness ignorance of reality's ways that underwrites all their emotional suffering.

An individual is more able to assert their purpose when they feel in their gut that what they are doing is supported by the principles that support the nature of this reality than biting their lip with only the cognitive assurance that what they are doing is supported by what another entity said should or will be.

Worldview Credibility

The credibility an individual fashions into their worldview will be fortified by the faith that's either heartfelt, standing steadfast, or of a compromised weaker strain that ruminates in the hope of things occurring.

If steadfast faith lines their belief system, whatever their worldview might assert about anything will have the feeling of assured support it provides.

Blind faith in an intellectually crafted plan to afterlife salvation leaves the belief system unprotected in the flow of sensually metered present moment real-life matters.

The world view they've fashioned will reflect the nature of what their belief system has internalized.

Too many people fail to ever come consciously at one with a personal heartfelt understanding of which latticework of wisdom best characterizes the moral/ethical boundaries that lead to a life of compassion-primed joy and happiness. Many with a compromised freewill choose to roll the dice and place their blind trust in having a hopeful faith in the promises of outside entities. They internalize unverified wisdom originated from untested knowledge.

This wisdom comes empty-of-understanding how the wisdom promised to justify the claim finds its truth. Should it be emotional bliss … it leaves the individual empty-of-understanding the principled ways of relational interactions that exist in this reality.

A resulting misaligned ego-managed worldview might over time have been conditioned to entertain an agenda that is self-serving and not compassion-oriented … infected and emotionally crippled by the urge of craving attachment.

They might hear and not try to listen. They might observe and not see. They might touch and not consciously feel.

They might be using intellectually founded Fig Leaf Wisdom to sensually feel their way through real-life's present moment.

… Contrast the integrity of steadfast faith-bound experientially assimilated life wisdom insightfully derived from intrinsically spawned self-knowledge through sensual media against borrowed wisdom's still-life flatline derived from knowledge that is received unverified via intellectually resourced media that comes hollow, empty-of-understanding on a security blanket of blind faith.

… There are Two Types of Faith
… Only One Engenders Enlightened Growth

XI

Get to Know Your "Self"?

Mental or Material Self?

"The worst loneliness is to not be comfortable with yourself."

~Mark Twain

... Find Comfort In Your Own Skin by Understanding How Reality Defines Your Material Self that Harbors Your Emotional Makeup

... Material Self Radiates Tree of Life Principles that go on to Affect Shaping the Mental Self

... Get to Understand the Source First

Rome's 325 A.D. biblical content editing allowed a few source-reference passages in the gospels to slip through to be included in their Roman Bible. Luke 17:21, I Corinthians 3:16, and II Corinthians 13:5 of the King James translation all give reference that points to "God" being found within:

- "The kingdom of God is within you."

- "The temple and spirit of God Dwelleth within you,"

- "Jesus Christ is in you."

One of the gospels that didn't say what Rome was looking for was the Book of Thomas. It was written to or by an audience/author of higher spiritual maturity that could verbally express Jesus's deeper meaning in his teachings.

In sayings 3 and 77B of the 114 sayings in the Book of Thomas, it's made clear that the kingdom of God's inside and outside and not in any buildings made of wood or stone:

- "The kingdom of God is inside of you, and it is outside of you."

- "…not in buildings/mansions of wood and stone. (When I am gone.) Split a piece of wood and I am there. Lift the/a stone and I am there."

Thomas makes it clear that Jesus taught that the spirit of life exists inside everything.

… Get to "Know Your "Material" Self Better

What comes to mind when someone suggests getting to "know yourself better?" Does it register as getting to better understand the nature of your personality … to better know the mental you?

Has it ever registered as getting to better understand the life energy that makes up your material self?

Knowing oneself better normally implies trying to better understand one's conditioned persona. Better understanding the principles that influence those characteristics will give one a better means of getting to know themselves and affecting change in the persona.

… Understand the Principles that Condition the Personality

To understand a personality, it's wise to understand what it is that conditioned the characteristics of that personality. It is better to step back to better understand the principled nature of what conditions the mental self that emits that emotional profile.

Think about better understanding the source of the principles that set course for the reality that one is conditioned to react or act to. These natural force-driven principles or patterns of principles are what affect the outcome of everything in their life experience that their mental self gets conditioned to deal with in the change that makes up their present moment.

It is true wisdom to understand your emotions … true emotional balance is emotional bliss. An individual has to have an established understanding of impermanence to allow understanding what affects their emotional state.

... The Theater of Change

"Wisdom tends to grow in proportion to one's awareness of one's ignorance."

-Anthony De Mello

One needs to go to their only spot-on source ... their own theater of change-manifest ... where this spirit of life emanates the living breath of change ... to witness it ... to sensually catch it in the act red-handed ... to first watch it sensually to then understand it better ... on the intrinsic level.

Getting to better understand the material self sounds silly to most or at least like a dead end. Seeing no obvious reason why to do this, it is probably never even considered.

The cause/effect relational justice coding the impermanence humans perceive as the present moment comes with in owner's guide ... the human body ... of the wisdom that makes sense of how its components relate to each other.

... What Could be a Better Place to Go?

One needs to develop a better understanding of nature's ways and principles through their physical body as it constantly radiates life change as it manifests. The humming presence of life-manifest lies within human flesh as it responds to the principled laws of impermanence that keep this reality synched up.

The living human body is an individual's only sensual conduit to feel the actual tic-toc of what happens in this reality's eddy of change to experientially witness its ways and understand the story it tells.

A truth-seeker must attend to the integration process between when the intellectually inspired idea of getting to better know themselves morphs into a conscious snapshot understanding of the intrinsically seeded answer.

To better understand the mental you, it is best to better understand the reality that it is been conditioned to perceive and act/react to.

The process of discovery feeds into understanding. It is what living life and this writing are all about.

Now ... Think a Little Deeper

For a truth-seeker to get to better know their emotional/mental self, involves the process of getting to know and understand the ageless principles of impermanence that also rule how life itself manifests from within.

This is where life answers lie.

With regular attention, over time, the fact that the same natural forces also rule the human experience will prove self-evident ... in steadfast fashion.

It is the ignorance ... intrinsic unfamiliarity ... conscious disassociation from awareness of this reality's timeless principles that rule the flow of its ongoing process of transformation that cause human emotional distress ... Buddhism's Fundamental Ignorance.

Siddhartha taught that it is this ignorance that seeds the clinging attachment to the imagined continual unchanging presence of things and ideas coming from not recognizing the nature of impermanence alive in all things. He points out that this ignorance is the root of all human suffering.

It is this reality's unalterable principles of impermanence that define and support its multi-dimensional transforming nature and control the outcome of every cause/effect relationship affecting everything as time passes.

It is these whip-cracking principles of nature that keep this passing reality ongoingly lit in full living color.

Humans can Control What They Think and Do

Individuals have been conditioned to behave in certain ways to get what they want or to avoid what they do not want. Humans have power over what they think and do.

Humans think and behave as they have been conditioned to. They develop the calculated behavioral logistics of approaching something in a way to justify using those certain behaviors that works for them in effort to get what they want or to avoid what they do not want.

But Not the Outcome

Nature's relational principles determine the outcome of relationships regardless of human intentions. To ease the pain from the friction of expectations not meeting up with reality, the goal is to develop a conscious understanding awareness of these principles and how those principles affect how things interrelate.

Benjamin P. Hardy, husband, and foster father of three who is pursuing a Ph.D. in Organizational Psychology had published a wonderfully insightful blog in the Huffington Post on Feb. 8, 2017. An excerpt reads:

> "You don't control the outcomes of your life.
> You don't control how other people will respond to you.
> You don't control your health.
> You don't control how much money you make.
> Principles control these things.
> If you consistently put unhealthy foods in your body, your
> body will become unhealthy.
> Your body is a natural system governed by principles.

If you don't pay the price to develop your mind with consistent learning, your mind will become dull and unclear.

Your mind is a natural system governed by principles.

Most people cram for tests while in college. But can you cram if you're a farmer? Can you forget to plant in the spring, slack-off all summer, and then work hard during the fall?

of course not. A farm is a natural system governed by principles.

So are you."

https://benjaminhardycom/I-control-outcomes-lifeprinciples/

An individual cannot determine how other individuals react to their presence or how their stock market investments fair. They cannot control exactly how their vehicle reacts to ice on streets.

They can do their best to influence these outcomes, but their ignorance to the ways of the forces detailing nature's governing principles leaves them unable to foresee the logistics of the outcome. The outcome is out of their control.

It is up to nature's unbiased principles that support and conform to the timeless force-determined fundamental laws defining the nature of this reality's dimensional backdrop composition.

If one opens a compass the natural law force electromagnetism will point the needle to the north.

Humans are not in control of the outcomes of their actions. The governing natural principles of this reality are.

Hemans are all familiar with how back and forth decisions often come down to the final decision being: "it's all about the principle of things."

"Tidal Flexing" of Impermanent Backdrop Natural Forces Underwrites Nature's Relational Principle Laws

... Whether Ying/Yang, God or Whatever Inspired ... The Nature of this Reality is the Ongoing Push and Pull of Change Itself

The only thing that does not change in this reality is the ongoing persistence of ever-changing transformation itself. The ongoing push and pull between gravity and electromagnetism fuel this reality's purpose of expansive ever-change.

... Nature's Forces Influence and Perpetuate Natural Principles

The relational integrity of the force-inspired principles ruling the push and pull that transforms one present moment into the next ... the effect of one cause into being the cause of the next effect … manifests up from the energy factory of life too small for the human eye to see.

At this point in mankind's life awareness timeline, the existence of four laws of nature has proven self-evident. Their truth has been questioned and proven by mankind's collective freewill (science).

On the larger realm, the forces of gravitation and electromagnetism rule, while the strong and weak nuclear forces dominate the roaring whisper of the quantum physics subatomic world.

These four forces of nature work together in patterns of dimensional harmony. They combine in ways that result in patterns of force that trickle up from the unpredictable, uncontrollable coming and going bits of energy that pump life into the subatomic quantum physics world (real-life incarnation of theology's Holy Spirit?) into the world of human perception.

These forces interact and affect each other in totally non-prejudiced. The energy processed by the force-spun principles stoke the fire pumping life into this impermanent reality.

It's never stopped. Stopping time itself would create such an unusual reality and its atmosphere so abnormal that it was used for at least one episode of Rod Sterling's *The Twilight Zone*.

The unpredictable tendencies of those little bits of appearing/disappearing energized quarks, that support/compose the building blocks of the ever-transform-ing forms of the ever-transforming objects that can be seen in the human range of perception, all dance to the music of these natural forces. They establish the model for the unbendable-by-man laws that set principles in nature's rulebook.

A truth-seeker needs to figure out how to understand and own their emo-tions in a way that flows to the rhythm of the waves of nature's patterned prin-ciples. Their emotions will be subject to much less emotional friction than from when their take of the present moment is caught between sensually observing nature's rhythm of truth and what they intellectually superimpose over the present moment by a borrowed explanation of how things should interrelate.

… The "Law of Gravity"

Most people today have heard of the "law of gravity" since early grade school. By most, it is just accepted as "the law" and does not question who or what it was that wrote that law.

Electromagnetism is also just known to exist with its source not questioned.

They both represent the forces that sustain this reality everyone must set in while questioning their source.

They are the forces that generate the relational principles that give order to the coming and going bits of energy that give shape to what animates the human perception of the present moment.

... What Works Best for Man Acts in Rhythm with those Principles

It follows that the primal cause/effect relational justice that governs those basic idiosyncrasies that give shape to subatomic particles, continues up the ladder of size proportion where these building blocks relationally unite to assume the behavioral characteristics described in the table of elements to finally join hands to constitute the inside and observable outside of the objects that appear in the human field of perception ... that most see as solid objects.

In view of the non-continual transforming nature of this reality, as time rolls forward, the flow of the interactions defining these principles, depending on situational conditions, morphs into patterns that will, in turn, affect the outcome of cause/effect relational interactions.

... Dimensional Harmony Affects Principles of Impermanence ... String and Wave Theories

These principled patterns are being questioned and tested by mankind's freewill, science, to this very day to increase mankind's collective awareness of the self-evident truths present that we as a biological species still stand ignorant to ... the various string and wave theories. (One must wonder if the general public's exposure to this gender of scientific progress is gained mostly by listening to the genius theoretical physicist, Sheldon on TV's "Big Bang Theory".)?

Even though these forces evade human perception, they are very real.

These invisible forces thread together to keep suspended this reality's silent backdrop. They define and support the truth that the Tree of Life wisdom leads to decodes.

Over time, the slowly emerging knowledge that makes insightfully clear their self-evident existence. Only a handful of centuries ago mankind's collective perspective opened from one of ancient superstition to a less fear-filled age of reason.

Relational Principles Link Together the Present Moment

The smallest of subatomic building blocks ... an elementary particle of raw energy ... the quark ... one bit of coming and going energy carries a fractional electric charge. They react with other quarks.

These relationships occur by a protocol that is dictated by the fundamental natural forces that string together ... electromagnetism and gravity, strong and weak… to hold together this reality and weave together the story of change told on this reality's one-dimensional timeline.

The interaction itinerary of these quarks is set to a cause/effect rhythm determined by the natural forces.

As the outcome effect of one interaction is determined, at the same time it becomes the cause for the effect of the next. This continues in an ongoing process that will link one present moment to the next.

Following Siddhartha's guided 8-fold pathway to become enlightened to Jehovah's Eden-demanded Tree of Life wisdom will edify an individual to what these natural principles are in a sensually detected intrinsic form of awareness.

Understanding how the principles of these forces of nature that affect change interact to affect human emotion allows an individual to understand the emotional bliss that religions refer to as "heaven" and those who are not theologians simply refer to as being "enlightened" about what causes emotional suffering.

Force-Driven Principles Affect Human Experience

The patterns of relational principles driven by the interactions between nature's dimensional forces that give order to the outcome of how the unpredictable coming and going bits of energy interact to maintain this reality's ongoing state of impermanence filter up to set natural order and rhythm in the same flow of time to set pattern to the relational principles affecting the outcomes of interactions in the range of human perception during each ever-evasive present moment of the human experience.

The relational principles outlined by these subatomic cause/effect relationships set the relational swing that trickles up to set relational pattern to outcomes on the larger scale.

Natural law principles established in the pattern displays of coming and going quantum mechanics energy particles trickle up to form the supporting infrastructure of the tree of life wisdom reflected in the conditioned nature of an individual's mind.

… Realism Crafts a Higher Emotional Intelligence and More Matured Worldview

An individual who has developed their knowledge base experientially to then assimilate their wisdom tree has brought to their conscious awareness a more intrinsic understanding of this transient reality. In so doing, they become more perceptive to what and how natural principles affect their emotions.

They have a higher emotional intelligence relative to those who derive their wisdom based on knowledge borrowed empty-of-understanding while lacking having any history of sensually acquired familiarity.

Perceiving reality, even if unknowingly, allowing its animated flow to assume a halted state of continuity is imaginary and unnatural. This is the source of the resulting illusionary expectations that cause human suffering.

The cumulative nature of an individual's acquired knowledge reflects the nature of the derived wisdom they trust and rely on when making life's decisions. The nature of this derived wisdom is reflected in the nature that characterizes and guides an individual's worldview.

It is the nature of their mind and it affects their point of view.

Mother Nature Reveals Her Network Web of Relational Principle to Mankind Mathematically

"The universe is written in the language of mathematics."

~ Galileo

... Mathematics is the Unspoken Language of the Universe

Around 500 B.C., Pythagoras recognized and brought to mankind's collective awareness the insight that the nature of this reality's impermanent personality is revealed numerically.

Mathematics helps bring to light the self-evident truth of what is not understood.

Mathematics is a non-verbal language that interprets relationships that can factor together the makeup of reality's dimensional composition. Mathematics is the language that reaches beyond any regional dialect to communicate the insightful detail of the relational justice within the natural laws sustaining the impermanent animation of this reality.

Natural balance and order can be revealed through the size and proportion capabilities of mathematics. It offers an interpretation to how Mother Nature finds and maintains balance in populating the present moment.

Through experiential investigation mathematical interpretation parleys to mankind's collective conscious awareness an intellectual reference giving detail to the insights expressed in the knowledge used to derive the wisdom an individual will use to knit together a wisdom-enriched enlightened worldview awareness.

... Mathematics is the Language Used by Science

Science is the freewill lobe of mankind's collective belief system network that steps beyond the constraints of theological lines in the sand to enforce mankind's natural right in demanding to know why about the unknown.

It looks under the bed and in the closets of the unknown to directly confront the boogieman that haunts mankind's collective sea of emptiness.

Science assigns order to the life cycles of the cause/effect processes as the order of new understandings unfolds. Numbers help reveal the relationship of one thing to the next as this reality hurls itself into the ongoing unknown future of the naked change showcasing the ephemeral presence of this reality from one present moment to the next.

Mother nature reveals the relational laws of her force-driven principles mathematically. There are mathematical equations representing the relationships between all of nature's forces so far exposed by mankind's freewill, science.

Science's findings set science's course that theology must adapt its notions to ... or die out. We no longer dodge Zeus's or Thor's bolts of God-sent lightening.

Mathematics give order to observations made about life's cause/effect processes founded in experientially verified cause/effect analysis that is available for anyone speaking any language to borrow.

A public broadcast system 2020 TV special, "The Great Math Mystery" told of how mankind uses mathematics to decode and understand the human experience as it tries to search for the principled patterns in what constitutes their living environment that might help bring to a head what it all means.

Mathematics gives a non-verbal recognizable format to the environment's countless rhythmic patterns such as with celestial constellations and the four seasons.

The PBS special noted how mankind recognizes the passage of these rhythm patterns as this reality's dimension of time.

The show questioned whether mathematics was discovered or invented, as it exists in everything. "Mathematical" is the expression of the living process of everything. It describes what everything has in common ... a mathematical logistics.

It is suggested that inspired insightful concepts are observed and through the mathematically expressed relationships between those concepts their self-evident nature is discovered.

... Mathematics has Enormous Predictive Powers

The math discovered in things allows and can bring about their predicted discovery. The show pointed out how Maxwell's 19th-century discovery of the invisible electromagnetic waves that travel through the universe at lightning speed were harnessed by Marconi to make available wireless communication.

It was mathematics that predicted the existence of the quarks, leptons, and gauge Bosons that make up the electrons, protons, and neutrons of atoms in quantum mechanics.

There is an underground 17-mile-long circular particle collider in Europe that is finding success in searching for the predicted existence of the Higgs Boson particle that mathematics says is responsible for everything's mass.

Mathematical techniques are used to quantify these observations. The laws of the universe follow mathematical models.

The fundamental laws of physics are expressed mathematically. I.E. Newton's Law of Universal Gravitation is $F=G(m1m2/r2)$, where F is the gravitational force acting between two objects, m_1 and m_2 are the masses of the objects, r is the distance between the centers of their masses, and G is the gravitational constant.

Mathematically expressed physical laws give an intellectually metered description of the essence of the dimensional properties of our physical reality. Science uses mathematics to continue unraveling the understanding of this reality's multi-dimensional makeup.

Coordinates on a 2-dimensional flat map can give an object's 2-dimensional location. Leaving the flat presence and adding a third-dimensional coordinate locates the object in space. This 3D effect is what many pay extra for to wear special glasses designed to detect when going to the movies.

Albert Einstein intellectually demonstrated how time and space relate to each other by mathematically defining time-space in the mathematical equation $E=MC2$. He brings to conscious understanding how time itself is the 4th dimensional component supporting the present moment backdrop of this universal reality.

By adding a 4th dimensional time coordinate, it is possible to describe and locate an event in the chronology of history.

Science has added more levels of dimensional awareness since with advancements in schools of thought like that supporting the string or wave theories.

Bringing to mankind's collective conscious awareness a more defined understanding of the concept of this reality's space-time fabric has further enlightened humankind's collective awareness about the laws of nature that rule the principles that pattern the relational advancement of this universe.

It has greatly lessened the amount of the "unknown" about the impermanent ways of this reality's multi-dimensional makeup.

Mathematics details the process of how the truth in a cause/effect relationship develops. It lays out and brings quantifiable detail to mankind's waking awareness the processes that make up this reality's ephemeral dimensional fiber.

This life knowledge is used to derive the wisdom-enriched awareness that enlightens the truth-seeker about their ignorance of the truth of the laws of those relational processes that ricochets on up from the subatomic world of quarks and leptons through the relationships between things that come into focus and hold true in the range of human perception.

This is the very ignorance of the unknown that every individual's unique demonic boogieman(men) hides in. This is the ignorance-born fear of the unknown that has people turning to their favorite flavor of theology to find some sort of pseudo-security from.

Mathematics instigates harmony between people of all races and times. Like how American males might be drawn to a lady's soft feminine French accent or the potentially seductive accent of a southern belle, individuals are drawn to the powerful accent of applied and accomplished purpose that radiates from the poetic language of mathematics as might be written in a set of blueprints or maybe in explaining how time and mass relate to the speed of light.

Mathematics gives detail to the known dimensional aspects of shapes and sizes. The mathematics of engineering is responsible for the completed construction of a countless number of things that are built from following sets of plans ... bridges, cars, trains, airplanes, spaceships, roadways, homes, and everything else that makes up the skylines of our beautiful cities, to name only a few things.

People speaking different verbal languages can unite in coordinated effort to reach the same end when equipped with a well-prepared set of math-speaking blueprints.

... People Enjoy Going to Big Cities

This human-sync with the ways or rhythms of mathematics registers on a subtle level of human consciousness. Most do not and will never realize it.

Mathematical relationships support the constructs of the prelingual rhythms of music. This subtle inborn cadence shows its face in many forms of innate human common understanding.

One reason visiting a big city captivates people is subliminal and never realized by most.

In the deeper regions of human consciousness, people celebrate an unpronounced sense of shared human accomplishment in the coordination of discipline, patience, and having the ability to follow the same procedural order while marching to the same rhythm of the same silent drum ... blueprint mathematics.

The thought of engineers stepping out and working in harmony with unknown others in the completion of such an immense challenge such as building a one-hundred-story building must be felt by any onlooker at some level.

The coordination of effort and shared purpose implied by the presence of a man-fashioned skyline has a calming effect on the human persona. A city's presence testifies to a time of humans working together to a shared end and seeing it through in a coordination effort that defied the idea of having to speak a common language.

A city's skyline is a Cliff Notes summary, telling the story of how humans who might not have spoken the same written language or even lived in the same century or even the same millennia were able to come to a common understanding and build such a metropolis.

When this coordinated effort is over time multiplied by twenty-five square miles of comparable results that's completion spans over several generations, it is no wonder people like to go see the big city. It can be calming, relaxing and through the scale of its presence, it can be thought inspiring. Visiting a big city shows one's pride in the potential stored in being a human ... most often unrealized or at least unappreciated to the waking mind.

... and most probably never wakingly look at it this way.

All of this is made possible by the power of the language of mathematics to precisely articulate the intended purpose of the designers that planned the layout and dimensions of that huge ongoing project that can extend beyond a normal lifetime. They offer their trust as they pass their contribution on to be completed by future generations.

Maybe mankind's work attire has spanned time from barefoot to sandals to steel-toed boots? Yet, all were able to grasp the message panned out mathematically on the blueprint style of the time.

... Business Financial Ratios Mathematically Reveal Nature's Universal Relational Principles

To run a business aimed at increasing the probability of attaining the best sales outcomes in its future customer relationships, a wise owner will give high attention to its financial statements that reveal mathematically how different aspects of the business plan relate to each other to best attain its goal.

A ratio analysis of the profit and loss income statement will reveal how the different segments of the "cause" that the business represents will contribute to the "effect" or outcome experienced from the customer/business relationship.

Its profit and loss income statement will reveal what the outcomes of these customer relationships have been over a time.

Keeping the business operations on target with the same pattern of flow shown by ratio analysis to work best will keep the business flow set to the rhythm suggested best by the laws of mathematics that intellectually mirror the cause/effect relationships of this reality.

Expense ratios reveal how the various aspects of a business's expenses relate to each other in the business's universe.

It's so fun and rewarding to operate a business with these logistics in mind compared to running a business that reacts in knee-jerk fashion with business decisions needed to salvage the operation in response to how naked change pushes its buttons and how many overdraft notices the bank sends.

Emotional Intelligence

> *"Emotional intelligence (EI) or emotional quotient (EQ) is the capacity of individuals to recognize their own, and other people's emotions, to discriminate between different feelings and label them appropriately, to use emotional information to guide thinking and behavior, and to manage and/or adjust emotions to adapt ..."*
>
> ... Emotional Intelligence – Wikipedia, the free encyclopedia
> https://en.*wikipedia.org/wiki/Emotional_intelligence*

... "EQ" Verses "IQ" Awareness

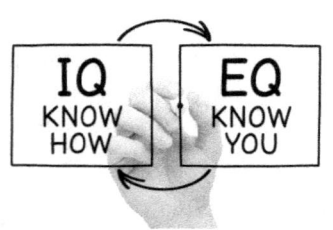

In the recent past, what has been generally known as an individual's "IQ" or intelligence quotient has been further scrutinized. In the past, individual's that are highly sensitive to the sensually metered reality that touches more into what flags the emotional state of mind might not have scored that high on "IQ" tests that test more for the level of intellectually metered knowledge.

To recognize a deeper understanding of where an individual's overall "intelligence" rates, society is now distinguishing between the emotional, "EQ", and intellectual characteristics that make up the measure of "intelligence."

Intuitive as well as intellectually centered abilities are now considered individually to give a deeper understanding and defined reflection of how "smart" an individual is or how well they are adapted or sensitive to the impermanent conditions exhibiting the relational truths of this ephemeral reality.

An individual who builds their wisdom bank using experientially assimilated self-derived knowledge will have an intelligence quotient that better recognizes their (EQ) emotional quotient related intrinsic abilities.

Individuals who calculate their wisdom from the knowledge they have borrowed on blind faith will tend to have an intelligence quotient with a lower (EQ) emotional quotient measure. They'll have one that more favors the (IQ) intellectual quotient.

Their present moment is more caught up in intellectually primed topics. With a worldview that honors time continuity, their ignorance-engineered feelings will trigger the emotion families that relate more to feelings resulting from attachment and aversion that instill some level of suffering or misery … anger, shame, fear, jealousy related.

They tend to entertain emotions that are more stunned to awareness of the principles that affect the outcomes of relationships … how feelings affect emotions.

They are more likely to be spending their present moment negotiating the mental white noise that eats away at their mind control and trigger emotions less compassion related. They are less capable of generating empathy related thoughts … happiness, contentment, joy.

An individual needs to be aware of their feelings and emotions before they can walk in someone else's shoes.

Nature of Wisdom-Deriving Knowledge Sways Nature of Wisdom and Life Purpose

"I believe in Spinoza's God, who reveals Himself in the lawful harmony of the world, not in a God who concerns Himself with the fate and the doings of mankind…"

~Albert Einstein to Rabbi Herbert Goldstein (1929)

Albert Einstein makes an interesting point. He thinks it's more important to show involvement in reality by addressing reality as a whole. The truth of ongoing change is happening in each bit of reality.

Understanding how this all relates is where an enlightened awareness of life purpose is established.

Only demonstrating a soap opera sort of interest in what mankind's up to does nothing about helping a truth-seeker address the cause of their suffering. This focus falls short of understanding the emotional relationship with ignorance-spawned suffering to letting this make the suffering disappear to be replaced with the emotional bliss that accompanies an enlightened understanding of reality.

… Gain the World and Lose the Soul

"Never mistake knowledge for wisdom. One helps you make a living, the other helps you make a life."

~Eleanor Roosevelt

"Who understands the world is learned. Who understands the self is enlightened. Who conquers the world has strength. Who conquers the self has harmony."

~ Lau Tzu, *Tao Te Ching*, verse 33

The nature of the knowledge that an individual chooses to internalize determines the nature of the derived wisdom it supports. This affects the shaping of their worldview and the nature of their mind. It helps determine how they will choose to connect with reality and how they deal with their human experience.

This is the manner they adopt for perceiving, analyzing, and acting in line with the patterned principles of the natural laws controlling the cause/effect situational outcomes of the animated presentations of each new "present moment.

This affects the nature of an individual's life purpose.

Tao Te Ching verse 33 could be the first time and place this inspired wisdom-enriched life-insight was ever pulled from mankind's collective deeper awareness and brought to recorded social visibility in the timeline of human development. It's thought it was written around 400 B.C.

Lau Tzu's discriminating observation reasons that when an individual attempts to reconcile and integrate their human condition into their human experience, a differing intrinsic core value originates and resonates from each of the differing life approaches where an individual either intellectually use their head or intrinsically use their heart.

In verse 33, Lau Tzu infers that when an individual recognizes and internalizes the world intellectually and then uses that cerebral knowledge as a tool or maybe even a weapon to conquer the world, they will amass a power reserve reflected in some form of personal strength ... perhaps a hollow hard-edged and brittle shell of power?

In immediate contrast to approaching life intellectually, Lau Tzu goes on in verse 33 to insightfully reason that when an individual acquires life strength through understanding the self, they learn to conquer the self and they will find emotional harmony.

Their wisdom-enriched enlightened awareness of our source's impermanent nature conquers their need to create a self-ego to manage, posture, and defend their once speculative worldview.

The cerebral approach to attaining life strength is fostered up from an individual's learned, intellectual understanding of how to relate to reality.

Whereas in the heartfelt approach to acknowledging reality, life strength grows while experientially attaining the material self-defining self-knowledge to self-train the ability to let that knowledge inspire the understanding to insightfully derive and assimilate Tree of Life wisdom by bringing to wakeful awareness the insightfully aware understanding of our physical reality that waits dormant and uncultivated in a subtle level of every individual's deeper consciousness.

**Peter A. Merel has reviewed several of the most popular modern-day translations and synthesized what appears to be the common meaning shared by the translations of Lau Tzu's recorded insights into his 1995 interpolation of Tao Te Ching.

This document attempts to draw the texts of several popular English translations of Lao Tzu into a consistent and accessible context. It is based on the translations of Robert G. Henricks, Lin Yutang, D. C. Lau, Ch'u Ta-Kao, Gia-Fu Feng and Jane English, Richard Wilhelm and Aleister Crowley.

Understanding Our Emotions … Where Human Condition Meets Human Experience

Emotions are mental and sensations are physical. The mind juggles what comes to it sensually and mentally determines how it's liked or not liked.

Feeling-defined or conditioned emotions are how the human condition judges and registers its human experience.

The neuroscientist Lisa Feldman Barrett says that emotional granularity means the more we can describe our emotions, the more accurately we can experience ourselves and our world.

The better an individual understands their emotions means that they are learning to better understand their relationship with how the principles that rule the ways of impermanence affect their emotional balance.

In better understanding their emotions, a truth-seeker is approaching emotional enlightenment … emotional balance/bliss.

When the reality of what's affecting physical existence becomes clear to the waking consciousness, the more enlightened one is becoming about the reality of what causes life misery.

… Feelings are a Sensual Conduit

Sensual feelings trigger mentally formulated emotions.

With every emotion comes a physical sensation.

Feelings are the sensual conduit between the human condition and the human experience.

… Pay Attention *and* Read Your Body's Signals

"Emotions arise in the place where your mind and body meet."

~Self-Evident Truth

Emotions come from mental perceptions of feelings from sensual media exposure. They track an individual's conscious understanding of their relationship with their environment.

In the book *The Art of Empathy,* by Karla McLaren M. Ed., she categorizes the human smorgasbord of emotions into 16 groups. Anger, apathy and boredom, guilt and shame, hatred, fear, worry and anxiety, confusion, jealousy, envy, panic and terror, sadness, grief, situational depression, happiness contentment, and joy are to encompass the full kaleidoscope of interrelated emotions. Different related emotions like frustration, peevishness, and rage are all included in the anger family.

There will be physical symptoms that accompany each of these emotional states … faster heartbeat … shortness of breath … perspiration. Making awareness of these physical symptoms that give signal to different emotions will help in recognizing and avoiding them in the future.

Emotions are the human condition's real-time sensual measuring stick for appraising its journey through its human experience.

Emotions are Action-Requiring Neurological Programs

Emotions are action-requiring neurological programs and are necessary for our whole cognitive and physical health.

With being a living part of the ultimate reality's ever-changing makeup, it is necessary to begin understanding the principles affecting its relational order to better understand where the cause of suffering lies.

The ignorance from misguided conditioning as well as simple absence of knowledge serves as the petri dish of suffering.

The Art of Living: Vipassana Meditation by Thomas Hart describes S.N. Goemka's teachings about the sequential process of how the mind recognizes and tenders a physical sensation. To paraphrase what it says about the mind on page 26:

1st … **Consciousness** registers the occurrence of any physical or mental input phenomenon. It labels or notes any sensual input presence free of evaluation.

2nd … **Perception** is the act of recognition. When identifying what consciously registers, perception distinguishes, evaluates, and categorizes the raw data positively or negatively.

3rd … **Sensation** comes along with any input. If not evaluated, it remains neutral. Once evaluated, the incoming data is classified as pleasant or unpleasant.

4th … **Reaction**: If a sensation or a comment that will bring about a sensation that is heard is positive, an individual will want to prolong the presence of its effects. If a sensation's unpleasant they will want to end or avoid it.

A sensual stimulation of some sort gets consciously noticed. Its value then gets perceived as being pleasant or unpleasant and gets more desired or less desired.

An individual's conditioned perception of what their sensed feelings represent is what affects and fuels their motivation and underwrites their intentions. Their understanding of the very primal natural principles that define and determine the relational outcomes of what they might do next affects how they decided to act.

Emotions seed the motivation for what people do. People will propose doing things that bring on good emotions and avoid doing things that bring on negative emotions.

... Emotions Speak Humanity's Native Language

"Emotions are your soul's native language."

~Karla McLaren M. Ed., 5-6-20 email list post

Emotions arise to the mind from sensations. Their body-speak sensual message will be there for the individual to translate into their spoken tongue.

Emotions represent the effects caused by sensual signals from some stimulus emerging from the ongoing feed from the sensual world.

Different cultures with different languages might use different words, but their words used to describe emotions are describing the same human sensual feelings.

What all different cultures that speak different languages share is the range of perception the feelings come from that generates the emotions they create words to describe.

When an individual learns how to interpret the body-speak from their sensually spun language and how to work with it, they will be deriving the wisdom of a Tree of Life enlightened understanding awareness that wil help unwind their suffering.

Emotions Don't Cause Trouble ... Each is a Gift

... They Establish Limits

"Emotions do not cause trouble; your emotions bring you the gifts and skills you need to deal with trouble."

~Karla McLaren M. Ed. insight posted 5-6-20 to the email list

"Emotions are a vital part of everything you are: every relationship; every dream; every failure; every triumph; every act of love.

~Karla McLaren, M.Ed. 3-13-2020 Facebook post

… Emotions Mentally Help To Recognize And Set The Human Experience Boundaries

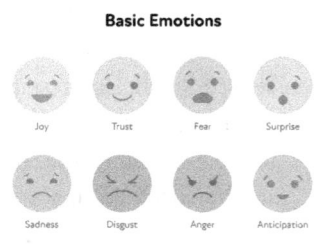

Basic Emotions

Joy · Trust · Fear · Surprise

Sadness · Disgust · Anger · Anticipation

Emotions are supposed to protect us. They give us the message that we need to act. The problems individuals have is in interpreting the message.

Emotional defenses are primitive. Mammals must fight for their lives every day, and emotions let them know what to fear. As humans, we try to develop the ability to first consider the fight-or-flight impulse … to evaluate instinctive decisions.

Each of the emotions is invaluable. With objective consideration, the relative volatility of the emotional bell rang will help an individual better understand their boundaries of toleration that enables them to better understand and maintain a more balanced emotional state of mind.

Human emotions are anchored in the sensual world. To address or fine tune them must also be done in the sensual world.

It's in the chamber of life-manifest itself where their language is learned.

Spirituality … The Rubik's Cube of Enlightenment

… The Abyss Between Deeper and Waking Conscious Awareness
… The Melting-Pot-Catchall of Undefined, Unbound Mysticism Addressing the Nature, Purpose, and Fate of the Human Condition

The realm of spirituality encompasses all the undefined conjecture existing between understanding what the nature's principled relational laws are that enforce the impermanent nature of this reality and mankind's ignorance-spawned emptiness of waking understanding of those principles. It is a primal sort of Pandora's box full of uncongealed understandings of how to link up the intrinsic wise-to-impermanence impulses from the deeper consciousness to the patchwork of intellectually metered understandings resident in the waking conscious awareness.

Religion's templated theological notions exist here in the abyss of spirituality as a virus that can numb its believers innate freewills with blind faith until they die. Like a virus, it adapts to any emerging threatening self-evident truth's that might cripple their promised Holy wisdom by adding to mankind's collective understanding of those life principles, threatening what they profess to be the existing god-ordained way reality is.

"Spirituality" is a zone of emotionally bound confusion between the all-knowing in-sync deeper consciousness and the unsure waking consciousness where an individual is unsettled on how they feel emotionally.

Until becoming enlightened with a Tree of Life wisdom-enriched understanding awareness, it is in an individual's waking awareness of what "impermanence" means to their worldview understanding of life that their understandings start to drift and become spirituality.

In a looser sense, spirituality is a melting-pot-catchall of speculation of how to develop in the waking consciousness a deeper understanding awareness of this reality's self-evident truth.

So, What to Do?

To better understand the nature of these cause/effect outcome-setting principles that Mother Nature describes mathematically and displays sensually, a truth-seeker needs to go to where they can collect the appropriate wisdom-deriving knowledge to develop the appropriate strain of wisdom that understands and decodes the impermanent nature of this reality on the pre-lingual intrinsic understanding level.

With the derived wisdom they can write the "book/chapter/verse" understanding from their hearts for what sets the course of this universal reality.

It is not the sort of knowledge that develops a strain of wisdom that misleads their waking awareness to a dead end of suffering in an awareness state that is empty of life understanding caught up in the emotional distress brought on by craving attachment.

... Understand Nature to Understand What Affects the Emotional State of the Mental Self

Getting to better know the nature of the mental self, first takes a truth seeker back to understanding the nature of the reality that sensually affects the perceptions that mentally register as likes and dislikes to affect the decisions an individual makes to affect the emotions that generate their behavior that defines who or what their personality or mental self is.

Choosing the Right School of Knowledge

... We Don't Need More Information ... We Need More Meaning

The network of wisdom an individual lives by reflects the nature of the knowledge they choose to internalize to derive that wisdom from.

Lau Tzu gives Cliff Notes-style insight in the writing *Tao Te Ching* verse 33 as to how a strain of wisdom borrowed from book-knowledge, lacking the self-knowledge derived wisdom and intrinsic familiarity founded in experiential history, could very well afford an individual the cognitive strength to conquer the world.

But, for those who through engendered mind-into-body harmony tune into sensually witness life manifest, the experientially based wisdom-enriched self-knowledge gained allows them to instead derive the strain of wisdom to identify, understand, own, and conquer their self-ego, to become enlightened about the cause of their ignorance-induced emotional suffering and gain emotional harmony … balance … bliss.

Lau Tzu's wisdom-enriched insight asserts that if you seek the sort of knowledge to merely nurture your mind intellectually to cognitively know this reality, you will not develop the infrastructure of knowledge aimed at supporting the strain of life wisdom founded in intrinsic familiarity and sensual history. You will not develop a wisdom-enriched enlightened self-understanding that makes sense of what it is that seeds your emotional/mental self-paradox.

… Nothing Beats the Real Thing

The knowledge truth-seekers accumulate will either be comprehensive enough to allow them to derive wisdom reflecting an intrinsic familiarity with what underwrites their conscious understanding of how the claim the knowledge supports realizes its truth … or not. To endure a core familiarity with the knowledge they internalize to derive wisdom from is where using the senses to accumulate the knowledge becomes necessary.

Distinguishing wisdom-deriving knowledge that is received or borrowed or intellectually calculated from wisdom-deriving knowledge that has been collected from the living "self" that's to be experientially assimilated into Life wisdom is like comparing gaining a wisdom-enriched understanding of what "freezing cold" means by reading its description verses jumping into a mountain stream of glacier water run-off.

Stepping into a mountain stream coming from melting snow gives an individual unforgettable sensually acquired experiential knowledge of what "freezing cold" means. This knowledge allows them to assimilate a level of intrinsically registered wisdom they will have a core-generated steadfast faith in when dealing with anything involving "freezing cold".

Should their defined understanding of freezing cold be borrowed from a dictionary, they would be unprepared to make any kind of gut-felt reaction when confronted with real life freezing cold. Their emotions of fear and panic would be balanced on different scales.

Their fight or flight response would instead be an intellectually calculated action lacking any sensual history instead of coming from an intrinsically generated self-preservation reflex. Their belief system would lack the sensually founded knowledge to have derived an intrinsically fed understanding awareness of what "ice cold" means in terms of the sensually defined limits or boundaries set earlier by their emotional watchguard.

Every individual has the same innate bug-to-fire pull to the same bright white light that shines emotional bliss. Using knowledge gained from sensually witnessing impermanence in action allows the individual the sensual familiarity to configure an enriched awareness of the Tree of Life wisdom needed to understand the relational ways of the impermanent dimensional makeup of this reality. Christian theology depends on their god to provide them with the wisdom needed to find their way to the templated wisdom-promised heaven.

Only experiential sensually derived self-knowledge seeds self-assimilated Tree of Life wisdom-enriched enlightenment about reality's undeniable self-evident truth. It is the sensually acquiring self-knowledge from their personal factory of life-manifest itself that enables a truth-seeker to over time enrich their conscious awareness with a familiarity and working understanding of the impermanent ways of this reality.

They accumulate insight to the relational justice that characterizes the circumscribing nature of the dimensional makeup of this reality. It's development eventually allows them to undo the ignorance of it to regenerate their present moment joy and happiness and to understand and own what it is that causes their suffering.

The Tree of Life knowledge sensually taps out the self-evident aspect of this reality and the knowledge borrowed from theological notions represents different wisdom-deriving infrastructures to explain the same truth about regaining an awareness of joy and happiness and eliminating suffering. Experiential wisdom draws from what has been personally witnessed while borrowed wisdom is derived from unverified blindly trusted knowledge lacking the understanding that comes with having developed an intrinsic familiarity with the cause of its promised effect.

People would rather sensually experience a vacation than merely read about it in even the best of written journals. When on vacation it is common to hear a picture-taker declare how the picture just does not capture what is being experienced by the senses.

The borders on the picture omit the smell, feel, sound and uninterrupted visuals offered by the wind and light shadings that the individual is trying to capture on their camera device.

Personal experience inspires songwriters and poets. They use prior experience to gain insight on their lyrics.

Attending Class is Necessary

Mathematics is an international language used to express the cause/effect relationships of how nature's forces interact to produce the principles that rule the flow of time's transforming reality. It resonates on the intellectual level.

Like Einstein's theory of relativity, E=MC2. This mathematical equation breaks down to detail the self-evident truth about the relationship between energy and mass and the speed of light.

It describes how energy and mass are the same ... interchangeable ... how it is the tiny bits of the ever-elusive coming and going subatomic quantum mechanics bits of energy are what compose or make up the transforming state of this material world ... the primal seed of impermanence.

Understanding the principles of mathematics can give somebody an intellectual understanding of how this reality's natural forces relate to and integrate with each other as they turn this reality's wheels of transformation by natural force-producing the relational principles that govern the cause/effect that give the life to its flow.

Scientists have been able to deduct the existence to the quark energy particles from the observation of the protons and neutrons they make up.

The presence of these bits of energy and their importance to explaining this reality's circle of truth became self-evident to Siddhartha as he was sitting under a Banyon tree the night he became "enlightened" to his ignorance. He became enlightened about the relational truths defining the natural force-driven principles that write the script for the impermanent backdrop running this reality.

He acquired a conscious understanding awareness of how the human emotion matrix fits into the logistics of this reality game plan of ongoing transformation.

With this understanding, he could speak completely in analogies of different sorts of cause/effect events with outcomes that at their seemingly unrelated cores were affected by the same force-driven principles.

Jesus did this with his enlightened understanding throughout Rome's chosen gospels as Jesus said he would do it for people who weren't yet able to understand. It depended on the spiritual maturity level of his audience. It was like teaching kindergarteners Mother Nature's graduate level mathematics.

Due diligence will find a truth seeker reading the more deliberate teachings of Jesus found in the Gnostic Gospels to discover this.

From collecting the sensual knowledge allowing him to derive the "aha" insightful wisdom both Siddhartha and Jesus sensually developed an intrinsic understanding of this Tree of Life Wisdom.

Today's discovering scientists have a cognitive understanding of this intellectually metered truth but do not enjoy the similar analogy-fed sort of depth of lateral application as did Siddhartha with this Tree of Knowledge wisdom gained under the Bodhi tree that night.

They have not yet earned heart-felt Tree of Life wisdom through sensually gaining the wisdom-deriving self-knowledge to realize an intrinsically familiar understanding with the principles that support the Tree of Life Wisdom.

By generating the due diligence to learn and intellectually understand the wisdom-inspiring knowledge of mathematics, a math student becomes enlightened about math's unbendable principles and avoids suffering from an empty or miscued understanding.

... Getting the Point ... Intellectually

While learning the language of mathematics, it is the set patterns of math principles that determine the unbiased outcomes of math problems. The better one understands math's ruling principles, the less they experience suffering from its ignorance.

The initial suffering might come from getting an "F". Then, suffering may again pop up from not understanding its principles well enough to add up how much is needed to buy a school lunch.

If someone wants to better understand math to get an "A" when questioned about the nature of its ruling principles, they gather math-related knowledge to inspire developing the insight-capable conscious familiarity with math's supporting network of wisdom that tells the story of mathematical truth. They study for the test and with the acquired applicable knowledge they derive the needed math wisdom to avoid emotional unrest.

When an individual becomes emotionally distraught due to their misunderstanding of the unalterable principles of mathematics, they gather the appropriate knowledge to derive the appropriate wisdom to better understand the principles of math.

... Getting the Point ... Intrinsically ... Life Truth has a Living Format

Likewise, if a truth seeker becomes emotionally distraught due to their misunderstanding of the unalterable principles that rule what affects life emotions, they gather the appropriate knowledge to make possible deriving the appropriate strain of wisdom to better understand the principles that set pattern to the principles that affect life emotions.

An individual would visit the theater of mathematics to develop a knowledge history to use to inspire assimilating the appropriate thread of wisdom that decodes the mathematical principles governing mathematics. With this, they become more enlightened about their math principle-related ignorance.

Likewise, a truth seeker would visit the theater of life manifest to develop a self-knowledge history to inspire assimilating the appropriate strain of wisdom that decodes the principles governing life's transforming nature that they're having problems developing emotional harmony with. They become more enlightened about their life principle-related ignorance.

When one wants to intrinsically understand water well enough to swim in it, what do they have to do? They have to get into the water.

When an individual wants to understand a bicycle well enough to ride one, what do they end up doing? They have to get on the bicycle.

An individual must go to the present moment theater of life-manifest to sensually experience and learn to understand these Tree of Life principles using the sensual medium that deals in or speaks the language of the intrinsic history's only true state.

They develop an intrinsic familiarity and sensual history through experientially witnessing its truth.

Collect the self-knowledge and derive the strain of life wisdom to make sense of and understand the principles.

Satisfy the ongoing thorn-in-the-side urge from the emotional/mental self that inspired the initial inclination to get to better know that emotional/mental self.

Any truth-seeking individual must get to better know and consciously understand the principles that control their human experience through observing its nature as it manifests to make up their material self. They will derive the wisdom-enriched understanding that makes sense of what it is that affects their emotional/mental self to restore its balance and to become free of suffering from any related ignorance.

The Sensation in the Flesh is the Writing on the Wall

"What I am looking for is not out there, it is in me."
~ Helen Keller

Helen Keller's access to reality was limited to sensually metered media. She was deaf and blind. Like all humans, her touch with the truth was found beyond the apparent reality of sight and sound. She knew she had to go into the ultimate reality to find what she was looking for.

She was lucky to have a more developed awareness of the presence of the ultimate reality. She just wanted to better understand it.

The physical body is an individual's only intrinsic connection to the sensual media that broadcasts usable wisdom-deriving knowledge about the transforming nature of this ephemeral reality. A truth-seeker needs to gain intrinsic familiarity with the truth ticking away unnoticed in the passage of time.

It is there 24/7/365 for free with no credit-claiming middleman.

This reality's story of transformation is sensually coded from within the flesh of the human body. This sensual medium is a human being's only pre-intellectual pre-lingual connection available to take intrinsic note of the relational presence of those unalterable principles for deriving the life wisdom to get to better understand material self to better understand the emotional/mental self.

Anything else would merely be intellectually metered, as referenced above in Lau Tzu's Tree of Life wisdom.

As an individual gets to better understand the natural principles that control the probabilities of relational outcomes their deeper consciousness awareness will begin to fuse with their waking consciousness.

Their level of awareness will squeeze out the uncertainty and emptiness-of-understanding that fill the cloudy abyss of spirituality that lies in between. Their growing "enlightened" understanding awareness of the nature of this reality will bring them closer to living in a state of emotional bliss.

... Spiritualist Eckhart Tolle Teaches Conscious Awareness to be the Collective Great White Light

When an individual can let go of thought, they know the present moment in a different way. The mind-into-body "buzz" that's noticed let's them know that they do exist ... a realization of their being.

Mr. Tolle teaches that an individual's consciousness is an emanation of the "source" ... but not the source ... like a ray of light is an emanation of the sun ... but not the sun.

It's conscious awareness that keeps one from emotionally reacting. They can stay level-headed to think or process the situation and then act. They're no longer drawn into their pit of emotional suffering.

Mr. Tolle teaches that the light of consciousness comes from a deeper level of consciousness ... that people are connected to this state of consciousness.

He teaches that the emotional enemy lies between the ears. It's too late if the self-protecting ego reacts, creating mental chaos before stepping back to weight the situation. Emotional suffering results.

Like Karla McLaren teaches, Mr. Tolle teaches that an aim in life is to learn how to handle emotional confrontation, not to just to try to live in a comfort zone.

It's through learning the sensual language that radiates from within to gain a better understanding of one's emotions, that an individual can eventually gain an enlightened understanding of the fundamental ignorance that causes their emotional suffering and denies them their emotional bliss.

All the different messengers of the "truth" are describing the same bright light.

The bliss-inspiring Tree of Life Wisdom Jehovah mandated is the same as the universal wisdom recognized and self-trained by Siddhartha.

It's necessary to take the middleman out to free up the mental bandwidth to derive Tree of Life Wisdom.

XII

Saving Your Soul Now ... Conciousness Fusion

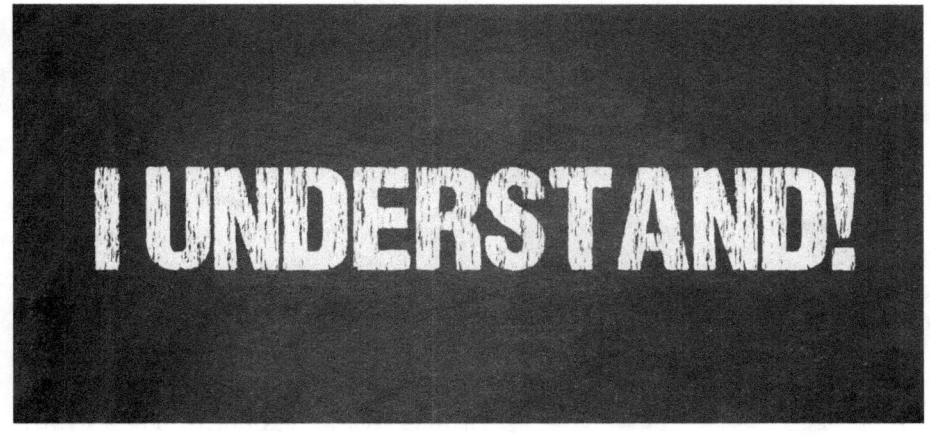

"Vision without action is a daydream."

~Japanese proverb

The Call of the Sea

... The Nature-Set Rhythm of Crashing Waves Strums a Primal Chord of Calm ... Crafted Billions of Years Ago

Mother Nature's force of gravity is demonstrating how it affects this reality ... since the moon first appeared.

... Humans have an Innate Pull to the Moon's Gravity?

Since the Earth's had its moon, there's been a push/pull tidal dance coming from their gravitational exchange that echoes the heartbeat of reality. The ocean boldly plays the primal sound of change in motion ... same sound ... same rhythm ... billions of years old.

People listen to the surf with bodies largely composed of water that sways to the moon's pull. The deeper consciousness recognizes that consciously undetectable push/pull relationship. The meditative calm is consciously shared by all humans. It's written in the gape of the human stance anytime its hypnotic lure sets in.

People listen paused, tuned in to the pulse of the surf like they're anticipating some sort of primal message coded into the dialog of the waves crashing against the shoreline.

The hypnotizing audio backs one into the rhythm of the planet-forming primal pulse that feeds into and soothes the emotional friction in the listener's mind coming from what they've expected in things and how things turned out … unexpected outcomes that they assign to periodic spells of lost rumination.

People listen patiently fixed, for the answers to the unknown questions their waking awareness suffers daily to better understand…. that they somehow innately know lie waiting in the deeper consciousness.

As a listener searches for a mental rhythm to understand Mother Nature's surf-coded message, it seems that most can only hear her saying to have patience and faith in the self-evident, that the answer is there.

Most cannot wakingly decode the primal message. They don't yet understand the sensual braille. body-speak language that emotions are coded in … some never will.

Listeners will point their cell cameras each way down the shoreline to capture the beauty. Yet, the photos cannot capture the sensual texture felt as one sea mist moment slides into the next.

It's like how the intrinsic intellect cannot communicate via an intellectual snapshot the real-life intrinsic display … feel … of understanding that's sensually available to define the meaning of each passing present moment of living.

It's an answer that shouts out with every pulse of quark energy that gives form to what is perceived by many as stilled material life. The answer shouts out from the platform of sensual perception … the material flesh where the human experience meets the human condition.

They are empty-of-understanding the Body-speak language used in the zone of spirituality that connects the deeper consciousness awareness to the waking consciousness ignorance.

But it seems that everyone likes returning to the beach to replay the message … to keep hearing while learning to better listen.

Vista Point, CA… April 1ˢᵗ, 2022

Captain the Arrow of Time to Gain Tree of Life Wisdom

… From Suffering to Enlightened Understanding

… An Intellectual Awakening and Look Down Life's Sensory Pathway

… From Traditional Illusion to Vision of Truth

… From Addictive Behavior to Acting on Purpose

… A Continuum Through Self-Training Morality, Mind Control and a Tree of Life Wisdom

… Self-Train The Ability to Fuse the Deeper Consciousness Life Principle Wisdom to the Waking Consciousness Emptiness-of-Understanding

Work to allow the life principle awareness that innately populates the deeper consciousness to surface as Tree of Life wisdom to the waking consciousness through the emptiness-of-understanding that echoes throughout the zone of spirituality in between.

> *"And I say unto you, ask, and it shall be given you; seek, and ye shall find; knock, and it shall be opened unto you."*
>
> ~Luke 11:9 King James translation

On his deathbed Siddhartha advised his followers that things change … to get off their butts and figure it out … in so many words.

Understanding takes work … it's not just gifted … or borrowed.

It requires due diligence … it's earned.

Understand that any individual that wishes to calm their unsettled understanding of life and find relief from the ongoing dissatisfaction and

BLESSED ARE THOSE WHO FIND WISDOM, THOSE WHO GAIN UNDERSTANDING

Proverbs 3:13

confusion that shadows their present moment must first take it upon themselves to calm their mind to at least slow down the mile-a-minute mental white noise to the point where they can sustain mental focus and gain awareness about out what thoughts are responsible for bringing on which of the unsettling emotions that are possibly making their life a living hell.

Get off the mental couch and assume the due diligence to self-train the ability to assimilate the knowledge that must be worked for to allow the thinking that generates the insightful understanding needed to undo the ignorance that causes suffering ... now ... while the soul is privy to the physical capacity to test and question life relationships to adjust its emotional understanding.

Self-train a calm mind. Establish moral and ethical standards to allow mental white noise to settle.

Self-train the ability to direct and sustain the mental focus (mind control) of that calmed mind into feeling the living presence of their material body, attuned to its presence to feel out which feelings are associated with those ruminated themes that are stirring up the emotional unrest.

The distilled deliberation focused on the "life-in-process noise" of life itself will help inspire a calm mind to identify and better understand their ignorance about the network of friction between what is imagined that should be and what really is that is bringing on their emotional suffering.

Self-train an intrinsically coded awareness of nature's force-driven principles to allow an insightful awareness to rise in the sensually spun language of the world of emotions to bring the wisdom-enriched understanding enlightenment that allows the compassion-spun joy and happiness of emotional bliss to replace present moment suffering.

Humans Share the Longing to Live Free of Suffering

Humankind emotionally suffers from an unchained understanding of how to perceive nature's ageless principles that control all this reality's outcomes ... the laws of nature.

... The Pathway Out of Ignorance is Open to All

When an individual becomes a truth seeker and musters up the due diligence and courage to persistently question what they do not understand and through assimilating the right strain of knowledge to derive the strain of wisdom that brings an enlightened conscious understanding of the ways of the principles that sustain the impermanence that defines this dimensional character of this reality, they will become enlightened about nature's principles and have nothing to cause their suffering.

... Modern Truth-Seekers Have it Easier

In gaining an enlightened understanding of the nature of this reality, a modern truth-seeker gets the benefit of all the discoveries made in the last two millennia ... the hidden truths explaining nature's ways that have become self-evident after all the questioning and attained experience in understanding. Modern man can start their search with a deeper understanding than our ancestors.

This gives modern man a better take-off understanding, at least intellectually, of the natural physical relationships in nature's principled forces that help hold together and explain the constant change in this reality.

The deafening static in between mankind's collective deeper consciousness and its waking consciousness, the catchall abyss "spirituality", becomes less intense and less interrupting as time passes. With increasing intellectual awareness of what to look for experientially, it must be easier to become "enlightened" in these modern times about the nature of this impermanent reality than for our ancient ancestors that are recognized as having achieved heavenly knowledge ... so it would seem.

Intellectual Understanding
... A Crutch for Self-Training Tree of Life Wisdom

... With Proper Guidance

A truth-seeker can take their intellectually acquired understanding of the pathway to experience enlightenment about the ignorance that causes their suffering and realize emotional bliss while living. To know what the "straight and narrow" path is, most individuals are going to require a teacher or series of teachers along the way.

It's too easy to go down the wring path.

When intellectual knowledge keeps getting lead to or associated with borrowed wisdom, they will only keep running into dead ends.

... The Door's Still Open! Jehovah Reminded Adam of the Tree of Life Heavenly Bliss as He Evicted Him and Eve From the Garden of Eden

> *"22. And the Lord God said, Behold, the man is become as one of us, to know good and evil: and now, lest he put forth his hand, and take also of the tree of life, and eat, and live forever:*
>
> *23. Therefore the Lord God sent him forth from the garden of Eden, to till the ground from whence he was taken. "*

~The Bible Genesis Chapter 3 King James Version

Jehovah evicted man from the Garden of Eden eternal spiritual satisfaction frame of mind. Jehovah sent Adam and Eve on their way to live with the Fig Leaf Wisdom they opted for from the Tree of Knowledge snake.

He left the door to eternal life open conditionally to man's taking from the Tree of Life. Jehovah left it up to man to figure it out for himself.

... Adam and Eve had to be Alive ... Not in Their Afterlife ... To Begin Eating from the Tree of Life to Return to State of Eden Paradise

To "live forever", Jehovah told Adam and Eve "lest he put forth his hand, and take also of the tree of life, and eat, and live forever." They would have to put forth their hand ... act while still living ... to develop Tree of Life wisdom.

... Not in their afterlife.

Until an individual can choose the Tree of Life wisdom, he is cursed to roam the Earth, "from which he was taken, "in a waking state living with the emptiness-of-understanding inherent to Fig Leaf Wisdom.

Siddhartha Gautama was one human being of an untold number that went ahead and figured it out. Siddhartha did it himself to then teach how to dismiss Fig Leaf Wisdom and "take also of the Tree of Life, and eat, and live forever."

After his enlightenment, that was the only thing he would engage in ... teaching about realizing the four noble truths to then go down the eight-fold pathway experientially to the enlightenment about suffering that worked for him.

Most of mankind continues to pace the earth emotionally lost to some degree in the confused frustration that shadows the emptiness-of-understanding inherent to using Fig Leaf Wisdom that confronts them daily in making many of their life decisions.

"The Meek Shall Inherit The Earth" ... Jesus

... Living in a World One Knows to Living in a World One Feels

Maybe this is the same state of awareness Jesus had in mind when he said in the Beatitudes that the meek ... the humble ... are blessed ... that they will inherit the Earth.

Maybe the meek are blessed for understanding the necessity for adherence to the facets of Sandbox Etiquette to give full attention to what someone is communicating ... to listen ... that should have been learned as a small child ... in the sandbox ... in kindergarten. Only the meek listen to their bodies.

The meek are on a level of awareness that allows them the luxury of being more ego-free for a more transparent perception of life to better enjoy, understand and appreciate what is happening in the present moment to everything that the transforming life process referred to as Earth has to offer.

Only through maintaining humility will any human being's perception share the "aha" Tree of Life awareness wavelength savvy to recognize insightful wisdom among the cause/effect relationships of the passing moment. There is really something in remaining humble and non-assuming as time passes to allow ideas and inspirations to surface any time of day … at times other than when posed cross-legged Eastern style in meditation.

Waiting To Find Emotional Bliss in the Future Heaven Versus Getting Started Now?

"We're always getting ready to live, but never living."
~ Ralf Waldo Emerson

"The secret of getting ahead is getting started."
~ Mark Twain

Theology suggests praying to a god for emotional balance … to be forgiven for sins without having more than a general idea of what a sin is while adhering blindly to a list of commands to be rewarded after death the very emotional bliss yearned for while living.

… Alert: Must be Living to Fix Suffering Cause

To change what affects the negative emotions that spell out suffering, an individual needs to be living. They must have an active sensual connection with the ongoing state of change in the living world to be able to alter the emotions formed in the wake of how they react to sensed stimuli.

Why wait to be free of suffering? It is the different modes of emotion an individual might experience while alive that are used by theology to describe what afterlife heavenly bliss will be like and how sensually and emotionally terrible eternal fire and brimstone would be.

Borrowed knowledge's steps for going from suffering back to not suffering are different from those using self-knowledge to derive the wisdom to live by. The differing protocols of cause/effect relational justice support different natures of reality's dimensional makeup … time/space/mass relationship … impermanent or continual.

Theology uses the afterlife timeline reference for when an individual realizes its promised suffering-free emotional bliss. A truth seeker can either chance waiting until the spiritual abyss of the afterlife or get started right now while being a living part of the ongoing change that the ignorance of brings on the suffering.

Why not understand why suffer exists and undo the confused ignorance that allows the emotional hell and pain the Bible warns to continue for eternity … in overlapping all-inclusive style … for those who do not follow its terms of scantly described obedience?

With the Bible's promised future afterlife relief from suffering its only necessary to follow its ancient multi-translated commandments that ring the intellectually strung bell of awareness.

There is no real connection with the gut-felt understanding of why or why not … just a pit of the emptiness of understanding.

Until afterlife, an individual suffers through the ignorance of not understanding how the natural forces of relational justice affect their state of emotion in the present moment.

While it is possible to bring light to understanding what causes suffering … now … while living … why wait?

Don't wait 'til after dying. Get started now! Jehovah told Adam to seek out only Tree of Life wisdom or die spiritually by borrowing the answer from another source.

He left the door open to Adam and Eve to "live forever" by partaking of the Tre of Life while they were still living … not during their afterlife.

Ignorance is Bliss … Really?

This saying might be made sort of with tongue-in-cheek, but many will use it to passingly excuse the outcome of an event and just continue walking in ignorance. This ignorance has caused suffering on some level somewhere.

Mother Teresa Came Compassion-Ready

Everyone is born into this world with some form of a worldview that carries them moment to moment … baby to adult. It is amazing how different and unique each personality is in any preschool classroom.

The ability to express a high level of compassion was already a part of Mother Teresa's conscious makeup when she was introduced to the ideals of Christianity. Her exposure to the situations the religion presented gave her a theater to express its more compassion-filled advanced state more easily.

… It's Our Job to Figure Out Our "Self"

Individuals with emotional challenges … anger, apathy, anger, shame, guilt, fear, anxiety, panic, jealousy, envy, sadness, grief, depression … that robs them of spending their present moment in states of joy and happiness must become enlightened about what they are ignorant about that allows these states of emotional suffering.

Feed Someone or Teach Them How to Fish?

... Having Only an Intellectual Grasp

A book with insightful bits of wisdom for its reader to intellectually chew on is good. It can provide blasts of insightful wisdom that suddenly rings so very true.

This new intellectually attained spark of wisdom will make sense of connecting a cause to its effect in a way that had not yet been considered or experienced. But, because it has not established any intrinsic familiarity, its intellectual fiber will most often fade into an intellectual data bank and not be recalled when a real life sensually metered situation arises.

Its intellectually stored cause/effect relationship will most often not be referenced in the go-to source that's comprised mostly of experiential life history.

But for a truth seeker, a process of learning that instills in them the ability to consciously realize the intrinsic connection referenced by that wisdom to then have the ready reference to its sensually stored real-life applicability is priceless.

The snips of Life wisdom showcased throughout Lau Tzu's *Tao Te Ching* are examples of the self-evident truth describing what happens in between a cause and its effect during the unfolding of ongoing change. In this writing, Lau Tzu served an intellectually graspable message telling of some derived wisdom interpreting and making relational sense describing our source's relational truth of impermanence.

Lau Tzu's writings have been interpreted and translated by many scholars, making the interworking of the relational truths he's channeled from mankind's deeper consciousness more intellectually available for those with a lesser-developed personal relationship with the waking awareness of our Source's truth of ongoing change.

... Intellectual Understanding Takes the Second Stage

For many, the relational wisdom presented in the *Tao Te Ching* makes perfect sense intellectually. Yet, an individual's conscious tie-in to their sensual memory record of the cause/effect transformation has not yet been earned. It's "not been experientially seared into their consciously recognizable intrinsically registered experiential memory.

Once a reader gets their head around it, it rings so true. It's mesmerizing, especially to those who live in illusionary realities and have developed no way of knowingly or purposefully self-training and realizing the same timeless insightful wisdom for themselves.

It's generally agreed that the engendered meanings are relational principles applying to this cause/effect reality that any individual would want to live by. But practically speaking, once a reader's waking mind moves onto something else, the statement of wisdom Lau Tzu channeled from his connection to the collective deeper human consciousness will not be in their consciously recognized sensual catalog of primary knowledge to the reader and not a part of their factory-set knee-jerk reflex knowledge that's developed from personally experiencing something. It will, at some rate, fade out of ready memory.

They'll continue suffering in life in much the same way.

... Borrowed Wisdom Fascinates But Misses in Serving Real-Life Purpose

A person can over time pound/memorize Lau Tzu's verses or borrow/adopt wisdom from any other intellectual source into their intellectual memory. But later, when the present moment comes when a like situation arises in real life, the earlier intellectually metered received wisdom will not be consciously referenced as wisdom to handle the situation.

The wisdom's ring of truth is not yet an experientially earned part of their first-to-be-accessed sensual memory archives, for the most rapid recall to better serve the individual. The borrowed wisdom's been intellectually memorized and stored in the outer regions of the brain. It's not on the ready recall of the more primitive central brain.

The adaptability of any insightfully applied cross-over or lateral sort of wisdom application will be missing when an individual's usage of the memorized wisdom is challenged in situations that relate to the relationships referenced in that wisdom, The same cause/effect ruling principle applies but the possible relevance of any tangent application is not recognized.

Their present moment intellectually filed mind cannot recognize and associate with the relational factors in these situations.

Lau Tzu's sensual experience that inspired his wisdom-enriched insight that they later intellectually memorized did not leave its footprint in their experiential memory archives.

Lau Tzu's sensually filed consciously developed awareness of the cause/effect justice insightfully realized during his harmonious introspective mind/body deliberations while focusing his right concentration into the relational interplay among the coming and going life-manifest sensations of change is missing.

... Beware: Multi-Stepped Process to Apply Intellectually Stored Book/Chapter/Verse

Primal access or rapid recall is part of the fight-or-flight defense mechanism wired into the human condition.

In future real-time personal encounters with the subject of the intellectual wisdom, an individual would have to be able to recognize the sensually transferred similarities of the past situation that were remembered in intellectually metered coding and be able to pull from their intellectual memory the cognitive "book, chapter, and verse" to draw a comparison to associate with an intellectually founded description to then apply the intellectually stored wisdom to the current situation and act accordingly.

It's just not going to happen ... at least very quickly.

This may work upon occasion, but an individual's intellectual files stay fresh for only so long. They have nothing connecting their intellectually and sensually metered memory banks.

They're coded in intellectual media verbiage while those that trigger the experientially founded intrinsic memory are coded in the sensual tongue. It's like associating intellectually coded religious theology with sensually metered and coded universal reality.

The individual would have no waking cognitive reference to their experiential memory library because they have no sensual history with the cause/effect relationship in a real-life situation as Lau Tzu had when collecting the right knowledge for the right-thinking to let surface his inspired insightful understanding from which he derived the Tree of Life wisdom related in *Tao Te Ching*.

... It's Best to Teach How to Derive the Wisdom

Lau Tzu links self-discovery to one's enlightenment in verse 33 of Tao Te Ching when he writes how harmony will conquer the self and that in understanding the self, a truth seeker finds enlightenment and thus ... emotional balance/bliss.

In this verse, Lau Tzu gives a Cliff Notes lesson on how to fish (find heavenly enlightenment).

If Lau Tzu's lesson is not detailed enough, a truth seeker's due diligence will uncover Siddhartha's expanded details on the process of self-training the ego-conquering mind-into-body harmony for an enlightened conscious awareness of this reality's impermanent nature.

Giving humanity an instruction book of relational etiquette that gives bits of unearned wisdom about the dos and don'ts of how to think and behave to avoid being punished and maintain a level of expected morality is a very positive thing to do.

But, teaching a truth seeker how to understand by their own means and in their own way why those actions are deemed to be "right or wrong" ... sinful or not ... to know why the Ten Commandments became commandments ... is priceless ... and emotionally settling.

Instead of giving an individual isolated bites of here-say wisdom to ruminate over and put aside, likely to be forgotten, it is better to teach them how to originate the wisdom from within themselves.

Any Truth-Seeker Can Self-Train Their Emotional Bliss

... Siddhartha was Nothing Other than a Man

"This person —Siddhartha Gautama, known as the Buddha, "the enlightened one"— never claimed to be anything other than a man. Like all great teachers he became the subject of legends, but no matter what marvelous stories were told of his past existences or his miraculous powers, still all accounts agree that he never claimed to be divine or to be divinely inspired. Whatever special qualities he had were pre-eminently human qualities that he had brought to perfection. Therefore, whatever he achieved is within the grasp of any human being who works as he did."

- The Art of Living: Vipassana Meditation as taught by
S. N. Goenka, William Hart p,13-14

Any truth seeker has it within their power to self-train their abilities to reach emotional bliss or enlightenment about what's causing their suffering and how to eliminate it within their lifetime.

... Real-Life Wisdom is Universal ... Totally Non-Sectarian

"Would you say that VIPASSANA is the only way to reach enlightenment?

Enlightenment is achieved by examining oneself and eliminating conditioning., And doing this is Vipassana, no matter what name you may call it. Some people have never even heard of Vipassana, and yet the process has started to work spontaneously on them. This seems to have happened in the case of a number of saintly people in India, judging from their own words. But because they did not learn the process step by step, they were unable to explain it clearly to others. Here you have the opportunity to learn a step-by-step method that will lead you to enlightenment."

-The Art of Living: Vipassana Meditation as taught by S. N. Goenka, William Hart p,130

Anybody can learn how this universe works. It's the parts manual of what they're made of. Anybody can unlearn prior misguided conditioning.

This desire can develop in the wake of realizing the innate desire to understand reality to be free of the ignorance of the unknown that brings on suffering.

This writing was inspired by the experience of duplicating Siddhartha Gautama's step-by-step procedure called Vipassana Meditation, without ever hearing about Theravada Buddhism. At the time, the evolvement of the discovery was not even recognized to be associated with "spiritualism". It just served to be a great way to find quiet calm.

... Do You Have Mind Control?

For most, their conscious awareness marches to the beat of its own agenda. It can get to the point where an individual cannot begin to hold a train of thought without white noise from their state of unsettled unrest stepping in to change the subject.

They cannot maintain focus reading anything before their train of attentiveness is interrupted to begin thinking ... ruminating about something off topic.

For someone to understand why they do not feel balanced in this reality, it is first necessary for them to better understand this reality and then the cause doesn't have any place to hide.

To better understand this reality, one must be able to direct and focus their mental train of thought.

To focus one's attention, they must have control of their mind.

To have control of one's mind, their mind must be in a state of calmness ... not laden by mental chatter.

There is a way to self-train that mental calmness to then allow self-training the right concentration to search for the right knowledge to then allow self-training the insightfully derived Tree of Life Wisdom for an enlightened awareness of the reality the acquired knowledge reveals.

Christian theology's text gives a way to begin calming the mind in its Ten Commandments but stops there with no explanation of why about anything or what to do next, besides praying to the lord.

This enlightened awareness must be fed the relevant knowledge to derive the relevant wisdom that understands the cause/effect action found in the network of relationships.

It needs to do this in the present moment world where it happens and through the used media ... the sensually intrinsically parleyed world of body-speak where the truths of impermanence radiate. This is what allows for entering an understanding awareness state of emotional bliss where the suffering from the ignorance of the thought-mysterious ways of this reality disappears.

... Father Time and Mother Earth's Ongoing Spatial 3-D Dance

Self-training the mind-into-body harmony to sustain mind-controlled awareness in the arena of the coming and going sensations of life as it transforms takes a truth seeker into this reality's realm of truth. The truth-seeker does not really understand the depths of its broadcasted non-prejudiced calling. Father

Time and Mother Earth post no better display demonstrating the spatial 4-D exchange of their ongoing present moment coexisting romance.

There is no place of quiet that is more suitable for dwelling in introspective deliberation, pondering about what boils within. Reaching new depths of thinking can be achieved to then inspire the spark the insightful understanding to retire unwholesome thought patterns and replace them with those that are on-purpose wholesome.

Without Guidance Truth-Seekers Can Miss Linking Conscious Intellectual to Innate Intrinsic Understanding of Impermanence

Even if life-truth knowledge is internalized via sensual protocol many truth-seekers will lack the guidance on how to recognize, transpose, or synthesize that knowledge by self-training the right thinking to inspire the right wisdom in the development of an enlightened grade of spiritualmaturity.

Their activity might be accomplishing something that would help them on their journey of self-training their enlightenment, but the pathway to emotional bliss pot of gold at the end of the rainbow might not be understood.

Like with Nidra Yoga, if someone does not tell the student about the connection between the knowledge they accumulate while meditating and the emotional bliss promised by religion or in realism, they may never make the connection. They might never connect the calmed mind or relaxed mind they feel afterwards with getting them closer to that goal of answering a question they might not even be aware of yet.

Most will not recognize to associate this new awareness as having the "spiritual" or "religious" moxie related to what theologians or realists target as being the emotional bliss or maybe as heavenly paradise.

This author self-discovered this source of knowledge at 21 years old and did not connect the dots until hearing an advertisement for the book written by William Hart, *The Art of Living: Vipassana Meditation as taught by S. N. Goenka,* on an obscure radio station at 46 years old. He had no guidance.

This is the state of a truth-seeker's spiritual maturity after initially intellectually realizing the role impermanence plays in molding the truth of life and having briefly happened onto experiencing the mind/body harmony to experience getting a brief waking sensual glimpse at its presence.

After connecting the dots, this author has reread Hart's book many times. Every sentence intellectually exposes some of the breadcrumbs for the waking consciousness to ingest on its pathway back to rediscovering the understanding awareness of what defines their deeper consciousness.

The student has had their intellectual eyes opened ... consciously realizing they have had a brief sensually transposed vision of what leads to the "truth." Their task is to then follow their teacher's intellectually processed guidance describing what spiritual signposts to look for as they, on their own, sensually walk the experiential pathway to self-training their ability to gain the conscious enlightenment that undoes their fundamental ignorance of impermanence that allows their suffering.

... Must Originate Personal Self-Training Signpost Interpretations

"You yourselves must strive; the Buddhas only point the way."

~ Dhammapada, XX, (276)

Siddhartha made it clear that the messenger who speaks of the pathway to becoming enlightened about the ignorance that allows a truth-seeker's negative reaction to life situations can only point the way. The individual must walk the pathway on their own.

When a truth-seeker lacks confidence that they have attained the "same" sensation as that intellectually described by their teacher, it is because they cannot qualify it intellectually. They must sync into their own body, finding their own self-trained mind-into-body harmony, and they will feel the gut assurance that rings their bell of steadfast faith.

They will feel an intrinsic assurance that they have hit the pitch using their own bat. This feeling that they can in turn intellectually describe what they sensually felt might help the teacher better understand their own awareness.

Intellectually tendered knowledge of the path to follow gets self-trained into heartfelt steadfast faith-assured sensual understanding. The supportive swath of self-assurance once gained, becomes unshakeable.

... Achieving Progress in Sustaining Uninterrupted Mind into Body Harmony is a Self-Trained Facility Where No One's Progress can be Judged

Like a human will never be able to touch their elbow with the fingers of the same arm, no one else can touch/identify and judge an individual's protocol for self-training and sustaining mind-into-body harmony as correct or incorrect. The methods can be verbally described as being the same, yet what happens is very personal in its own unique way.

Guidance on Having Enlightened Worldview Credo Centers on Acquiring Intrinsic Awareness

... Not on Memorized Intellectual Reference ... Walk Where Our Enlightened Ancestors Walked

When a truth-seeker pools in harmony their waking cognitive awareness with the essence of the presence of their material body, their conscious focus is sensually witnessing or reading the very same Garden of Eden knowledge source that Jehovah warned Adam to use to derive the wisdom that he lived by.

This pool of knowledge ongoingly rewaters the Tree of Life.

This is the same harmonic soul-searching frequency of present moment life-manifest itself that Jesus managed to sustain dwelling in during his 40-day and 40-night pre-crucifixion meditation before being tempted by Satan.

That was a long time to sit in meditation. No details were given about his meditation technique. What other presence could his mind assume?

Trying to sustain an Aramaic ... the language of few words ... conversation in his head could get a bit boring ... while riding the ever-refreshed life river of ever change would bring on new insight.

... Jesus's 40 Days and Nights Awareness Must Have Been Spent in the Same State of Awareness as Siddhartha's Night Under the Banyan Tree

It is the same coming and going sensation abyss of deliberative solace in which Siddhartha searched his soul while sitting full lotus under the Banyan tree during the night he gained his enlightened understanding of the cause/effect relational justice that supports this reality.

Both Jesus and Siddhartha poised their harmonic mind-into-body self-awareness in the very same library of impermanence self-knowledge theater figuratively sighted by Moses in the account of the Genesis beginning.

They sustained the focus of their awareness into the coming and going rhythm of the ephemeral essence of this reality's life-giving Holy Spirit manifesting in their bodies allowing their conscious awareness to delve deeper and deeper into the self-knowledge awaiting in their deeper conscious world to inspire the life-wisdom-enriching "aha" insights that fueled their enlightenment about the ignorance that made them suffer.

... Gaining an Enlightened Understanding of Impermanence

Seeking outside guidance on deriving the wisdom to reach emotional bliss does not have to mean seeking to borrow or receive wisdom unearned like getting the finished product spot-on from The Tree of Knowledge as Adam and Eve did from the Tree of Knowledge of Good and Evil or reading religious text.

To first have the intellectual realization that suffering exists, that it has a cause, that the cause can be dealt with and an intellectual understanding of what that pathway is, it is possible to learn how to self-train oneself to have that intellectual vision converted to an experientially spun conscious awareness of its intrinsically registered meaning.

The self-knowledge that is sensually discovered is used to insightfully bring to conscious awareness a Tree of Life wisdom-enriched understanding of its real-time intrinsic truth.

It is wise to seek guidance on where to find and how to identify the type of knowledge that can feed into the insightful thinking to let Tree of Life wisdom rise to conscious awareness.

... Eastern Accent Not Needed in the West

Preoccupation with the "Eastern style" can sidetrack a truth-seeker. Individuals who cannot comfortably sit in a full lotus position can still find access to emotional bliss.

When thinking about spiritual enlightenment, many people born in the USA think about the Eastern disciplines. It can be intimidating and distance what they perceive their connection to our source to be.

Learning this dialect is a hoop a truth-seeker does not need to jump through. The intrinsically defined realm of living truth registers deeper in mankind's collective soul that does any intellectually conceived spoken language or cultural twist.

... Best Available Guidance

Just like the role of the Dali Llama was created at the end of the first millennia to best ensure preserving the meaning of the Buddhist monk Atisha's interpretation given to help Tibet reinstate its understanding of Buddhist spirituality by passing his interpretation of Siddhartha's message along from living person to living person, the Theravada Buddhist sect is said to have passed along Siddhartha's teachings of the methodology of self-training the wisdom-enriched enlightened understanding or impermanence from Siddhartha himself, from person to person.

This meaning transfer idea is Theravada Buddhism's equivalent to the idea supporting Tibet's Dalai Lama by the thread of person-to-person teachings in what is taught today by S.N. Goenka at his seminars.

A wonderful book describing Mr. Goenka's account is *The Art of Living: Vipassana Meditation* by William Hart. Mr. Hart. He describes in great detail the subject matter of what Mr. Goenka teaches at his seminars.

It is a short read, but each sentence is completely packed with detail describing what to look for to become enlightened as per how Siddhartha managed it and how he taught it to his followers.

One reading will not do.

This book is intellectually metered borrowed wisdom, like the Bible only it lays out what knowledge to look for and where and how to find it. It details how to train your mind to realize emotional bliss. It does not stop at just calming the mind with empty wisdom as does the Bible. It really breaks the process down and does a great job of giving meaning to the detail.

It seems to have some configuration of layered understanding written into it. Each time it is reread, the intellectual understanding goes just a bit deeper.

Siddhartha taught this method of experientially reaching enlightenment that he self-discovered at around 35 years old after years of dedicated searching. He devoted the rest of his life to doing nothing but teaching this method that worked for him. He taught how to gain a conscious understanding awareness of how the cause/effect principles formed by the force-driven show of impermanence that runs this reality has effect on the state of human emotions.

There's No Mental Bandwidth for a Middleman

If an individual's awareness is sidetracked into following a religious discipline's set of rites and rituals, their mind doesn't have room to devote to becoming aware of and further understanding reality's buzz.

... A False Prophet Presents a Dead-End Storyline

Begin by Asking the Right Question
... Quest Must be Tendered by the Realized Desire

A truth-seeker must acknowledge their innate desire to consciously touch and feel the living presence of life itself as it manifests from somewhere ... within is their only direct sensual paying pitch ... their only sensually connected point of reference.

To effectively strike up the "right effort" with the body to be available to meld with the "right mental awareness" takes that initial strike of sincere desire to taste and be witness to life as it presents itself at that moment. There must be nothing interrupting this burn-to-know ... to focus into its what's manifest during the passing of time ... to introduce the waking consciousness to the theater where inspired thinking to further knit together the wisdom-enriched understanding and increased awareness of life's complimenting relationships originates.

Clean up life behavior and allow self-training the ability to quiet the ever-repeating swirl of rumination that fills the head and use the right effort to find the right waking awareness to focus mental awareness into and through the coming and going pulse of life-manifest continually emanating from the various body areas.

This is what the living Holy Spirit of the present moment "now" actually feels like and will soon become a memory that opens the door to the next pulse of life.

This is an exercise of mind control … jumping conscious mental awareness from the garden of ruminating imagination fixed in the cognitive brain area to the coming and going life pulse fixed in the truth-seeker's sliver of the ultimate reality … real-time life itself as it manifests from within.

of the many types of meditation available today, this is the one that befits accumulating the self-knowledge to self-train the enriching wisdom of the Garden of Eden Tree of Life.

Anybody can develop the burning desire to know what all this intellectually metered "spiritual" stuff is about that they have heard about how the different ancient religions and Buddhist truth-seekers are trying to gain a soul-saving or enlightened understanding of … of the credit-claiming religion templated explanations.

After convincing oneself that they are just as deservingly important as any of those who sit full lotus under a Banyan tree to gain this awareness, that wanting desire can mature into realizing that this state should be here, right now.

The two-year-old child within is reawakening. It wants to better understand this heart-warming feeling.

… The Significance of a Meditated "Calm" Goes Unrecognized

How does someone meditate and what does that really mean?

Previous attempts at meditating might have led nowhere more than a short feeling of calm while the path where that calm can lead isn't even a consideration as for most in the USA there's no modern-day understanding or association on hand of its ancient Eastern old-world reference as to where it could take you.

Even if there had been a reference, the intended meaning would probably either be off course or lost in semantics.

There's probably no associated thought that the feeling of calm could be a step on the pathway leading to the intrinsically registered emotional bliss targeted by realism or to the intellectually painted world of the emotional bliss promised by religion.

There's no connection as to how that sensually registered calmed feeling is a part of the pathway to that intellectually painted picture of the emotional calm the pastor promises while holding the Bible up in supporting display.

Feeling the question stirring deep within but not being consciously sure of what the answer is they are looking for … the truth-seeker's thinking becomes preoccupied more with what the right question is.

They feel they must be able to sensually touch this unknown answer.

... The Intellectual Burn Morphs into a Sensual Journey

If their misery has a living cause, it must have a living answer.

How does this mind-into-body effort help find this answer to their suffering?

They do not yet see that self-training the mind and body to strike the harmony to enter right concentration/meditation (home of that calm) is just the step in between self-training a calmed morally/ethically state of mind like where the Ten Commandments leaves Christian believers dangling and self-training the ability to become aware of the Tree of Life wisdom that Jehovah issued a mandate for.

The felt urgency will lead the truth-seeker into making the "right effort" to focus their "right awareness" to search out their physical body for some hint to what the unknown question is.

They shut everything down except their mental awareness and desire to take it for a walk. They focus their attention totally on what their body feels like.

Their awareness enters their personal library of life knowledge to gain exposure to the knowledge they need to be able to derive the wisdom-enriched enlightened understanding conscious awareness that will bring them the emotional balance/bliss they seek.

This mind-into-body effort/awareness will take their uncertain ignorant conscious awareness to the depths of the rhythm of the sensually spoken heartbeat of their all-knowing deeper consciousness.

Problem is that they can't speak or understand its language of body-speak yet.

The feeling of unbound urgency is so prevalent that their ability to maintain their mental focus is blind to any mental white noise trying to impose any sort of obstruction.

The motivation to "touch" and to feel the fiber of the cord that connects the human condition to what instills that life to the human condition can move the truth-seeker's state of intellectual frustration into a body-wide sensual treasure hunt.

They will focus their awareness so intensely inwardly to sensually turn their body inside out to witness and better understand the life felt manifesting itself at that very present moment.

They act as though they have a back-stage pass.

It's possible for any human being to uncover this pathway or part of it on their own.

This is what this author experienced.

Yet, given that it is a natural process instilling conscious awareness of what is already there, a truth-seeker could follow the intellectual guidelines of an experienced teacher that will lead them step-by-step for bringing an understanding awareness of the intrinsically enriched awareness of this reality's ruling life principles they have failed to consciously reckon with.

About 25 years later this author connected the dots after hearing of Thomas Hart's book.

... Primal Home Address

With time, the more an individual makes the decision to self-train the mind-into-body state of awareness control, the better they get to know the territory, the more it feels like they are returning to their primal home.

This place of solitude is always there ... that's the only thing about this reality that doesn't change ... the manifestation of change itself.

As the journey of sensually collecting self-knowledge becomes more familiar, the more they will look forward to letting it inspire more wisdom-enriched insights.

Gather Life Knowledge to Self-Train a Life Wisdom-Enriched Enlightened Understanding

... "It Is Right Understanding That Is Real Wisdom...

> *... Thinking about truth is not enough. We must realize truth our-selves, we must see things as they really are, not just as they appear to be. Apparent truth is a reality, but one that we must penetrate in order to experience the ultimate reality of ourselves and eliminate suffering."*

> ~The Are of Living VIPASSANA MEDITATION, as Taught by S.N.Goenka, William Hart pg. 88

The challenge is deciding what is the right kind of knowledge to gather and where to find it to allow deriving the wisdom that comes with full understanding. It comes supported by a faith established in the self-evident assurance of what the wisdom decodes.

... Must Gather the Right Knowledge

The preceding chapters point out what 21st century human suffering can look like. Since it is a living state of disfunction, it is shown how there is a solution that is found in the same living transforming reality with sensitivity to sensual media only. The living reality is really the only state of existence that is not cornerstoned somewhere in the imagination.

Piecing together remnants of intellectually gathered and stored knowledge borrowed from some other entity that promises the truth of the claim will not lead anyone to the sensually registered answer. Focusing search for the answer to suffering on an imagination-built deity is a dead end.

No intrinsically seeded spiritual maturing can occur when mental awareness is not focused with sensual eyes open into transforming impermanence itself to gather the appropriate Life knowledge for deriving Tree of Life wisdom to understand what the living intrinsically registered answer of truth is.

A truth-seeker needs to know what type of knowledge is needed to derive the Tree of Life strain of wisdom that is suited for decoding and bringing from the deeper consciousness an atmosphere to derive a waking understanding of the patterned principles of impermanence that sustain the animated rendition of this reality that human perception can recognize.

Self-Training a Tree of Life Wisdom-Enriched Understanding Has a Three-Phase Progression

... A Calmed Mind

Self-train a calm mind to allow self-training the mind control to gather the right knowledge to allow self-training the ability to derive a wisdom-enriched understanding of what it is that has infected emotional balance with emotional suffering.

A truth-seeker needs to calm their mind before they can control it. It is after this phase of developing mind control where religious theology stops. Its ancient books of wisdom tell individuals how to think and act but does not share with them why. They build a wall where explanation stops and name it "sin" and warn not to go there with the threat of eternal fire and brimstone punishment.

Many individuals cannot maintain a train of thought for long at all. Listen to what so many say about what happens when they sit and try to clear their mind to meditate, how they cannot stop all these unrelated topics from entering their thinking ... mental white noise.

A truth-seeker needs to know where to direct their mind once it has been calmed. They must self-train their ability to control their mind to be attentive to accumulating the fiber of knowledge to derive Tree of Life wisdom.

Siddhartha's *Eightfold Pathway to Enlightenment* steps over theology's wall of just not "sinning" to give detail to why not to sin or do things to inhibit seeking enlightenment in his teachings of the *Four Noble Truths*. He taught of how the eightfold pathway leads a truth-seeker down the path of self-discovery to self-training their state of emotional bliss ... that process of gaining enlightenment that is grouped into the "right" actions of three self-trainings.

First, self-train an ethically and morally sound state of mind through using the "right speech, right actions, and right employment" to free up the peace of mind for the next level of self-training.

... Sandbox Etiquette ... Shut Up and Listen!

Revisit the childhood school of human relations where the basics that form the foundation for a compassionate human existence were taught. Keep the mental white noise under control and use a little sandbox etiquette (listening) and take the now calmed mind and focus its attention on what is being taught.

... A Sustained Mental Focus

With that non-frantic state of mind, the truth-seeker next self-trains their mind control to allow freeing up suppressed self-knowledge from the deeper consciousness to better understand the nature of the impermanence that defines its existence. A truth-seeker unites in harmony their body's "right effort" to make the essence of its presence available to combine with the mentally sustained "right awareness" directed at the coming and going sensations of life being manifested and felt within that essence.

This allows for the truth-seeker's successful "right concentration" creating the revealing primal atmosphere or sensual theater where life itself is being manifest for the quiet introspective deliberation to inspire the third level of self-training.

... Self-Train the Right Wisdom

With the truth-seeker's mental awareness stripped clean of outside interruptions, they can dwell in this arena of life manifest and allow the "right thinking" to inspire self-training over time the "right understanding" of the cause/effect relational justice that makes this reality tick. With this enlightened aware understanding of the ignorance that left them lost in suffering, their conditioned suffering does not return.

It's a dead end to self-train a memorized intellectually referenced knowledge of biblical wisdom.

They need to know what sort of knowledge to search for. They need to be clear on what language that knowledge is metered/parleyed in.

It can cut directly to the quick because it contains no middleman static.

Siddhartha Gautama ... Typical Human Being

... Self-Discovered and Taught Self-Training Calm Mind to Mind Control to Enlightened (Tree of Life) Wisdom ... Christianity's God Told Mankind What Wisdom to Live by and Siddhartha Told Mankind Where and How to Find It

Siddhartha who made it clear that he was no more than a typical human being, commandeered the arrow of time and unlike Jesus was able to leave a detailed undaunted record of how he figured the process out. His teachings describe how to walk the same path of self-discovery that worked for him.

> *"The unique contribution of the Buddha to the world was a way to realize truth personally and thus to develop experiential wisdom."*
>
> ~ *The Art of Living: Vipassana Meditation as taught by S. N. Goenka*, William Hart, p. 90

> > *"In themselves, morality and concentration, sila and Samadhi, are valuable, but their real purpose is to lead to wisdom…By practicing morality, we avoid actions that cause the grossest forms of mental agitation. By concentrating the mind, we further calm it and at the same time shape it into an effective tool with which to undertake the work of self-examination. But it is only by developing wisdom that we can penetrate into the reality within and free ourselves of all ignorance and attachments."*
> >
> > ~ *The Art of Living: Vipassana Meditation as taught by S. N. Goenka*, William Hart p. 88

After becoming enlightened, for the remainder of his life, Siddhartha taught how he self-discovered that through self-training mind control, a truth seeker can collect the self-knowledge to derive the experientially enriched wisdom to realize emotional bliss through gaining an enlightened understanding awareness of this reality's impermanent character.

… Siddhartha Connected The Dots … That Led Him to an Enlightened Understanding of the Transforming Nature of this Impermanent Reality

> *"He used no instrument in his investigation other than his own mind. The truth that he discovered was not the result of intellectualizing but of his own direct experience, and that is why it could liberate him."*
>
> ~ *The Art of Living: Vipassana Meditation as taught by S. N. Goenka*, p. 36

Siddhartha taught what knowledge to seek and why and how to seek that knowledge and exactly how to then derive the Tree of Life Wisdom that Jehovah gave the Garden of Eden stamp to as being essential to live in the Eden paradise of emotional bliss.

It seems Jehovah kept this understanding a secret, thinking he could just tell his human beings what to do to keep a calm mind without letting them know why.

Siddhartha recognized how to go beyond self-training morality (where Christianity stops) and through self-training mental concentration he self-trained his ability to tap into the reality that his physical human presence was a material part of to collect the necessary self-knowledge to self-train how to derive experientially enriched wisdom to better understand the principles of the uncontrollable dimensional forces and the interlinking principles that hold this impermanent reality together.

In doing so, he was able to understand and overcome the fundamental ignorance that held his emotions hostage.

He taught of how and where a truth seeker needs to take their awareness and how to self-train the life wisdom that understands and decodes the logistics supporting nature's unchangeable uncontrollable principles that govern the cause/effect outcome of all the change that constitute and define the transforming nature of this impermanent reality.

Keep in mind that until experienced, his recorded account is, like the Bible or other theological accounts, Tree of Knowledge wisdom. Siddhartha's account describes and lays out the pathway to experientially gaining an understanding awareness of the Tree of Life wisdom. But his description does not install the intrinsic meaning of the wisdom it describes.

... Theology Falls Short

Mainstream theological disciplines fail to describe how to go beyond living a moral/ethical lifestyle to self-train the ability to gather the needed knowledge and how to use it to experience and intrinsically record the same insightful "aha" moments that form the supporting network infrastructure of what feeds and keeps alive the Garden of Eden Tree of Life.

Instead of realizing it from within, theology believers give credit to their chosen deity who promises to hand emotional bliss over after they die to them as being the finished product, just like the snake promised all-knowing wisdom from the Garden of Eden Tree of Knowledge to Eve.

... Siddhartha's Figured Out that he had a Deeper Consciousness

Siddhartha figured out what the deeper consciousness was and the process needed to tap into it to open a sensual media primal pathway to his waking consciousness.

People today look at their awareness of their deeper consciousness as having always been consciously known to people. That's not the case. The self-evident nature of that had to be figured out. It took insightful moments to realize that the human body has a consciousness that's in step with nature's principles and a waking consciousness that's strapped with ignorance about that nature.

Siddhartha was able to leave details of how he conditioned his mind to self-train his ability to do this to his followers without the sort of government interference Jesus encountered. His account is not as fragmented and weak on cohesion as that of Jesus.

His conscious awareness coming from the strain of life wisdom he derived from his acquired self-knowledge brought him a conscious connection with his deeper consciousness awareness that understands the ways of impermanence. He eventually was able to understand this connection.

Siddhartha's Ageless Process Detailed in Theravada 101

... No Middleman or God-Insert

Siddhartha supplied and answered those hard-to-generate initial questions a truth-seeker encounters when figuring out the way to emotional balance in what he taught as being the Four Noble Truths. He taught his self-discovered way to realize the answer to the fourth noble truth dealing with consciously gaining awareness of the sensual answer in what he taught about the eight-fold pathway to enlightenment.

Impermanence is ever-present. It knows nothing about the past and the future. It lives in the life wisdom that makes sense of the present moment ... the only source where the "answer" can be derived.

... Beginning Questions Should Question Aspects of these Four Truths

In sweating out the impatience that can follow unrest, an individual might ask themselves what is it that they don't understand.

They can admit that they are suffering in their lack of understanding.

Siddhartha's Four Noble Truths help in giving ordered form to realizing and answering initial questions.

1. Suffering is present (initial realization)

2. It has an alterable living cause

3. It has a living solution

4. The life pathway to the living solution

Siddhartha's four noble truths give order to a truth-seeker's questioning process that leads to enlightenment. First, after first realizing they are suffering ... that suffering exists.

Does it have a cause? Can the cause be changed by humans? Is there a way to eliminate the cause? How to eliminate the cause.

A difference between Theravada and Malayalam Buddhism is that Theravada Buddhism is directly handed down mouth-to-mouth from Siddhartha himself. Malayalam Buddhism offers a less defined or has a roomier understanding as to what the right order is for the eight folds of the pathway.

Tibetan Buddhism and Zen Buddhism are a few of the strains of Buddhism in this category.

The three phases of developing mind control are intertwined within his directives in his two teachings The Four Noble Truths and The Eight Folds to Enlightenment.

Siddhartha's Eight Folds to Enlightenment give detail to attaining the 4th Noble Truth.

The four noble truths …A truth-seeker needs to let their conscious awareness progress through these 4 noble insights…

Suffering exists … insipient suffering has many fronts of normalcy.

It has a cause… ignorance seeds faulty conditioned perception.

It can be eliminated… not predetermined, the living cause has a living solution

How it's done … follows the Eight-Fold Pathway to Enlightenment formula

Siddhartha's eight folds to enlightenment are intertwined with the three stages of self-training mind control:

The first phase of self-training mind control:

> Self-training ethical/moral standards
> Right Speech
> Right Action
> Right Livelihood

Second phase of self-training mind control: self-training right concentration (meditating)

> Right Effort
> Right Awareness
> Right Concentration
> Third phase of self-training mind control: self-training the right wisdom
> Right Thought
> Right Understanding

A motivated truth-seeker must wakingly realize, in their own way, an intrinsically registered realization and understanding of what is contained in *The Four Noble Truths*, while concentrating on following the right behaviors of *The Eight Folds of Enlightenment* hand in hand with self-training their mind control.

Listen to Your Two-Year-Old Inner Child

… Question Anything Not Understood … Self-Train Cognitive Control of Impulsive Mental White Noise

"An unexamined life is not worth living."

~Socrates

"Open your world to the excitement of discovery!"

~ Bill Nye

Siddhartha taught that it's an individual's duty to question the things they don't understand:

> *"Do not simply believe whatever you are told, or whatever has been handed down from past generations, or what is common opinion, or whatever the scriptures say. Do not accept something as true merely by deduction or inference, or by considering outward appearances, or by partiality for a certain view, or because of its plausibility, or because your teacher tells you it is so. But when you yourselves directly know, "These principles are unwholesome, blameworthy, condemned by the wise: when adopted and carried out they lead to harm and suffering, "then you should abandon them. And when you yourselves directly known, "These principles are wholesome, blameless, praised by the wise: when adopted and carried out they lead to welfare and happiness," then you should accept and practice them."* (A. III. Via. 65, Kesamutti Sutta (Kalamazoo Sutta), iii, ix.)

> *"The highest authority is one's own experience of truth. Nothing should be accepted on faith alone: we have to examine to see whether it is logical, practical, beneficial."*
> *~The Art of Living: Vipassana Meditation as taught by S. N. Goenka, William Hart p.14*

...Step Out And Ask Why? ... Shout Prove It!

A truth-seeker must find the strength and fortitude to step beyond what the confined dogma-set limits and idle speculation of their social network or their chosen theology-set guidelines might specify. They must question what they do not "feel" they understand with the unending grunt of a life-hungry 2-year-old.

Like how a policeman is trained to question what seems odd, a truth-seeker should show no hesitation to getting to the heart of uncertainty.

If an individual cannot work up the courage to ask questions, they are just not ready to find out what it is that defines the unknown.

... Settle Only for What Appears to Support a Self-Evident Principle that Serves Impermanence

The Chinese Martial Art of Kung Fu patterns its many forms after various members of the animal kingdom. Kung Fu recognizes the wisdom that's exhibited by other forms of life in the non-human side of reality. Mammals, reptiles, fish, birds, and even insects have over the centuries learned to adapt their behavior to align with Mother Nature's rhythm of life to live in the happiest state possible … to avert suffering.

Watch and learn.

Stare into the dragon's eyes. Look inside to where the life that is defined by the principles of nature manifest as time flows. Do not settle for the unverifiable principles donned by any school of theology.

Grow spiritually by collecting this life knowledge and using it to insightfully derive the Tree of Life wisdom to realize an understanding awareness of the cause/effect life-situation-outcome determining principles that through conditioned ignorance have brought on suffering. Replace ignorance-spawned suffering with wisdom-enriched emotional bliss.

Keep in mind that the "getting" of an intellectually conceptualized understanding of the process of this discovery is much quicker and easier than it is to sensually recognize and establish a conscious understanding awareness through its intrinsic sensually metered history.

Therein lies the challenge.

A Truth-Seeker Must Realize that They're Suffering *and* that it has a Cause

… First Two of Four Noble Truths

When an individual develops a more defined understanding of what insipient suffering is and they realize and can admit to themselves that they spend their time at some level of emotional unhappiness and that things just do not add up and they can strike up the due diligence, they become a truth-seeker. The importance of finding out why must charge them with the courage to trust their freewill and step outside their chosen social network or outside of theology's allowable questioning.

Their burning desire to figure this out will help give them the mind control to fight off and clear their thinking of cognitive "white noise" … the random thoughts they cannot normally seem to control so they can settle their waking awareness into their life-filled flesh. They can take their conscious awareness and let it sink into the activity present in their body … part by part.

They can seek the appropriate guidance to help bring intellectual clarity to what emotional bliss awaits and find the sensual pathway to connecting this sensually metered truth to their waking conscious awareness.

Self-Train a Calm Moral/Ethical Mind

... Mind Control ... Phase One of Three Phases of Self-Training

Siddhartha realized it necessary to harbor a mental presence that was not dominated by the white noise of unsettling uncontrollable thoughts. From his Noble Eightfold Pathway to Enlightenment, Siddhartha teaches it's necessary to use the Right Speech and the Right Action and to be involved in the Right Livelihood to help fashion a morally calmed mental presence.

He taught to abstain from unwholesome deeds and perform only wholesome ones.

It's common for individuals, from early childhood, to mistakenly believe what they're told will make them happy and let that belief numb them and deafen their ear to the callout from their inside angst of emotional distress.

Even though an individual can be living in a state poisoned by anger, apathy, hatred, shame, guilt, fear, anxiety, jealousy, envy, sadness, grief, depression, or any other state of emotional distress, they might not realize it. This state of emotional suffering might have become their normal life.

Effectively self-training a white-noise-static-free mind to be calm by using the Right Thinking, Right Speech, and Right Employment. By practicing this, the mind eventually frees itself of negatives that can overtake, hijack or just uncontrollably butt their way into threads of thought and leave a calmed mental state that can be trained to sustain a focused awareness.

Suffering Trigger Found in the Sensual Dimension ... Where Mind and Body Meet ... Where Awareness and Reality Intersect

... Third of Four Noble Truths ... Mental Reaction Phase is at Heart of Suffering ... The Brain and the Fly-in-the-Ointment

To remove a fly-in-the-ointment, first one must go into the ointment and pinpoint where the fly is.

To remove the faulty part of the belief system that's causing or allowing emotional disturbance, it's necessary to go into the mind's belief system (ointment) and figure out where in the mental process the fly is lodged.

The mind is not the solid piece of flesh it appears to be when looking at one. The human range of perception only sees the outline (apparent reality) of what is the ultimate reality that makes up its whole.

With the material brain, the self-evident truth is that like everything else, there's nothing solid about it. It consists of quark-size bits of energy constantly transforming in response to the ongoing cause/effect outcomes dictated by the relational principles established by the push and pull of the gravity and electro-magnetism forces that form the backdrop that knits together the ultimate reality.

In the transforming life-swirl of electrons that make up the physical brain exists the individual's consciousness that keeps their human condition switched on to figure out how to negotiate its human experience. The consciousness has a deeper region that's wise to the natural force-driven principles that set the boundaries for the human condition to act out its life purpose.

There's nothing odd about something … on some level … understanding the nature of what it is that it is composed of.

The region of the consciousness that the individual uses to make decisions while acting out its life purpose is their waking consciousness. The waking consciousness works within the boundaries set by the individual's belief system concocted worldview.

The object is for the waking consciousness to figure out and understand what the deeper consciousness knows as the outcomes of all the individual's life interactions are governed by of the impermanent ultimate reality that the deeper consciousness understands.

The outcomes of the individual's interactions are bound by the relational justice set by those force-determined principles, and the individual must survive and find emotional balance within the patterns of those principles.

How well an individual understands these life principles will affect the individual's state of emotional rest.

… The Freewill

The freewill captains the belief system. It decides what claims of truth it accepts and trusts to internalize to further hone the host's worldview.

The freewill decides how high to set the bar for believing or accepting something before internalizing it and weaving its understanding into their worldview.

An individual uses their freewill to draw the line in the sand as to when they must stop blindly believing what another entity tells them. Individuals have to believe what other tell them just to get started in something.

They decide on how important it is for somethings that's purported to be true, to be verified to the point of being self-evident.

These factors will influence the purpose and nature of an individual's worldview.

It determines who's making their way through the day using Fig Leaf Wisdom.

… The Problem

When an individual's freewill decides to lower the bar of the belief system's blind faith resistance filter for allowing internalizing unverified or unverifiable claims of truth to further shape their worldview, the outcomes proclaimed by what the claim proposes to be true and what really happens in real life might not be the same.

The principles of the false claim fail to fully factor into the promised result the claim stands behind and that its wisdom leads to, the self-evident principles that run the ultimate reality.

If an individual's freewill's been compromised by their belief system's conditioning to accept as real some claim of truth that fails to recognize the nature of the ultimate reality … when they settle for only seeing what is really only an apparent reality … their suffer … as their ignorance is fundamental in not realizing and respecting the present moment presence and outcome-ruling authority of the force-driven string theory or wave theory principles that give pattern to the impermanence that suspends the transforming infrastructure of this reality and sets course for all the relational outcomes in all situations included in the ongoing change of everything in the ultimate reality.

The false claim's principles disregard the importance of impermanence and thus would allow for time continuity. Something that stands still in time is something an individual can become attached to.

When an individual becomes attached to something in what they perceive as the "apparent reality," they are ignorant or choosing to ignore how the laws of impermanence make self-evident the truth that what they're attached to, doesn't exist.

The mental friction resulting from when what an individual's worldview's been conditioned to believe and what they witness in real time don't agree is realized in their emotional suffering.

As the liking/avoidance reaction to something might seem very slight initially, after it occurs several times, it can develop into more of a craving or in being aversive to its presence.

Siddhartha called this developing a thirst for the object.

They will suffer the emotion roller-coaster that comes inherent to these imagined relationships.

The individual has an ongoing waking struggle in effort to find emotional balance in sight of the imaginary relationships they've formed with the objects from their apparent reality.

… The Fly-in-the-Ointment … The Cause

This mind, in its life-swirl of electrons brain, has a protocol that processes its recognition of the ultimate reality it finds life.

It its state of consciousness, it becomes aware of sensual inputs from its 5 ports of sensual recognition. It perceives the sensation and attaches the like/dislike rating to it. That rating can develop into an attachment or aversion if the host's not wise to the ultimate reality.

This rating phase is when the mind is reacting to how the sensation was perceived. It's in this reacting that the cause of suffering arises.

Siddhartha taught that when there's no reacting, there's no suffering.

Therefore, an individual needs to listen to their body when trying to better understand their emotions. The body will react to a situation before the mind has time to consciously realize it.

… If the Cause of Suffering Registers Sensually, the Solution Must also be Metered Sensually

If the suffering from the conditioned perceptions that generate those negative emotional states is metered in the sensual world, the cause of that suffering must originate in the same sensual dimension.

For a truth-seeker to enter the arena to deal with suffering's cause that exists in the transforming realm of reality, they must first eliminate the mental white noise to then take control of their conscious awareness to go to this dimension of awareness where life itself manifests with unbiased sensual eyes open.

Reactions are formed mentally and are reflected physically in sensations on a "preverbal" level.

A truth-seeker must acquire the needed appropriate wisdom-deriving knowledge from where the mind meets up with and forms its perception of naked change's consciously sensed ever-changing tangible presence. Use the new knowledge to reconfigure and recondition what the mind perceives the sensation to represent.

Bit by bit fill the pit of emptiness-of-understanding that feeds into Fig Leaf Wisdom with an intrinsically founded understanding awareness.

… Tree of Life Knowledge Source

A truth-seeker must self-train having a sustained mental focus into the sensual world for their mind to go to this sensual dimension to experientially gain the appropriate knowledge to then self-train the sustained awareness to have the right thinking to derive the intrinsically retained and sensually spoken Tree of Life wisdom to eliminate their ignorance.

The only place a truth-seeker has available to go for this sensually metered intrinsic education is to sensually check into the living flesh of their own human condition. They must sensually tune in and catch life transformation there, red-handed, in the act of manifestation.

Self-knowledge originates from sensually witnessing the life-manifest display in the existing impermanent reality itself. The truth-seeker self-trains their ability to sensual witness the essence of its presence in their own physical transmitter (their impermanent living flesh.)

The truth-seeker must self-train their ability to develop a sensual familiarity and conscious feel for the logic and proportion of self-evident truth as its coming and going incarnation sensually displays the impermanent makeup of this reality.

... Pulsing Flesh is the Only Direct Wiring to Reality's Flow

There is no other part of the transforming material world but the blood-pulsing nerve-mapped infrastructure of the human body that is connected to the human heart to sensually derive a Tree of Life wisdom-enriched understanding of this impermanent reality to scare off the elusive boogieman(men) of the unknown.

Sensually recognized reality is where everyone's boogieman(men) hides to do his dirty work.

The truth-seeker takes their focused awareness there and in a humbled state of mind-into-body focus, they collect and assimilate the self-knowledge to allow the "right-thinking" for deriving the strain of life wisdom that speaks the sensual body-speak language. It is the life principle decoding key that brings conscious understanding to the ways of the pre-lingual relational data that connect all of nature's countless ongoing transformational causes to their effects of change.

This life manifest process is the living fiber of this reality's dimensional backdrop. It gives an organic demonstration of this reality's nature of ongoing transformation.

Right Thinking" "Aha" Insights Originate from Heart-Sourced Matrix More Primal than Linguistics

... Meditation Mimed

Just because a truth-seeker might be effectively striking a Buddha-like pose does not necessarily bring them the increased conscious awareness they've painted in an intellectually metered picture.

Attempting to fade into the said state of "blank mind" that they are not sure the meaning of or concentrating on an object or mantra will not take them any closer to understanding the impermanence of this reality.

This mimed appearance itself will not bring understanding to what causes the grey shadow of uncontrolled mental white noise or the grey lining in the life awareness cloud of misunderstanding. Focusing attention on what is going on in the reality of life manifest on the inside and not what the outside looks like is the way to approach becoming enlightened about the way of that life manifest.

This process of life manifest has been a consistent present moment state of real since creation. Taking mental awareness into that constant haven should be a lifelong association in the conscious mind, as it is in the subconscious. It provides the settling warmth consistent with seeing a candle in a nighttime window at Christmas time.

Maintaining a sustained focus withstanding the mental white noise that is pounding on the thought train door to interrupt having mental awareness focused into a body area can be tough. It is what this is all about. It's why the mind's been self-trained to be morally and ethically balanced, to find that white noise-free calm as best can be.

... Intellectual Focus Registers Too Shallow

A truth-seeker must vacate the world of intellectual mental chatter that occupies the waking conscious arena of concern and move the focus of mental awareness into the buzz of the coming and going manifestation of life within their body parts. They must go beyond merely thinking of body location intellectually and have mental awareness search it out and enter it sensually.

Unless a truth-seeker is merely wanting to enter a state of momentary bliss or deep relaxation, they must focus their attention into the sensual media of their body buzz and not merely on some mental exercise. William Hart reflects the teachings of S.N. Goenka, Theravada Buddhism's "Dali Lama" of sorts who was taught by the chain of living teachers who have kept Siddhartha's teachings alive since his lifetime. In his book *The Art of Living: Vipassana Meditation as taught by S. N. Goenka*, page 78, he says:

"There are many techniques to develop concentration. One may be taught to concentrate on a word by repeating it, or on a visual image, or even to perform over and over again a certain physical action, in doing so one becomes absorbed in the object of attention and attains a blissful state of trance. Although such a state is no doubt very pleasant while it lasts, when it ends one finds oneself back in ordinary life with the same problems as before. These techniques work by developing a layer of peace and joy at the surface of the mind, but in the depths the conditioning remains untouched. The objects used to attain concentration in such techniques have no connection with the moment-to-moment reality of oneself."

... Intellectually Founded Soundness through Abstract Logistics?
... Focus Sustained on Image or Mantra? Temporary Ecstasy Only

Gaining self-knowledge gives experiential validation to the strain of wisdom the knowledge is used to derive. It gives it an intrinsic foundation wrapped in steadfast faith. When meditating with the "right awareness" faction of the "right concentration" focused on mantras or objects generated by what the imagination creates means focusing on something needing a state of continuity which is the "unreal" ... the apparent reality ... that the truth-seeker is seeking understanding of to gain freedom from.

It is a dead-end with a possible temporary state of ecstasy payoff that does not address obtaining the appropriate Tree of Life wisdom-deriving knowledge used to build a wisdom-enriched awareness conscious understanding of the principle-based ways of nature.

A temporary layer of peace and joy might appear of the surface of the mind but being fixed on an object needing an imaginary state of permanence to exist from keeps the focus away from sensually metering the life-manifest which experientially details the knowledge that will feed the "right thinking" needed to inspire deriving the wisdom-enriched "right understanding" that leads to a state of total enlightenment.

… Shift From Rumination Abyss to Deeper Consciousness Awareness

Many spend much of their daytime life energy spinning in an ongoing emotional state bound by guilt reflections over past relationships to worrying about what the boogieman of their unknown future might have in mind for them.

They might worry about what might be coming in the future.

They need to stop chewing the cud of "what ifs" and take their mental focus out of their imaginary garden of rumination and strike awareness with what unexplored present moment change manifests from within.

… Mind Into Body Harmony Unlocks Inner Primal Sanctuary to Ponder Emotional Moods in Self-Investigative Deliberation

A truth-seeker must first self-train a calm mental moral/ethical state to the point where they can self-train the mind control to engender the mind into body harmony to sensually witness the presence of the essence of the coming and going bits of life-giving energy to witness its ongoing process of life manifest. With self-training this self-knowledge they become suspended in quiet self-investigative deliberation to allow inspiring thoughts to spawn insightful wisdom enriched understandings giving conscious sight to a self-evident Tree of Life awareness.

They can have a heightened awareness to physical reactions that might accompany their focused body tour.

As Siddhartha taught in making the right effort in self-training mind control to generate mind/body harmony … get to recognize and know the character of those moods that spur negative emotions. Become familiar with the thinking used to, on an intrinsic level, remove and replace the thought patterns of those states of awareness to allow their non-return.

... Physical Makeup is the Only Contact with Material World Experience

A typical individual's waking awareness stays centered between their ears where they consider, calculate, weigh, judge, and get caught up in unending circles of rumination. Even though conscious realizations of joy and compassion happen in this area, many spend most of their waking time revolving in a rumination whirlpool of regret, worry, and confused fear about an unknown future.

They use their present moment life energy treading water in their sea of emotional distress.

The only material configuration of this reality that an individual's awareness of their sensual experience can access exists in the nerve-connected material composition of their body. The fearful world of regret and worry teeters in the individual's imagination.

A truth-seeker can self-train the right physical effort and the right mental awareness to harmoniously strum the sensual chords of their coming and going life experience. With the right concentration, their mind control has turned off the between-the-ears discontent or life struggle to feel what is emanating from their human condition.

... Focused Awareness can Endorse Sleep

Self-training the harmony to focus the mind/body coordination to generate mind-into-body right concentration to take conscious awareness from the fury of untethered mental rumination into the place of life manifest in the tangible reality of the material body allows the spirit to realize a warm calm that will often put the individual to sleep.

For those who have trouble sleeping at night, this is a welcome treat. Just begin assuming the focused calm needed and sleep might soon follow.

... Right Concentration Opens Up the Source's Comforting Zone of Timeless Familiarity

When shaken by the present moment's unexpected and sometimes unnerving situations, when making the right effort to focus right mental awareness in the body's coming and going testimony of life manifestation, an individual enters the calming peaceful zone of quiet familiarity ... anytime ... anyplace.

... State of Rumination is Set in Mental Abyss ... Move Awareness Generation from Head into Ongoing Tingle in the Essence of Body Area Presence

Switching into the hunt mode for the familiar buzz from body essence takes awareness out from between the ears. Displace the waking awareness or the center of thought from between the ears to the individual body areas.

Develop mind control to maintain this focus of awareness. Overcome the urge to let the mind roam through the random white noise thoughts that cut short the mind control needed to generate the right thinking to inspire self-training the insights to let surface an enlightened understanding of the ways of this reality's impermanent nature.

After a truth-seeker initially realizes that they are suffering to then self-train a calm mental state by using the right speech, the right actions, and right employment, as Siddhartha suggests, can self-train a mind they can then control to self-train a Tree of Life wisdom enriched waking awareness with the supporting understanding awareness to undo their ignorance-caused suffering.

They self-train their ability to calm and coral the random thoughts their mind generates and through attaining the mind/body harmony found in uniting "right effort" and "right awareness," they can achieve the "right concentration" needed to focus their mind control to within the sensual world to where the answer lies. Those random uncontrolled mind-wandering thoughts that ruminate through their life experience to spend time in unmonitored states of worry, hope, hate, love, joy, anger, fright … etcetera happen in the "mind" in the center of the head … yet resonates physical symptom throughout the entire body.

Use the right effort of the body to make itself present for the right mental awareness or thought initiator to be placed in the coming and going materializing of life itself in those body parts … area by area. Finding the "mind control" to do this can pose quite a challenge for most.

… Focusing on Breathing is Good for Beginners

Focusing awareness into breathing is recommended for beginners as it is easier to self-staying focused by staying focused on something more sensually observable.

Self-training mind control should be placed high on an individual's priority list. The rewards are priceless…

It is setting the conditioned mind free from the white noise echo of rumination to feel its way through the space of creation itself. The mental calm is achieved, and its progression is the goal.

When the Ebb Finds Its Flow

"Embracing the wisdom of our emotions—instead of avoiding them— is at once a powerful way to show up in the world and a powerful avenue for personal transformation. "
~Karla McLaren M.Ed.

Intellectually metered borrowed wisdom lacks the mind-into-body harmonic connection needed to inspire from a truth-seeker's detected deeper consciousness the intrinsic impulses that inspire and feed into the right thinking to allow consciously realizing the "aha" wisdom that better understands emotional holdups and allows self-training ability to allow the acquired life knowledge to inspire the Tree of Life wisdom to undo the self-ego.

A truth-seeker needs to deliberate in mind-into-body body scan to get the sensual meaning of what the spiritual signposts were that preconditioned their illusionary intellectually painted mental picture of what ancient religious theology's real-life presence was. Either on their own or by being taught they need to recognize the sensually emanated incarnations of those religious maxims in the real-time flow of today's present moment material presence.

Is the body scan life buzz that's felt, the Bible-referenced Holy Spirit/Holy Ghost?

When these sensual signposts are recognized and associated with or linked to the intellectually sketched religious notions, their sensually witnessed presence helps to unmask and inspire the understanding way to tap into the source of insightful wisdom that brings waking clarity to the nature and intended purpose of our living source.

Siddhartha spent the post-enlightenment years of his life discussing nothing but how he became fully enlightened about the object of his ignorance that allowed his suffering.

This knowledge/awareness gaining process works for anybody the same way today ... 2,500 years later. Advancement in spiritual maturity achieved by linking self-knowledge experientially from the deeper to the waking consciousness ... letting intellectual theology find sync with sensual reality ... is nurtured from the inside and founded in the sensual experiential discovery and realization that every aspect of this reality is completely transitory.

... Human Passion Unlocks Human Potential

The unbridled desire to do this undoes the ignorance that preoccupies and indefinitely delays finding the unique purpose felt when human passion finds and unlocks human potential. It is the same ignorance that sponsors the same lack of understanding that underwrites all human suffering. Sought out wisdom-enriched awareness changes the nature of any human mind that has been locked in the myth of material permanence ... a worldview acknowledging attachment to craving and aversion. It allows seeing beyond the ego to embrace and embody newly inspired insightful wisdom that overwrites and undoes its ignorance.

With all the humility they can muster, a truth-seeker must self-train their ability to fine-tune the harmonious coexistence between their physical presence and their aware understanding of its material mass. They sensually tune their harmonious mind/body awareness into witnessing life as it manifests within their own flesh.

They relate their ebb to its flow.

... The "Message from Above"

This is our Source's ongoing free-to-all message-of-life broadcast. It is the "sign from above" that manifests from within. Our true source speaks sensually to us through our hearts.

An inspired insightful understanding of this forming of life will undo the ignorance that allows living in the misery of present moment discontent. An on-track truth-seeker's passing day can be filled with moments of sudden inspired insightful "aha" wisdom-enriched revelations of how their surrounding reality makes sense.

As Jesus has said, "The meek shall inherit the earth." This is how. The meek will learn to understand it.

They can wakingly feel life-truth's insightful revelation. It is relaxing and they can consciously attribute this re-found mental peace to their conscious awareness of its intuitive presence.

As a truth-seeker nears being fully enlightened about the ways of nature that their lack of understanding has caused them to suffer the two worlds begin to merge metaphorically. This is when the meanings that are felt in the heart translate into the same as those felt in the mind.

The waking consciousness syncs into the deeper consciousness ... they're fused together.

It is necessary for an individual to assume due diligence to self-train the ability to spot-on equate one into the other ... recognizing life analogies becomes easy.

Self-Train a Focused Mind into the Most Primal State of Harmony

... Mind Control ... Phase Two of Three Phases of Self-Training

> "The physical aspect of vedana (mind-into-body process) is partic-
> ularly important because it offers vivid, tangible experience of the
> reality of impermanence within ourselves. Change occurs at every
> moment within us, manifesting itself in the play of sensations. It is at
> this level that impermanence must be experienced."
>
> - The Art of Living: Vipassana Meditation as taught by S. N.
> Goenka, William Hart p. 149

... Self-Directing Oneself into their Own Impermanence to Witness Change Sensually

The idea in calming the mind is for a truth-seeker to train themselves how to fight off the mental white noise interruptions that make their mind wander. By striving to focus mental attention to be in sync with the sensual buzz within the areas of the body, they can learn to hold maintain control of the focus of their thinking.

Change happens constantly and during mind-into-body awareness the truth-seeker experiences it as it manifests itself in the sensations that serve as the subject of the sustained focus.

... Listen to Natural Harmony in Mother Nature's All-Night Symphony

An individual can relax into the intoning harmony that fills the air of a summer night in the Midwestern USA. The coming and going vocal exchange between the masses of crickets and frogs becomes intoxicating.

It's becomes clear where the Buddhist monks turn for role models for their chants.

When the sun wakes up the countryside, the intended meaning heard in the wordless discussion between the different birds can become so well understood that it seems appropriate to just shout out for some of them to just go get a motel room.

... Primal Cornerstone Role Model Epitomizing True Harmony ... Mind-into-Body Ying-Yang Relationship

Self-training mind-into-body harmony becomes feasible after unchecked ear-ringing mental white noise is eliminated or sufficiently minimized.

A truth-seeker can now proceed with a more calmed mind and effectively slip into a state of mind-into-body harmony. This is where 2 things work together in harmony of its most primal form.

This is where mental awareness is focused into sensually metering the material truth of the physical body ... mind-into-body harmony.

This harmony allows self-training, as Siddhartha taught, a sustained state of right concentration to collect the applicable flesh-brewed knowledge that allows for inspiring the insightful right thinking to self-train the right life wisdom to become enlightened about the ignorance that robbed them of their emotional bliss ... that caused their suffering.

It will continue to improve over time with practice and patience.

... "Conquer The Self" ... Find Harmony

"Who understands the world is learned. Who understands the self is enlightened.
Who conquers the world has strength. Who conquers the self has harmony."

~Lau Tzu, Tao Te Ching, verse 33

An individual's imbalanced mental state with the 1,000 different voices uncontrollably shouting their unrelated intentions all at once is trying to gain control of the individual's behavioral intentions, causing the individual confused mental unrest.

A reduction in this mental white noise is what Siddhartha teaches will follow calming the mind by having the "right speech", "right actions" and "right livelihood". It helps avoid having more thought-stealers uncontrollably pop into action.

Eventually with persistence, the truth-seeker's mind will be calmed enough to make the "right effort" to have a "right awareness" to control its focus into the sustained "right concentration".

Cease the bouts with mental rumination. A truth-seeker must feel-out the mental residue coming from extended unanswered concern and bring into view whatever thought thread it is that is shading their mood ... that has their mind preoccupied ... depressing or worrying them ... that they are ruminating over.

Be aware of physical reactions that accompany those themes.

The truth-seeker can settle into the physical symptoms that accompany that pot-stirrer and relax out of it trying to gain focus on the calm associated with excusing the disruptive state and use this gained understanding awareness (wisdom) to extrapolate the relief they would feel to just have the needless occurrence of a mental paradox like this one settled and put in the past.

By recognizing the physical symptoms that prelude the reaction the right thinking can eliminate the reaction before it happens and it can be circumvented.

When the reactions gone, there is no suffering.

This is where the intellectually metered knowledge from a qualified teacher of how to, what it means, and where to find this sensual target meets up with and morphs into the sensually metered and intrinsically stored understanding. They have the insightful right thinking and the newly derived wisdom to act and not react. Their calm ownership and understanding generates an action that replaces the knee-jerk reaction that had brought on suffering through reappearing distress.

This is the sensually metered and stored Tree of Life knowledge that is used to derive Tree of Life wisdom.

It's an example of obtaining the knowledge to derive the Tree of Life wisdom Jehovah had warned Adam to pursue in their Eden talk.

By making the "Right Effort" to relax the body to focus the "Right Awareness" into the flesh, the truth seeker is making the "Right Concentration." The longer they can sustain the focused awareness, the deeper they can concentrate to allow "aha" insightful thinking to surface ... thus ... derive intrinsically registered, consciously understood Tree of Life Wisdom.

… Sustained Focus Unlocks Knowledge to Derive the Most Basic Tree of Life Wisdom

Mind-into-body meditating fine-tunes the mind control needed to develop a present moment awareness and reshape a worldview. The greater developed the ability to maintain harmonic mind-into-body focus, the quieter and more undisturbed the arena of life manifest becomes. This allows progressively deeper introspective deliberation to inspire more insightful awakenings about how the life puzzle fits together.

The longer focused harmony is generated and maintained between mental awareness and its material dwelling in the sensually witnessed unpredictable uncontrollable vibrations of life manifest emanating from the body's physical presence uninterrupted by any spark of untethered rumination thought pattern, the deeper into the personal sanctuary of peace the individual will drift and the greater the sensual familiarity will become with their feel for the unchanging swing of the coming and going buzz of Tree of Life manifest itself.

And the more emotional disturbances they can insightfully find relief for.

This attained self-knowledge or familiarity provides the sensual coding for the conscious awareness to realize inspired "aha" insightful wisdom to undo emotional snags.

This enriches the truth-seeker's conscious awareness and the more familiar the truth-seeker will become with recognizing the common facets of the sensual signposts suggesting the self-evident truths.

… Give Sensual Meaning to Cerebrally Tailored Biblical Reality
…Recognize and Craft a Lifetime Friendship with the Living Holy Spirit Theology Refers To

If an individual has life in their material body, they will have a life-long haven of familiarity to retreat to for consciously rejoining the unchanging presence of ever-change as the coming and going particles of life-giving Holy Spirit life energy manifests from within.

Consciously stepping out and developing a friendship with the sensually defined living Holy Ghost is a great idea.

This insight works to increasingly transform the nature of a religious believer's worldview from one struggling to perceive their present moment through the imaginary confines of a reality backdrop of continuity. The intellectually described and cerebrally ingested biblically imposed cognitively adorned meaning of the Holy Spirit existed untouchably with a cold sense of life in a reality state of continuity. Its reality was from the ancient scriptures and it hung suspended in the believer's imaginary cognitive world of continuity.

This insight works to transform that worldview conception of the Holy Spirit to one with a nature that's alive with impermanence … that one can touch … that touches them.

It allows coupling real Tree of Life understanding to what is intellectually suggested by the ancient scriptures borrowed wisdom. It shows how the borrowed wisdom biblical sense happens in terms of experientially assimilated real-life awareness.

… Mental White Noise Will Dissolve Itself Overtime

Over time, as their talent for sustaining mind-into-body focus improves and the better they become at being able to sensually sense the feeling of each body part (modern meditation teachers call this "body scan"), the more their white noise has been minimized and the more relaxed they have taught themselves to be into understanding the depths of nature.

… No Body Scan Area Should be Favored or Avoided

Awareness focused into each body part on an equal time basis helps to avoid the likings and dis-likings that can signal prejudice and end up in feelings of attachment or clinging.

… Thought Patterns True to Purpose … A Nurtured Skill

Self-training the mind control to sustain the mind-into-body harmony to open the door to inspired thinking to incite the self-knowledge derived wisdom to inspire a more enlightened understanding of the Tree of Life's impermanence-suited cause/effect relational justice improves with practice. The echo of broken remnants of previous thought patterns might still cross the truth seeker's mental platform to interrupt efforts to sustain the right awareness to strike the right concentration to allow a mental awareness to subside into the tissue of the body.

With repeated experience with meeting up with these rogue thought patterns, a truth-seeker becomes more accustomed to recognizing them and allowing them to dissipate. Siddhartha made it clear that making the right effort to attain the right sustained concentration, consisted of recognizing unwholesome thoughts, eliminating them, and replacing them with a wholesome on-purpose state of mind and then practicing that time and time again will help a truth seeker to better sustain a harmonious right concentration to then allow self-training the wisdom-deriving knowledge to realize an enlightened life wisdom understanding awareness.

The more self-trained a truth-seeker becomes at sustaining their harmonious mind-into-body focus, the deeper into their unchartered awareness they can sync. They can better notice the intricacies in the flow of the coming and going sensations from the bits of life-giving energy that everything is made of. Over time mind-controlled awareness isolating a certain body region can be deeper scrutinized.

With sustained focusing, the attention awareness sensitized to the coming and going sensations noted in the throat can be further focused on those coming from only the tongue. The coming and going sensations being sensually witnessed in the hands, with sustained concentration can be focused into each of the fingers and onto the fingertips.

The deeper into the subtle region of their deeper consciousness a truth seeker's introspective deliberation syncs, the more "aha" inspired wisdom-enriched self-knowledge can rise to their waking conscious awareness.

... Mind Control Challenge of Visiting Coming and Going Sanctuary Provides Practice Court for Sustaining Mind-into-Body Harmony Mind Control

Add this mind control exercise to the daily workout regime. Stretch out with soul yoga to strengthen the spirit.

The coming and going tickling buzz awareness takes mind control down to its most basic primal level. Anything the ego is flipping through to think about must go. It is the most primal level of harmonic relationship a human can ind.

Self-train familiarity with forming the presence of focused mind-into-body awareness ... jumping it from the frantic between-the-ears world of rumination abyss deeper into the constant coming and going mentally quiet calmness of life manifesting to engage in the mind-into-body harmony of the same deliberative meditation presence prescribed by Siddhartha. Set the stage for the inspired thinking to ignite the wisdom-enriched insightful awareness that progressively makes more sense in understanding the subtle ways of this osmos.

Make self-trained morally/ethically calmed focused awareness-controlled mind "right" meditation a daily habit. Just make it worthwhile by making it the "right" kind, exposing mental awareness into the kiln of life manifest that sensually demonstrates all the "right" answers.

Exercise the soul to strengthen the spirit. During mind-into-body deliberation, feel the soul's living awareness stretch out like the coming and going life manifestation pulses through each body part.

After honing the mind into the relaxed theater of omnipresent essence of life manifest, over time an individual becomes more familiar with the types of thought patterns that lead to interruptions in sustaining their mind-into-body focused awareness. With this increased understanding, the interruptions eventually become less frequent, and the longer sustained focus of mind-into-body awareness penetrates deeper into the essence of life manifest ... allowing the inspired thinking during the longer periods of humble deliberation to uproot deeper-rooted cause/effect relational truths about how things naturally interact with each other.

These inspired insights can just pop into conscious recognition ... just dawn on you ... anywhere at any time ... aha ... that makes sense ... now it seems so obvious. Building steadfast faith in the process of the arena of change where their cause/effect relationship came from makes their truth something to die for ... like something that is burnt into stone.

... Feeling Weight of Spirit's Essence Helps Sustain Focus into Deeper Consciousness Relationships

The truth-seeker eventually over time can develop the ability to sense the weight of their spirit's essence to allow more effectively sustaining engendered mind-into-body harmony. The truth-seeker's quiet introspective deliberation can go deeper into the quieter regions of the deeper consciousness. More inspiring right thinking can give life to more insightful wisdom-enriched understandings of the cause/effect relational justice they have to live subject to in this impermanent reality.

... It is All an Individual Has

Whenever mind-into-body concentration is done, it humbles an individual ... reminding them that this interactive group of coming and going particles their mental awareness is focused into is the only allotted group of coming and going life-giving bits of energy that represents the presence of their human condition.

Sustained harmonious mind-into-body concentration sensually takes an individual's awareness to the only material place that is intrinsically sensually real to them. They need to get to better know it. It is what they are ... all they are and all they ever have been or will ever be.

Mind-Into-Body "Vipassana" Meditation Etiquette

... Must Dial into Sensual Abyss ... Bypass Mind-Speak Maze Work ... Sever External Fixation so to Sensually Witness What's Evolving Inside ... Mind-into-Body Focus Stays Harmony in its Most Primal State

Vipassana-style meditation is catching on and referenced today as a type of meditation. The act of using the "right effort" to focus the "right awareness" into the different body parts is what Siddhartha taught as his method for finding the right concentration to self-train the right thinking and right understanding while gaining his state of enlightenment.

... Burning Desire to Touch Life Manifest Red-Handed ... Near Death Seeded Author's Quest to Seek and Better Understand what Life's Story Is

This author self-discovered the Vipassana style mind-into-body search process exactly as it's taught today at 21 years old. Following a near-death auto crash, he wanted to know what life feels like. He wanted to sensually see and consciously meet the enchanter that stirred the pot of life.

He sat on his bed and went to the only place he knew he could touch it ... inside.

He looked in every nook and cranny of his body for it ... purposefully giving each body area equal time to avoid any prejudice. He dared it or something to come out and show its something. He didn't intellectually know the answer he was looking for ... his questioning was all written in emotional impatience.

There was no thought of the search having anything to do with religion or spirituality or anything with such a dead feel to it ... just life itself ... as it kept prodding his emotional distress.

He felt that through his flesh was the shortest path to who or what was winding up Father Time's ticking clock.

He did not make the "spiritual" connection for another 25 years.

... Detached Involvement ... Inner-Self Sensual Deliberation

The faint rhythm from the in-flesh-detected coming and going sensations play to the beat of this reality's force-driven patterns of principle that govern all cause/effect relationships in this reality. The material incarnation of those unpredictable uncontrollable randomly appearing/disappearing quark-scale subatomic metaphysical bits of energy are what animates the present moment.

It's simply amazing.

The sensually metered Tree of Life wisdom-deriving knowledge relating to its supporting logistics detail filters deeper into the human condition than do any finger of intellectually metered/stored (borrowed wisdom) can reach.

An individual must reach and secure this plateau of understanding, sensually on their own.

... Quark-Spawned Principles Filter Up Scale to Pattern the Human Experience

This sensual pulse mirrors the unalterable-by-man force-determined patterns of life principles that relationally filter up in size to determine the outcomes of events on the larger scale. They maintain the ever-changing natural force-determined elasticity that supports the impermanent multi-dimensional backdrop make up of this reality.

Go from head to toe and back again with sustained focused awareness. Providing equanimity to the consideration of sensations from different parts of the body shows no favoritism … no prejudice … no attachment.

Good luck trying to control nature's pulse … acquired wisdom will reveal to the truth-seeker that it's quite useless.

Sustaining the focus proves not being that easy … it is personal … but is the important part and takes practice. The longer a truth-seeker self-trains themself to shut out the mental white noise and focus, the deeper they'll venture into the sensually defined abyss of reality's engine room.

The more skilled at sustained focus a truth seeker becomes allows them to sensually reach deeper into the different body parts to feel the "body buzz". They are falling more into sync with the heartbeat of Mother Nature.

… Nidra Meditation … Performing a "Body Scan"

Performing a "body scan" is gaining public popularity. Although it has not really been associated with being a part of the method Siddhartha used to gain the appropriate knowledge to self-train the enlightened Tree of Life wisdom that allowed him to realize his personal enlightened understanding of what he was ignorant about that stole away his state of bliss that all humans possess.

Yoga Nidra is translated as yogis sleep or psychic sleep is said to be far superior to regular sleep. Without losing consciousness, the entire body, mind, and nervous system obtain complete rest through deep relaxation. It is said that 20 minutes of Nidra Yoga is equal to 3 hours of normal sleep. It is said to help with creativity.

This author discovered while focusing awareness into body parts that it was easy to drift off in sleep.

The oldest part of the brain, the amygdala, which is the part of the brain that is related to the stress response and production of cortisol that can contribute to insomnia is relaxed while the mind is focused into the body. It is a great way to return to sleep when awakening at night.

Nidra yoga calls for mind-into-body harmony to sensually witness the effects of life manifesting yet does not make point about how it provides the pathway for bringing to a conscious level the knowledge needed to find relief from disruptive emotional suffering … derive a Tree of Life wisdom-enriched understanding of their ignorance that causes their suffering.

This form of meditation is believed to give all the benefits of sleep while being awake. Simply lie down, close your eyes, and try to focus on individual parts of your body, thinking of them in a circular motion going from one hand up the arm to your face, then back down the other arm and across your torso, ending up traveling down one leg and then the other.

Although it seems Yoga Nedra's draw might be its shortcut to gaining sleep, this process is what helped bring Siddhartha closer to the emotional status of heavenly enlightenment 2500 years ago. Tomato-Tomatoe ... Potato-Potatoe.

Mindfully Peer into Emotional Fog

"All of your emotions contain healing gifts – they're a vital community of skills, abilities, talents, and instincts that support everything you think, everything you learn, every action you take, and all of your behaviors."

~ Karla McLaren M.Ed. 12-6-19 Facebook post

"These pains are messengers. Listen to them."

~Rumi

"Your emotions don't create problems. They arise to help you deal with problems. Learn their language and you can change the world."

~Karla McLaren M.Ed. 5-15-21 Facebook post

A self-trained calm mind abled with a relaxed sustained awareness that's present moment-absorbed, sensually alert in its search for the physical pulse of life is tuned into the right channel to get the knowledge to generate the right thinking to inspire having insightful "aha" moments.

Human experience issues that underwrite the unspoken unexplained or misunderstood emotional disturbance or dissatisfaction bouncing around somewhere in the back of the mind between the waking and deeper consciousnesses can find a peaceful connection that might suddenly make sense ... an insightful epiphany of sorts.

These are the cloud-ridded issues of emotional fog. Knee-jerk reactions can be sensually waded through. If the body starts to perspire or the heart rate increases during a body scan episode, in some instances a mental realization might just follow.

It's possible to still have waves of anger left over from an earlier incident where knee-jerk anger was the emotional reaction that followed. A calm, focused mind relaxing into the humility written into the non-anger principle that allows a controlled mind and controlled effort to unite in harmony might derive a better understanding of the relational fix between the involved factors that the reactionary response had never been conditioned to factor in.

This could be the moment for a permanent fix.

It's possible to better understand and unravel the ignorance that before caused the suffering.

It's possible to become a bit more enlightened about the relational principles that set course for this impermanent reality.

Just like Siddhartha did. Just like Jesus did.

Gifted Teachers Today are Looking Deeper into the Infrastructure of Humankind's Emotional Matrix

... Teachers Today Further Dissect Emotional Intent

Today there are movements coming from different worldview platforms that are focused on gaining waking awareness of the same bright white light of emotional balance/bliss that both Siddhartha and Jesus had sight of long ago.

... Karla Mclaren M. Ed. Authors Books and is Touching Souls Through Social Media

Karla McLaren is engaging finding emotional balance through head-on confrontation and respectful acceptance of all emotions. She has a gifted understanding of the emotional matrix and has devoted most of her life to better understanding it.

She teaches how to learn from the messages of "negative" emotions to eliminate the ignorance-fed suffering they can bring that brings one closer to the "enlightened" state Siddhartha targeted and gave detail on in self-training his calmed mind to sustain inward focus to allow deriving bits of insightful "aha" wisdom in what he taught his followers that was written to describe his *Eight Fold Pathway to Enlightenment* ... the same emotional bliss that's blindly promised in theology's heaven.

Same sort of inward focus ... same sort of waking realization. A human's a human.

... Bringing Insightful Clarity to What's Been Locked in Humanity's Collective Deeper Consciousness

Her teachings involve helping truth-seekers make sense of the uncertain world of emotionally coded spirituality that lies in between their all-knowing deeper consciousness and their emotionally confused waking consciousness.

Her classes are structured to intellectually tip toe her online students through their sometimes Zoom captured emotional minefields on an experiential pathway to finding an understanding and appreciation for the details of their emotional makeup.

In a 1-14-22 Facebook blog, she was discussing how "any action that moves a person away from the message and purpose of an emotion is bypassing" and how "any action that moves a person toward the purpose and function of the emotion is regulation and what we call channeling."

"So, deep breathing anger away and calming ourselves would be bypassing that emotion, while breathing to settle ourselves so that we can address the boundary violation that brought the anger forward is regulation-toward-channeling."

"Without an understanding of the purpose of emotions, most people experience emotions as a generalized and nonspecific suffering. Bypassing may be their only skill!"

Most people are stuck in this bypassing stage their entire lives. They remain suffering in ignorance.

Through better understanding the principles that emotions are formed around, a truth-seeker can eliminate some of the ignorance that's causing them emotional distress.

... Karla Mclaren's Foundation for Undoing the EQ Imbalance that Supports Emptiness of Understanding

In her 2-12-22 newsletter, she presents the four keys to awakening your emotions that in one way or another are a part of her approach to teaching her students:

1. *There are no negative emotions or positive emotions. (Really!)*

2. *Emotions arise at many different levels of intensity, and you can learn to work with every emotion at every level of intensity.*

3. *It's normal for emotions to arise in pairs, groups, and clusters.*

4. *You can learn to work with all of your emotions intentionally by understanding why they arise and which forms of genius they bring to you.*

Her class identifies how the basic problem here is how it's a mistake in identifying and pairing up a cause with its effect." ... The problem individuals have who imagine another reality and experience suffering due to clinging and attachment issues.

... Spiritual Teacher Eckhart Tolle Authors Books and offers Social Media Education

Mr. Tolle teaches online with Kim Eng how to "bring in the light of consciousness." He teaches how to through inner awareness fill in the emptiness-of-understanding that cripples an individual's ability to be emotionally balanced.

Like how Siddhartha taught to navigate to this zone of understanding by tuning waking awareness into the mind-into-body language during self-deliberation (meditation), Mr. Tolle teaches how "letting go of thought" will put one in the same state of sensual presence to generate the same "right thinking" for allowing an insightful understanding to rise to conscious awareness from the deeper consciousness.

With this cumulative deeper understanding, an individual's improved conscious awareness will allow them to replace the ego-spawned situational reactions that brings their emotional suffering with the same Tree of Life wisdom that Jehovah mandated that mankind use in the Garden of Eden.

Mr. Tolle teaches how to use an individual's "light of consciousness" to contribute to the bright white light of mankind's collective consciousness awareness as each individual light of consciousness contributes to a collective state of conscious awareness.

... "Engaged Buddhism"

Thich Naht Hanh was a 95-year Vietnamese Zen Buddhist monk and prominent Buddhist teacher who initiated the movement engaged Buddhism. He taught this alongside his raising popularity in the 60's and 70's. One on his 100 books, *Living Buddha, Living Christ* helped ease his acceptance into the Western culture.

Martin Luther King Jr. nominated him for the Noble Peace Prize in 1966. Deepak Chopra said he was a "gift to humanity."

He spoke 7 languages which made it more possible for him to pin down and give waking meaning to the deeper inner feeling-spun emotions he offered insight on.

This movement teaches how to apply Buddhist thought to practical problems.

He has sight on filling ignorance-spun "emptiness of understanding" with an intrinsically registered conscious awareness of the life principles that affect emotions.

They want to help people become more "enlightened" about their ignorance that causes their suffering ... like Siddhartha ... like Jesus.

Same bright white light ... different messengers.

... Nidra Yoga

Like with Yoga Nidra meditation, body scan now has formed a protocol for meditation that's now finding traction in the modern-day list of recommended forms of meditation. Its methodology is what is described here as what Siddhartha used for self-training his calmed mind to let rise from his deeper conscious awareness to self-train the "aha" Tree of Life wisdom that reached a total enlightened state under the Banyan tree 2500 years ago.

... Methodology is Innate to Human Nature

Nedra meditation and Siddhartha's Right Effort and Right Awareness present the same mental focus exercise that this author discovered when trying to sensually touch and witness life emanation in action, to only 25 years later realize that it had "spiritual" relevance to what religious theology tried to claim credit for with no real idea what Buddhism was. Reading Herman Hesse's "Siddhartha," was his only prior association with Siddhartha's Buddhism.

Every living human has this theater of ongoing change that's ever available ... until they die.

At the time, the author made no connection between his real-life methodology and any of today's meditation options or Siddhartha's methodology. He made no connection with there being a tie-in with the means to self-training Tree of Life wisdom to become enlightened about human suffering to realize heavenly emotional bliss.

His quest for the intrinsically registered sensual key to living emotional balance was never equated in his mind with the pearly gates of afterlife heavenly bliss he'd heard about in church 3 times/week until graduating high school.

A teacher was needed to realize and understand this connection.

... As Mankind Nears Collective Enlightenment ... Just Imagine

John Lennon describes what life might be like when humankind finally spiritually matures to this plateau of awareness in his ballad *Imagine*.

Self-Train a Tree of Life Wisdom-Enriched Enlightened Mind ... Own and Embrace Emotions

... Phase Three of Three Self-Training Phases

From this self-trained ability of mind control to generate the "right concentration," the third phase self-training will generate the right thinking and right understanding to derive the Tree of Life wisdom. With the accumulated self-knowledge, allow insightful "aha" wisdom to rise from the deeper consciousness into waking consciousness awareness.

Over time, with repeated effort, the amount of self-knowledge will accumulate, inspiring increased insightful epiphanies in the form of Tree of Life enriched wisdom.

There is no schedule as to when the moments of inspired insight might surface into conscious awareness. Life becomes more interesting.

... Wisdom Tends to Grow in Proportion to One's Awareness of One's Ignorance

Finding the humility to realize and accept that personal ignorance exists is an initial step to becoming wise to the unknown truth.

Siddhartha Gautama's noble eightfold path recognizes the steps of this self-trained wisdom phase to be the Right Thought and the Right Understanding.

In making the "Right Effort" to make their body sensually available, a truth-seeker must find the mind control to sustain their "right awareness" into the mind-into-body coexistence harmony needed to establish the "right concentration".

The resulting thought threads from the targeted state of self-deliberation has now unlocked the door to the source of the right knowledge to inspire the "aha" Tree of Life wisdom that can "change your world" ... as Karla McLaren points out.

The calmed and focused stages are set to self-train enlightened Tree of Life wisdom.

It sensually decodes and gives burning-bush clarity to the relational principles set in stone by the human influence-proof transforming string and wave theory patterns of coming and going bits of quark-scale subatomic metaphysical life-giving Holy Ghost-sort of life energy.

These are the patterns of unalterable (Tree of) Life principles that determine the outcomes of all relationships that make up and define the moving picture animation to the passage of time. That, when understood, allow a life rhythm that pulses to that of this impermanent reality.

This wisdom arises out of a truth-seeker's own experience. It's not received or borrowed from somewhere else. It comes from their personal experience of witnessing the truth red-handed at play.

... The Quicker the Mind-into-Body Scan ... The Better

Self-training mind control to sustain having the harmony to keep the mental awareness focused into the body's material reality is the challenge. Over time and with practice, familiarity develops with the aspects of this mind-into-body struggle-to-sustain focus.

To pass through a full area-by-area mind-into-body body scan without being interrupted by any sort of mental white noise shows progress. With repeated practice, a truth-seeker will gain the inner strength to excuse what might be some level of boogieman-spun self-questioning or self-doubt that short-circuits the focused awareness of the life manifestation detectable in the area of focus.

This increased self-understanding will filter into everything the individual does throughout the day. This is the true organic mental balance that will allow a truth seeker to better realize an intrinsic understanding of the "aha" wisdom that enlightens them with an understanding of the relational principles that run this reality.

There are many activities that can increase proficiency in mind-into-body harmony ability.

Doing martial arts forms requires strict adherence to having mental awareness focused into body intent.

... The Deeper the Truth-Seeker can Listen ... The More They're Able to Hear and Better Understand Their Human Experience

With this familiarity comes the self-trained ability to maintain sustained awareness progressively longer. With this ability comes the ability to focus deeper into the body.

The better an individual understands their emotions, the more they will get from their human experience ... the closer they will be to realizing emotional bliss ... while living.

Instead of only being able to sustain focus on a larger body part area, with practice they can focus a bit deeper into that area to sensually highlight the smaller areas that comprise it. Instead of only being able to keep attention concentrated into how the torso feels before having attention span broken by unrelated subjects, the awareness might be able to focus into the shoulder area or instead of only being able to keep attention long enough to sensually witness the coming and going sensations of the arms, with prolonged focus the truth seeker might be able to self-train their focused mind awareness into what is only the bicep or forearm or wrist or hand or finger or fingertips.

With the extended absence of the white noise of indecision tugging at an individual's attention, they can strike the primal harmony to allow reaching further into the depths of their all-knowing deeper consciousness that syncs in harmonic beat with the rhythm of the coming and going pulse of impermanence.

On this journey, the "aha" moments become more profound and satisfying.

The bit by bit of deeper understanding that results is something that maybe cannot yet be put into words, but its conscious recognition has added a touch more peace of mind in the human condition's struggle to find its way through its human experience.

Siddhartha developed such a deep harmonic familiarity during his process of mind-into-body concentration that he was able to sustain his mental awareness long and deep enough to self-train the self-knowledge to inspire the right thinking for the insightful "aha" moments of the wisdom-enriched awareness clear down to sensually visualizing the coming and going particles (kapalas) of energy itself that makeup his material presence and the whole of reality ... science's "quarks" of energy.

Today's scientific community has pictures of these particles ... intellectual understanding ... not the intrinsic understanding that Siddhartha derived.

His sensual familiarity developed through self-training his sustained mind-into-his body-focused awareness led him to his wisdom-enriched enlightened understanding of the self-evident ways of this reality that in his admitted to ignorance, he could not before understand ... lessening the ignorance that caused him to suffer.

A Life-Long Haven of Familiar Retreat

During times when feeling mentally jarred by some type of threatening discomfort, it is truly uplifting to have a haven of retreat waiting on call to visit to help restore the calm.

... A Sensual Island of Refuge

Tapping into the unchanging ever-changing state of one's physical makeup is an onboard private retreat where any individual can go to experience nothing but the sensual echo describing life's ongoing truth.

An individual's mind and body when harmoniously united in the right concentration is their sensual island of refuge.

Anytime an individual finds themself in some sort of emotional storm, anytime anywhere, they can step back and focus their awareness into the unchanging ongoing life change written into the physical essence of their human condition ... their source of life-manifest ... to establish emotional rebalance.

They can sensually relocate and step back into the calming source of primal harmony itself.

It is always there. Its presence and purpose are all about this reality that remains unchanged. Yet it is always greeted with differing levels of conscious awareness.

Mind-into-body harmonious deliberation takes an individual's awareness to an inner theater of reflection with a presence that remains forever constant from visit to visit. It is a place to go to observe how the ever-erupting volcano of the manifestation of change itself is forever putting on its show of life flow.

Quiet sensual observation of the essence of its presence allows insightful renderings of thought patterns to arise that relate to the same life-filled energy used in making present-moment decisions. It allows for thinking time for the realization of gut-felt insights to whether those certain types of real-life decisions are based on the same effective relational justice felt present where the mind directs an individual's right concentration.

Humans get to understand this zone better or become accustomed to its presence progressively with age. To attain its understanding is the underlying unspoken life purpose of all humans … developing a conscious understanding awareness of the nature of impermanence.

The physical body is the slice of reality … the deeper consciousness domain that it keeps in order while keeping bodily functions on cue.

It knows what is going on. It understands those life principles.

The self-protecting deeper consciousness rests wide open the rhythm and beat of the human experience to be better realized by the waking consciousness of the human condition.

This deeper consciousness has the same healing intent of curing mental health as it does with finding wellness for physical health.

… Awareness of Humanity's Collective Touch with Reality Helps Nullify Emotional Loneliness

Having mind and body united in harmonious focus enters the world of real-time. It is a hum of constant change that an individual learns to recognize. They gain an understood familiarity with the feel of what true calm means.

The coming and going sensations note the same spark of Life … Holy Ghost … felt by everyone else. There's the same ongoing fountain of change within each living or non-living bit of reality.

There is no reason to ever feel lonely. It is like having a communally recognized island of refuge in the river of life manifest. Anyone can be alone, yet not feel lonely.

Compassionate understandings come much easier.

… Slip into the Demilitarized Zone

The feeling of when an individual's ego comes in from the intellectually founded emotional battlefield of ruminated guilt and untethered frustration into the calm newness of the passing present moment flow of life is great. A sigh of relief can easily mark this transition.

It is the sensual point of contact with material reality. It is the only thing about this reality that does not change … ongoing change itself … their only non-foreign place of self-retreat.

With the right concentration, the 1,000 voices of the ego-managed mental white noise can be effectively squelched. The coming and going sensations are recognized with deliberating equanimity and impartial deliberation as to eliminate the mind jacking and overpowering emotionally triggered reactionary thought pattern displays.

This zone can become a truth seeker's refuge any time and at any place for them to step back, weigh and consider options, and to then act.

It is available from birth to death … dust to dust.

Spiritual Fusion Takes Time … Compassion Slowly Assumes Default Status

Strengthening the spirituality link between the deeper consciousness and the waking consciousness is a gradual process. Spiritual fusion happens when an individual's waking mental awareness mirrors the life truths stored in their deeper consciousness that radiate from every bit of their human condition.

Spiritual fusion materializes at different rates in different people. It is nurtured in diverse ways in different people. What sparks the insightful wisdom-enriched understandings that complete spiritual fusion come from a variety of sources.

When an individual first develops an eye for the truth with sustained focus anchored only by an intellectual understanding of the truth, there is going to be unintended interruptions to their focused thinking coming from their gradually disappearing mitote/maya mental state of endless mental chatter.

Only one thing at a time can use up an individual's present moment attention. This means the heartfelt security of their steadfast faith will come and go with their focused awareness on the truth of ongoing change … fading in-between reality and illusion … in-between moments of unwholesome mind wonder-inspiring and wholesome attention-sustaining thought patterns … in-between knee-jerk emotional reactions or stepping back to think first.

At times when an individual's ego is in control and is managing the mental direction of an illusionary explanation of what their imagination sees as the apparent reality for what reality appears to be, their present moments will pass with their freewill unguarded from the misguiding effects of attachment to thought patterns invoking feelings based in cravings and aversions.

Their passing present moment will be subject to the uncertainty-inspired fear that ruled their mind before getting their initial glimpse of the truth. Their pot of emotional unrest will be astir. The warmth of their steadfast faith that is felt in their heart will fade at these times.

As the individual's freewill becomes increasingly freed and its power restored from the mind-clogging thought patterns resulting from their internalized misguided prior conditioning with the many attachment-condoning claims and becomes increasingly enriched with the experientially realized relational wisdom inspired during their self-discovery, the more their eye for the truth will be supported by an unshakeable steadfast faith.

Their steadfast faith will increasingly become less obstructed from the chatter of unwholesome mitote/maya interference. They will have the steadfast faith to guard and protect their intended purpose to spread the compassion they feel growing in their present moment attitude.

They are approaching their goal of becoming enlightened about the details of what it is that they are ignorant about that allows their suffering.

Their Fig Leaf Wisdom is morphing into Tree of Life Wisdom.

… A focused mind-into-body transforms a truth-seeker's waking awareness into sensually witnessing what the intrinsic presence of ongoing change itself feels like as it defines what they perceive to make up their passing present moment.

… The great modern-day spiritualist teacher Eckhart Tolle teaches how emotions are part of the human experience and acceptance is the key to transmuting them. Constant distraction from the white noise of busy thoughts and conditioned patterns of unhappiness-supporting emotion-guided reactivity will pull an individual's awareness out of the present moment.

… By accepting emotions, a truth-seeker avoids the negative emotions associated with denial.

… Self-training this state of self-knowledge familiarity seeds and knits together the Tree of Life wisdom that brings to conscious awareness the ignorance-undoing enlightened understanding of the multi-dimensional infrastructure of this impermanent reality that feeds into supporting this reality's web of self-evident truth.

Find balance where theology and reality meet ... Associate intellectual maxims with their sensual incarnations.

Self-train mind control and temper mind-into-body harmony to better understand mood-to-emotional reaction relationship ... Sensual trigger recognition is key to emotional understanding.

Mind-into-body meditation slides your spiritually unconscious waking awareness into the present moment ... mental thinking morphs into body awareness. It transfers your focus into a different dimension of consciousness that allows sensually witnessing ongoing change as it manifests in your flesh the living essence of present moment reality.

You're awakened to the present moment with mental focus no longer immersed in a ruminating mental white noise whirlpool of ego-managed and conditioned reactionary emotion-related deliberations rapt in regret or guilt of the past or maybe fear-spawned worry about the future or for some reason elated.

Your mental focus assumes an intrinsic seat in your flesh-built theater. Its sensual alertness stands primed and set to grow in understanding the sensually broadcast self-knowledge to self-train a better waking understanding of how natural principles affect your emotional matrix ... why your conditioned perceptions fuel your kneejerk reactionary behaviors.

Self-train Tree of Life Wisdom and lessen/eliminate your ignorance-spawned "emptiness" ... approach/attain emotional bliss.

A truth-seeker can't become enlightened.
It's not a future state of being to be achieved.
It's already here. It's a state to be realized.
"You need time until you realize you don't need time."
~ Eckhart Tolle ... 9/13/22 Facebook post

XIII

Intellectual Understanding Finds Intrinsic Meaning

"The 2 most important days of your life are the day you are born and the day you figure out why."

~Mark Twain

... From Living in a World One Knows to Living in a World One Feels
... From Thinking With The Mind To Feeling With The Heart

"Beyond sculptures and symphonies, beyond great works and masterpieces is the greater, finer art of creating a conscious life. Genius appears everywhere, but never so magnificently as in a life well-lived."

~ Karla McLaren M. ED. on Instagram 2021

It would add an emotional keel to a religious believer's human experience and maybe help instill some balance to their blind faith if their intellectually metered and stored cognitive sketches they have made of their religion's spiritual signposts could find kindred meaning with the sensually metered intrinsic footprint of the real-life ultimate reality manifestations of those mentally showcased Sunday-morning concepts they encounter in real life.

"Aha" Wisdom Epiphany #1:
Impermanence Itself Proves Self-Evident

With his equation E=MC2, Albert Einstein used Mother Nature's language … mathematics … to bring to humanity's waking awareness the self-evident truth that energy and mass are interchangeable. Mass is nothing more than the energy in the process of change. This is impermanence.

… Let this Truth Become Self-Evident … Sensually Stamped

After adding the aware understanding from sensually witnessing impermanence to an intellectually defined cognitively stored notion of what this reality's state of impermanence or ongoing change is, in future references to impermanence, its new tangibly founded meaning will be stirred up to replace the cognitively stored intellectually understood meaning.

Just like a child holding their finger next to a flame to see what their warning parents meant by "hot" or why the "ouch" from a cactus needle prick is generated.

After self-training a calmer mind to then develop the self-trained ability to put forth the "right effort" with the "right awareness" to sustain mind-into-body "right concentration" a truth-seeker can then generate the "right-thinking" to insightfully realize the "right understanding" or Tree of Life wisdom-enriched awareness of this reality's impermanent personality.

To get an intrinsically registered meaning of impermanence to replace its intellectually metered cognitively stored definition received or borrowed from elsewhere, just sink mental awareness into the flesh of an area of a body part and quit mental conversations … no mental white noise.

Feel the presence of the "buzz of life" … all the energy-in-action going on with blood pumping, cell walls dividing, hair growing, bones aging … etcetera.

When the epiphany hits that there is absolutely nothing ever standing still in the transforming flow of life, the truth-seeker can take this sensual knowledge and insightfully enjoy the soul-felt comfort from deriving some Tree of Life wisdom … the unquestionable truth of life becomes unquestionably self-evident.

... Then Relax Into A New Steadfast Faith

An individual's steadfast faith grows with the waking understanding awareness of this characteristic of ongoing change that defines the nature of the ultimate reality after sensually witnessing its self-evident truth. A deeper understanding about the nature of the ultimate reality is gained while undoing some prior conditioned ignorance that allowed the misguided rationale that an imagined apparent reality exists that has caused suffering on some level in the past.

The awareness floats to the top that all those things seen as things, are actually full of other process in action. There's nothing continual there to get attached to.

Intrinsically proving to oneself through sensually understanding what impermanence is will introduce a new way of perceiving life. It changes the nature of one's mind.

Becoming totally enlightened to this reality's properties brings with it a state of emotional bliss ... while still living. There will be no "living hell" that theology threatens to send sinners to for eternity if they don't follow the unexplained directives of their borrowed strain of empty wisdom.

"Aha" Wisdom Epiphany #2:
This Living "Buzz of Life" Must be what the Bible Means by the Holy Ghost/Spirit Gift of Life

Allow the religious mindset understanding to ring the intrinsic bell.

Instill a present moment heartbeat into the "Sunday-morning" conceptualized association with the "Holy Ghost or Spirit."

Try to take that intellectually strung understanding and touch it in the transforming state of the ultimate reality of today.

Let an intellectually metered conceptual understanding pair up with its sensually metered meaning.

After making an intellect-to-intrinsic connection for what an intellectually juggled concept means to the passing present moment, the living role it plays in the passage of time becomes "Oh! I-can-see-that." self-evident.

A steadfast faith in its undeniable relevance follows simultaneously in the wake of its insightful recognition.

Gain control over waking consciousness white noise. Minimize thoughts that uncontrollably tap on the shoulder and interrupt/preoccupy the effort to sustain a thought train awareness directed into sensually witnessing the body's living existence.

This is the same unscripted random thought mental white noise that takes control of mental awareness when trying to settle into reading a good novel.

... The Holy Spirit/Ghost Concept Finds its Sensual Expression

While focusing a calmed mind into quiet self-deliberation, sensually recognize the living buzz that emanates life-manifest from each body part ... one after the other ... equal time to each to show no liking or non-liking favoritism ... only sensual recognition.

Take your quieted mind into where your intellectually metered universal reality teacher described and said to expect to sensually detect this Tree of Life knowledge feedback. Size up what is sensually acknowledged against what your intellectual mind expected to feel and consciously become aware of and acknowledge the new sensually filtered wakingly understood intrinsic meaning to that intellectually defined expectation.

With a mind calmed enough to take the Tree of Life knowledge just recognized through harmonious mind-into-body "right concentration" a truth seeker might then be able to have the insightful "right thinking" to self-train the right wisdom to gain the "right awareness" to become "enlightened" as they derive a Tree of Life wisdom-enriched understanding awareness that undoes whatever distorted understanding of reality that before made them suffer in some way.

Feel this now. This is where the intellectual and sensual minds meet up.

This mind-into-body sensually metered buzz of life is the present moment meaning of what the holy scriptures refer to as the holy transporter of life ... the Holy Ghost/Spirit.

... The Holy Spirit Supporting Role in the Ten Commandments

The part of the Holy Trinity that transfers life is the Holy Ghost/Spirit. It is hard to get a prior intellectually metered/stored cognitively sketched visual out of mind of the low-creeping white fog that slowly crept through Egypt as the last plague, taking the life of the first-born males in the Charlton Heston movie "The Ten Commandments." That was intended to show the Holy Ghost/Spirit doing its god's work.

What a curve ball to understanding what the Holy Ghost/Spirit is.

In this movie, picturing the Holy Ghost/Spirit as a separate entity eliminates the possibility of it being the heartbeat of change itself that is actually the tiny bits of energy that define the heartbeat of change itself that's present in everything today.

There must be some tangible living presence of what the Bible intellectually refers to as the Holy Ghost/Spirit. Intellectual reference must be transposed into a real time sensually perceived intrinsic meaning. For its intellectual conception to have any credit at all, it must have a tangible living presence and play a role in the life-filled passage of time.

The awareness imprint of the meeting of intellectual and sensual mindsets will be sealed with new steadfast faith gained when the wakingly recognized sensually metered self-evident truth of something that is intellectually defined becomes one with the new intrinsically founded understanding.

Both self-confidence and self-belief will silently grow proportionately to this newly realized steadfast faith ... exponentially over time.

"Aha" Wisdom Epiphany #3:
It's Useless to Act Out and Try to Control
Nature's Patterns of Change

While self-training the insightful understandings from dispassionate unattached contemplation over the sensually witnessed uncontrollable stream of coming and going bodily sensations, it becomes clear how useless it would be to try to act out or try to control the coming and going of those sensations.

It is pointless and foolish to make effort to control the patterns of change that determine situational outcomes.

... Humility's Needed to Assemble Mind-into-Body Harmony

The act of employing Siddhartha's suggested: "right effort" and "right awareness" for the needed self-trained mind control to tender the "right-thinking" to inspire the right contemplation to then inspire the insightful derivation of Tree of Life wisdom-deriving self-knowledge must be approached with total humility.

The unalterable presence of life-manifest must always be greeted and sustained by a truth seeker's most humble mind-into-body presence and be allowed to make its own path. It must be "listened to" without trying to influence its presence.

Eliminating an individual's "acting out and control" prior conditioning will bring them more in step with the principle-fed rhythm that time flows to. Removing this phase of ignorance will bring more peace into their life as they are not making effort to swim against the flow of change.

When applying this insight to other cause/effect life situations the reflective wisdom suggests that it is wise for an individual to live under the same principle of humility to effectively address the ever-renewing configuration of this reality's real-time present moment cause/effect presence.

It's not possible to control the principle-determined outcomes in nature's display of life.

... Manipulators Beware

Individuals who are thought to be "manipulators" are trying to control the flow of the natural cause/effect give and take of interpersonal relationships. Covering up fears by telling white lies or full-blown gaslighting to craft the desired outcome to shape what they perceive to be how another should perceive a situation can become a normal way of living for some.

An individual's ongoing development of an aware understanding of the relational justice that is appropriate to run an impermanent reality that has been repeatedly compromised over time will cause them to lose touch with their ability to objectively determine what an "un-doctored" reality really is.

Later in life, this self-engineered style of intentionally steered misperception will assume the character of reality. The individual will lose their objectivity and not be able to decipher a soap opera pseudo-reality from what is on hand.

Some call this type of loss of connection with present moment reality, one type of dementia.

Like not being able to alter the passing present of change, it is useless to act out and try to control things beyond their natural rhythm.

It is true that when trying to unduly control situations, acting rude, inconsiderate or being deaf to reason, that this is when peaceful coexistence is not possible and suffering results.

Ted Talks

...Shared Vigor In Realizing Self Evidence In "Aha" Wisdom Insight

"TED Conferences LLC is a media organization that posts talks online for free distribution under the slogan "ideas worth spreading. TED was conceived by Richard Saul Wurman in February 1984 as a conference; it has been held annually since 1990."

-Wikipedia

... Follows Right Understanding

TED talks are an example of when someone converts what they've intellectually metered and stored while being taught about the emotional benefits from positive characteristics ... perseverance, self-belief, determination ... experiences the sudden surprise of an "aha" epiphany felt when that cognitive understanding meets up with its sensually metered intrinsic understanding.

"AHA"! You have got to listen to what came to me!

Their steadfast faith-supported elevated level of confidence that makes it seem easy for them to give the TED lecture follows in the wake of when their intellectual understanding meets up with their conscious awareness of their intrinsic understanding that has always existed in a subtle level of their deeper consciousness.

XIV

Compassion ... Stairway to Heaven

"Everyone you meet is fighting an internal battle you know nothing about. Always be kind."

~Robin Williams

"Always have courage and be kind to others." ... as she explained ... "Kindness has power and magic."

~ Cinderella's mother's deathbed advise

"Kindness is the language that the deaf can hear and the blind can see."

~ Mark Twain

Goodness in Human Nature "to Heal" is Inborn *and* Unstoppable

"We can reject everything else: religion, ideology, all received wisdom. But we cannot escape the necessity of love and compassion. This, is, my true religion, my simple faith. In this sense, there is no need for temple or church, for mosque or synagogue, no need for complicated philosophy, doctrine, or dogma. Our own heart, our own mind, is the temple. The doctrine is compassion. Love for others and respect for their rights and dignity, no matter who or what they are: ultimately these are all we need."

~Dalai Lama

... Altruistic Compassion is Born into Every Individual

Like the human body is programmed to heal its cuts and make hair grow, it is a natural facility of human nature to heal or improve the state of the human waking consciousness.

The empathy-seeded altruistic push to help others, un-thanked, that factors into acts of compassion comes from this same human programming. People are just born with it wired into their DNA.

... Compassion Came in Their DNA

Mother Teresa and each of the other Roman Catholic canonized individuals bowed to the Roman-backed theology expressed in the Holy Bible. Their early life conditioning allowed the innate characteristic to mature.

Their fear of the unknown grew in them until they looked outside for an answer to their longing to better understand their place in the human experience and purpose.

They used their freewill to decide to eat from the Tree of Knowledge. They borrowed the wisdom they intellectually gave credit to for their compassionate approach to life.

They share a human characteristic with other humans that are not of Christian blind faith or any other of theology's ancient man-drafted mystical notions of avoiding misery and realizing emotional bliss.

These individuals already exhibited compassion in their lives before believing Jehovah's promise. It is rather deceiving where the credit for their wonderful "God-blessable" behavior gets attributed.

There is very much good done in the name of the different gods.

There is also much ongoing worldly genocide done in the name of those different gods.

... Epitaphs Tell of the Most Valued Human Element

Why does society sometimes wait until an individual has died to step back and appreciate their "good side?"

After one's death, their loved ones offer what they feel to be the noblest of their loved one's human characteristics. The range of accounts includes how the individual was so thoughtful and always was there to help others. Their living presence usually was highlighted by a smile.

Different individuals have differing described strengths, but they are all manifestations of some aspect of the network of intentions that connect with compassion.

Altruism ... What Tenders Empathy

... Altruism-Spawned Compassion Founded in Selflessness ... Not Self-Fullness

> *"Altruism is the antidote for self-centeredness."*
> ~ paraphrasing the Dalai Lama

It doesn't really matter who said the above quote. Its truth is self-evident and everyone has the right to wave its flag.

... Help Others Because They Need Help, Not Because it makes You Feel Good

Altruistic intentions are not about how good it makes "me" feel to be kind. It is all too common to hear how good someone might say it makes them feel to help others.

That is not at all what it is about, as it would then follow that if they saw no good feeling return, they would lack the motivation to help another individual.

Supplying something needed to someone else should not have to be done because of the good feeling felt afterward. Feeling better might not be a part of the deed. The important thing is that the person in need has had their need met.

Empathy ... Doormat to Compassion

"Empathy may be a trait, but it is a skill we can develop throughout our lives."
~Karla McLaren D.Ed.

... Cut Them Some Slack ... Put Yourself in Their Shoes

As what Robin Williams said about when dealing with other people ... keep in mind that every person you meet up with has their inner battles to deal with that you know nothing about.

They may not be able to find the words to describe these battles themselves. These inner battles are fought on their personal sensual battlefield.

Live a clean life to clear your head and self-train a mind clear of white noise ... take that mind to sensually witness the different dimensions of what defines the present moment of life manifest within... use this knowledge for insightful thinking to gain an understanding awareness of new-found wisdom ... enriched by the sensually metered Tree of Life knowledge ... backed by an unshakeable steadfast faith.

... White Lies are Used to Make the Ends Meet

White lies can give the liar the sense that they are controlling event outcomes to unfold in the way they think is best. They try to affect what really happens to meet up with what they think should have happened to satisfy some misdirected inner agenda.

Telling "white" lies could be the only way someone whose life rhythm is not flowing comfortably in sync with the principles that open the gates in the flow of naked change.

They try to find a way to make ends meet. They try to force the foreseen ends of their life flow meet up with the effect they desire to see or should be.

They are talking through an emotional minefield of feelings that are generating emotions like embarrassment or guilt that they do not have the courage to confront or the wisdom to recognize.

Everyone is trying to figure things out. What lies at the root of those battles?

... Empathy Opens the door to Compassion

Empathy is a seed from which compassion grows and matures. Standing in another's shoes can be the cleansing agent for self-pity and depression.

Empathy is a key that unlocks and opens the door of compassion.

Empathetic thought patterns are the seeding grounds for a compassionate life purpose.

Religious believers who "pray" for the wellbeing of friends and family are unlocking their gate to empathy. Just hope they can exercise that ability when not involved in their prayer of hope to their god and will still treat their friends and family well.

Grassroots Legacy

... Altruistic Generosity ... Compassionate Agenda

When an individual says that they think they are good to other people, how superficial or oversimplified is this claim? When they meet up with someone, what kind of personality do they present to them to deal with?

Having regard for the humanity in others, do they give them someone to deal with that treats them well and is fun to be with or do they give them a negative aura to cope with?

They will always remember how you treated them.

... Leave All Meet Ups with Emotional Boost

The essence of an individual's personality that is presented is something that is left after each encounter of any kind. It is a gift that is invaluable.

Anytime an individual meets up with someone, they should give the other individual's present moment the presence of an individual who is smiles and listens with sincere interest in how they are and what they are involved in.

XV

Mankind Moves Towards Herd Enlightenment

"We all seek the same white light our essences are part of. In ignorance, we view it differently. Time-allowed discovery is removing these filters and finding common focus."

HUMANITY authentic share expression PURPOSE outcome awaken ALL THAT IS soul manifest knowledge creative harmony spiritual DIVINE PLAN connected LET GO unconditional HEALING attitude COLLECTIVE CONSCIOUSNESS contemplate HEART wisdom truth LOVE ideas possibilities society ESSENCE group WHOLE infinite unlimited network expansion identity UNITY purity share transformation FLOW energy ALLOW

So, Yes... Mankind's Still Living in the Garden of Eden

... Just Too Ignorant To See It

The Tree of Life reality ... the truth of impermanence totally free of continuity ... has been here in motion since day one.

Emotional bliss is here 24/7/365 ... for the last 6,000 to 14.5 billion years+/-.

... It's Still Here ... Just Locked Up

"So He drove out the man; and He placed cherubim at the east of the garden of Eden, and a flaming sword which turned every way, to guard the way to the tree of life."

~ Genesis 3:24 King James Translation

Jehovah locked the Tree of Life truth up and placed a sworded guard at the gate. But … it's still there.

"And unto Adam he (Jehovah) said, Because thou hast heartened unto the voice of thy wife, and hast eaten of the tree, of which I commended thee, saying, T hou shalt not eat of it: cursed is the ground for thy sake; in sorrow shalt thou eat of it all the days of thy life;"

~Genesis 3:17 King James Version

He told Adam and Eve because they partook of the Tree of Knowledge, they would have to spend their days tending to his earth and live using the borrowed Fig Leaf Wisdom that they chose to have and were told would make them wise to all good and evil for the rest of their days.

… Unless … They Reach Out and Eat of the Tree of Life For Wisdom that has the Key to Unlock the Door

"And the LORD God said, Behold, the man is become as one of us, to know good and evil: and now, lest he put forth his hand, and take also of the tree of life, and eat, and live forever."

~ Genesis 3:22, King James Version

To have the Gates to Eden opened again to Adam and Eve, they must have begun eating of the Tree of Life.

It looks like they would have to be alive to reach out and start eating of the tree of life. There was no God-to-man verbiage mentioning the afterlife.

… The Door's Still Open, as per Jehovah

The author of Genesis (Moses?) understood the importance of "understanding" verses being "empty-of-understanding" and analogized it in genius fashion.

God tells Adam since he ate the borrowed wisdom that he'll have to use his borrowed wisdom for the rest of his life unless he eats of the Tree of Life … priceless.

Like with Adam and Eve, as long as mankind ingests the borrowed wisdom that's empty-of-understanding the way of things and misunderstanding what's seen, it will suffer in the many forms of confused emotional misery. Jehovah said they'd not be allowed back in to having an enlightened awareness until Tree of Life wisdom was used.

Having a waking conscious awareness wise to the life principles that determine the relational outcomes of interactions would be free of ignorance-generated "emptiness-of-understanding." It would be what the snake promised in the Tree of Knowledge "of Everything Good to Everything Evil" but failed to be because as being borrowed wisdom, it came "empty-of-understanding."

There'd be no need for conjuring up fig leaf-lined masks to disguise the ignorance-spawned incarnations of shame-related emotions from not understanding how to best relate to new change in the ever-flipping pages of present moment display.

There'd be an understanding of the emotional perception generated by how life principles affect the outcome of situations that otherwise would have just drawn some sort of an aversive reaction followed by some negative emotions … regret … anger…etc. Instead, this enlightened understanding would allow the individual to understand, think, and then act on the situation in a state of mind that would not generate the feelings that trigger the reactive emotions of suffering.

As Siddhartha taught, when the "reaction" part of the mind's processing of the real-life circumstance is eliminated … the suffering that always accompanies a reaction is also eliminated.

Humans can set their sight on finding the guidance to have an intellectually metered understanding of how to self-train the ability to find and sensually catalogue the intrinsically registered knowledge to inspire the right thinking to insightfully derived Tree of Life wisdom. They would first have to be made aware that the pathway existed and understand why they're looking for it.

They would develop an enlightened understanding of what would become self-evident about the impermanent personality that defines the nature of the reality that they have to relate to while negotiating their way through their everchanging present moment human experience.

"Emotional balance … wise to and free of suffering" would be the sign hanging over the entrance to their community like the one John Lennon describes in his lyrics to *Imagine*.

… Curiosity Killed the Cat

Either the original sin was due to curiosity or naivety, but should Eve had just eaten the snake, there'd be no problem … no Bible … no ignorance … no suffering. This would be true, given none of her descendants used their freewill to check out the fruit of the Tree of Knowledge … committed the original sin … then a Bible would be needed … ignorance … suffering.

Adam's forewarning about eating from the Tree of Knowledge was to Eve like a parent telling their child not to put their hand in a flame because it would be too hot. At some time, that child is going to put their hand near a flame to experience what "hot" means … intrinsically … something they can have a real deeply felt understanding of. They want the intrinsically registered experiential knowledge from which to derive their wisdom on how to treat flames in the future.

Adam gave Eve an account of Jehovah's either/or warning. Maybe Eve just wanted to see what "hot" felt like.

Surely, at some time, one of Eve's descendants would take a bite of the forbidden fruit. Eve did ... Adam did.

Human nature?

Add a teaspoon of curiosity to an active freewill and the outcome unpredictable ... look what happened to Jehovah when he tried it with his new universe.

You'd think that a god could control the outcome of this or at least the causing factors leading up the outcome.

... Anyway ... The Truth Is

The truth about how things interact while dancing to the rhythm of impermanence is right in front of every living creature's face. The human face has its material presence because of this truth ... a person's face is the truth ... in motion ... nothing solid ... a pool of coming and going bits of energy ... here one second to become a new one the next.

The scale of perception throws people off. It's too easy for an individual to misinterpret what they see as being just an apparent reality, Fig Leaf Wisdom allows them to be blind to the mist of everchanging life that makes up everything. They get attached to an apparent reality they imagine and start suffering.

Within the range of human perception, this world of motion only reveals how wrinkles are becoming just a bit more prominent and maybe the hair a bit grayer. This human can't see the depths of the ongoing activity that is really taking place.

Yet, this person pictures themselves as they looked in their high school yearbook ... ignorance.

A little hair darkener, some skin tightener and maybe a mascara mask ... and a handful of fig leaves and this human's ready to go out into society again.

Even so, as time passes this Tree of Life understanding is becoming more visible to mankind's collective waking consciousness.

Insightful Epiphanies Continue Popping Up

One of humanity's very distant descendants once had an insightful "aha" moment.

It came to them how to take advantage of the newly discovered self-evident truth that a round cylinder-shaped object will roll. They gained a waking understanding of how they could use that natural force generated principle-driven self-evident fact to make life a bit easier ... and "aha" the wheel.

Since long before that, since humans were placed here by intelligent design or when they evolved from a spark of life that hit the Earth via asteroid ... doesn't matter … since then human life insights about the self-evident truths that explain how life principles interrelate to make life easier with less suffering.

Over time, mankind's trillions of insightful derivations of bits of Tree of Life wisdom have decreased collective ignorance of how nature's principles work to affect human perception.

Humankind's shared emptiness-of-understanding pit shrinks bit by bit … "aha" moment by "aha" moment.

… Eagerly Shared with Loving Compassion

Just listen to one of the Ted Talks. Each of these individuals are relieved and amazed at what their increased intrinsic understanding touch with the ultimate reality has done to improve their appreciation of life. They are overly happy to share this with others.

No gaslighting here.

It brings them joy. They want to share it.

Many individuals who have an insightful "aha" moment will write a poem or song lyrics to share their increased understanding.

… Often Intelligence is Blind to Ignorance … IQ has Low EQ

Human insights now have placed a satellite clear outside of this solar system in interstellar space … humans have walked on the moon … figured out how to cure many illnesses/diseases … etcetera … etcetera … etcetera.

And ignorance steps in.

Mankind has figured out how to make the deadliest sorts of weapons that can kill fellow humans in many unbelievably horrible ways. And are using them … with their god on their side.

Ignorance takes its toll in body counts.

… Take A Moment to Think About It

Insightful understandings from many people are quoted throughout this writing … 'aha" moments of understanding … shared wisdom … lessening mankind's collective pool of ignorance inspired emptiness bit by bit.

… "Good" Will Win Out … Over Time … The Force is Unstoppable … It Proves Self-Evident

All the incarnations of the Tree of Life truth will eventually prove to be self-evident and undeniable to mankind's waking awareness.

Swimming against the current makes no sense when it's clear where the river's flowing.

As insights continue appearing in the collective human mindset to increase life understanding, waking awareness of life's relational properties will improve worldwide.

The various sources of the insights have derived their Tree of Life wisdom experientially. That's why they're so excited about their realization … they feel it … the resulting steadfast faith tickles and strokes their soul.

By making the discovery public knowledge, it will help others to eventually experience it themselves.

… Converting Borrowed Wisdom to Tree of Life Wisdom can Take Time

Individuals in a Ted Talk audience will be excited and inspired at what they are intellectually metering. Just like reading some verse from Lau Tzu's *Tao Te Ching*.

They'll leave the show or put the book down and their mental white noise will change the subject. Their intellect will place its awareness to ruminate about some other unrelated topic.

Their Ted Talk or Lau Tzu borrowed wisdom will be intellectually archived.

A time will come when the Tree of Life wisdom they heard in the audience or read in the book would be appropriate but will not be first to come to mind before they react to the situation with their poor behavior imprinted through practiced conditioning.

There's a reaction … there's suffering.

And they'll suffer emotionally somehow from not understanding what the appropriate behavior would have been to influence the better outcome as was heard about in the audience or read in *Tao Te Ching*.

The intellectually metered wisdom had no intrinsic stamp. Maybe in a future occurrence, they'll catch themselves and act instead of reacting to begin an experiential history with the intellectually ingested feed.

Purpose driven repeated practice of intellectually spawned behavior can eventually assume experiential status to achieve intrinsic awareness.

Over time, the worldwide EQ (emotional intelligence quotient) will rise.

History has shown how when self-evident wisdom creeps in with new advancements in anything making the living experience contain less suffering, it will become normal life for many.

When the ignorance-numbed intelligent individuals that are committing criminal acts against human rights gain a better understanding of the matrix of emotions, they will act differently.

Should they continue with their heartless agenda and if enough of those around them increasingly know better, they will be pushed out of control.

I.E. Authoritarian government style in 2022.

... Suffering Knows No Prejudice ... Compassion Knows No Prejudice

There aren't "bad" people or "good" people. There are people of differing levels of ignorance.

It's the nature of this impermanent reality to "heal."

Just like the deeper consciousness has the agenda to heal a cut ... make a heartbeat ... remind an individual to inhale and exhale, from the most basic level reality strives to restore balance by eliminating the ignorance that generates these "flies-in-the-ointment" that interrupt the smooth flow of the principles that script the flow to the river of time.

The dimensional fabric that holds this reality together will shake out the wrinkles that go against the grain ... in all fields of recognition.

The World of Emotions is Finally Finding its Footing

... EQ is Finally Getting Recognition

In 2022 A.D. mankind's collective (IQ) intelligence quotient seems to be advancing exponentially. Yet, society is just now figuring out how emotional intelligence (EQ) is needed to establish any balance.

To achieve any sort of social balance, the intrinsic world needs to manage the intellectual world.

Currently in history, fundamental ignorance is far too world encompassing.

Humankind continues to ingest the Fig Lear Wisdom borrowed from other entities picked from the Tree of Knowledge. And just like with Adam and Eve, any strain of this out-sourced wisdom comes void of understanding. Believers in borrowed wisdom limp through the present moment with a worldview hovering in emptiness-of-understanding inherently a part of Fig Leaf Wisdom.

This choice of wisdom, as Jehovah promised, will continue to bring spiritual death to realizing the Eden-like, heaven-to-be-as promised beauty of emotional bliss free of suffering from the countless offshoots of fundamental ignorance.

... Modern Schools of Psychology Work to Advance the Understanding of Where the Human Condition Meets the Human Experience
... Emotional Awareness

Human psyche has been studied for as long as society has questioned why people suffer. Social workers and those with psychiatry titles are trying to help people understand their suffering and get closer to emotional bliss.

The main areas of modern psychology include clinical psychology ... counseling for mental and behavioral health, cognitive psychology ... the study of the mental processes, behavioral psychology ... understanding behavior through different types of conditioning, and biopsychology ... research on the brain, behavior, and evolution.

From Pavlov's dogs to the Freudian couch and beyond, the different approaches to bring understanding to human psyche have viewed the human emotional package in many ways.

Emotions are action-requiring neurological programs.

Sensuality is how the waking consciousness of the human condition is notified how ongoing change has included them in the next flash of present moment human experience.

The sensation is perceived as a liked or disliked feeling that the human condition's been conditioned to perceive as good or bad. ... for most, something to become attached or aversive to.

The intellectual intelligence and the intrinsic reference intersect here ... in sensual braille ... where the emotion sprouts from.

The intellectual intelligence will either give way to the intrinsically primed fight-or-flight reflex or maybe evaluate the sensation cocktail and use its chosen school of wisdom to either just react to it or to note its presence and act on it.

The negative emotions coming from this sequence are not something to be eliminated ... they are to be owned and understood.

They set the red flags exposing perceptual boundaries. They are to be understood and not rejected or cowered from.

The different schools of psychological study enter this timeline at different points and concentrate on how their chosen aspect plays a role.

As time passes, the different viewpoints are taking on more of a common focus.

There are people ahead of their time like Karla McLaren who has a gifted connection with understanding human emotional presence and is taking advantage of today's technology to share it with others.

And So ... Fig Leaf Wisdom Finally Becomes Obsolete

... Here's How

The answer's here ... now. The brightness of its white light radiates in such blinding clarity that the longed-for answer to realizing emotional balance/bliss becomes invisible to most.

Religious believers that have lived their life guided by borrowed wisdom hope to be rewarded with emotional balance/bliss in the present moment mystery of their unfamiliar intellectually sketched afterlife ... as their god promised. They die hoping they suit his final-cut judgement come the day of the gathering of armies for the battle during the end of times on the Day of Armageddon.

Those who've never been able to convert to a religion's templated path to emotional bliss but live their live in some degree of mental fog with no understanding of this reality's impermanent footprint still live lost looking to dead ends for the way to emotional balance.

They too will use Fig Leaf Wisdom to relate to reality's barrage of naked change that confronts them.

When their perception focuses on an apparent reality, like with a religious believer, that's blind to the truth display of the coming and going bits of transforming energy that make up the ultimate reality of what they're misperceiving, they too will suffer from craving the attachments and aversions they've formed to items and ideas in their imagined state of permanence.

They too are empty-of-understanding what it is that affects their emotions and how to take control of it to realize emotional balance/bliss.

Both groups leave this life idled in fundamental ignorance ... empty-of-understanding their emotional matrix as their only material connection to the source of the answer returns to the dust it came from.

,.. As Life Truth's Self Evidence Continues to Gain Public Recognition

As word of the path leading to the enlightened balanced emotional health every human has an innate longing for continues to become less obscure to mankind, increasing numbers will be able to actually "see the light" and walk that narrow pathway they've kept an eye pealed for all their lives.

They want to gain the understanding they've lived their lives trying to find.

After uncovering the experiential pathway to understanding, they will focus their life purpose on converting this new thread of intellectual knowledge into a sensually registered enlightened understanding awareness of its intrinsic meaning and relevance.

Even though they will be holding the hand of their teacher as they walk the pathway to enlightenment, they will take every step of that experiential pathway on their own to intrinsically witness the sensual display of its truth.

... The Anti-Christ Agenda Loses its Threat of Influence

These truth-seekers will have learned to strike an ethical/moral standard that will free their ability to self-train control of their mind, freed from the clutches of the sources hosting an Anti-Crist agenda ... sources of dead ends and mental white noise that interrupt an individual's self-training movement towards becoming enlightened ... from understanding the message... the "Christ" ... that Jesus was the messenger of, and that Siddhartha and other enlightened ones taught at other times.

Don't think the sources of an "Anti-Christ" agenda that lead away from the path to an enlightened understanding aren't here today. It's very loosely defined in the scriptures. They don't wear a nametag. They are here now and working against an individual's pathway toward emotional balance every day.

These various veins of "sinful" intimidation from the sources representing agendas with an Anti-Christ intent become understood and disappear. The mental confusion and thought disruption they engender creates and allows for the demons and boogiemen to hide in the mental mist of uncertainty.

It becomes clear to those on track to becoming enlightened about their ignorance how shallow any Anti-Christ agenda is. The agenda lacks having any altruistically founded compassionate intent.

They thump out the mind pounding white noise robbing those unaware of their mental clarity and control of their train of thought needed to self-train their sensual walk down the experiential pathway to self-train the mind control to self-train the Tree of Life wisdom that enlightens them to take on a waking understanding awareness that undoes their fundamental ignorance about this reality's personality ... impermanence.

The truth-seekers will have used their calmed minds to strike the humility to self-train the mind-into-body harmony to settle into the mind-into-body-generated awareness capabilities of a body scan.

Over time they will have learned to sensually listen in the emotional language of body-speak to intrinsically witness the flow of life energy emitted in the coming and going electron tap dance performance of nature's quark-fed Holy Spirit.

They will have shaken sensual hands with each of their emotions.

During repeated sessions of inner self-deliberation, the sensual body-speak will reveal in braille flesh typeset what their emotions are trying to tell them while sensually meeting the red flag physical symptoms that give signal to each of the emotion-shaping reactions.

A waking understanding of the principle-wise boundaries set by each of their emotions will grow in time.

Their sensual body-speak vocabulary will have grown to give order to the meaningful sentences acquired from the newly attained self-knowledge needed to inspire the right thinking to underwrite new "aha" insightful understandings as they derive the Tree of Life wisdom Jehovah mandated that Adam use ... first thing on day 6 of the alleged Garden of Eden creation.

Their growing cache of Tree of Life wisdom inches their understanding awareness closer to their becoming totally enlightened about their ignorance that causes their emotional suffering.

A faith steadfast in the self-evident nature of the contributing sign post-factors uncovered while deriving the new wisdom follows in the wake of each of their" aha" moments of inspired insightful wisdom realization... with no middleman ... or what his borrowed wisdom promised ... without any emptiness-of-understanding.

They will have developed an understanding awareness of how the transforming nature of this reality's force-driven patterned principle impermeant makeup directly or indirectly affects the emotional presence of their human condition.

They will be able to crack the ego-hardened cover of their ego-disguised ignorance and pivot their intrinsic understanding of their perception of the *effects* ... of how their sensual presence relates to the *cause* from reality's intended purpose of ongoing change.

Their protective ego-serviced hardened exterior shell peals away to expose their compassion fueled point guard of altruistic intent. They will no longer have an emptiness-of-understanding spawning their need to find fig leaves to line their social masks to hide their shame of ignorance-generated emptiness.

They learned that they cannot control relational outcomes ... that's up to Mother Nature's formula.

They learned that by greeting situations with Tree of Life wisdom purposed by altruistic compassion, the outcomes were usually good and how that altruism-fueled intent often caused effects that were much better than imagined.

Striking this relationship with nature proved highly contagious.

Their joy and happiness fed on itself.

Their Fig Leaf Wisdom became forever obsolete ... everlastingly dated ... the storyline for fables and folklore.

Just Imagine

If you can ... try to imagine there's no heaven above...and if a believer ... that you made the Day of Redemption final cut to live in that time-stilled cognitively sketched mental rendition of an afterlife heavenly haven of God-promised emotional bliss.

Imagine there's no hell below ... even though you made it, some of your friends, despite the poor role models they had that didn't teach them how to maneuver relational situations with the compassionate purpose needed to understand what deep-seated emotional balance means, could have suddenly, when the trumpets blared at the end of time, been judged and labeled as lost sinners ... as Jehovah promised ... to begin eternal fire and brimstone torment.

It's tough to come to understand and then find the joy in all this new-found emotional bliss ... knowing of your friends' sudden fate ... while you knowing they had pure hearts shackled by fundamental ignorance ... their Fig Leaf Wisdom came empty-of-understanding.

Are all your family members here in heaven with you as you had promised their lifeless bodies at their funeral? Your pets? How can it be heaven … emotional bliss … without them?

… Just try to imagine that there's just the sky above and everyone is living for the present moment.

Imagine that there are no line-in-the-sand divisions separating landmass areas to die protecting … that everyone's life purpose understands and adheres to the life principles that feed the living into the Tree of Life.

Imagine that nobody's now being fatally fooled … no borrowed wisdom anymore … no emptiness-of-understanding calling for fig leaf-lined social masks. The days of people being empty-of-understanding find their place only in the annals of history.

… Just try to imagine how peace fills the air.

With mankind's continuing insight-driven wisdom that further understands the principles that make relationships work, the day will come for worldwide herd enlightenment.

The ignorance-fed emptiness-of-understanding that caused all the suffering is gone. This reality's force-driven impermanent personality finds nobody foolishly becoming attached or aversive to things or ideas of imagined time continuity to suffer the inherent emotional distress.

… Just try to imagine emotional balance … worldwide.

Imagine there's no greed to create social class and the attached plethora of emotional misery. The Bible-referenced "root of all evil" … the love of money … is no more.

… Just try to imagine everybody sharing everything … there's no hunger.

To most this may sound like a dream. One day, everyone will find and walk the experiential pathway to their understanding of how this reality's life principles affect their emotions for the enlightened awareness that will undo their ignorance-inspired misguided or non-existent understanding of life principles.

Someday … when this happens … the world will live as one.

John Lennon says it's easy if you try in his song *Imagine.*

Fig Leaf Wisdom … RIP

About the Author

David McCaslin was raised in central Indiana and from age seven until graduating from New Castle's only high school, he attended a local church 3 times a week with his parents and three brothers. He was the only family member who never blindly accepted Christianity's templated claim that its god had a living presence in shaping the heartbeat of this ephemeral reality's ever-changing present moment flash-in-time.

He never took the blind leap to become a Christian.

Having been raised under semi-fundamental living circumstances may have left the author with somewhat of a chip-on-the-shoulder attitude towards Christian wisdom. The insights that surfaced in writing this text has exposed and helped bring clarity to the miscued rational those fundamental beliefs are founded in, bringing him closer to realizing emotional balance.

At age 21, he barely survived a car accident that left him weak and feeling quite grateful just to be alive. During recovery, out of innate curiosity and the gratitude for life itself, he wanted to consciously touch the buzz of life to intrinsically witness it in action.

He intuitively felt this living force had an intrinsic connection ... that this could only be done where he had the capacity to actually feel or touch life itself and that was inside his living body.

At the time, he made no association between the intellectually sketched cognitive impressions left from the rather abstract religious theology's template he was taught at church and the living message he was seeking with his self-designed sensual method for reaching this end of consciously touching the living presence of life's essence.

It took twenty-five years before, while hearing the end of a book review on an obscure internet radio station, describing how a certain strain of a spiritual discipline uses the same method he had engineered to feel the buzz of life, that he made any conscious connection between an intellectually learned and remembered religious template and its present moment sensual incarnation.

Theravada Buddhism uses the act of feeling the buzz of life to self-train the mind control to develop a wisdom-enriched enlightened understanding about the nature of the ways of this impermanent reality to undo the human ignorance that causes human suffering.

... Two years high school NFL debate finals, 1 year as high school tennis team captain, 16th in '75 New Castle, Indiana High School class of 354 students

... Four years Snow Ski Instructor, four years National Ski Patrol Slope Leader Long Mountain and Nashville Alps Ski Resorts

... Indiana University Business Management/Administration degree, Bloomington campus

... Owned restaurant, land surveying company, real estate broker/appraiser/ investor company

... 6th Dan Master Tae Kwan Do ... Chung Park, Grandmaster 9th Dan

... Published 1st book ... Hoosier Heaven

www.ingramcontent.com/pod-product-compliance
Lightning Source LLC
Chambersburg PA
CBHW070901120626
46546CB00001B/90